F HOENIX
SCOTTSDALE & SEDONA

KATHLEEN BRYANT

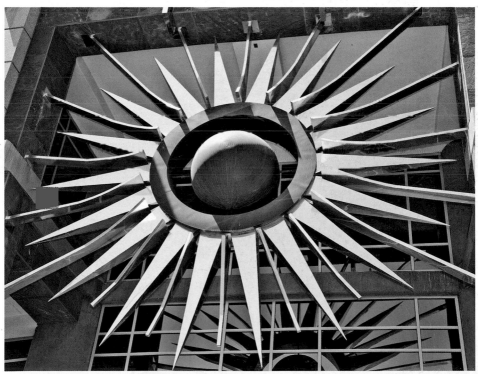

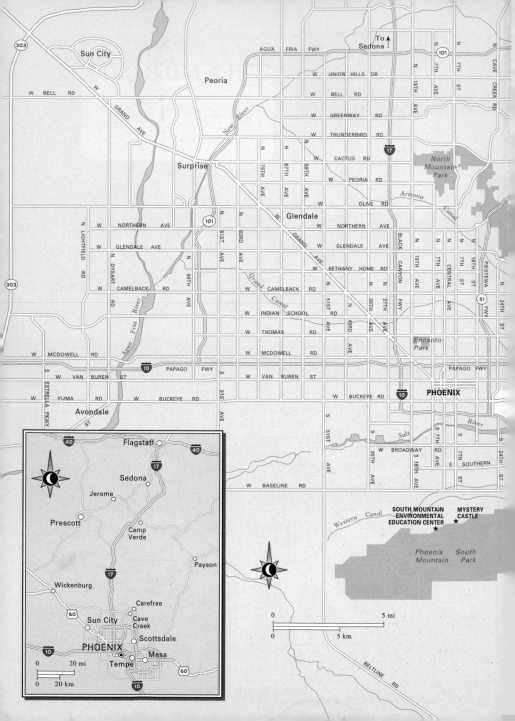

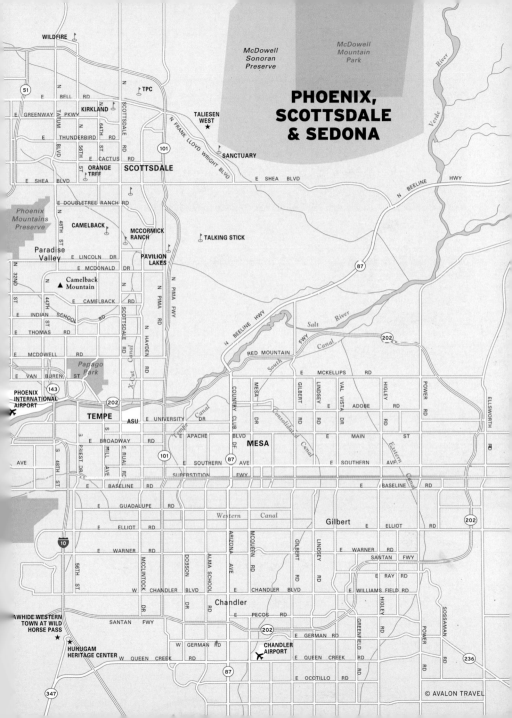

Contents

Discover Phoenix, Scottsdale & Sedona

"The only constant is change." This saying attributed to Heraclitus could easily be the motto of Phoenix, an energetic city that reinvents itself every decade or so. Phoenix, Scottsdale, and surrounding communities—together known as the Valley of the Sun—make up one of the country's fastest growing metro areas, enticing new residents with abundant sunshine, mountain vistas, and a resort lifestyle.

This desert playground boasts more than 200 golf courses, countless swimming pools, and miles of hiking and biking trails. Skyscrapers mark its status as the Southwest's commercial center, yet it's mountains, not architecture, that truly define the skyline. The McDowells, Superstitions, and other ranges encircle the Valley of the Sun, and the distinctive outline of Camelback stands a thousand feet above seas of red-tiled roofs and emerald green resorts.

While growth may be the city's lifeblood, the Sonoran Desert is its soul. The desert's twice-yearly rain pattern supports a surprisingly lush assortment of plants and animals, including the iconic saguaro cactus. Many species that have adapted to cope with local conditions are found nowhere else in the world.

Humans, too, have learned to conform to desert living. Hohokam farmers who settled here 1,500 years ago relied on a complex system of

canals, and the advent of air-conditioning set the stage for the city's post-WWII boom. In this metropolis of four million residents, cacti, coyotes, and lizards coexist with people.

Blend the exotic landscape with welcome winter sunshine and colorful cultural traditions, and you have a place where even locals live like they're on vacation, hiking before work or enjoying a late-night swim, booking their weekends with festivals or visits to the high country. Follow their lead: Taste the best Sonoran-style cuisine this side of the Mexican border. Enjoy Scottsdale's two favorite pastimes—shopping and nightlife. Discover centuries-old Native American traditions. Venture north to the red-rock monoliths of Sedona and the leafy oasis of Oak Creek Canyon.

Just remember to leave plenty of time to kick back on the patio and watch a desert sunset. Change may be constant, but the desert endures, an ever-present reminder of antiquity and grace—especially as the mountains turn purple and swatches of orange, vermilion, and magenta streak across a darkening sky.

Planning Your Trip

▶ WHERE TO GO

Phoenix

The Sonoran Desert's brilliant light and warmth permeate every aspect of Arizona's state capital, now the sixth-largest city in the country. With approximately 300 days of sunshine annually, it's possible to dine alfresco, play golf, or hike year-round. The jagged mountains that surround the Valley of the Sun are prime spots to explore the area's diverse desert landscape. For urban delights, visit downtown Phoenix and the college town of Tempe, where you'll find fascinating museums, cultural attractions, and popular restaurants.

Scottsdale

Phoenix's best-known suburb calls itself "The West's Most Western Town," but Scottsdale's is a modern West, blending chic resorts, restaurants, and

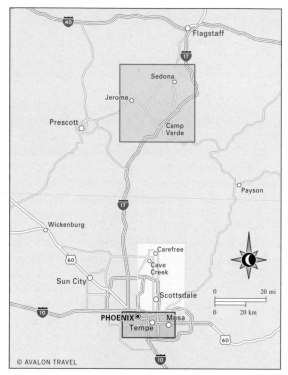

© AVALON TRAVEL

Phoenix Museum of History

golf course in Scottsdale

prickly pear cactus in Sedona

Oak Creek Canyon

IF YOU HAVE . . .

Heard Museum, Phoenix

- **THREE DAYS:** Visit Phoenix and Scottsdale.
- **FIVE DAYS:** Add Sedona.
- **ONE WEEK:** Add Jerome, Montezuma Castle, and Oak Creek Canyon.

nightspots with desert golf courses and eclectic boutiques selling cowboy boots, trendy brands, and luxury goods. The city's galleries support the country's third-largest art market, and its five-star spas are among the finest in the world. Scottsdale's commitment to the arts harks back to the 1930s, when architect Frank Lloyd Wright established his winter home and design incubator at Taliesin West.

Sedona

It's easy to understand why Sedona is called Red Rock Country. Its monumental sandstone formations and intricate spires—colored in shades of buff, gold, maroon, and orange—lure travelers and outdoor lovers. Explore on a Jeep tour or hike along miles of forest trails, then be pampered at a luxury inn or resort. Browse charming galleries, visit the stunning Chapel of the Holy Cross, and take a scenic drive through the green oasis of Oak Creek Canyon. Visit neighboring Verde Valley, where historic and cultural attractions include wineries and tasting rooms, the ancient cliff dwelling of Montezuma Castle, and the Old West mining town of Jerome.

red bird of paradise in summer

Phoenix's Desert Botanical Garden in December

► WHEN TO GO

Locals like to joke that the Valley of the Sun has three seasons: beautiful, hot, and "it can't get any hotter." And though there's some truth to that sentiment, savvy Phoenicians find ways to take full advantage of the sunny, desert climate year-round.

In spring, splashes of colorful wild-flowers and cactus blossoms greet visitors. Temperatures peak in the 70s and 80s during the day and cool down to "sweater weather" at night. Residents spend most of their time outdoors, taking advantage of the numerous golf courses, hiking spots, open-air shopping centers, and annual events like Major League Baseball spring training and the Phoenix Open.

You might just fall in love with Phoenix in the summer when it sizzles—or it may be the bargain rates at luxury resorts and spas that help you embrace the heat. The searing temperatures and constant sun send visitors and residents to the nearest swimming pool or air-conditioned building in midday. Cooler mornings and late nights provide relief, and dramatic monsoon storms deliver a refreshing reprieve many evenings in July and August.

Fall kicks off the social season. Residents eagerly return to their outdoor haunts in October and November, lingering on patios and gathering for festivals and concerts. Whether you're an art lover or outdoor enthusiast, it's an ideal time to visit.

By winter, the mercury dips into the 50s and 60s, but the sunshine is deliciously warm, and Phoenix becomes a mecca for snow-weary travelers. It can get downright chilly in Sedona (though never too cold for an invigorating hike), and the occasional light dusting of snow on the red rocks is a spectacular sight.

Explore Phoenix, Scottsdale & Sedona

▶ THE BEST OF THE VALLEY OF THE SUN

An extended weekend in Phoenix and Scottsdale can combine culture, adventure, and R&R. Instead of trying to check off a lengthy list of sights, choose a few highlights that match your interests, then savor the landscape like a local to experience its unique flavor.

Day 1

Make the most of your time by catching an early flight to Phoenix Sky Harbor International Airport. Drive the short distance to Tempe and have lunch before heading across Tempe Town Lake to get to know the Valley from its geographic heart, Papago Park. It's an easy scramble up a rounded, red-hued butte to the Hole-in-the-Rock formation, where you'll be rewarded with a spectacular view of the city. Within the protected reserve, you'll also find the Desert Botanical Garden, an impressive collection of the diverse cacti and plants that make their home in the Sonoran Desert. On your way back toward Phoenix, visit Pueblo Grande Museum and Archaeological Park, the remains of the ancient Hohokam settlement from which the modern city of Phoenix rose. Check into your hotel in Central Phoenix, and then have dinner at one of the independent restaurants that regularly earn praise from foodies, such as Pizzeria Bianco, The Tuck Shop, or Barrio Café.

Day 2

Rise with the sun and pick up coffee and a quick bite at Lux Central or La Grande Orange. Head out for a round of golf at one

Tempe Town Lake

Camelback Mountain

of the city's championship desert courses or hike Camelback Mountain, a Valley of the Sun icon. Spend the rest of your afternoon relaxing, either poolside at your hotel or shopping at the open-air Biltmore Fashion Park. Later, enjoy a glass of wine or a cocktail at one of the patio-centric establishments that locals frequent, like Postino, The Vig, or Chelsea's Kitchen.

Day 3

Fuel up with a hearty meal at Matt's Big Breakfast, or America's Taco Shop, then drive north to Taliesin West, Frank Lloyd Wright's winter home and architecture school. Learn how Wright's revolutionary work blended modern design with the Sonoran Desert landscape. Continue your architectural tour at Cosanti, the home and workshop of Paolo Soleri, a Wright acolyte. Keep heading south to Old Town Scottsdale and have a fabulously fresh lunch at Arcadia Farms or Café Monarch, then wander the grassy mall, stopping to visit the Old Adobe Mission, Scottsdale's first

Catholic church. Head across Scottsdale Road to the art districts of Marshall Way, 5th Avenue, and Main Street, where the city's chic galleries showcase contemporary and Western art. Have dinner at one of downtown's numerous restaurants, such as Cowboy Ciao or The Mission, and barhop among Scottsdale's hip clubs and lounges, including AZ88, Geisha A Go-Go, and Axis/Radius.

Day 4

Spend your last morning in Phoenix at South Mountain Park, either hiking or biking one of the desert trails or exploring on horseback. Afterward, enjoy an alfresco brunch at Morning Glory Café. Alternatively, linger downtown to check out the Desert Modernist Burton Barr Central Library, then get a dose of culture at the Phoenix Art Museum or the Heard Museum, one of the nation's finest collections of Native American art and artifacts. Grab a gourmet Pane Bianco sandwich for lunch before you have to catch your flight home.

Sure, it's tempting to kick back by the pool or to spend another day on the golf course, but Arizona is the land of rugged cowboys, desert rats, and adrenaline junkies. Put down the margarita–the state's wild side is calling.

ON HORSEBACK

Get honest-to-goodness, "no frills" lessons in cowboyin' at **Arizona Cowboy College.** From half-day sessions on horseback riding and roping to the comprehensive six-day course, learn authentic cowboy skills by working at this cattle ranch in Scottsdale.

ON THE ROAD

Head for the hills on the scenic **Apache Trail,** which leads through the fabled Superstition Mountains and the mining towns of Globe and Superior. If you'd rather let someone else do the driving, arrange a Jeep tour with **Arizona Trails,** blending scenery with history and, if you're game, a gold-panning lesson.

Former racer Bob Bondurant and his team coach thousands of students every year at **The Bob Bondurant School of High Performance Driving,** a custom-designed, 60-acre facility near Phoenix's Firebird International Raceway. Single-day courses cover skills ranging from introductory racing techniques to highway survival.

OFF-ROAD

Romp around Sedona's red rocks with popular **Pink Jeep Tours.** Charismatic guides describe the geology and ecosystem as they drive beefed-up Jeep Wranglers over steep boulders and along slickrock benches.

AT NIGHT

Catch a glimpse of the nocturnal desert by donning night-vision goggles on a tour with **Scottsdale's Stellar Adventures.** Spot bats and coyotes, and hunt for scorpions using UV lights that cause their exoskeletons to glow.

IN THE WATER

Fill a cooler with your favorite beverage and float on an inner tube provided by **Salt River Recreation** through Salt River Canyon, where you might catch a glimpse of a desert bighorn or wild pony.

TAKE A HIKE

Leave blacktop and rooftops behind on a hike into the Red Rock–Secret Mountain Wilderness Area near Sedona. The moderate climb to the natural rock arch known as **Devil's Bridge** blends scenery with geology.

IN THE AIR

Tempt both gravity and death by flying a plane on a "combat mission" over Phoenix's East Valley at **Fighter Combat International.** Even beginners learn to take the stick during air-combat tactics, "smoke chases," lead-and-follow drills, and weapons training.

the pink jeeps of Sedona's Pink Jeep Tours

▶ FAMILY ROAD TRIP

Phoenix, Scottsdale, and Sedona offer a diverse range of activities for the whole family. Start in the Valley of the Sun and explore downtown Phoenix's museums and parks, then head north to Sedona for a series of outdoor adventures. Finally, make your way back to Scottsdale for some Old West fun.

Day 1

Fly into Phoenix Sky Harbor International Airport and check into your resort. You've got plenty of time to explore the city, so spend the afternoon taking advantage of the resort's amenities, which range from water parks and tennis courts to day camps for kids.

Day 2

There's no better place to begin your trip to Phoenix than at its ancient foundations, the Pueblo Grande Museum and Archaeological

SOUTHWESTERN CULTURE AND HERITAGE

The American Southwest is a rich blend of Native American roots, vibrant Latino culture, and cowboy flair. Experience colorful festivals, enjoy the layered flavors of regional cuisine, and learn about traditions that reach back a century or more as you explore Arizona's largest city and the desert beyond.

PHOENIX

- Learn about Phoenix's past at **Pueblo Grande Museum and Archaeological Park.**

- At the **Heard Museum,** you'll find an unmatched introduction to Native American art and culture, as well as lively celebrations like the annual Indian Market or the world hoop-dancing championship.

- If you're downtown, get a quick snapshot of the Wild West at the **Wells Fargo History Museum,** displaying an authentic 19th-century stagecoach, antique guns, and a softball-size nugget of gold.

- In the East Valley, at Mesa's **Arizona Museum of Natural History,** you can pan for "gold" or lock yourself in a territorial jail cell. Nearby, the **Arizona Temple** visitor center provides an introduction to the state's Mormon pioneers.

- The Valley's agricultural past is being rediscovered at farmers markets and restaurants highlighting locally raised ingredients, such as the **Farm at South Mountain, Phoenix Public Market,** and family-oriented **Schnepf Farms.**

- For a taste of desert heritage cuisine, head for **Kai** restaurant at the Gila River Indian Community's Sheraton Wild Horse Pass Resort.

SCOTTSDALE

- The Wild West meets the New West in **Old Town,** where you'll find everything from kitschy souvenirs to classy galleries.

- The **Scottsdale Mall** anchors downtown's lively arts district and a few historic sites, including the **Old Adobe Mission,** built by Mexican and Yaqui Indian families in 1933. From mid-January through mid-April, the mall hosts free noontime festivals of **Native American music, dance, and food.**

- Downtown Scottsdale is home to several of the Valley's most popular Mexican-style restaurants, from the classic—**Old Town Tortilla Factory** and **Frank and Lupe's Old Mexico**—to the chic—**The Mission.**

- For Western flavor, head north to **Pinnacle Peak** steakhouse or **Reata Pass,** a cowboy-style eatery that began in the 1880s as a stagecoach stop. Next door,

Park. Go inside reconstructed pit houses and learn more about archaeology in the interactive gallery. Head to neighboring Tempe Town Lake, where you can rent paddleboats or let the little ones run wild in the water-soaked Splash Playground. Have lunch at one of Mill Avenue's many family-friendly restaurants before crossing back over the lake to Papago Park to tour the Phoenix Zoo, where you can touch stingrays or duck into the walk-through Monkey Village. In the evening, sample tacos and fajitas at Macayo's

Depot Cantina or dine inside Tempe's oldest building, Monti's La Casa Vieja.

Day 3

Begin your third day in the Valley at Matt's Big Breakfast or Scramble. Afterward, visit the Arizona State Capitol, restored to its original look in 1912, the year of Arizona's statehood. Nearby, the Wells Fargo Museum highlights the state's Wild West past. Consider a picnic lunch at Civic Space Park, where kids play in the grass or splash around

Greasewood Flat hosts Western music and dancing on weekends.

SEDONA

- Red-rock canyons and limestone bluffs shelter enigmatic rock art and cliff dwellings, such as those at **Palatki Heritage Site** and **Montezuma Castle National Monument,** home to the Sinagua people from about 1150 to 1400.

- To learn more about Sinagua culture, visit the **Verde Valley Archaeology Center** in Camp Verde.

- **Fort Verde State Historic Park** offers a glimpse of the frontier soldier's life.

- In the mountainside town of **Jerome,** the boom-and-bust business of mining takes center stage.

- When Jerome was booming during the early 1900s, nearby Cottonwood was a bustling commerce center, with mercantiles, blacksmiths, and a brisk bootlegging business that employed secret rooms and tunnels. For a legal taste of the grape, tour the **wine-tasting rooms** that line Main Street in **Old Town Cottonwood.**

- Sample farm to-table fare at **Crema** in Cottonwood or gourmet Mexican cuisine at **Elote Café** in Sedona.

Montezuma Castle National Monument, Sedona

Papago Park, Phoenix

in the water features, or Encanto Park, home of Enchanted Island Amusement Park. If it's too hot to be outdoors, grab a bite at the Arizona Science Center, a delightfully interactive museum in Heritage and Science Park. Younger kids may prefer the Children's Museum of Phoenix, across 7th Street. Older teens may enjoy a tour of Phoenix's progressive art and design at the Phoenix Art Museum and the Burton Barr Central Library, which offers brilliant views of the Phoenix skyline. Tonight, try dinner at one of downtown's pizzerias, like Cibo or the renowned Pizzeria Bianco.

Day 4

It's time to immerse yourself in the Sonoran Desert, with a morning hike in South Mountain Park, the world's largest municipal park. Hunt for ancient Native American petroglyphs or explore the pristine trails on horseback. Reward your adventurous spirit

with a hearty, gourmet brunch at the open-air The Farm at South Mountain. Explore the mountainside Mystery Castle, a private home built from objects found in the desert, or you may want to take the kids to Rawhide Western Town. The 1880s-themed Old West burg features dusty streets, stagecoach rides, and old-fashioned carnival games. After lunch, cross to the East Valley to pan for "gold," visit a territorial jail, and scope out the three-story Dinosaur Mountain at the Arizona Museum of Natural History in Mesa. Relax poolside at your resort before staking out a good spot for viewing the sunset.

Day 5

Today, discover Arizona's rich Native American history. Spend the morning at the Heard Museum, an impressive introduction to Arizona's original inhabitants and culture. Head north on I-17 to Montezuma Castle National Monument. The stunning five-story

Heard Museum, Phoenix

cliff dwelling near Camp Verde was once inhabited by the ancient Sinagua people. Shady tables near Beaver Creek make a good spot for a picnic (unless, of course, you stopped for lunch at the Rock Springs Café and sampled their famous fresh-baked pies). Just up the interstate, you can witness more Sinagua ingenuity in the petroglyphs, cliff dwellings, and early irrigation ditches at Montezuma Well, one of Arizona's unique geological wonders, a limestone sinkhole fed by 1.5 million gallons of water every day by underground springs.

From there, take I-17 to SR 179 and Sedona, driving into town on the Red Rock Scenic Byway to admire the monolithic Bell Rock, Courthouse Butte, and Cathedral Rock. Stop to tour Chapel of the Holy Cross, an elegant, Modernist church that appears to rise out of the red rocks, offering panoramic views. Check into your hotel, and after dinner, consider a Sedona Stargazing Tours adventure with an astronomer who will guide you around Sedona's star-studded nighttime sky.

Day 6

Have a hearty breakfast at Coffee Pot Restaurant and stroll the easy trails at Red Rock State Park or Crescent Moon Ranch Picnic Area, which features postcard views of Oak Creek and Cathedral Rock. Also, you can't come to Sedona without venturing into the backcountry on one of the ubiquitous Jeep tours. The guided journeys are a fun way to learn the names of Sedona's rock formations while getting an introduction to geology and wildlife. Pick up sandwiches at Sedona Memories or Indian Gardens before continuing north on SR 89A to explore the leafy refuge of Oak Creek Canyon. Hike the streamside West Fork Trail or plunge down the 80-foot-long natural rock slide at Slide Rock State Park. Explore the courtyards and stairways of Tlaquepaque Arts and Crafts

South Mountain Park, Phoenix

Cathedral Rock and Oak Creek, Sedona

Village and get a treetop view while you dine at Oak Creek Brewery and Grill or The Hideaway Restaurant.

Day 7

Take a side trip to the Old West mining town of Jerome. The hillside community was once called the "Wickedest Town in the West," and today it's a National Historic Landmark, welcoming visitors with a host of small cafés, shops, galleries, and saloons. Have lunch at Quince and learn about the Little Daisy Mine at the Jerome State Historic Park. Before driving back to the Valley of the Sun, consider a stop at Tuzigoot National Monument or Dead Horse Ranch State Park, a lush stretch of the Verde River that offers hiking, mountain biking, fishing, and equestrian areas. Make the 90-minute drive back to Scottsdale, where you check into one of the city's sprawling resorts.

McCormick-Stillman Railroad Park, Scottsdale

Day 8

Reacquaint yourself with the Valley of the Sun at Camelback Mountain. The moderately difficult trails are among the best in the area, although you may want to take the little ones to McCormick-Stillman Railroad Park, where they can ride the popular train or beautifully restored carousel. If your family includes a budding musician, spend the afternoon at the fabulous and fun Musical Instrument Museum, taking a break for lunch at the museum's excellent cafeteria. Or keep heading north on Scottsdale Road to Frontier Town in Cave Creek. Continue the Wild West theme with a steak dinner at Pinnacle Peak or Reata Pass, a historic stage stop.

Day 9

Today, you may want to camp out at your resort to enjoy the pools, tennis courts, and golf courses. However, if you're looking for a little adventure, travel east to explore the Superstition Mountains via the Apache Trail. Stop at Lost Dutchman State Park or the recreated mining town of Goldfield, or join a steamboat tour of Canyon Lake. Tonight, have dinner at one of Scottsdale's iconic Mexican restaurants, and then venture into the hidden nocturnal desert on an outing with Stellar Adventures to spot wildlife with the aid of night-vision goggles.

Day 10

On your last day in Scottsdale, wander the Western-themed streets of Old Town to pick up last-minute souvenirs and gifts. Hop on and off the free Scottsdale Trolley, which stops in the three arts districts and at Scottsdale Fashion Square. Grab lunch at The Orange Table or The Sugar Bowl before you have to catch your flight home.

► *LA BUENA VIDA:* DESERT CHIC

Brilliant light, rugged mountains, sculptural plantlife—few landscapes create such an evocative setting, but the Sonoran Desert also has a luxurious, cosmopolitan side, which lures pleasure-seekers and stressed-out vacationers to its resorts, golf courses, and award-winning restaurants and five-star spas. Even if your budget is limited, you can live *la buena vida* by scoping out off-season rates or sampling fine cuisine during happy hour, when several top-notch restaurants offer small plates or tapas. It doesn't cost a thing to window-shop at Scottsdale's boutiques and malls or to browse galleries in the art districts downtown. Lively cultural events are often free, and so are many attractions. During your charmed and chic week, sip margaritas poolside in Scottsdale, then retreat north to Sedona's red rocks.

Day 1

Arrive at Phoenix Sky Harbor International Airport and head to Papago Park to get your bearings in this sprawling city. The park's rounded, red-rock formation is an easy ascent, and its views of the desert metropolis will help you blow away the travel cobwebs. Visit the park's Desert Botanical Garden to learn about spiny cacti, green-bark paloverde, and colorful wildflowers. Afterward, head for your Scottsdale resort. Relax poolside or on a veranda overlooking the Valley of the Sun and enjoy—literally—the fruits of the desert in a delicious prickly pear margarita. Have dinner at one of Scottsdale's acclaimed restaurants, or order room service for a romantic meal on your private balcony.

Desert Botanical Garden, Phoenix

Old Adobe Mission, Scottsdale

Day 2

Wake up early to experience the desert at sunrise. Consider a leisurely hike up Pinnacle Peak or a round of golf at your resort. Reward your efforts and soothe any aching muscles at one of Scottsdale's deluxe spas, like the canyon-inspired Willow Stream Spa or the renowned Golden Door Spa, set against the Boulders Resort's namesake rock formation. Linger to savor a healthy lunch or enjoy a glass of bubbly while you take advantage of spa amenities like lush gardens, whirlpools, and cabanas. While away the rest of the afternoon at Kierland Commons and Scottsdale Quarter, shopping for resort wear and gifts or seeking out a cozy restaurant for dinner.

Day 3

Take a morning to explore the shops in Scottsdale's Old Town. If you've had enough retail therapy, opt instead for history and culture at the Old Adobe Mission and the Scottsdale Museum of Contemporary Art. Break for brunch at Arcadia Farms or graze gourmet-style at Bodega. Continue your cultural adventure by hopping aboard a free trolley or picking up a map for a self-guided walking tour of downtown's public sculptures. Pause en route to visit galleries showcasing edgy modern pieces along with traditional Southwestern canvases and bronzes. End your art tour at Scottsdale Fashion Square and SouthBridge along Scottsdale's waterfront, watching sunset colors reflect in the Arizona Canal. Spend the evening sampling Scottsdale's dining and nightlife scene or take in a concert at the Musical Instrument Museum.

Taliesin West, Scottsdale

Day 4

Set aside the morning to enjoy your resort's amenities or a leisurely horseback ride through the desert north of Scottsdale. Afterward, drive south on Scottsdale Road to Paradise Valley, where Paolo Soleri's quirky Cosanti bell foundry and artist community reveals the architect's theories on environmentally responsible design. Investigate the boutiques and cafés at the charming Tuscan-style Borgata mall. As evening approaches, enjoy a handcrafted cocktail at Sanctuary on Camelback Mountain Resort & Spa's stylish Jade Bar, where you can catch Mummy Mountain bathed in a desert sunset. For an elegant Western-style dinner, try the historic Lon's at the Hermosa Inn or go modern at the sleek Bourbon Steak.

Day 5

Tour Frank Lloyd Wright's winter home, Taliesin West, a stone, sand, and glass masterpiece that incorporates indigenous

Cosanti bell foundry

GREEN ARIZONA

Sugarloaf Loop, Coconino National Forest's Red Rock Ranger District

Visitors who expect to see a bare expanse of sand are often surprised at how green the Sonoran Desert can be, especially after summer or winter rains create an explosion of life. But, as Kermit the Frog would say, it's not easy being green, at least not for desert cities, dependent on air-conditioning and huge amounts of water.

For a list of certified green hotels, contact the Arizona Lodging and Tourism Association (www.stayinaz.com). The state's tourism board (www.arizonaguide.com) offers tips on greening your vacation through volunteer projects. But perhaps the simplest way to go green is to leave your car behind and spend more time exploring the outdoors on foot or bicycle. Great places to start:

IN THE CITY
The paved paths of the **Desert Botanical Garden** are an easy way to get to know native plants.

Phoenix's **mountain preserves** cover 35,000 acres and offer 200-plus miles of trail, including the popular but challenging trail to the top of Piestewa Peak, where long views reward hikers.

The largest municipal park in the country, **South Mountain,** includes a visitor center, picnic areas, and 51 miles of trails for hiking, horseback riding, and biking.

ON THE EDGES
Scottsdale's **McDowell Sonoran Preserve** protects 21,400 acres of lush and mountainous desert. Access points for hikers, bikers, and equestrians include the LEED-certified **Gateway Trailhead** near Bell Road.

Lost Dutchman State Park, east of the metro area, is an outstanding spot for wildflower viewing in February and March.

OUT OF TOWN
The 2,873,200 acres of **Tonto National Forest** include four sparkling reservoir lakes east of Phoenix, popular for boating and fishing.

Red Rock State Park near Sedona has educational exhibits, easy interpretive hikes, and a creekside setting that is ideal for bird-watching.

Coconino National Forest's **Red Rock Ranger District** boasts more than 200 miles of hiking trails, some suitable for mountain biking.

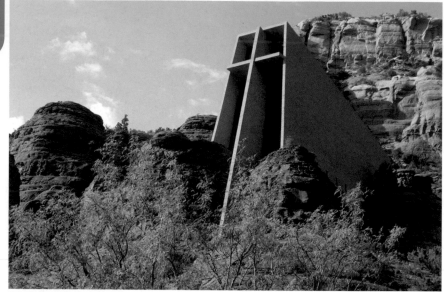

Chapel of the Holy Cross, Sedona

materials and blends indoor and outdoor spaces. Afterward, get a brief introduction to Native American art, culture, and design at the Heard Museum North, an intimate branch of the respected museum in downtown Phoenix. Continue north to have lunch at the charming El Encanto or stylish Café Bink before picking up I-17 to drive to the red-rock wonderland of Sedona. Stay in the heart of town in a luxury inn like El Portal, or escape to the Boynton Canyon Enchantment Resort and Mii Amo spa. Though you may never want to leave the shelter of the canyon's soaring cliff walls, a short drive back to town as the sun sets will reward you with awe-inspiring views and a delicious meal at Elote Café.

Day 6

This morning, survey the red-rock buttes from the sky while floating over Sedona in a hot-air balloon, gaining a bit of perspective of the vast scale of the region's rocky formations. Alternatively, explore Sedona's metaphysical

side with a guided vortex tour, followed by a spa treatment at Ayurveda Sedona or a private class at 7 Centers Yoga Arts. Afterward, visit the Chapel of the Holy Cross, a stunning church that seems to emerge from its red-rock foundations. Spend the afternoon browsing the boutiques and galleries at sycamore-shaded Tlaquepaque village. Stay for dinner at one of Tlaquepaque's restaurants or dine creekside at L'Auberge in Uptown.

Day 7

On your last morning, linger over an alfresco breakfast in one of Sedona's charming courtyard restaurants, such as the Heartline Gourmet Express or Secret Garden Café. Spend the rest of the morning shopping in Uptown or along Gallery Row, where you may find a piece of locally made pottery or a handmade Navajo rug to take home. Drive 90 minutes back to Phoenix and Sky Harbor International Airport to catch your return flight.

PHOENIX AND VICINITY

Phoenix, the Sonoran Desert's largest city, is old and new, urban and wild. Glittering high-rises are backdropped by purple-blue mountain ranges. Native saguaros, prickly pears, and paloverde trees sidle up to emerald green golf courses. Coyotes and bobcats wander into suburban neighborhoods. The historic Yaqui village of Guadalupe is surrounded by subdivisions, and the suburbs are in turn surrounded by Akimel O'odham (Pima) and Pee Posh (Maricopa) communities and national forest. Rising above it all, sending shadows across ancient stone calendars and recharging thousands of solar cells, is the ever-present desert sun.

Phoenix and its surrounding cities, towns, and suburbs are known as the Valley of the Sun.

In recent decades, this sprawling metropolitan area was one of the fastest growing in the nation. With rapid growth, the only constant is change, and Phoenix has been reinvented time and again by each influx of new residents: Hohokam villagers, Mormon pioneers, ranching and farming families, health-seekers and retirees, college students and technology workers.

Today's Phoenix is a cultural hub, with a host of new, architecturally significant museums, arts districts, sports arenas, and revitalized neighborhoods, now linked by a light-rail network. But underlying modern Phoenix is a 2,000-year-old city, its ancient canal system forming the skeleton of today's concrete-lined waterways, the outlines of villages still visible from busy freeways.

© CHRIS CURTIS/123RF.COM

PHOENIX AND VICINITY

HIGHLIGHTS

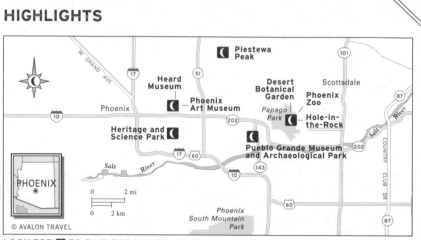

© AVALON TRAVEL

LOOK FOR TO FIND RECOMMENDED SIGHTS, ACTIVITIES, DINING, AND LODGING.

Heritage and Science Park: Get a glimpse of Phoenix's original Victorian-era townsite. Heritage Square's eight historic homes now house small museums and popular restaurants and bars, and its futuristic Arizona Science Center is the perfect spot to escape the summer heat (page 34).

Heard Museum: Learn about the rich culture of the state's original inhabitants at what is perhaps the finest collection of Native American art in the world. The Heard Museum is one of Arizona's great treasures (page 37).

Phoenix Art Museum: Browse galleries featuring a diverse selection of American, European, and Latin American artists, as well as Asian art and fashion design. The building is sleek and contemporary, and so are its events, from film screenings to gallery talks to the First Friday art walk (page 38).

Hole-in-the-Rock: Head for the rounded, red sandstone formations of Papago Park and scramble up to view an opening in the rock that was once used by the ancient Hohokam civili-

zation for astronomical observations (page 41).

Phoenix Zoo: Ride a camel, walk through a jungle with chattering squirrel monkeys, or meet some of Arizona's native species—coyotes, javelinas, wolves, and more. It's been voted one of the nation's top five zoos for kids, but grown-ups can have plenty of fun here as well (page 42).

Desert Botanical Garden: Get a taste of the Sonoran Desert without leaving the city. The garden easily claims the world's largest collection of desert plants, with thousands of cacti, shrubs, trees, and colorful wildflowers (page 42).

Pueblo Grande Museum and Archaeological Park: Discover Phoenix's ancient roots. The site of a Hohokam village that stood here from about A.D. 100 to 1400, Pueblo Grande offers a fascinating into the city's past (page 43).

Piestewa Peak: Do as the locals do and make your way to the top of this peak in the Phoenix Mountains Preserve. The Summit Trail is steep, but the rewards are views in every direction and a chance to commune with saguaros, lizards, and other denizens of the desert (page 71).

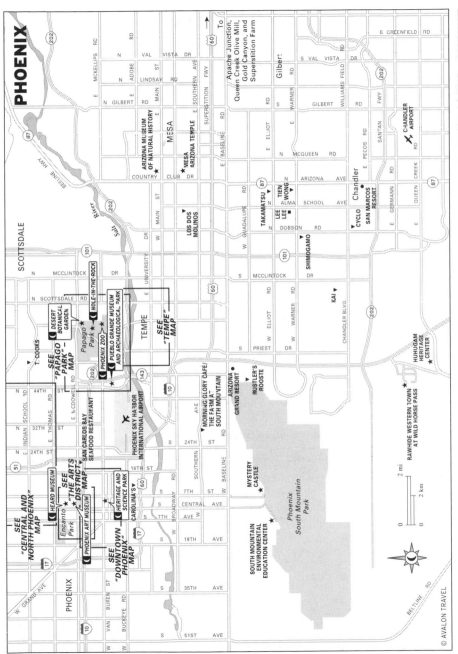

PHOENIX

SCOTTSDALE

MESA

TEMPE

Gilbert

Chandler

PHOENIX

ARIZONA MUSEUM OF NATURAL HISTORY

MESA ARIZONA TEMPLE

LOS DOS MOLINOS

TAKAMATSU

TIEN WONG

LEE LEE

CYCLO

SAN MARCOS RESORT

SHIMOGAMO

KAI

HUHUGAM HERITAGE CENTER

MOLE-IN-THE-ROCK

DESERT BOTANICAL GARDEN

Papago Park

PHOENIX ZOO

PUEBLO GRANDE MUSEUM AND ARCHAEOLOGICAL PARK

SEE "PAPAGO PARK" MAP

SEE "TEMPE" MAP

SAN CARLOS BAY SEAFOOD RESTAURANT

PHOENIX SKY HARBOR INTERNATIONAL AIRPORT

MORNING GLORY CAFE/ THE FARM AT SOUTH MOUNTAIN

ARIZONA GRAND RESORT

RUSTLER'S ROOSTE

SEE "CENTRAL AND NORTH PHOENIX" MAP

HEARD MUSEUM

SEE "THE ARTS DISTRICT" MAP

Encanto Park

PHOENIX ART MUSEUM

HERITAGE AND SCIENCE PARK

CAROLINA'S

SEE "DOWNTOWN PHOENIX" MAP

MYSTERY CASTLE

Phoenix South Mountain Park

SOUTH MOUNTAIN ENVIRONMENTAL EDUCATION CENTER

RAWHIDE WESTERN TOWN AT WILD HORSE PASS

0   2 mi
0   2 km

Apache Junction, Queen Creek Olive Mill, Gold Canyon, and Superstition Farm

CHANDLER AIRPORT

tiger at the Phoenix Zoo

Hints of the past are everywhere—a glimpse of enigmatic petroglyghs carved into a large boulder, the intoxicating scent of citrus blossoms on a spring breeze, the sounds of mariachi music on a festival day—linking residents and visitors to the generations who grew this vibrant, livable city out of arid desert.

With more than 200 days of sunshine annually, the Valley of the Sun is a recreational nirvana, offering mountain hikes and horseback rides along with world-class golf courses and pampering spas. Warm days by the pool or on the links melt into a blazing sea of color at sunset. The heady mix of sun and fun has tempted many to make a permanent move, and Phoenix is thick with transplants from all parts of the nation. More than a few remember shoveling snowy driveways and sidewalks, and if you ask them about torrid summers, they'll be the first to hand you that hoary Arizona line, "Yeah, but it's a dry heat."

The people who have moved here brought with them foods and festivals, adding to venerable Latino and Native American traditions, creating a rich blend of cultures and flavors, from bougainvillea-draped adobes to dazzling high-rises, salsa to sushi, Western swing to Chicago blues. Sprinkle in some desert mystique, and you have the unique flavor that defines Phoenix.

To get to know the city and its residents, hit the trail that climbs Piestewa Peak, dine on corn tortillas and carne asada at a neighborhood taqueria, or join the crowd milling around the stadium before a Diamondbacks game. Discover the ancient culture of the region's Native American people at the Heard Museum, and meet desert denizens at the Phoenix Zoo or Desert Botanical Garden. But don't explore by checking off a long list of tourist sites. Instead, spend your time gathering experiences: listening to bees crowding a sweet-smelling mesquite tree, tasting a freshly picked orange at a farm stand, sipping a local ale on a shaded and misted patio. The memories you make will linger long after a suntan begins to fade.

PLANNING YOUR TIME

Plan to spend at least three days in Phoenix, balancing sightseeing with cultural events and the bounty of outdoor activities. Consider a hike or a round of golf in the morning and afternoon visits to the Phoenix Art Museum, Heritage Square, or the world-renowned Heard Museum, a rich repository of Native American art and artifacts. A week is even better to make the most of a trip to the Valley of the Sun. Phoenix and the surrounding suburbs each offer pockets of pedestrian-friendly neighborhoods to explore, and you can add a day looping through the legendary Superstition Mountains east of the city.

Families will find a lot of kid-friendly activities in the Valley. Most of the year, kids will want to spend morning, noon, and night soaking up the local pools and water parks, a recreational specialty found at many resorts. When the weather is a bit cooler, though, the Phoenix Zoo and the Old West–themed Rawhide Western Town can be fun diversions. Kids and grown-ups alike find plenty of amazements and amusements in the Sonoran Desert landscape. Hikers, mountain bikers, and horseback riders of all levels can explore the cactus-dotted peaks that rise within and around the city. You can even get up-close and personal without leaving pavement, watching white-winged doves gorge on cactus fruit at the Desert Botanical Garden or strolling among the red sandstone buttes of Papago Park.

One of the largest urban centers in the United States in terms of land area, the Valley of the Sun covers 2,000 square miles. To explore, you'll definitely need a car. The Valley's four million residents crisscross the city daily thanks to a large web of freeways. Fortunately for visitors, many of the best sights, parks, restaurants, and shops are clustered in a central strip running from South Mountain through downtown Phoenix and Tempe to North Scottsdale. The main commuter arteries are I-10, Loops 101 and 202, the Piestewa Freeway, Central Avenue, and Camelback Road.

The weather, in all likelihood, will shape what you do and when you do it. October through April, Phoenix is heavenly, with warm days and cool evenings. In winter, nighttime temperatures occasionally drop below freezing. Summer is a different story. Count on triple-digit temps June through September, making a swimming pool or air-conditioned escape mandatory. But don't let summers scare you away. As the locals say, "It's a dry heat." When you emerge from a pool into the desert's arid climate, you'll find yourself shivering, and most local businesses keep air conditioners cranked to arctic levels. But you won't be trapped inside if you take a cue from desert dwellers and use the cooler early morning to hike or play a round of golf. Summer is also the opportunity to indulge at luxury resorts for bargain prices.

HISTORY

Phoenix is called a "young" city so often it's easy to forget that an entire ancient civilization is buried underneath it. Native Americans have called the Sonoran Desert home for thousands of years, but the Hohokam people dug the first irrigation canals fed by the Salt River about 1,500 years ago. They improved and expanded the system over centuries using nothing but wood and stone tools, simple leveling devices, and their own labor. Some canals were as long as 20 miles and carried thousands of gallons of water through a complex series of main lines, laterals, and small ditches. At its height around 1300, the system watered more than 10,000 acres scattered across most of what is now metro Phoenix. The Hohokam's corn, beans, squash, and cotton crops supported as many as 50,000 people, making the Salt River Valley one of the largest settlements in prehistoric North America. But after nearly a millennium of growth, Hohokam society began a slow collapse, likely triggered by a combination of drought, environmental stresses, and conflict. Some archaeologists say the Hohokam's canal network was destroyed by flooding. Whatever their reasons, by the end of the 1400s, the people had abandoned their pueblos and canals for small farming villages scattered across the region.

Modern Phoenix didn't get its start until 1867, when a man named Jack Swilling passed through and saw that the Salt River Valley looked like a good place for farming. The broad, fertile valley was filled with desert grasses, mesquite, willow, and cottonwood trees, and best of all, the wide, winding river that flowed down out of the mountains to the northeast. The onetime army scout, gold miner, cattle rancher, and saloon owner returned home to Wickenburg, a mining town about 50 miles northwest of present-day Phoenix, and convinced a group of local residents to back him. With their funds, Swilling organized a company to dig irrigation canals and establish farms in the desert valley.

It wasn't long before he and the dozens of settlers who followed discovered that digging up the ancient Hohokam canal system was an easier way to bring water to their fields than starting from scratch. So it was that an erudite settler named Lord Darrell Duppa suggested they name their new town Phoenix, after the mythical bird that rises from its own ashes after being consumed by flame.

By 1900, the young town's population had grown to 5,554, thanks to a long growing season and new railroads that took farmers' crops from Union Station downtown all across the United States. Modern technology didn't solve all their problems, though. Snowmelt and rain regularly sent the Salt River over its banks. The worst flood on record occurred in February 1901, swelling the river to three miles wide in some places, wiping out crops, houses, and the all-important railroad bridge. The brand-new territorial capitol west

of downtown was inundated, too, destroying many early records. Luckily, President Theodore Roosevelt rode to the rescue with a bold plan and several million dollars.

Roosevelt tasked the newly formed federal Bureau of Reclamation with building a hydroelectric dam on the Salt River in 1911 to control flooding and generate electricity. It was the first project the new agency tackled, and it tamed the free-flowing river by diverting it into an expanded canal system, triggering one of the city's first big boom periods. With an economy fueled by the "Five C's"—citrus, cotton, cattle, copper, and climate—Phoenix's population mushroomed to nearly 30,000 people by 1920, then added almost 20,000 more by 1930, matching the Hohokam's previous record of 50,000 inhabitants in just 50 years.

Following World War II, soldiers (many of whom had trained at air bases located in Phoenix for its flying-friendly weather) returned to the area and its burgeoning aerospace industry. As air-conditioning became widely available and early technology-manufacturing companies moved here in search of cheap land, the population grew past 100,000 by 1950 and neared an almost-unimaginable 440,000 by 1960.

Today, some 1.5 million people live in Phoenix, making it the sixth-largest city in the nation behind New York City, Los Angeles, Chicago, Houston, and Philadelphia. Growth has come with a price, however. Ozone alerts, blowing dust and particulates, and the destruction of pristine desert for new subdivisions have impacted the quality of life in recent years. But the same spirit that drove Phoenicians to build a metropolis in less than 150 years is pushing them to dream up new solutions, including a light-rail system and solar energy development, putting the city at the leading edge of sustainable architectural design.

THE VALLEY OF THE SUN

© ANTON FOLTIN/123RF.COM

a new home under construction in Phoenix

Phoenix, now the sixth-largest city in the country, is merely a part of an immense metropolitan area known as the Valley of the Sun. And, thanks to nearly 300 days a year of sunshine, the nickname isn't just a tourism slogan. "The Valley," as locals call it, is ringed by mountain ranges, and after decades of suburban sprawl, the population has crept beyond the valley floor. Since 2000, more than 1 million people have moved here. Developers have consumed huge swaths of agricultural land and pristine desert. Formerly independent cities and towns now blend from one into another, connected by a giant system of freeways. In fact, the U.S. Census Bureau now designates all of Maricopa and Pinal Counties as part of the Phoenix metropolitan area, a mammoth conglomeration of 60-plus municipalities, Native American lands, and 4.2 million people.

The East Valley was the first to experience a huge surge of arrivals in the 1980s and 1990s, when small cities like Chandler and former agricultural centers like Gilbert, Queen Creek, and Apache Junction became stucco-home boomtowns. Bedroom communities like Fountain Hills and Ahwatukee expanded practically overnight. Scottsdale in the Northeast Valley experienced significant growing pains after annexing huge portions of land.

A decade later, master-planned communities—like Anthem in the north, Gold Canyon in the east, and Maricopa in the south—pushed farther into the desert. Developers in the West Valley turned huge tracts of land into subdivisions that now house hundreds of thousands of people. Glendale and the retirement community of Sun City were soon engulfed by Surprise, Avondale, Goodyear, Peoria, and Buckeye. Civic leaders scrambled to find the best ways to turn their small towns into big ones.

With the housing bust in 2008, the Valley's growth-dependent economy stalled, and the Phoenix real estate market was one of the hardest-hit in the country. "For Sale" signs and foreclosure auctions are now a common sight, and decade-low prices are drawing real estate investors and out-of-staters looking for retirement home bargains. How all this will shift future demographics isn't clear, but Phoenix is a city well accustomed to change.

Sights

Phoenix is a sprawling expanse of neighborhoods and suburbs, and its attractions are scattered throughout. You'll need a car to navigate the Valley of the Sun, though the new light-rail conveniently connects some of the most popular sights, including the Heard Museum, the Phoenix Art Museum, the Arizona Science Center, and Tempe's university neighborhood along Mill Avenue.

DOWNTOWN AND THE ARTS DISTRICT

Like any Old West town worth its salt, Phoenix has endured boom-and-bust cycles since its founding in 1870. However, unlike its ghost town brethren, Phoenix has a knack for reemerging from hard times, and downtown Phoenix has risen to glittering new heights.

In the city's early days, farmers and ranchers came to town to see a show or to pick up supplies. Following decades of suburban flight and urban decay, an estimated $3 billion was spent redeveloping the 90-block area dubbed **Copper Square** (602/495-1500, www. coppersquare.com). Businesses and, more importantly, people, are returning to downtown's stadiums, museums, and concert venues, supporting new restaurants and bars. The construction of a new convention center and Arizona State University's downtown campus has brought nighttime pedestrian traffic to the once-empty streets. The light-rail in particular has given the area a new lease on life. Phoenix's downtown was built in an easy-to-navigate grid, but if you have any questions or need directions, look for one of the Copper Square "ambassadors," easily identified by their orange shirts.

Arizona State Capitol

When Tucson, Arizona's original territorial capital, was declared a Confederate hotbed, the capital was moved to a log cabin in Prescott before finally being settled in Phoenix in 1889. In an effort to prove to the federal government that Arizona was ready for statehood, the territorial legislature constructed a capitol building between 1898 and 1901. The domed design was modified by legislators, who scaled back its size and added features appropriate for the desert climate, like thick masonry walls for insulation and ventilating windows. They painted the dome copper as a tribute to one of Arizona's essential economic resources.

As the state grew, so did the demands on the building. Part-time Arizona resident Frank Lloyd Wright submitted plans in 1957 for Oasis, a massive capitol complex that would have transferred the legislature, governor, and Supreme Court from downtown to Papago Park—at a whopping cost of $5 million. It was immediately rejected. (The Capitol museum collection includes a model of Wright's proposal, and you can see one of the 125-foot-tall spires for the project at Scottsdale Road and Frank Lloyd Wright Boulevard in North Scottsdale.) Instead, the state House and Senate were relocated into bunker-like buildings on either side of the capitol in 1960, and the governor moved to the Executive Tower behind the capitol.

A renovation in 1981 restored the capitol to its appearance in 1912, the year of Arizona's statehood, and the dome was finally given a proper copper plating: 4.8 million pennies-worth, a fitting number for the 48th state. That same year, the **Arizona Capitol**

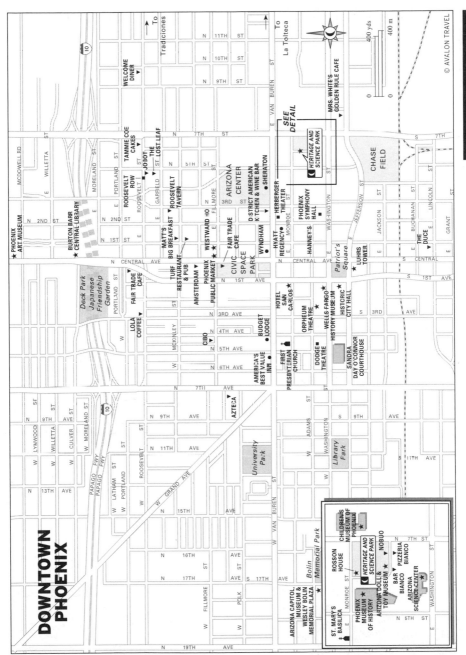

© AVALON TRAVEL

DOWNTOWN PHOENIX

Museum (1700 W. Washington St., 602/926-3620, www.lib.az.us/museum, 9 A.M.–4 P.M. Mon.–Fri., free) was opened, allowing visitors to see the old House and Senate chambers, offices of the governor, and changing exhibitions about Arizona's history. Displays include state symbols, memorabilia about the Harvey Girls, and artifacts from and photos of the USS *Arizona,* the battleship sunk at Pearl Harbor.

Civic Space Park

Part of an effort by city leaders to transform downtown into a vibrant urban space, Civic Space Park (424 N. Central Ave., 602/262-4734, http://phoenix.gov/parks, 5:30 A.M.–11 P.M. daily, free) brings green design to the neighborhood, with three acres of rolling lawns, dancing water fountains, and leafy trees that are expected to shade as much as 70 percent of the park once they mature.

Her Secret is Patience, a massive fabric-net sculpture that hangs over the park from steel rings, has garnered some controversy, both because of its abstract shape and its $2.4 million price tag. Artist Janet Echelman named the piece after a line in a Ralph Waldo Emerson poem ("Adopt the pace of nature; her secret is patience"), saying her work was inspired by Arizona's monsoon clouds and saguaro cactus blossoms, though some liken the funnel-shaped sculpture to a giant jellyfish or purple tornado. The kinetic sculpture billows in the wind and glows in brilliant shades of violet and orange after sunset, part of the nighttime transformation that makes this park so unique. During the day, solar panels on the park's shade structures collect energy. At sunset, a dozen LED-lit poles put on a show at the south end of the park while whimsical water features for kids glow purple. There is even space for movies and small concerts, which attract students from Arizona State University's adjacent downtown campus.

Wells Fargo History Museum

For a snapshot of the Wild West, duck into the Wells Fargo History Museum (145 W. Adams St., 602/378-1852, www.wellsfargohistory.com/museums, 9 A.M.–5 P.M. Mon.–Fri., free), where you'll be greeted by an icon of Arizona's history—an authentic 19th-century stagecoach that still bears the scars of a hard life roaming the West's bumpy trails. The small collection of memorabilia includes antique guns, Western artwork by N. C. Wyeth and Frederic Remington, and a softball-size nugget of gold. Plus, kids can try their hands at the telegraph or climb aboard a replica stagecoach.

St. Mary's Basilica

Phoenix's citizens built their first Catholic church in 1881 from hand-formed adobe. It was replaced in 1902 by St. Mary's Basilica (231 N. 3rd St., 602/354-2100, www.st-marysbasilica.org, 10 A.M.–4 P.M. Mon.–Fri., 10 A.M.–6 A.M. Sat., 8 A.M.–1 P.M. Sun., free), a Spanish Colonial Revival church that celebrates mass daily. Pope John Paul II named St. Mary's a minor basilica in 1985, and two years later he visited this Franciscan church on a trip to Phoenix. The basilica's collection of stained-glass windows is the largest in the state, and its bright interior is worth a stop. The gift shop is open Thursday–Sunday.

◖ Heritage and Science Park

Heritage Square (115 N. 6th St., 602/262-5071, http://phoenix.gov/parks) is a bit of an anomaly in car-loving, tear-it-down-and-build-something-new Phoenix. The historic park protects the only remaining residential buildings from Phoenix's original 1870 townsite. Today, the eight historic structures house small museums, offices, shops, and restaurants. **Rosson House** (115 N. 6th St., 602/262-5070, www.rossonhousemuseum.org, 10 A.M.–4 P.M. Wed.–Sat., noon–4 P.M. Sun., $7.50 adults, $4 children 6–12) is the most ornate, and even

BUILT IN PHOENIX

The term "Southwest Style" often brings to mind the seas of tile-roofed tract homes surrounding Phoenix, but the city can lay claim to several indigenous architectural styles and 35 historic districts.

Prehistoric villages (A.D. 1-1450): More than 2,000 years ago, the Hohokam people built semi-subterranean pit houses of mud and brush. Later, they puddled layers of adobe to make multistory pueblos. Home to 50,000, the Salt River Valley was one of the largest population centers in North America. Today, visitors can tour an 800-year-old platform mound village at **Pueblo Grande Museum and Archaeological Park** (4619 E. Washington St., 602/495-0901, www.pueblogrande.com).

Pioneer period (1880-1915): The handsome redbrick houses of **Heritage Square** (115 N. 6th St., 602/262-5071, www.phoenix.gov/parks) are what remains of the city's original townsite. Today, they serve as restaurants and museums, but in the late 1800s, they were home to territorial merchants and traders. **Rosson House** (115 N. 6th St., 602/262-5070, www.rossonhousemuseum.org), a stately 1895 Eastlake Victorian, is open for public tours.

Boomtown (1920-1935): Downtown Central Avenue hints at a former frontier town's big-city aspirations. The renaissance-revival **Hotel San Carlos** (220 N. Central Ave., 602/253-4121, www.hotelsancarlos.com) and the Art Deco **Westward Ho** (618 N. Central Ave.) opened in 1928 as luxury hotels that attracted Hollywood stars, politicos, and gangsters. Also in 1928, **City Hall** (125 W. Washington St.) was completed. In 1929, the Art Deco **Luhrs Tower** (45 W. Jefferson St.) provided office space and a members' lounge, and the Spanish Revival **Orpheum Theatre** (203 W. Adams St., 602/534-5600, www.

orpheum-theater.com) opened as a vaudeville venue. The Friends of the Orpheum Theatre (602/495-7139, www.friendsoftheorpheumtheatre.org) offer free tours twice monthly. Call for times.

Midcentury Modern (1948-1970): With the end of WWII and the advent of air-conditioning, Phoenix boomed once again. Frank Lloyd Wright designed several homes and businesses, including **Taliesin West** (12621 N. Frank Lloyd Wright Blvd., 480/860-2700, www.franklloydwright.org, 9 A.M.-4 P.M. daily, closed Tues.-Wed. July-Aug.), his winter home and studio since 1937. In 1956, Wright's acolyte Paolo Soleri designed his own studio home, **Cosanti** (6433 E. Doubletree Ranch Rd., 480/948-6145, www.arcosanti.org). Good examples of midcentury design include the 1964 **Phoenix Financial Center** (3443 N. Central Ave.) and the 1948 **Hanny's,** downtown's first "modern" department store, now a restaurant (40 N. 1st St., 602/252-2285, http://hannys.net). Local architect Al Beadle designed many iconic ranch houses in the **Paradise Gardens** neighborhood near the Phoenix Mountains. Nearby **Marlen Gardens** was designed and built by Arizona architect Ralph Haver. In late March, **Modern Phoenix** (www.modernphoenix.net) hosts a tour of midcentury residences.

Desert Modernism (1990-present): In recent decades, Phoenix architects have embraced light and space. Good examples of Desert Modernism include three public libraries, the Will Bruder-designed **Burton Barr Central Library** (1221 N. Central Ave.), the Richard+Bauer-designed **Desert Broom Library** (29710 N. Cave Creek Rd.), and the Gould Evans and Wendell Burnette-designed **Palo Verde Branch Library** (4402 N. 51st Ave.).

when it was built in 1895 by Roland and Flora Rosson for $7,525, the Victorian home's octagonal turret and shaded veranda were considered extravagant. Flora, who came from a wealthy family, purchased the entire city block, allowing plenty of space for the 2,800-square-foot

home's 10 rooms, now restored with period furnishings and pressed-tin ceilings. Docent-guided tours are available.

Nearby, the 1901 Stevens House is home to the **Arizona Doll & Toy Museum** (602 E. Adams, 602/253-9337, 10 A.M.-4 P.M.

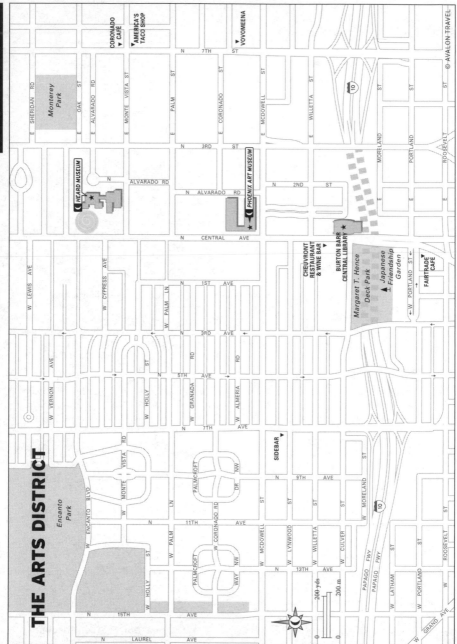

THE ARTS DISTRICT

© KATHLEEN BRYANT

Arizona Science Center has interactive exhibits.

Tues.–Sat., noon–4 P.M. Sun., $3 adults, $1 children under 12), which showcases antique dolls, vintage toys, and a reproduction of a turn-of-the-20th-century one-room schoolhouse.

Arizona Science Center

One of the best museums in the Valley and a hit with kids, the Arizona Science Center (600 E. Washington St., 602/716-2000, www.azscience. org, 10 A.M.–5 P.M. daily, $14 adults, $11 children 3–17) packs 350 interactive exhibits into 40,000 square feet of gallery space, making science seem cool and even a little scary: Climb a rock wall, race up a pulley system, make clouds, or lie on a bed of 1,000 nails. Noted architect Antoine Predock designed the sprawling concrete-and-metal building, creating soaring spaces for the large displays. The museum's high-tech IMAX theater and planetarium feature a series of shows throughout the day, and nationally traveling exhibitions regularly make a stop here. There's a gift shop and an on-site café.

Children's Museum of Phoenix

It seems fitting that Jackson Pollock's old elementary school should find new life as the splashy Children's Museum of Phoenix (215 N. 7th St., 602/253-0501, www.childrensmuseumofphoenix.org, 9 A.M.–4 P.M. daily, $11), a hands-on, 70,000-square-foot gallery dedicated to little ones 10 and under. Would-be Picassos and Pollocks will find more than finger-paints here, though. In 2008, the historic Monroe School Building was transformed into a playground designed to "engage the minds, muscles, and imaginations of children." Kids can navigate through the Noodle Forest, climb up a makeshift tree house, pedal through a tricycle car wash, or simply enjoy a little reading in the comfy Book Loft. It's a great place for exploring on a hot day.

◖ Heard Museum

For thousands of years, people have made their home in the Southwest. The Heard Museum

© KATHLEEN BRYANT

The Heard Museum highlights Native American art.

(2301 N. Central Ave., 602/252-8848, www. heard.org, 9:30 A.M.–5 P.M. Mon.–Sat., 11 A.M.–5 P.M. Sun., $18 adults, $7.50 children 6–12) documents millennia-old traditions, offering an impressive introduction to Native American art and Arizona's original inhabitants. Experience what it is like to live in a Navajo hogan, or learn how the intricate weavings and beadwork found in many clothes, baskets, and rugs reflect a tribe's unique history. The museum displays sand paintings, Barry Goldwater's collection of 437 Hopi kachina dolls, and boldly imaginative works by contemporary artists, as well as photographs documenting the indignities of those forced to live on reservations and in boarding schools in the 19th and 20th centuries.

The museum started as the personal collection of Dwight and Maie Heard, who built the first incarnation of the Spanish Colonial building on their private grounds in 1929 to house the art and artifacts that had begun to overtake their home. Dwight died of a heart attack as the display cabinets were being installed, but Maie forged ahead, overseeing the museum until her death in 1951. The Heard has been significantly expanded over the years, and its grounds, beautifully landscaped with native plants and trees, also provide space for music and dance performances, special events, and festivals, like the annual Indian Fair and Market. The gift shop sells art and jewelry by Native American artisans, and the ironwood-shaded café serves posole, tepary bean hummus, and other Southwestern specialties.

(Phoenix Art Museum

For years, the Phoenix Art Museum (1625 N. Central Ave., 602/257-1222, www.phxart.org, 10 A.M.–9 P.M. Wed., 10 A.M.–5 P.M. Thurs.–Sat., noon–5 P.M. Sun. $15 adults, $6 children ages 6–17, free after 3 P.M. Wed.) limped by with a small but respectable collection of art. That all changed in 1996 when the museum

© KATHLEEN BRYANT

Phoenix Art Museum

launched an ambitious makeover that tripled its size and gave new focus to its acquisitions and exhibitions. A later $50 million expansion added a grassy sculpture garden and a dramatic, glass-enclosed lobby and entry plaza.

Today, you'll find a broad cross section of art, with European, American, and Latin American artists like Claude Monet, Pablo Picasso, Georgia O'Keeffe, Mark Rothko, and Frida Kahlo, as well as a nicely curated Asian art gallery. A new four-level wing has space for large-scale contemporary pieces, photography, and the museum's 4,500-piece fashion design collection, with garments by Balenciaga, Chanel, Dior, and Yves Saint Laurent.

The museum hosts film screenings, lectures, live concerts, and blockbuster traveling exhibitions, which have featured Impressionism, Rembrandt, Richard Avedon, and the glassworks of Dale Chihuly. Admission fees are waived after 5 P.M. Wednesdays and on the first Friday evening of every month, when the museum joins downtown galleries and studios in hosting the popular art walk. There's a gift shop and café on-site.

Encanto Park

Encanto Park (2605 N. 15th Ave., 602/261-8991, http://phoenix.gov/parks, 5:30 A.M.–11 P.M., free) has been a leafy Phoenix retreat for generations. On most weekends, you'll see kids running toward the playground, young couples lying under shady trees, and large families hauling coolers and bags of food to the old picnic tables. The 222-acre "enchanted" park was designed to be an oasis for escaping the heat, and its quaint neighborhood of Spanish Colonial homes and historic bungalows turns back the clock to the Phoenix of 50 years ago. There are plenty of amenities—basketball and tennis courts, softball fields, and a municipal swimming pool and golf course—but it's the small lagoon that gives the park its unique character. Bring your fishing pole or head down to the boathouse and rent a paddleboat or canoe ($10 for 30 minutes). Encanto also is home to the **Enchanted Island Amusement Park** (1202 W. Encanto Blvd., 602/254-1200, www.enchantedisland.com, open Wed.–Sun.), which offers a splash playground and a charming collection of rides, bumper boats, games, and a carousel. Check the website for detailed information on hours and prices.

Burton Barr Central Library

Phoenix embarked on a cultural renaissance in 1988, when voters approved an ambitious, architecturally daring series of public works projects that included the Phoenix Art Museum and Burton Barr Central Library (1221 N. Central Ave., 602/262-4636, www. phoenixpubliclibrary.org, 9 A.M.–5 P.M. Mon. and Fri.–Sat., 9 A.M.–9 P.M. Tues.–Thurs., 1 P.M.–5 P.M. Sun.). The iconic building's rectangular, rusted-steel facade resembles a red-hued mesa. Phoenix architect Will Bruder, a pioneer in the region's Desert Modernism movement, gracefully incorporated natural daylight throughout the design, including a glass-and-steel central stairwell and elevator atrium, called the "Crystal Canyon." At noon on the summer solstice, the sun shines through round, lens-covered skylights in the 43,000-square-foot fifth-floor reading room, creating a brief but dazzling light show.

Japanese Friendship Garden

A lush, peaceful oasis on three and a half acres, the Japanese Friendship Garden (1125 N. 3rd Ave., 602/256-3204, www.japanese-friendshipgarden.org, 10 A.M.–3 P.M. Tues.–Sun., Oct.–May, $5 adults, $4 children) is a pleasant contrast to the desert cityscape that surrounds it, with some 50 varieties of plants, flowing streams, a koi pond, and a 12-foot waterfall. This joint effort between Phoenix and its sister city, Himeji, Japan, is tucked into the southwestern end of **Margaret T. Hance Deck Park** (on top of the I-10 freeway underpass, between Central and 3rd Avenues). The beautifully manicured grounds feature stone footbridges, yellow and purple irises, water lilies, and artfully placed boulders. Some allowances for the desert climate have been made, like the neatly trimmed bonsai that are shaped from hardy olive trees.

PHOENIX INDIAN SCHOOL

Part of the federal government's plan to assimilate Native Americans, the Phoenix Indian School opened in 1891. It was one of several boarding schools established around the country that forced Indian children to speak English, cut their hair, wear Anglo clothes, and attend church. Students were also required to abandon their tribal traditions and leave their families behind, a particularly difficult sacrifice for close-knit Native American communities.

By 1900, the coed school had grown to 698 students from 23 tribes across the West. Its 160-acre campus had a large schoolhouse, dining hall, several dormitories, and work space to teach vocation skills. It finally closed in 1990, and a decade later, a third of the land was redeveloped as **Steele Indian School Park** (300 E. Indian School Rd., 602/495-0739, www. phoenix.gov/parks, 6 A.M.-10 P.M. daily). Only three of the school's original buildings remain, including the restored Memorial Hall, an auditorium that was opened in 1922 to honor former students who had fought in World War I. Beautifully landscaped, the park features a Native American design representing the Circle of Life, centered by a water feature. The amphitheater holds a full symphony orchestra, and the park is the site of Phoenix's annual Fourth of July fireworks event.

You can join a tea ceremony on the second Saturday of the month during regular public hours, though reservations are required ($22, including garden admission).

PAPAGO PARK

Think of it as Phoenix's answer to New York's Central Park, a natural refuge in the middle of the city, where residents can hike, fish, or play a round of golf. Papago Park (625 N. Galvin Pkwy., 602/256-3220, http://phoenix. gov/parks, 5 A.M.–11 P.M. daily, free) is one of the city's great resources, and the large desert sanctuary's paved trails, small lake, baseball stadium, and softball fields—not to mention its museums and cultural attractions like the Phoenix Zoo and Desert Botanical Garden—make it a popular destination.

◖ Hole-in-the-Rock

You can see Papago Park's rounded, red-hued buttes from the surrounding communities of Phoenix, Tempe, and Scottsdale, but the sandstone formations should be explored up close, especially the unique "holes" formed by water erosion over millions of years. It's a short, easy trek to the landmark Hole-in-the-Rock, a natural window through which you can survey the city. Phoenix's first residents, the Hohokam, used the opening for astronomy and to track the seasonal movements of the sun. You can also make the short walk to **Hunt's Tomb,** a white pyramid that serves as the final resting place of George W. P. Hunt, Arizona's first governor (as well as its second, third, sixth, seventh, eighth, and tenth; he set a national record for number of terms served).

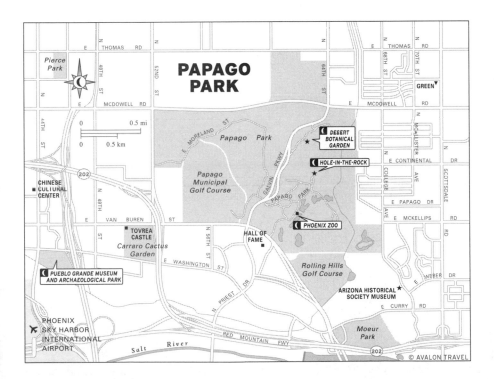

© AVALON TRAVEL

Arizona Historical Society Museum

Some wild things have happened in Arizona— Old West gunfights, copper rushes, gubernatorial impeachments—and the Arizona Historical Society has been there to document it all since its formation in 1864 by the first territorial legislature. Today, four museums across Arizona preserve some three million artifacts, with the facility at Papago Park (1300 N. College Ave., Tempe, 480/929-9499, www.arizonahistoricalsociety.org, 10 A.M.–6 P.M. Mon.–Thurs., 9 A.M.–4 P.M. Fri., $5 adults, $4 students and seniors, children under 11 free) specializing in the Phoenix area from the 20th century on. A particularly interesting exhibition documents how the state came of age during World War II with the bombing of the USS *Arizona* at Pearl Harbor. You can learn how Camp Papago Park, not too far from the museum, experienced the largest mass escape of POWs in the United States. On the first Tuesday of each month admission is two-for-one.

(Phoenix Zoo

Lions and tigers and desert tortoises— oh, my! The Phoenix Zoo (455 N. Galvin Pkwy., 602/273-1341, www.phoenixzoo.org, 9 A.M.–5 P.M. Jan.–May and Oct, 7 A.M.–2 P.M. June–Sept., 9 A.M.–4 P.M. Nov.–Dec., daily, $20 adults, $10 children 3–12) is one of the nation's largest privately owned zoological parks, with some 1,300 birds, slithering reptiles, and furry mammals. You'll find habitats with elephants, zebras, and playful orangutans, but it's the newer exhibits that are blurring the boundaries of the animal kingdom, like Monkey Village, where visitors can walk through a cage-free enclosure where a dozen squirrel monkeys hop from tree to tree. For an extra $3, you can plunge your hand into Stingray Bay and feed a school of small sharks and stingrays. Or set your little ones free in Yakulla Caverns to explore the geologically

themed water park's dripping stalactites and refreshing waterfalls.

(Desert Botanical Garden

First-time visitors to the Sonoran Desert often expect to find a lifeless expanse of sandy dunes. A trip to the Desert Botanical Garden (1201 N. Galvin Pkwy., 480/941-1225, www.dbg.org, 8 A.M.–8 P.M. daily Oct.–May, 7 A.M.–8 P.M. daily Jun.–Sept., $18 adults, $8 children 3–12) quickly dispels any misconceptions. The Sonoran is quite lush, and a third of the garden's 50,000 cacti, agaves, succulents, shrubs, trees, and colorful wildflowers are native to the region, with the remaining plants originating from Australia, South America, and Mexico. The garden easily claims the world's largest, if not finest, collection of desert plants, including 139 rare, threatened, or endangered species. The park began in 1939 with a mission "to exhibit, to conserve, to study, and to disseminate knowledge of the arid-land plants of the world." Since then, it has evolved beyond a plant refuge, offering classes and hosting a series of social events throughout the year that range from spring concerts to workshops to arts festivals.

Try to come early in the day or late in the evening, when the sunlight is incredible. Or, for a different perspective, flashlight tours are held during the summer, a fun opportunity for children to see the nocturnal desert's nighthawks, snakes, insects, and night-blooming flowers. Of course, the springtime wildflowers are always a highlight, and the annual Las Noches de las Luminarias in the winter has become a Phoenix holiday tradition. There's an on-site café and gift shop, and twice a year the garden holds plant sales.

Hall of Flame Museum

Firefighters and gear take center stage at the Hall of Flame (6101 E. Van Buren, 602/275-3473, 9 A.M.–5 P.M. Mon.–Sat., noon–4 P.M.

© KATHLEEN BRYANT

Desert Botanical Garden

Sun., $6 adults, $4 children 12–18), which displays fire engines, helmets, and other apparatus from the 18th century on. The National Firefighting Hall of Heroes honors those who have died in the line of duty or who have been decorated for heroism.

◀ Pueblo Grande Museum and Archaeological Park

This is where the modern metropolis of Phoenix honors the ancient foundations from which it rose. Pueblo Grande Museum and Archaeological Park (4619 E. Washington St., 602/495-0901, www.pueblogrande.com, 9 A.M.–4:45 P.M. Mon.–Sat., 1–4:45 P.M. Sun., closed Sun. and Mon. May–Sept., $6 adults, $3 children 6–17) is the site of a Hohokam village that stood here from about A.D. 450 to 1450, supporting as many as 1,000 people. The valley looked quite different then, when water flowing from the Salt River fed lush plants along its banks, as well as a complex system of canals

that irrigated crops. Those well-engineered waterways served as a framework for the rebirth of Phoenix in the 1860s—and today's canals still parallel their original paths.

The Hohokam lived in adobe pit houses—wood-frame homes, built over shallow pits and covered with adobe. Because these natural materials were so vulnerable to erosion, none of Phoenix's early dwellings still exist, though you're now able to go inside full-size replicas. You can also see an excavated ball court and an example of a compound, homes surrounded with large walls to create private courtyards—a practice adopted by Mexican architecture and modern suburban housing developments. The museum's three indoor galleries highlight the Hohokam villagers' tools, shell and stone jewelry, and unique red-on-buff pottery. Interactive exhibits demonstrate how archaeologists dig at sites and sort through relics to piece together the history of an ancient civilization. There isn't much shade on the outdoor

© KATHLEEN BRYANT

Tovrea Castle has a fascinating history.

trail, so be sure to visit on a cool day or early in the morning.

Tovrea Castle and Carraro Cactus Garden

More than a few Phoenicians regularly drive by this turreted, three-tiered white building known as Tovrea Castle (5041 E. Van Buren St., 602/256-3220, http://phoenix.gov/parks, weekend tour hours vary by season, available through Tovrea Carraro Society, 800/838-3006, www.tovreacastletours.com, $15 adults, $10 children 2–12, reservations necessary) on Loop 202 with no clue to its colorful past. In 1928, Italian immigrant Alessio Carraro purchased 277 acres of undeveloped land east of downtown Phoenix, armed with grand plans for the desert hilltop. He envisioned a luxury housing development that would be crowned by a massive cactus garden and a posh resort, built to resemble a rococo castle from his native Italy. His dreams were dashed by the arrival

of the Great Depression and of Edward and Della Tovrea's ranch and slaughterhouse next door. With few options, Carraro sold the castle in 1931 to an anonymous buyer: Della Tovrea. Edward died the following year, but Della would live in the castle until 1969, when burglars broke in and beat the 80-year-old woman. She eventually died from her injuries. The city of Phoenix renovated the abandoned home and replanted the garden with 5,000 cacti, including 352 saguaros.

TEMPE AND THE EAST VALLEY

The vibrant, progressive-minded college town of Tempe (pop. 162,000) is an island surrounded by its more conservative neighbors. Unlike Phoenix, Scottsdale, Mesa, and Chandler, the 40-square-mile city can no longer spread into the desert. Instead, Tempe meets the demands of a growing population by becoming a city where residential, retail,

THE WRIGLEY MANSION

A Valley landmark, the Wrigley Mansion sits atop a small hill in Central Phoenix's Biltmore neighborhood, like a Spanish Colonial citadel safeguarding million-dollar homes and golf courses. Chewing-gum magnate William Wrigley Jr. built the 24-room, 16,000-square-foot mansion in 1931 as a "winter cottage" and gave it to his wife, Ada, for a 50th anniversary present. The couple only stayed a month or two a year, and the mansion was the smallest of the family's five homes.

Long gone are the days when the Wrigley family wintered at the house while they managed their fortunes, a business and real estate empire that included California's Catalina Island and the Arizona Biltmore Resort. And though the home's pristine desert view has evolved into a sprawling cityscape, the mansion retains much of its original 1930s appeal, from hand-carved doors to an elegant rotunda ceiling. Even the 17 bathrooms, which reflect the Art Deco tastes of the era, have been carefully restored, reviving the chartreuse, turquoise, black, and royal blue tiles that were made in the Wrigley family kiln.

Historic architectural details include a two-story patio and balcony that formed the mansion's northern facade. The space has been converted into an intimate lounge and restaurant, **Geordie's at the Wrigley Mansion** (2501 E. Telawa Trail, 602/955-4079, www.wrigleymansionclub.com, lunch 11 A.M.-3 P.M. Wed.-Sat., dinner 5-9 P.M. Thurs.-Sat., lounge 4 P.M.-close Thurs.-Sat.) named after the mansion's last owner, the late heir to the Spam fortune, George "Geordie" Hormel. Big picture windows offer unobstructed views of the city lights at night. Due to neighborhood zoning restrictions, the Wrigley Mansion must operate as a private club, and the Hormels have instituted an egalitarian $10 yearly fee that is donated to Valley charities. Trial memberships of $3 are offered to anyone who would like to join a guided tour, enjoy a meal, or have drinks in the lounge.

---

and commercial buildings coexist rather than retreat to their respective neighborhoods. The city's developers, recognizing the success of pedestrian-oriented **Mill Avenue**—a popular spot for dining and shopping—are now moving beyond the street's nostalgic redbrick buildings and creating a modern cityscape along Tempe Town Lake.

The city isn't new to experimental design. The **Tempe Municipal Building** (31 E. 5th St., 480/350-4311, www.tempe.gov), unveiled in 1971, is an inverted glass-walled pyramid that shades itself from the summer sun. More recently, the **Tempe Center for the Arts** (700 W. Rio Salado Pkwy., 480/350-2829, www.tempe.gov/TCA, 10 A.M.-6 P.M. Tues.-Fri., 11 A.M.-6 P.M. Sat., free) made a splash on the banks of Tempe Town Lake, with an elaborate silver roof reminiscent of local mountain ranges.

Nor has Tempe bulldozed its past. At the northern end of Mill Avenue, you can see the tall silos and remains of the **Hayden Flour Mill.** Charles Hayden originally built the river-powered mill in 1874. His Hayden Ferry connected Phoenix from the north banks of the Salt River to a road to Tucson. A small community grew up along this "Mill Avenue," and many old brick buildings and quaint bungalows have been repurposed as retail and restaurant space. The Hayden family's adobe home still stands as **Monti's La Casa Vieja,** a perennially popular restaurant. (In 1912, Charles Hayden's son Carl became Arizona's first congressional representative.)

Tempe Town Lake

If you build it, they will come—or so city leaders hoped in 1989 when they adopted the ambitious Rio Salado Master Plan, which converted two miles of the usually dry Salt River into a reservoir for boating, rowing, and fishing.

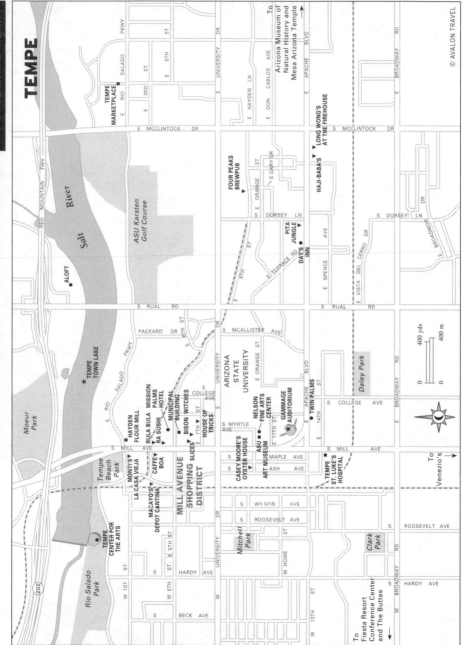

TEMPE

Tempe Town Lake (620 N. Mill Ave., 480/350-4311, www.tempe.gov/lake, free) opened a decade later, created by inflatable rubber dams and encircled by five miles of paths for biking and jogging. The adjacent **Tempe Beach Park** has become one of the Valley's prime spots for festivals, concerts, and events, and little ones will love the $1.3 million **Splash Playground** (10 A.M.–7 P.M. daily Apr.–Sept., free) when the temperatures start to climb. The monsoon-inspired water park features rain showers, misters, waterfalls, and large squirt guns.

Arizona State University

Much of Tempe's progressive attitude—and the abundance of inexpensive restaurants, bars, and shops—can be credited to the presence of Arizona State University's main campus (University Dr. and Mill Ave., 480/965-2100, www.asu.edu). ASU was founded as the Tempe Normal School in 1885 while Arizona was still a territory. Since then, it has expanded into the largest public research university in the country, with 67,000 students on four campuses in the Valley.

Those interested in design and architecture should head south on Mill Avenue to see two significant buildings. The **Nelson Fine Arts Center** is a Modernist concrete complex that is perfectly suited to its desert home, drawing inspiration from Native American architecture and creating brilliant subterranean spaces that highlight the desert's stark contrasts of light and shadow. Inside, the **ASU Art Museum** (51 E. 10th St., 480/965-2787, http://asuartmuseum.asu.edu, 11 A.M.–5 P.M. Tues.–Sat., free) has a modest collection that features contemporary, Latin American, and ceramic pieces.

Just south, you'll find **Gammage Auditorium** (1200 S. Forest Ave., 480/965-5062, tours: 480/965-6912, www.asugammage.com), the last public commission of Frank Lloyd Wright,

© KATHLEEN BRYANT

Nelson Fine Arts Center has performance stages and galleries.

© TEMPE TOURISM OFFICE/NICK DOAN

Gammage Auditorium

at the edge of ASU's campus. Wright's concept for the auditorium was a modified version of a never-built design for an opera house in Baghdad, Iraq. "I believe this is the site," he said. "The structure should be circular in design, and yes, with outstretched arms, saying 'Welcome to ASU.'" Those arms became flying buttresses that serve as pedestrian ramps and echo the building's interlocking-circle motif. Both Wright and ASU president Grady Gammage, who is credited with landing the commission, died before its completion in 1964. The Gammage hosts Broadway shows and other events.

Arizona Museum of Natural History

One of the Valley's best-kept secrets, the Arizona Museum of Natural History (53 N. MacDonald, 480/644-2230, www.azmnh. org, 10 A.M.–5 P.M. Tues.–Fri., 11 A.M.–5 P.M.

Sat., 1–5 P.M. Sun., $10 adults, $6 children 3–12) appeals to kids—dinosaurs!—and even adults who aren't "museum people." Formerly known as the Mesa Southwest Museum, it explores the region's natural and cultural history with plenty of hands-on, interactive, sound-and-light, try-this-on excitement. Pan for "gold," visit a territorial jail, and scope out the three-story Dinosaur Mountain, complete with a simulated flash flood and mechanical creatures. Those who revel in the nerdy joy of museums will love the in-depth exhibits on prehistoric Native American life and the assembled mammoth and mastodon fossils. The museum also cares for **Mesa Grande,** the platform mound where as many as 2,000 Hohokam villagers once lived.

Mesa Arizona Temple

Now Arizona's third-largest city, Mesa (pop. 440,000) was settled by Mormon colonists who lived in simple adobe and brush structures while they designed a townsite with broad streets (wide enough to turn a wagon around) and lots large enough for families to garden. The townsite was registered in 1878, and at its center, the Church of Jesus Christ of Latter Day Saints built Arizona's first temple. Dedicated in 1927, the Mesa Arizona Temple (101 S. LaSeur, 480/833-1211) is an elegant edifice of steel-reinforced concrete faced with eggshell-white tile and topped with carved friezes. It was the last of three LDS temples built without a tower or spire.

During the Christmas season, the tall palms along the reflecting pool are decorated, part of a magnificent display that includes music, a nativity, and thousands upon thousands of twinkling lights. Each spring, an outdoor Easter pageant featuring a cast of hundreds draws a large audience to the temple grounds. Though non-Mormons are not allowed inside the temple, guests can stroll around the manicured lawn and gardens and stop in at the temple's visitor center (525 E. Main St., 480/714-9164, 9 A.M.–9 P.M.daily, free), which has displays and artwork.

Commemorative Air Force

Plane buffs and military historians can make a sentimental journey to Mesa's Falcon Field, the home of the Commemorative Air Force (2017 N. Greenfield Rd., 480/924-1940, www.azcaf.org, 10 A.M.–4 P.M. daily Oct.–May, 9 A.M.–3 P.M. Wed.–Sun. June–Sept., $12 adults, $3 children age 5–12). Among the museum's displays is one honoring hometown hero Lt. Frank Luke, the WWI ace who became the nation's first pilot to earn the Medal of Honor. Part of the CAF's mission is to restore combat aircraft to flying condition, and they periodically offer flights ($95 and up) on B-17s, B-25s, and other vintage planes. Other events include big band dances and veterans' gatherings.

AHWATUKEE AND SOUTH PHOENIX

Look at Phoenix's southern horizon at night, and you'll see a cluster of blinking red lights marking the top of South Mountain. The lights comprise an antenna farm of 30-plus towers that beam radio and television transmissions from the mountaintop. They also serve as an important navigational marker for pilots flying into nearby Sky Harbor Airport. For the rest of us, the twinkling lights indicate southern Phoenix and, on the other side of South Mountain, its affluent bedroom community of Ahwatukee (pronounced ah-wuh-TOO-kee), a sea of stucco housing developments. This side of town is also home to a couple large resorts, Firebird International Raceway, the Yaqui village of Guadalupe, and the Gila River Indian Community, not to mention the largest urban park in the United States, which covers the mountain's broad peak and canyon-cut slopes.

South Mountain Park

The country's largest urban park, South Mountain Park (10409 S. Central Avenue, 602/262-7393, http://phoenix.gov/parks, 5 A.M.–10 P.M. daily, free) is where many Valley residents escape from the city to hike, bike, ride horses, and picnic. Don't expect large grassy meadows or shady forested hideaways, though. It's 61,000-plus acres of bona fide Sonoran Desert, preserving hardy creosote bushes, paloverde trees, and dozens of varieties of cactus. You may even come across a few critters, like jackrabbits and lizards. (Many of the snakes, scorpions, and coyotes that also live in the park tend to come out a night when it's much cooler, but you should still keep an eye out for them.) The park also protects hundreds of petroglyphs and pictographs created by the Hohokam and other indigenous tribes. These small drawings, carved or painted onto stones, depict people, animals, and geometric patterns, and anthropologists theorize they may have been a means of recording history, part of religious ceremonies, or even ancient "street signs" or boundary markers.

If you're not interested in exploring the more than 50 miles of trails on foot or by bike, there are a few scenic drives, including five-mile San Juan Road, which is open to cars the first weekend of the month. The road winds its way up the mountain to the summit lookout, where panoramic views reveal Phoenix's sprawling suburban growth.

Mystery Castle

"Life Visits a Mystery Castle," proclaimed the cover of *Life* magazine in 1948, featuring a teenage Mary Lou Gulley on a spiral staircase that overlooked the eccentric house her father, Boyce Luther Gulley, had built. The name Mystery Castle stuck (800 E. Mineral Rd., 602/268-1581, 11 A.M.–4 P.M. Thurs.–Sun. Oct.–May, $10 adults, $5 children 5–12), and although Mary Lou died in 2010, visitors are still welcome to tour her home. In 1930, after being diagnosed with tuberculosis, Boyce left his wife and daughter in Seattle, moving to the dry climate of Phoenix. He built Mystery Castle from a hodgepodge of found objects: rocks, adobe, glass, and even auto parts. Though he left his daughter behind so that she wouldn't witness his illness, he built the castle with her in mind, remembering how she would cry when her sandcastles were washed away by the Pacific's tides. When he died in 1945, a lawyer contacted Mary Lou and her mother, and they moved into the eccentric castle. Today, you can tour the 18 rooms, furnished with quirky pieces designed by Boyce as well as an original sofa designed by Frank Lloyd Wright. To reach the castle, head south on 7th Street, past Baseline Road, and make a left where the road dead-ends at South Mountain.

Rawhide Western Town at Wild Horse Pass

Rawhide Western Town (5700 W. North Loop Rd., 480/502-5600, www.rawhide.com, 5–10 P.M. Thurs.–Sun., free) moved from North Scottsdale to the Gila River Indian Community a few years ago, but it's still delivering 1880s-themed family fun. Check out the stunt shows in the dusty streets, or try your luck on the mechanical bull. Of course, there are easier rides in town, such as the desert train or stagecoach tours guided by a trained mule team. It's all a little hokey, but having an "old-time" photo made or stopping for ice cream or a sarsaparilla is fun for the whole family. Admission to the park is free, but there are small fees for activities or games. An all-day pass is $15. On Saturday nights in spring and fall, visitors can join an old-fashioned chuck-wagon cookout under the stars ($48 adults, $15 children 4–11), which includes a hayride, live music and dancing, and a marshmallow roast around the campfire.

Huhugam Heritage Center

Nearby, the Huhugam Heritage Center (4759 N. Maricopa Rd., 520/796-3500, 10 A.M.–4 P.M. Tues.–Sat., $5 adults, $2 children 6–12) is operated by the Gila River Indian Community's Akimel O'odham (Pima) and Pee Posh (Maricopa) tribes. The museum's small exhibits include historic photographs that illustrate tribal life and a fascinating ethnobotanical garden of desert plants. The building's architecture is strikingly modern, and at the same time it echoes the platform mound villages of the tribes' Hohokam ancestors.

GLENDALE AND THE WEST VALLEY

North and west of Phoenix are the communities of Glendale, Peoria, Sun City, and Avondale, which is home to Luke Air Force Base. These are mostly residential suburbs, though Glendale's charming historic downtown is a fun place to shop, especially for antiquers, and the West Valley can claim two major sports arenas, Phoenix International Raceway, and other attractions. Farther west, near the base of the Estrella Mountains, are some of the Valley's newest subdivisions, though the inexorable spread toward the White Tank Mountain Recreation Area seems to have stopped for now.

Deer Valley Rock Art Center

Long before the Valley's modern population began creeping into the desert northwest of Phoenix, the ancient peoples made it their home. These indigenous tribes literally left their mark on the landscape, carving more than 1,500 petroglyphs onto the basalt boulder formations in the Hedgpeth Hills. This impressive concentration of petroglyphs—geometric and anthropomorphic drawings carved onto rock—gives us hints of their stories, religious rites, and hunting practices. The Deer Valley Rock Art Center (3711 W. Deer Valley Rd., 623/582-8007, http://dvrac. asu.edu, 9 A.M.–5 P.M. Tues.–Sat. Oct.–Apr., 8 A.M.–2 P.M. Tues.–Sat. May–Sept., $7 adults, $3 children) also serves as a nature preserve for native wildlife and an ethnobotanical garden for the hardy crops that have been cultivated in Arizona for hundreds of years, including corn, beans, onions, squash, and cotton. Bring a pair of binoculars or rent some at the center to view the more distant petroglyphs.

Pioneer Arizona
Living History Museum

Settled across 90 acres a half-hour's drive north of downtown Phoenix, Pioneer Village (3901 W. Pioneer Rd. 623/465-1052, http:// pioneeraz.org, 9 A.M.–4 P.M. Wed.–Sun., summers 8 A.M.–1 P.M. Wed.–Sun. and 6–9:30 P.M. Wed.–Sat., $7 adults, $5 children) is the culmination of more than 50 years of hard work by a group of dedicated history buffs (including Barry Goldwater), who wanted to preserve a piece of Territorial Arizona for future generations. The village recreates an 1800s town complete with residences, schoolhouse, bakery, blacksmith shop, sheriff's office, and even a gallows. Among the historic structures are an opera house where Lily Langtry sang and a cabin from the Graham-Tewksbury feud between sheep herders and cattle ranchers (also known as the Pleasant Valley War) that inspired Zane Grey's novel, *To the Last Man*. The volunteer staffing is inconsistent, so it's a good idea to check the website for special events (and coupons) or to bone up on the exhibits before making the drive.

Challenger Space Center

In Peoria, the Challenger Space Center (211870 N. 83rd Ave., 623/322-2001, www.azchallenger.org, 10 A.M.–4 P.M. daily, $8 adults, $7 seniors/military, $6 children 3–12) has exhibits and activities relating to space travel, including a two-hour simulated mission ($23) that transports you to Mars or takes you on a scientific probe of the comet Encke.

Cerreta Candy Company

Even the severest chocoholics will be sated by a visit to Cerreta Candy Company (5345 W. Glendale Ave., 620/930-1000, www.cerreta. com, 8 A.M.–6 P.M. Mon.–Sat.). For four generations, the Cerreta family has been making chocolates, caramel, nut brittle, and other treats in this redbrick building in downtown Glendale. You can shop for a gift basket of Arizona-themed goodies, watch the video screens monitoring various production stations inside the factory, or go on one of the daily 30-minute behind-the-scenes tours (10 A.M. and 1 P.M. Mon.–Fri., free).

Entertainment and Events

Frequently overshadowed by Scottsdale's trendy clubs, Phoenix's nightlife takes a bit more work to find. If you're in town at the beginning of the month, you can join art lovers and hipsters at the First Friday art walk in downtown's Roosevelt Historic District. The rest of the month is good for meeting friends (or making new ones) at one of Phoenix's hip but low-key bars and lounges.

NIGHTLIFE
Downtown
BARS AND PUBS

The **Turf Irish Pub** (705 N. 1st St., 602/296-5043, http://theturfpub.com, 10 A.M.–2 A.M. daily) has booths, tables, a long bar, and a sidewalk patio ideal for kicking back and people-watching. The dark interior blends traditional and contemporary styles, and it's roomy enough to host live music Thursday through Saturday nights. The menu features classic pub fare, with a few Irish specialties like corned beef and boxtys (a Galway-style grilled potato pancake). The weeknight happy hour is especially popular before D-Backs games. To find the pub, look for the trompe l'oeil mural gracing its front.

The Rose & Crown (628 E. Adams St., 602/256-0223, http://theroseandcrownaz.com, 11 A.M.–2 A.M. Mon.–Sat., 10 A.M.–2 A.M. Sun.) has a full bar, imports galore from the British Isles, and loads of room outside on the front porch, patio, and lawn. The pool table, darts, and pop art paintings of Queen Elizabeth and Winston Churchill add some fun British style to this turn-of-the-20th-century bungalow in Heritage Square. Throughout the day, the scene changes from business lunches to families taking a break between the nearby museums and Science Center to a late-night, 20-something crowd.

LOUNGES AND WINE BARS

Like a good speakeasy, **SideBar** (1514 N. 7th Ave., 602/254-1646, http://sidebarphoenix. com, 4 P.M.–2 A.M. Mon.–Fri., 5:30 P.M.–2 A.M. Sat.–Sun.) can be tough to find. Enter through the side door on 7th Avenue and climb the stairs to the sleek loft-like space with exposed-brick walls, funky lights, retro seating, and classic films running on TV screens. There's a large lineup of specialty cocktails, dozens of beers, and 40-plus wines, and bartenders promise a hangover-free morning after, thanks to fresh-made syrups and juices. The signature White Rabbit is a loaded version of horchata (a traditional rice-based drink from Mexico).

The sleekly chic **Hanny's** (40 N. 1st St., 602/252-2285, http://hannys.net, 11 A.M.–1:30 A.M. Mon.–Fri., 5 P.M.–1:30 A.M. Sat.–Sun.) occupies a former department store that in later years was repeatedly set on fire as training for the city's firefighters. Opened in 1947 as an upscale men's store, the building is notable for bringing the clean lines of International Style to downtown Phoenix. Renovation has preserved much of the building's original character—airy ceilings, curving lines, department store windows, and a mezzanine—making a fine backdrop for classic cocktails, absinthes, and a long list of whiskeys.

Hotel bars can be hit or miss, but the **District American Kitchen and Wine Bar** (320 N. 3rd St., 602/817-5400, http://districtrestaurant.com, 11 A.M.–midnight daily) at the Sheraton Phoenix Downtown is a home run. The District specializes in American wines, beers, and cocktails. The prices here aren't cheap, but live music on the weekends makes this contemporary restaurant/lounge with low-slung furniture and floor-to-ceiling windows a fun place to settle in. The menu is American comfort food updated with artisanal ingredients from the restaurant's herb garden and local farms. Theatergoer specials make it handy if you're headed for the nearby Herberger or Symphony Hall.

Cheuvront Restaurant & Wine Bar (1326 N. Central Ave., 602/307-0022, http://cheuvronts.com, 11 A.M.–10 P.M. Mon.–Thurs., 11 A.M.–midnight Fri., 4 P.M.–midnight Sat., 4 P.M.–10 P.M. Sun.) highlights a wide-ranging selection of cheeses—creamy camembert, nutty *manchego,* robust monte enebro—and pairs them with an equally worldly list of wines, recently earning its fourth consecutive Wine Spectator Award of Excellence. Expect to learn something new by ordering a flight of wines, sampling the featured cheese, or making reservations for the monthly sommelier-hosted wine-tasting. Cheuvront's is popular for a post-work drink or after-theater nightcap, thanks to its contemporary urban decor, happy hour specials, and convenient light-rail access.

Can't decide between catching an indie flick or lingering over a couple glasses of wine? Enjoy both at **FilmBar** (815 N. 2nd St., 602/595-9187, www.thefilmbarphx.com, 5 P.M.–midnight nightly, till 2 A.M. Fri.–Sat.), a 70-seat theater and lounge in the Roosevelt District. Movie tickets are $7, but you can forgo the show and stick to the bar, which serves 25 craft beers and a dozen wines.

LIVE MUSIC

Listen for **The Lost Leaf** (915 N. 5th St., 602/258-0014, www.thelostleaf.org, 5 P.M.–2 A.M. daily) in the Roosevelt District, a gentrified area on the north side of downtown. This boho hangout features local artwork and, most nights, live music by regional or underground acts, as well as the occasional improv group or poetry reading. The 1920s bungalow (once home to an immigrant sausage maker) maintains much of its original character, including hardwood floors, exposed brick walls,

and the former kitchen, which now serves more than 150 types of beer and 20 wines. And it's not only the music that's live: The Lost Leaf hosts a monthly "anti-art school" with a life-drawing class.

GAY AND LESBIAN

Amsterdam (718 N. Central Ave., 602/258-6122, www.amsterdambar.com, 4 P.M.–2 A.M. daily) is the heart of the Valley's gay nightlife scene, but with so few dance clubs in Phoenix, everyone is welcome here. Clubbers will find a large dance floor fueled by thumping music, but you can give your eardrums a rest on the large back patio. There's karaoke on Sunday and the occasional drag show, but the Amsterdam's claim to fame is its menu of 200 martinis. Next door are the **Malibu Beach Bar and Surf Club** and **Club Miami.**

Central Phoenix
BARS AND PUBS

Desert Modernist style, happy hour specials, and a cool and capacious patio bar make **The Vig** (4041 N. 40th St., 602/553-7227, http://thevig.us, 11 A.M.–2 A.M. Mon.–Fri., 10 A.M.–2 A.M. Sat.–Sun.) a local hot spot. A mix of live music and DJs keeps things hopping from midweek through Sunday, or you can join a leisurely game of boccie ball. This modern take on the neighborhood tavern is a relaxed place to start your evening or while away a Sunday afternoon. A second location Uptown (6015 N. 16th St., 602/633-1187) offers patrons free transportation (602/328-6334) on weekends.

If you're seeking an antidote to the strong desert sun, **Shady's Lounge** (2701 E. Indian School Rd., 602/956-8998, 11 A.M.–2 A.M. daily) will wrap you in comforting darkness no matter the hour. The retro wood-paneled walls, fireplace, and leather booths might remind you of your uncle's basement bonus room, but the über-hip jukebox, craft beers, and signature cocktails draw a young crowd. Quirky movies (not sports) roll on the TVs, and there's a pool table in back.

Hop off the light-rail at the **George & Dragon** (4240 N. Central Ave., 602/241-0018, http://georgeanddragonpub.net, 11 A.M.–2 A.M. daily), and you'll think you've landed in merry old England as you are greeted by half-timber walls, stone fireplaces, and Union Jacks, with "footy" often playing on the telly. The "GnD" pours an impressive selection of libations from across the pond, including Scotch and Irish whiskeys and hard-to-find imported beers, with traditional fare from Cornish pasties to treacle pudding.

If you don't want to deal with stadium parking, or if you're a few states away from your favorite team, you can still catch your game at the upscale **Half Moon Sports Grill** (2121 E. Highland Ave., 602/977-2700, www.half-moonsportsgrill.com, 11 A.M.–2 A.M. daily). Scores of screens can be found throughout the restaurant, bar, and patio, and servers will make an effort to seat you near the game of your choice. Wondering why someone would name a sports lounge Half Moon? Your curiosity will be satisfied by the "moon shots" of weekend warriors. The original Biltmore area location has spawned a second in North Phoenix (288 E. Greenway, 602/993-6600).

Owned by a pair of Belfast natives, **Rosie McCaffrey's Irish Pub** (906 E. Camelback Rd., 602/241-1916, www.rosiemccaffreys.com, 11 A.M.–2 A.M. daily) is a classic, with plenty of dark wood and stained glass. The atmosphere is always festive, thanks to live Celtic music several nights a week. When it gets too loud, head for one of the outdoor patios. As you might expect, Rosie's serves up Irish ale and stout, along with pub fare and meaty platters.

Nearly hidden behind Starbucks, **The Swizzle Inn** (5835 N. 16th St., 602/277-7775, 10 A.M.–2 A.M. daily) has a surprising (for Phoenix) nautical theme, complete with

dartboard, pool table, jukebox, and a row of regulars holding down the bar. Though it's often fondly referred to as a dive bar, the bathrooms are clean, the drinks are strong, and the atmosphere convivial. You can even purchase a souvenir tee printed with the bar's motto: "Swizzle in and swagger out."

An atmospheric Mexican restaurant with a couple leafy outdoor bars, **Aunt Chilada's** (7330 N. Dreamy Draw Dr., 602/944-1286, www.auntchiladas.com, 11 A.M.–1 A.M. daily) was once the location of a general store serving miners in the Dreamy Draw area. Blend history with live music and some of the best margaritas in the 'Nix, and you've got a great spot to kick back after a hike up nearby Piestewa Peak. The pleasant patios make this a suitable choice for families and kids.

LOUNGES AND WINE BARS

The **Merc Bar** (2525 E. Camelback Rd., 602/508-9449, www.mercbar.com, 4 P.M.–2 A.M. Mon.–Fri., 6 P.M.–2 A.M. Sat.–Sun.) has earned Best of Phoenix accolades for its timeless candlelit ambience as much as for its well-made martinis and mojitos. Sure, drinks cost more here, but you're paying to play with a mixed crowd of businesspeople, Scottsdale party girls, and guests from the Ritz-Carlton next door, who number among them the occasional celebrity.

In-the-know Phoenicians have made the rooftop deck at the **Clarendon Hotel** (401 W. Clarendon Ave., 602/252-7363) one of their favorite hangouts, particularly at sunset when the city seems to glow and the sky is streaked with oranges and reds. During the daytime, the rooftop is a sunny place for a cup of coffee or lunch, but at night it transforms into a popular lounge—so popular, in fact, that hotel staff has had to get strict about occupancy limits. It's closed in summer, and hours vary throughout the year, so be sure to call ahead.

LIVE MUSIC

Char's Has the Blues (4631 N. 7th Ave., 602/230-0205, www.charshastheblues.com, 8 P.M.–1 A.M. Sun.–Wed., 7:30 P.M.–1 A.M. Thurs.–Sat.)—as well as live funk, soul, and jazz seven nights a week. The drinks are cheap, the cover is low (free Mon.–Wed), $6 weekends), and the varied music attracts a varied crowd. If you're crowd-shy, there's pool and darts, but most people come to this converted cottage to dance. Soul Power, a local favorite that covers R&B hits to Motown, is often in the week's lineup.

For top blues acts, head for **The Rhythm Room** (1019 E. Indian School Rd., 602/265-4842, www.rhythmroom.com, 6–8 P.M. to 1 A.M. or 2 A.M. Fri.–Sat.), a dark, intimate club that highlights some of the best jazz, bluegrass, and roots musicians, as well as touring acts that range from Bob Schneider and Cary Brothers to MGMT. Owner Bob Corritore, a local musician and DJ, grew up in Chicago and often invites some of his hometown heroes to the club to play with his house band. And if you work up an appetite on the dance floor, you can head out back most nights to pick up a sweet-and-smoky sandwich or plate of ribs at **Rack Shack BBQ** (602/279-0772, 6–11 P.M. Wed.–Thurs., 6 P.M.–2 A.M. Fri.–Sat.).

GAY AND LESBIAN

Kobalt (3110 N. Central Ave., Ste. 125, 602/264-5307, www.kobaltbarphoenix.com, 11 P.M.–2 A.M. daily) supports the Valley's GLBT community by hosting charitable events and fundraisers, and it shows the love every day with drink specials and themes that range from trivia to dart matches to the popular karaoke on Sunday and Tuesday nights. The Park Central Mall location has a large, shady outdoor patio, and the scene is more laid-back than downtown's Amsterdam.

Cash Inn Country (2140 E. McDowell Rd., 602/244-9943, www.cashinncountry.

net, 2 P.M.–1 A.M. Tues.–Thurs., 2 P.M.–2 A.M. Fri., noon–2 A.M. Sat., noon–1 A.M. Sun.) calls itself Phoenix's friendliest lesbian-gay bar. This saloon offers free line-dancing lessons every Thursday at 7 P.M., but the rest of the week you'll find live music, Latin dancing, or a DJ spinning tunes. Besides pool tables and dartboards, there's a Wednesday night poker tournament.

While the ladies are line-dancing at Cash Inn, gentlemen who'd like to give their cowboy boots a workout should head to **Charlie's** (727 W. Camelback Rd., 602/265-0224, www.charliesphoenix.com, 2 P.M.–2 A.M. Mon.–Fri., noon–2 A.M. Sat.–Sun.). Charlie's (which is also home to the Arizona Gay Rodeo Association) has recently expanded the musical lineup to include Latin and dance music.

Tempe and the East Valley
BARS AND PUBS

A Tempe mainstay, **Casey Moore's Oyster House** (850 S. Ash Ave., 480/968-9935, 11 A.M.–2 A.M. daily) has the feel of a sprawling yet genteel frat house party. College students, professors, hipsters, and neighbors mix at this historic bungalow-turned-restaurant, where you can hang out on the porch or patio, or head inside to the warren of rooms. (Some are said to be frequented in the wee hours by a female ghost wearing turn-of-the-20th-century clothing, but that may just be the beer talking.) Dine after five, or order pub grub—including homemade soup and oysters on the half shell—and wash it down with Casey Moore's good beer selection.

Four Peaks Brewing Company (1340 E. 8th St., 480/303-9967, www.fourpeaks.com, 11 A.M.–2 A.M. Mon.–Sat., 10 A.M.–2 A.M. Sun.), housed in an old redbrick creamery, is beloved by ASU students and alumni. The popular brewpub pours delicious ales, stouts, pilsners, and seasonal brews. The best known is Kiltlifter, a Scottish-style ale served at restaurants and bars throughout the Valley. If it's a hot day, head for the sidewalk patio, cooled by misters. Daily specials, good grub, and a Sunday brunch are pluses. You can drive to the recently added Scottsdale location (15745 N. Hayden, 480/991-1795), but you'll miss out on the collegiate vibe.

Rúla Búla (401 S. Mill Ave., 480/929-9500, http://rulabula.com, 11 A.M.–2 A.M. daily) means "uproar and commotion" in Gaelic, and this Irish pub certainly is lively. The Victorian brick building was home to a saddlery business, and the present owners have created a "merchant pub" theme, mixing tack room memorabilia with convivial regulars, imported beers, traditional pub fare, and "new Irish" cuisine. Faith and Begorrah, they even dish up a vegetarian shepherd's pie!

Though Tempe legend Long Wong's is long gone, it's been reborn as **Long Wong's at The Firehouse** (1639 E. Apache Blvd., 480/967-0167, www.longwongstempe.com, 10:30 A.M.–2 A.M. Mon.–Sat., 11 A.M.–2 A.M. Sun.). The new digs are in an old firehouse, and the aim is the same, to showcase local bands. On Sunday nights, stand-up comics take the stage.

CASINOS

South of Phoenix, the Gila River Indian Community operates three casinos. **Wild Horse Pass Casino** (5550 W. Wild Horse Pass, 800/946-4452, www.wingilariver.com) is the closest to the city and the largest. In addition to live poker, blackjack, and 875 slot machines, it offers live entertainment, a hotel, and several bar and restaurant options. **Lone Butte Casino** (1077 S. Kyrene Rd., 800/946-4452, www.wingilariver.com) near Chandler features 850 slot machines and 24 Las Vegas–style table games, including blackjack and Pai Gow. Southwest of Phoenix, **Vee Quiva Casino** (6443 N. Komatke, 800/946-4452, www.wingilariver.com) has slots, bingo, table games, and

a 14-table poker room with daily tournaments. All three locations offer **shuttle service** to and from various locations in the Valley. For reservations, call 800/946-4452, ext. 7256 or ext. 7342.

COMEDY

Located in downtown's CityScape, **Stand Up Live** (50 W. Jefferson St., 480/719-6100, www.standuplive.com) draws national and regional comedy acts. Shows usually start between 7 and 8 P.M. Thurs.–Sun., with double bills on weekends. Seating is first-come, first-served, and doors open an hour before show time (90 minutes before special events). Next door, the **Copper Blues** (50 W. Jefferson St., 480/719-5005, http://copperblueslive.com, 11 A.M.–10 P.M. Mon.–Tues., 11 A.M.–11 P.M. Wed.–Thurs., 11 A.M.–2 A.M. Fri., 4 P.M.–2 A.M. Sat., 4 P.M.–10 P.M. Sun.) lounge makes the wait easy with live music, food, and a lengthy list of beers.

PERFORMING ARTS

The Valley has numerous venues for catching a play, concert, or dance performance. **Phoenix Symphony Hall** (75 N. 2nd St., 602/495-1117) is home to the city's most respected cultural institutions and some impressive art, such as the 20-foot tapestries in the lobby. From October through April, the **Arizona Opera** (602/266-7464, www.azopera.com) stages perennial crowd-pleasers along with one or two surprises. The **Phoenix Symphony** (602/495-1999, www.phoenixsymphony.org) performs classics, chamber orchestra, and symphony pops throughout the year. Multiple award-winning **Ballet Arizona** (602/381-1096, www.balletaz.org) merged three struggling Arizona dance companies to become, according to the *Arizona Republic,* "a treasure." The company performs classic and contemporary ballet November through May. Symphony Hall frequently hosts touring companies and

Dance, by sculptor John Henry Waddell, in front of the Herberger Theater

entertainers, from Yo-Yo Ma to Crosby, Stills, and Nash.

Also in downtown Phoenix, the **Herberger Theater** (222 E. Monroe St., 602/254-7399, www.herbergertheater.org) is home to the Arizona Theatre Company, Actors Theatre, and the Center Dance Ensemble. Part of the Herberger's mission is to act as an arts incubator, hosting schoolchildren and sponsoring outreach programs around the state. The theater's three stages, gallery, and outdoor spaces are hopping during October's annual festival of the arts. Throughout the year, 30–45 minute lunch performances entertain downtown workers and other guests.

A 12-year, $14-million renovation transformed the **Orpheum Theatre** (203 W. Adams St., 602/534-5600, www.orpheum-theater.com), a 1929 vaudeville house, into a dazzling baroque confection complete with a projected ceiling of clouds and stars. The 1,364-seat hall hosts a wide variety of performances, from arts-themed events to Broadway shows. Nearby, touring shows, comedy acts, and concerts take the stage at **Comerica Theatre** (400 W. Washington St., 602/379-2800, http://comericatheatre.com). Originally known as the Dodge Theatre, this 5,000-seat venue has welcomed such wide-ranging acts as the Russian Ballet and Coldplay. With a revolving stage and intimate auditorium, the **Celebrity Theatre** (440 N. 32nd St., 602/267-1600, www.celebritytheatre.com) boasts that "no seat is farther than 75 feet from the stage." Boxing matches, plays, comedy acts, and musicians, including Martina McBride, Smokey Robinson, and Lyle Lovett, have appeared here.

In the East Valley overlooking Tempe Town Lake, the **Tempe Center for the Arts** (700 W. Rio Salado Pkwy., 480/350-2829, www.tempe.gov/TCA) hosts a plethora of arts events, including a songwriter's showcase, kid-friendly movies and workshops, rotating art exhibits,

© KATHLEEN BRYANT

Tempe Center for the Arts

and performances by the Tempe Symphony. Ballet Arizona's annual season opens here under the starry desert night sky. Nearby, on the Arizona State University campus, the Frank Lloyd Wright–designed **Gammage Auditorium** (1200 S. Forest Ave., 480/965-5062, www. asugammage.com) regularly hosts touring Broadway musicals and plays, as well as concerts and lectures. A block north, the Nelson Fine Art Center is home to university art galleries and the innovative **Galvin Playhouse** (51 E. 10th St., 480/965-6447, http://theatrefilm. asu.edu). The building's architecture also puts on a show, as light and shadow interact with the homage-to-the-desert design.

A few miles farther east, the boldly designed **Mesa Arts Center** (1 E. Main St., 480/644-6500, www.mesaartscenter.com) has four theaters for visiting acts and regional groups like the **Southwest Shakespeare Company** (480/641-7039, www.swshakespeare.org) and **Xico** (480/833-2327, http://xicoinc.org), which supports Latino and Native American art and culture.

FESTIVALS AND EVENTS

In spring and fall, the Valley's calendar is so packed with festivals and events that it can be challenging to choose among them. The winter holidays sparkle with light displays, including the Southwestern tradition of luminarias (paper bags filled with sand and glowing candles), but even in the heat of summer Phoenicians find reasons to celebrate.

January

The year kicks off with the **Fiesta Bowl** (1 Cardinals Dr., 480/350-0900, www.fiestabowl. org) at the University of Phoenix Stadium in Glendale. The big game, part of the NCAA Bowl Championship Series, is preceded by the **Fiesta Bowl Parade** in Central Phoenix, with dozens of floats, marching bands, cheerleaders, balloons, and equestrian groups.

Later in January, **P.F. Chang's Rock 'N' Roll Arizona Marathon** (800/311-1255, www.rnraz. com) runs through Phoenix and Scottsdale, with a triumphant finish at Tempe's Sun Devil Stadium. More than 60 live bands help keep the energy pumping along the route.

February

In mid-February, book lovers converge on the **VNSA Book Sale** (1826 W. McDowell Rd., 602/265-6805, www.vnsabooksale.org) at the Arizona State Fairgrounds, featuring more than half a million used, rare, and out-of-print books. Also in February, the **Arizona Renaissance Festival** (12601 E. State Route 60, 520/463-2600, www.royalfaires.com) descends upon Apache Junction in the far East Valley, for two months of ye olde fun. Enjoy raucous jousting tournaments, rides, live shows, and giant turkey legs fit for Henry VIII.

March

The **Heard Museum Guild & Indian Market** (2301 N. Central Ave., 602/252-8848, www. heard.org) in early March is the state's largest festival of Native American arts and crafts. An estimated 20,000 serious collectors and curious browsers attend the annual event, where they are able to purchase original artwork and enjoy authentic food and entertainment. Throughout March, Arizona celebrates **Archaeology and Heritage Awareness Month** (www.azstateparks.com) with fascinating tours into the state's past, including events at Pueblo Grande, Deer Valley Rock Art Center, and other locations.

Later in the month, downtown Tempe celebrates with a series of outdoor events, including the **Great Arizona Beer Festival** (80 W. Rio Salado Pkwy., 480/774-8300, www.az-beer.com). The **Tempe Festival of the Arts** (Mill Ave. and University Dr., 480/921-2300, www.downtowntempe.com) transforms Mill Avenue into a pedestrian-only zone, lined with artists' booths, food stalls, and concert stages. The hugely popular arts festival is repeated in October.

And for some quirky fun, head out to Chandler in mid-March for the **Ostrich Festival & Parade** (2250 S. McQueen Rd., 480/963-4571, www.ostrichfestival.com), featuring live races, a carnival, and lots of food and entertainment.

April

Hollywood comes to town in April for the **Phoenix Film Festival** (7000 E. Mayo Blvd., 602/955-6444, www.phoenixfilmfestival.org), which screens soon-to-be released features as well as documentaries, shorts, and independent and foreign films. Past attendees include Ed Burns, Peter Fonda, director John Waters.

Springtime sunshine means kicking back and enjoying live music outdoors. In mid-April (and in October), the **Arizona Jazz Festival** (602/244-8444, http://arizonajazzfestival.com) brings smooth stylings to the historic Wigwam Resort in Litchfield Park. **Country Thunder** (20585 E. Price Rd., 866/802-6418, http:// arizona.countrythunder.com), held southeast of Phoenix in Florence, is a rowdy mid-April gathering with camping and live music. Think Woodstock in the desert with country acts like Big and Rich, Keith Urban, and Alan Jackson.

May-September

Major outdoor events tend to fade like wildflower blossoms when the temperatures climb into the triple digits during summer, but a little hot weather doesn't wilt Phoenicians. If you're visiting in summer, do as locals do, and head out after dark for concerts in the park, art walks, or outdoor movies at Biltmore Fashion Park and other locations. Look for **flashlight walks** at the Desert Botanical Garden, Phoenix Zoo, Deer Valley Rock Art Center, and elsewhere, or sit back and enjoy performances by the **Glendale Summer**

Band, state's longest-running community band, at Glendale's 400-seat Murphy Park Amphitheater (58th and Glendale Aves., 623/930-2299).

On Cinco de Mayo, local restaurants and bars top the list of party-throwers, but the fifth of May isn't all *tacos y margaritas.* Honoring Arizona's Latino culture, **Cinco de Mayo Phoenix** brings a weekend of food, folklorico dancers, and art to downtown.

The Valley's version of **Juneteenth** (602/550-0034, http://vosjuneteenth.com), recognizing the Emancipation Proclamation of June 19, 1865, has grown over the years to encompass food, art, storytelling, step teams, and music galore.

On Independence Day, the **Fabulous Phoenix Fourth** held in Steele Indian School Park (3rd St. and Indian School Rd.) boasts free entertainment for the whole family, including the largest fireworks display in Arizona. The Phoenix Zoo also celebrates the Fourth with fireworks, then a couple weeks later, hosts **Winter in July** (www.phoenixzoo. org), when 20 tons of snow arrive to the delight of the animals and summer-weary humans.

Throughout August and September, the **Chandler Center for the Arts** (250 N. Arizona Ave., 480/782-2680, www.chandlercenter.org) hosts a free concert series inside its fine auditorium. In mid-September, expect to find firework displays around the Phoenix area marking **Mexican Independence Day,** September 16.

October

Fall festival season leads off with the **Arizona State Fair** (1826 W. McDowell Rd., 602/252-6771, www.azstatefair.com). The two-week carnival combines rides, deep-fried food, big-name concerts, and farm animal exhibitions for a bit of classic Americana.

November–December

On November 1, the Valley's Latino

Las Noches de las Luminarias at the Desert Botanical Garden

© GREATER PHOENIX CVB/ADAM RODRIGUEZ

community celebrates **Día de los Muertos,** or Day of the Dead. At the **Desert Botanical Garden** (1201 N. Galvin Pkwy., 480/941-1225, www.dbg.org), artists display ofrendas, altars with offerings of food, flowers, photographs, or other items, a traditional means of honoring the ancestors. Day of the Dead is also marked by exhibitions and events at the Mesa Arts Center (1 E. Main St., 480/644-6500, www.mesaartscenter.com) and the Burton Barr Central Library (1221 N. Central Ave., 602/262-4636, www.phoenixpubliclibrary. org), as well as a musical celebration at the Musical Instrument Museum (4725 E. Mayo Blvd., 480/478-6000, www.themim.org).

By mid-November, most of the Valley is gearing up for elaborate holiday events, like **Las Noches de las Luminarias** (1201 N. Galvin Pkwy., 480/941-1225, www.dbg.org) at the Desert Botanical Garden. Luminarias are a Southwestern tradition, and thousands are lit throughout the grounds of the desert garden, creating a spectacular sight. **ZooLights** (455 N. Galvin Pkwy., 602/273-1341, www.phoenixzoo.org) delights kids with elaborate light displays, carousel rides, and hot cocoa at the Phoenix Zoo.

In the West Valley, **Glendale Glitter and Glow** (58th and Glendale Aves., 623/930-2299, www.glendaleaz.com) lights up the city's historic district with illuminated hot-air balloons. At the end of the month, Tempe lures college football fans with the **Insight Bowl** (500 E. Veterans Way, 480/350-0900, www.fiestabowl.org) at ASU's Sun Devil Stadium and the wild **Fiesta Bowl Block Party** (Mill Ave. and University Dr., 480/350-0900, www.fiestabowl.org), one of the nation's largest New Year's Eve celebrations.

Shopping

Phoenix helped pioneer the outdoor mall when Biltmore Fashion Park opened in the 1960s, and recently expanded and renovated, it continues to be identified with high-end retailers and upscale dining. Shoppers who are looking for funky mom-and-pop stores and vintage boutiques should head downtown or to Central Phoenix, which offers some surprisingly affordable retail options. Also, Tempe's Mill Avenue shops attract students from neighboring Arizona State University.

DOWNTOWN
Shopping Districts and Centers
ARIZONA CENTER
Arizona Center (400 E. Van Buren St., 602/271-4000, 10 A.M.–9 P.M. Mon.–Sat., 11 A.M.–5 P.M. Sun.) is downtown's pocket oasis, with shade, waterfalls, and a palm-lined pond, surrounded by restaurants, bars, and shops specializing in Arizona-themed souvenirs and gifts. The garden makes a great escape from the heat (or from the office), but if you're seeking more chill, you can head for the center's 24-screen multiplex movie theater.

ROOSEVELT ROW
A growing collection of boutiques, galleries, and restaurants has turned Roosevelt Row (602/772-0083, www.rooseveltrow.org) into an art-oriented, pedestrian-friendly downtown neighborhood. RoRo's monthly **First Friday art walk** (602/256-7539, http://artlinkphoenix.com, 6–10 P.M.) filling Roosevelt Street from Grand Avenue to 16th Street, is a lively evening of gallery-hopping, when artists open their studios to the public. Some of the smaller shops come and go, but **Modified Arts** (407 E.

© GREATER PHOENIX CVB

The Arizona Center is a downtown oasis.

Roosevelt St., 602/462-5516, http://modifie-darts.org, first and third Saturdays 6–9 P.M., Fridays noon–4 P.M., or by appointment) is a mainstay on the alternative arts scene, featuring musical performances in addition to rotating gallery selections.

The **Downtown Phoenix Public Market** (721 N. Central Ave., 602/254-1799, http://foodconnect.org/phxmarket, 4–8 P.M. Wed., 8 A.M.–noon Sat.) hosts a twice-weekly, open-air market near Central Avenue and McKinley Street, where local farmers and artisans sell or-ganic produce and homemade goods.

The artists who run the collective **eye lounge** (419 E. Roosevelt St., 602/430-1490, http://eyelounge.com, noon–7 P.M. Thurs., noon–9 P.M. Fri., 1–5 P.M. Sat., 11 A.M.–3 P.M. Sun.) have established this space as the "Best Underground Art Scene," according to the *Arizona Republic.*

Like Etsy? You'll love **Made Art Boutique** (922 N. 5th St., 602/256-6233, www.

madephx.com, 11 A.M.–6 P.M. Mon.–Fri., 11 A.M.–5 P.M. Sat., 11 A.M.–3 P.M. Sun.), which sells fun books, T-shirts, jewelry, and decor. **Butter Toast Boutique** (908 N. 6th St., 602/258-3458, noon–7 P.M. Mon.–Fri., 11 A.M.–6 P.M. Sat.) has affordable vintage clothing and accessories.

Hip yet sophisticated, **Bunky Boutique** (1437 N. 1st St., 602/252-1323, www.bunky-boutique.com, 10 A.M.–6 P.M. Mon.–Fri., 10 A.M.–5 P.M. Sat.) is known for an eclectic and well-curated selection of men's, women's, and children's clothing and accessories. Hours vary throughout the year.

CENTRAL PHOENIX
Shopping Districts and Centers
BILTMORE FASHION PARK
Since opening in 1963, Biltmore Fashion Park (24th St. and Camelback Rd., 602/955-8400, www.shopbiltmore.com, 10 A.M.–7 P.M. Mon.–Wed., 10 A.M.–8 P.M. Thurs.–Fri.,

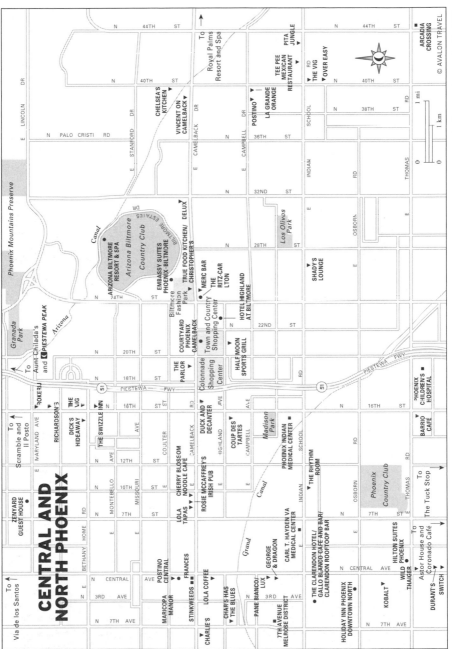

© KATHLEEN BRYANT

Biltmore Fashion Park

10 A.M.–6 P.M. Sat., noon–6 P.M. Sun.) has become a sort of public square for this posh neighborhood. The open-air shopping center incorporates landscaped courtyards, popular restaurants, and upscale shops, anchored by **Macy's** and **Saks Fifth Avenue**. Well-heeled clients, including the occasional celebrity, visit the mall's mini-boutiques or Elizabeth Arden Red Door Spa, while young hipsters head for the Apple store and lululemon. Not everyone approves of the recent remodel to a once-classic Midcentury Modern design, though it did add a new underground pedestrian walkway connecting the center to additional restaurants, a movie theater, and The Ritz-Carlton on the other side of Camelback Road.

MELROSE DISTRICT
The 7th Avenue Melrose District includes a mile-long mecca of thrift shops and vintage clothing stores, many of which stay open late on First Fridays. In March, the neighborhood hosts a popular street fair and car show. Inside **Zinnia** antiques mall (724 W. Indian School, 602/264-4166, 10 A.M.–6 P.M. daily), shoppers can browse an appealing jumble of everything from furniture to clothing. Next door, **Flo's** (4116 N. 7th Ave., 602/254-7861, 7 A.M.–5 P.M. Mon.–Fri., 10 A.M.–5 P.M. Sat.) is a large resale shop that supports the Florence Crittenton charities.

Retro Ranch (4303 N. 7th Ave., 602/297-1971, www.retroranch.net, 11 A.M.–6 P.M. Tues.–Sun.) specializes in mid-20th-century clothing, furniture, and accessories. If Danish Modern makes you drool, don't miss **Phoenix Metro Retro** (708 W. Hazelwood St., 602/279-0702, www.phoenixmetroretro.com, 11 A.M.–6 P.M. Wed.–Sun.).

Romantics will fall for the Euro-flair furniture and accessories at **Paris Envy** (4624 N. 7th Ave., 602/266-0966, 11 A.M.–5 P.M. Tues.–Sat.) and the shabby-but-elegant chic **Melrose Vintage** (4238 N. 7th Ave., 602/636-0300, http://shopmelrosevintage.com, 10 A.M.–5 P.M. Wed.–Sat.), whose inventory includes a wide selection of paper arts.

CHINESE CULTURAL CENTER

Just north of Sky Harbor Airport, the COFCO Chinese Cultural Center (668 N. 44th St., 602/273-7268, www.phxchinatown.com) combines graceful pagodas, statuary and arches, and traditional gardens with retail shops and restaurants serving Mandarin, Sichuan, and Shanghai-style cuisine. Stores include **Golden Gifts** (602/275-1311, 10 A.M.–7 P.M. Mon.–Sat., 10 A.M.–6 P.M. Sun.) selling bonsai, bamboo, and decor, and the **Chinese Herbal Shop** (602/244-9885, 10 A.M.–7 P.M. daily). The large, upscale **Super L Ranch Market** (602/225-2288, 9 A.M.–9 P.M. daily) has rows of imported goods, a bakery, and fresh produce and seafood.

Clothing and Gifts

A few interesting independents are clustered around Camelback Road and Central Avenue and its Medlock Plaza, including **Frances** (10 W. Camelback Rd., 602/279-5467, www.francesvintage.com, 10 A.M.–6 P.M. Mon.–Sat., noon–5 P.M. Sun.), where shoppers will have fun browsing an eclectic inventory of clothing, garden supplies, and great gifts for kids and adults. Nearby, sister store **Smeeks** (14 W. Camelback Rd., 602/279-0538, www.smeeks.com) sells candy and novelties (squirrel underpants? bacon Band-Aids?).

Even if you don't have room for another piercing, **Halo** (10 W. Camelback Rd., 602/230-0044, www.halopiercing.com, 11 A.M.–8 P.M. Mon.–Sat., noon–6 P.M. Sun.) has a wide selection of fascinating adornments, from earrings to wearable art.

Stinkweeds (12 W. Camelback Rd., 602/248-9461, www.stinkweeds.com, 11 A.M.–8 P.M. Mon.–Sat., noon–6 P.M. Sun.) is one of the city's last independent record shops,

specializing in up-and-coming bands, imports, and music from independent labels.

Home Furnishings

East on Camelback, **Red Modern Furniture** (201 E. Camelback Rd., 602/256-9620, http://redmodernfurniture.com, 10 A.M.–6 P.M. Mon.–Sat., noon–5 P.M. Sun.) is the place to go for original vintage pieces by Eero Saarinen, Arne Jacobsen, Knoll, Henredon, Gio Ponti, and Charles and Ray Eames. This hidden gem is a resource for some the nation's top interior designers and collectors. Inside, you'll find **Mint,** a collection of vintage clothing and accessories that run from glamorous cocktail dresses to disco threads. Farther east still, **Relics** (839 E. Camelback, 602/265-7354, www.relicsaz.com, 10 A.M.–5 P.M. Mon.–Sat. Sept.–May, 9 A.M.–4 P.M. Mon.–Sat. June–Aug.) has home and garden decor that looks as though it came from ancient Ephesus or a baroque palace.

NORTH PHOENIX
Shopping Districts and Centers
DESERT RIDGE

Behold yet another of Phoenix's outdoor "lifestyle centers" (aka mega-malls); at 1.2 million square feet, Desert Ridge (21001 N. Tatum Blvd., 480/523-7586, www.shopdesertridge.com, 11 A.M.–9 P.M. Mon.–Sat., 11 A.M.–6 P.M. Sun.) has something for every need and taste, conveniently situated near the JW Marriott Desert Ridge Resort. Barnes & Noble, Old Navy, Total Wine, and Target are among the national retailers who've staked a claim here, and specialty shops include Xi Clothing, Charming Charlie, and As You Wish Pottery Painting. Live bands entertain shoppers on weekend evenings. The Arizona Popular Culture Experience, a fun stop for trivia buffs, has displays featuring comic books, television series, and iconic toys like Barbie dolls and hula hoops. There's also an 18-screen movie theater, bungee jumping, and inside Dave &

Buster's restaurant, a video arcade and bowling alley.

OUTLETS AT ANTHEM

A few miles north of town, a bargain-hunter's paradise unfolds in the desert. The Outlets at Anthem (4250 W. Anthem Way, 623/465-9500, www.outletsanthem.com, 10 A.M.–8 P.M. Mon.–Sat., 10 A.M.–7 P.M. Sun.) is home to 75 brand-name stores loaded with merchandise at significantly reduced prices. You'll find Banana Republic, Gap, and J. Crew duds marked down by up to 70 percent. The shops are clean. The styles are new. A food court with just about anything you're looking for will fuel your search for bargains on outdoor gear, shoes, sunglasses, kitchenware, and more.

TEMPE AND THE EAST VALLEY
Shopping Districts and Centers
MILL AVENUE

A Main Street for Arizona State University, Mill Avenue became a little too popular for its own good in the 1990s, when high rents chased out mom-and-pop shops and bars. Enduring indies include **Lotions and Potions** (420 S. Mill, 480/968-4652, www.lotionsandpotions.com, 10 A.M.–9 P.M. Mon.–Thurs., 10 A.M.–10 P.M. Fri.–Sat., 11 A.M.–6 P.M. Sun.), where you can indulge in Crabtree & Evelyn or custom-mix your own scented body care, and the 1888 redbrick **Hackett House** (95 W. 4th St., 480/350-8181, www.hacketthouse.org, 10 A.M.–4 P.M. Mon.–Sat.), selling tea sets and other gifts, and hosting cooking classes.

In a karmic twist, many of the national chains that usurped local businesses didn't survive the economic downturn. While others have come and gone, **Urban Outfitters** remains to serve an eclectic crowd of students, suburbanites, and visitors, and "Mill Ave." continues to be one of the city's few spots for streetside shopping.

© KATHLEEN BRYANT

Tempe's Mill Avenue is lined with shops and restaurants.

TEMPE MARKETPLACE

A couple miles north, you'll find the sprawling Tempe Marketplace (Loop 202 and McClintock, 480/966-9338, www.tempemarketplace.com, 11 A.M.–9 P.M. Mon.–Sat., 11 A.M.–6 P.M. Sun.). The mega-complex of chain retailers boasts a lot of names you'll recognize from the mall, like Gap, Levi's, and Barnes & Noble, as well as a movie theater and dozens of restaurants and bars. Its light shows, outdoor fireplaces, and unique water features make it a great place to hang out at night, especially for the free Third Thursday concerts.

Bookstores

One of the stores that fled Mill Avenue, **Changing Hands Bookstore** (6428 S. McClintock Dr., 480/730-0205, www.changinghands.com, 10 A.M.–9 P.M. Mon.–Fri., 9 A.M.–9 P.M. Sat., 10 A.M.–6 P.M. Sun.) stocks

12,000 square feet with new and used books. Known for its regular book clubs, workshops, and events, the store's impressive roster of signings has included David Sedaris, Jimmy Carter, Hillary Clinton, Anne Rice, Luis Alberto Urrea, and Jodi Picoult. Collectors will find rare and modern first editions as well as author-signed copies.

On the ASU campus, the **Student Book Center** (704 S. College Ave., 480/966-6226, www.studentbookcenter.com, 8 A.M.–5 P.M. Mon.–Fri., 9 A.M.–5 P.M. Sat.) is an independent, family-owned business that sells textbooks (of course), Greek gear, and Sun Devil–themed clothing and gifts.

With stores in Phoenix, Mesa, and other Arizona locations, **Bookmans Entertainment Exchange** (www.booksmans.com, 9 A.M.–10 P.M. daily) lures bargain-hunters looking to buy, sell, or trade books, music, games, instruments, and outdoor gear. The Mesa store (1056 S. Country Club Dr., 480/835-0505) has a kids' corner with Saturday morning story times.

Clothing

Mere blocks west of Mill Avenue, **Here on the Corner** (714 S. College Ave., 480/377-0100, www.hereonthecorner.com, 10 A.M.–8 P.M. Mon.–Fri., 11 A.M.–7 P.M. Sat., noon–8 P.M. Sun.) has trendy finds from designer denim to ecofriendly handbags. On the third Thursday evening of each month, the store fêtes local designers (and customers) with food and music. Nearby, **Buffalo Exchange** (227 W. University Dr., 480/968-2557, www.buffaloexchange.com, 10 A.M.–9 P.M. Mon.–Sat., 11 A.M.–7 P.M. Sun.) sells an eclectic mix of new and used clothing. Hunt for vintage concert shirts, leather jackets, funky accessories, and high-end brand names.

Farmers Markets and Food Tours

Think nothing grows in the desert? You'd be surprised. Farmers markets are popping up all around urban Phoenix, but for even more flavor, drive a bit farther east or south, where grocery shopping approaches entertainment.

Tucked into the community of Guadalupe, a one-square-mile town predominantly inhabited by Yaqui Indian and Latino residents, you'll find the **Guadalupe Farmer's Market** (9210 S. Avenida del Yaqui, 480/730-1945, 9 A.M.–6 P.M. Mon.–Sat., 9 A.M.–5 P.M. Sun.). The market sells locally grown fruits and vegetables, as well as Latin American specialties like fresh tortillas, roasted chiles, and homemade salsas. While you're in Guadalupe, take time to pop into **El Mercado** (8212 S. Avenida del Yaqui, 480/831-5925), where you'll find imported products from south of the border, like ceramics and paper goods.

Gourmet Magazine called dining at the 12-acre organic **Farm at South Mountain** (6106 S. 32nd St., 602/276-6360, www.thefarmatsouthmountain.com, open seasonally) "a spiritual experience." The brainchild of Dwight Heard (who founded the fabulous Phoenix museum of that name), this ancient riverbed beneath South Mountain was planted with a hundred pecan trees. Current owners operate a spa, studio gift shop, and three farm-to-table restaurants on the property, often rented for weddings and other events. Restaurants go on hiatus during summer months, reopening in August or September, though you'll spot the farm's produce at local markets. Call 480/236-7097 to sign up for a tour of the biodynamic garden.

It's a farmers market. No, it's petting zoo. Wait, it's a summer camp for kids. It's…**SuperFarm!** (3440 S. Hawes Rd., 602/432-6865, http://superstitionfarm.com, 10 A.M.–4 P.M. Fri.–Wed., 10 A.M.–7:30 P.M. Thurs.). Also known as Superstition Farm, this fourth-generation dairy farm in Mesa has hayrides, tours, and a Thursday night farmers market offering everything from veggies to artisanal ice cream. The owners delight in showing urban-dwellers how the udder-half lives.

Southeast of Phoenix, the **Queen Creek Olive Mill** (25062 S. Meridian, 480/888-9290, http://queencreekolivemill.com, 9 A.M.–5 P.M. Mon.–Fri., 8 A.M.–5 P.M. Sat.–Sun.) raises 16 different types of olives in their pesticide-free groves. You can shop in the gourmet marketplace for local and imported gifts (including the farm's line of olive oil body treatments), have breakfast or lunch at del Piero, and take the Olive Oil 101 tour ($5) to learn more about growing olives in the desert.

Less than a mile away, **Schnepf Farms** (24810 S. Rittenhouse Rd., 480/987-3100, http://schnepffarms.com, 7:30 A.M.–4 P.M. Thurs.–Sun.) has been feeding Phoenicians for 70 years. Named an Arizona Treasure in 2006, the farm has organic orchards and gardens where you can pick your own produce May through June or, if you'd rather let them do the picking, a general store stocked with homemade preserves and country crafts. Breakfast (Saturday and Sunday only) and lunch are available at the store's bakery. Special events include festivals, tours, and chef-hosted dinners. Call for directions and seasonal hours.

WEST VALLEY
Shopping Districts and Centers
HISTORIC DOWNTOWN GLENDALE

Named by *Sunset* magazine as one of the nation's 10 best places to shop, historic downtown Glendale has a hundred antiques stores and boutiques. The walkable 10-block-square downtown comprises three shopping districts: Old Towne (Glendale Ave. and 58th Ave.), Catlin Court (Myrtle Ave. and 58th Ave.), and sandwiched between them, the Promenade, where you'll find a visitor center and free covered parking. Historic bungalows with white picket fences and shade trees line the Catlin neighborhood, many of them converted into small specialty shops, like **Country Maiden** (7146 N. 58th Ave., 623/930-7303, 10 A.M.–5 P.M. Mon.–Sat., 11 A.M.–3 P.M. Sun.) and **The Cottage Garden** (7142 N. 58th Ave., 623/847-3232, 10 A.M.–4 P.M. Mon.–Sat.).

If you have a sweet tooth, head east on Glendale Avenue for **Cerreta Candy Company** (5345 W. Glendale Ave., 620/930-1000, www.cerreta.com, 8 A.M.–6 P.M. Mon.–Sat.) a family-owned candy factory where you can swoon over cases chock-full of chocolates or go on a 30-minute behind-the-scenes tour (10 A.M. and 1 P.M. Mon.–Fri., free).

Sports and Recreation

Phoenix is "big league," home to the Arizona Diamondbacks (MLB), Phoenix Suns (NBA), Phoenix Mercury (WNBA), Arizona Cardinals (NFL), and Phoenix Coyotes (hockey). And it's not all about spectator sports—the city and its suburbs are nirvana for die-hard golfers, hikers, bikers, and adventurers. Don't let the summer heat stop you from taking advantage of the desert's incredible landscapes. Do as the locals do, and set your alarm clock early. Even in the hottest months, cool morning temperatures make a round of golf or jog along the city's canals downright pleasant.

AIR ADVENTURES AND BALLOONING

With nearly 300 sunny days a year, Phoenix skies are friendly for fliers. You can soar like a hawk over the spectacular desert scenery by taking a glider ride at **Arizona Soaring** (22548

N. Sailport Way, Maricopa, 520/568-2318, www.azsoaring.com). Twenty-minute flights start at $105 and come with or without aerobatics like loops and spins.

Act out all your *Top Gun* fantasies at **Fighter Combat International** (5865 S. Sossaman Rd., Mesa, 866/359-4273, www.fightercombat.com), where you can tempt both gravity and death by flying a plane on a "combat mission." Even beginners learn to take the stick during in-the-air training, learning maneuvering and weaponry, and engaging in air-to-air combat drills. The grand finale is a high-speed, low-altitude pass in front of family and friends watching from an observation deck. Prices range from $795 for a three- to four-hour adventure to $4,000 for a multiday experience.

Hot Air Expeditions (704 W. Deer Valley Rd., 480/502-6999, www.hotairexpeditions.com) flies its balloons over the Sonoran Desert for spectacular panoramas of the mountain-rimmed valley, often dipping below 400 feet to see jackrabbits, roadrunners, coyotes, and even javelinas, or to get close to saguaro cacti and other desert exotics. You will be welcomed back to terra firma with flutes of champagne and alfresco gourmet selections prepared by chef Vincent Guerithault. Three-hour trips cost about $175, and round-trip hotel transportation is available.

Aerogelic Ballooning (866/353-8329, www.aerogelicballooning.com) focuses on small balloons that hold two, four, or six people for flights over the Sonoran Desert outside of Phoenix, as well as some unusual itineraries, such as an adrenaline-inducing night flight (the only one in the United States). "Dawn patrol" flights start at $165, taking off 30 minutes before sunrise to show the city coming to life. Private charters for you and your special someone start at $700.

© HOT AIR EXPEDITIONS

For spectacular views of the Sonoran Desert, try a hot-air balloon ride.

DESERT AND JEEP TOURS

Get an up-close look at the Sonoran Desert on a tour with **Arizona Trails** (888/799-4284 or 480/837-4284, www.arizonatrails.com). Their Jeeps or Hummers will transport you to rocky canyons and streams, where you can visit a historic gold mine or even learn the art of panning for gold. **Carefree Adventures** (480/488-2466, www.carefreeadventures.com) heads into the surrounding desert and mountains for hikes, archaeological tours, or a flashlight-and-hard-hat exploration of an old mine tunnel. **Phoenix Tours** (800/303-5185, www.phoenixtours.us) brokers a wide range of itineraries, from city sites to ATV or Jeep adventures in the desert. Prices range $45–500, depending on the trip.

BIKING AND JOGGING

Phoenix's 181-mile system of canals (some of them a legacy from the prehistoric Hohokam) includes pleasant stretches for biking and running. One of the best is along the gravel banks of the **Arizona Canal** between Scottsdale Road and Central Avenue. The full distance is just over 11 miles, with the best parts at either end: Scottsdale hotels and neighborhoods carved out of old citrus groves near 68th Street and canal-side public art and the Biltmore Hotel on the stretch between Central Avenue and 24th Street.

One of the best introductions to mountain biking in the Sonoran Desert is the **Desert Classic** trail, one of several hiking and biking trails that start at the Pima Canyon Trailhead (9904 S. 48th St., near Guadalupe Road) of **South Mountain Park** (http://phoenix.gov/parks). The nine-mile out-and-back Desert Classic runs the gamut of terrain from steep-sided washes to single-track speedways and even a few rocky, technical climbs without becoming impossible for bikers who have at least intermediate skills. If that's not challenging enough, you can loop back to the parking area by taking the midsection of the **National Trail**. On its full 14.5-mile (one way) length, the National Trail traverses the 16,000-acre park for diverse views and rocky, steep descents.

Road bikers will have a hard time finding traffic-free pedaling in Phoenix, but on **Silent Sunday** (usually the fourth Sunday of the month), South Mountain Park closes its main access roads to motorized vehicles, reserving them for bikers, hikers, and runners. Across town at North Mountain Park, Silent Sunday is usually the second Sunday of the month. Contact the City of Phoenix Parks and Recreation department (602/262-7393, http://phoenix.gov/parks) for details.

Another paved hill climb can be found on **Valle Vista Road** on the south side of Camelback Mountain. The best approach is from the south, either on 48th Street or 56th Street, because the streets link up to form a loop back to your car (or to the light-rail stop at 44th Street and Washington).

HIKING AND ROCK CLIMBING

Walking through the Sonoran Desert is an eye-opening experience. For one, this desert is actually lush with fascinating vegetation, from tiny pincushion cacti to tall paloverdes, trees with smooth green trunks and yellow blooms each spring. For another, the mountain preserves around Phoenix offer stunning vistas in every direction. But sun protection and plentiful water are a must all year long. If you're new to desert hiking, heading out with a guide is a good option.

Take a Hike Arizona (866/615-2748, www.takeahikearizona.com) leads guided hikes to all destinations around metro Phoenix. Half-day excursions start at $65. Full-day hikes of five hours or more run about $99. Prices include water, snacks, and the use of poles and packs.

The steep canyons and rock spires that shape the mountains around Phoenix are a playground for rock climbers, but the sandstone terrain is often treacherous. The guides at **360 Adventures** (602/795-1877, www.360-adventures.com) offer instruction and equipment for beginners and the lay of the land for experts. Prices for rock climbing or canyoneering trips start around $150 per person for a half-day, depending on the size of the group.

◀ Piestewa Peak

No visit to Phoenix would be complete without hiking up Piestewa Peak. The short but challenging Summit Trail rises a little more than 1,200 feet in 1.2 miles, but it's worth it. The peak offers panoramic views of the city stretched out for miles in every direction, and when the wind carries the scent of creosote and citrus blossoms up from the valley below, it can be hard to begin the clamber back down. On weekend mornings, the trail becomes a mountainside promenade as throngs of tanned, supple hikers and runners (and those who wish to be so) make even panting by the side of the trail interesting. But it is the quieter weekdays when jackrabbits, lizards, and the occasional rattlesnake or coyote come out to sun themselves among the cacti and desert trees that pepper the hillsides. To reach the trailhead, turn east onto Squaw Peak Drive from Lincoln Drive between 22nd and 24th Streets.

North Mountain Preserve

Farther north, the 10.7-mile Charles Christiansen Memorial Trail (Trail 100) linking North Mountain, Shaw Butte, and Dreamy Draw is too long for most people to hike in a single go, but it serves as the spine of the entire **Phoenix Mountains Preserve** trail network and is a good jumping-off point to explore canyons and washes that feel like they're far from the surrounding city. Find information on the flora and fauna and get maps at the **North Mountain Visitors Center** (12950 N. 7th St., 602/335-1962, http://phoenix.gov/parks, 8 A.M.–1 P.M. daily).

South Mountain Park

The city's other must-hike destination is South Mountain Park (main entrance at 10409 S. Central Avenue, 602/262-7393, phoenix.gov/parks). Its 61,000-plus acres of mountains, arroyos, and flats crisscrossed by 51 miles of hiking trails make this the largest municipal park in the United States. San Juan Road, open to motor vehicles the first weekend of every month, leads to the highest peak, where you'll find picnic areas and a series of short hikes. The more challenging Alta Trail starts near the park entrance and runs along a ridge, offering 4.5 miles (one-way) of some of the most stunning city views anywhere. Rattlesnakes and other desert critters make regular appearances in the park, so be alert and give them a wide berth. Volunteers at the **South Mountain Environmental Education Center** (10409 S. Central Ave., 602/262-6412, 9 A.M.–2 P.M. Tues.–Thurs., 9 A.M.–noon Sat.) offer maps and trail information, and interpretive displays introduce the desert ecosystem.

Papago Park

Between Phoenix and Tempe, Papago Park offers easy, paved trails and fun rock scrambles. The short but sweet Hole-in-the-Rock trail is an easy 835-foot scramble up to a tunnel-like hole in the sandstone, used by the ancient Hohokam as a solar calendar. Enchanting views of downtown Phoenix make this one of the best places anywhere to watch a colorful Southwestern sunset. Get there by turning off the Galvin Parkway onto the Papago Park/Phoenix Zoo road. The trail begins from a picnic area on the northern end of the Ranger Office Loop road.

GOLF

Welcome to the Southwest's golf capital, luring professionals and amateurs with one of the finest collections of courses in the world. Championship greens dot the city, and some residents literally live on the links, thanks to dozens of golf course communities. Arizona State University graduates Phil Mickelson, Billy Mayfair, and Grace Park refined their skills here, and Tom Lehman and Annika Sörenstam were compelled to move here for the constant sunshine and top-notch fairways.

Scottsdale's luxury desert courses may be more well-known, but Phoenix and Chandler offer quality for a good price, with a broad mix of traditional and desert courses, as well as some unique landmarks. Many courses close for aeration and overseeding between seasons, so be sure to call ahead. Like hotel and resort rates, greens fees tumble as the heat rises, with even the best courses charging a fraction of their winter prices in the summer.

Consistently earning "best of" nods, **Wildfire Golf Club** (5350 E. Marriott Dr., 480/473-0205, www.wildfiregolf.com) at the JW Marriott Desert Ridge Resort showcases two 18-hole desert courses designed by giants Arnold Palmer and Nick Faldo. The scenic Palmer Signature Course has expansive fairways and rolling greens, while the Faldo Championship Course treats golfers to large bent-grass greens, tee boxes, and a bewildering 106 sand bunkers. If you'd prefer to hit a few balls and take in the views of the McDowell Mountains, though, grab a bucket at the 13,000-square-foot practice green, complete with bunkers and pitching areas.

A bit closer to town, **Lookout Mountain Golf Club** (11111 N. 7th St., 602/866-6356, http://tapatiocliffshilton.com) at the Pointe Hilton Tapatio Cliffs Resort is an award-winning par-71, 18-hole championship course that wraps around North Mountain Park and the Lookout Mountain Preserve, giving golfers a chance to appreciate the occasional Sonoran Desert rabbit or coyote along with their birdies and eagles. The medium-length course should appeal to most skill levels, though the back nine features a few challenging target holes. The

well-regarded golf academy may be a good place to grab a few lessons if you're new to the game, and its practice area has its own pitching green and separate chipping and putting areas.

City-owned **Papago Golf Course** (5595 E. Moreland St., 602/275-8428, www.papagogolfcourse.net) is not only one of the most loved slices of turf in the Valley, it is also one of Phoenix's best golf values. Golf course architect William Francis "Billy" Bell, whose roster of 100-plus courses includes Torrey Pines, designed it to showcase the red-hued Papago Buttes, Camelback Mountain, and downtown Phoenix. Opened in 1963, the course is now better than ever, thanks to a $5.8 million renovation that improved aesthetics and bunkering. Another favorite among the city's eight courses is **Aguila** (8440 S. 35th Ave., 602/237-9601, http://phoenix.gov/recreation), an 18-hole championship course designed by Gary Panks and located at the base of South Mountain.

Arizona State University boasts one of the finest collegiate golf programs in the country, so it's little surprise that their home course in Tempe should earn 4.5 stars from *Golf Digest*. The challenging **ASU Karsten Golf Club** (1125 E. Rio Salado Pkwy., 480/921-8070, www.asu-karsten.com) may force you to use every club in your bag, but with four sets of tees, you don't have to be PGA-bound to make par—or at least have fun. Designer Pete Dye incorporated his trademark mounding and inspired pot bunkers, as well as lakes, rolling hills, and well-protected greens. The Scottish links-style course books well in advance, so be sure to call early for a tee time.

Raven Golf Club (3636 E. Baseline Rd., 602/243-3636, www.ravenphx.com) features thousands of mature trees, including large African sumacs and 6,000 pines. You'll find water hazards, strategically placed bunkers, and a few challenging target holes on the par-72 course. Raven regularly gets high marks for

© CITY OF PHOENIX

Aguila golf course

its customer service and the Kent Chase Golf Academy, which offers private instruction and group classes.

The **Legacy Golf Resort** (6808 S. 32nd St., 888/828-3673, www.shellhospitality.com) sits on the former ranch of Dwight Heard—founder of the Heard Museum. Historic ranch buildings line the 18-hole desert golf course, where you'll have views of South Mountain and the downtown Phoenix skyline. Group instruction is available, as are private lessons by LPGA professionals Lynn Marriott and Pia Nilsson, who are regularly named among the best instructors in the country.

Arizona Grand Golf Course (8000 S. Arizona Grand Pkwy., 602/431-6480, www.arizonagrandresort.com) boasts a par-71 layout with unconventional fairways that wrap around South Mountain Park, creating dramatic elevation changes, unusual slopes, and stunning views. The ingenious design features a traditional front nine before switching over to a

desert back nine, which can be an exhilarating change during a mid-game slump.

Many say Arizona's reputation as a mecca for golfers began in Chandler, at the **San Marcos Golf Resort** (1 N. San Marcos Pl., 480/963-3358, www.sanmarcosresort.com). When it opened in 1913, the San Marcos boasted the state's first course with grass greens. Over the years, presidents and celebrities have played its wide, forgiving fairways. The stately historic landmark is a good value and should be considered if you're staying in the East Valley.

Chandler's **Ocotillo Golf Resort** (3751 S. Clubhouse Dr., 480/917-6660, www.ocotillogolf.com) is one of the state's most individual courses, as 24 of its 27 holes feature water hazards—from small lakes and cascading waterfalls to a few "island holes." This makes the challenging course refreshingly different, and many say it's one of the best-manicured in the city, earning accolades from several golf magazines.

Thirty miles east of Phoenix (and worth the drive), **Gold Canyon Golf Resort** (6100 S. Kings Ranch Rd., 480/982-9090, www.gcgr.com) is home to a pair of spectacular 18-hole courses tucked into the Superstition Mountains. The Dinosaur Mountain Course snakes through mountain passes (the fourth hole is postcard-pretty), while the Sidewinder wraps around the foothills.

HORSEBACK RIDING

For more than 40 years, **South Ponderosa Stables** (10215 S. Central Ave., 602/286-1261, www.arizona-horses.com, daily year-round) has been guiding visitors and residents over desert trails. Their "spread" is the 16,000-acre South Mountain, where 50 miles of riding trails lead almost everywhere through the park. Trail rides start at $33 per person for one hour. Specialties include sunrise and sunset rides, a petroglyph tour, and breakfast or dinner cookouts. Morning reservations are recommended, especially for summer days when the temperature can top 100 degrees.

Driving east to the Superstition Mountains turns **Saguaro Lake Trail Rides** (13020 Bush Hwy., 480/984-0335, www.saguarolaketrailrides.com, Oct.–Apr.) into an all-day adventure. The lush canyons, towering rock spires, and sparkling lake make this one of the more scenic spots to ride horses. Rides are $50–125 per person.

On the west side of the valley, **White Tanks Riding Stables** (20300 W. Olive Ave., 623/935-7455, www.whitetanksriding.com, Nov.–Apr.) leads one-hour to half-day trips through the saguaros and rock art of White Tank Mountain Regional Park. Rates start at $39 per person, and for children age 7 or younger, 20-minute pony rides are $18.

WATER FUN

As might be expected in a town where summertime temperatures regularly top 100 degrees, fun in the water doesn't end at the nearest pool. You'll be surprised when you see how many vehicles are carrying kayaks or pulling speedboats through Phoenix traffic. A favorite destination is the Salt River and its reservoirs, located about 40 minutes northeast of downtown Phoenix.

Tubing on the lower Salt River is a relaxed float through a pretty stretch of Tonto National Forest, where you might spot wildlife like great blue herons or mustangs. Though the concessioner warns that floating and alcohol don't mix, you'll also see (and hear) plenty of wild life (aka raucous partying). Tubes for picnic coolers are available, and buses stop at three different spots downstream, so you can float for two hours or four, as long as your sunscreen and cold beverages hold out. The tour company **Salt River Recreation** (480/984-3305, www.saltrivertubing.com, 9 A.M.–6:30 P.M. daily, water flow permitting, $15) will rent you a tube and give you a ride to and from the parking lot. Take Highway 202 (Loop 202) to Power Road in east Mesa and drive seven miles north.

If you'd rather be on the water than in it, **Desert Belle Cruises** (14011 N. Bush Hwy., 480/984-2425, www.saguarolake.net, May–Sept., $20 adults, $10 kids) operates 90-minute sightseeing tours of Saguaro Lake, one of four sparkling reservoirs tucked into the mountains northeast of Phoenix. Bald eagles have been spotted soaring along the cliffs around the lake, and the desert-scape of saguaro and cholla cacti slopes down to the water's edge. The marina is located about 13 miles northeast of Loop 202 off Bush Highway (Power Road).

For those who prefer adventures closer to home, Metro Phoenix has a wealth of water parks. The biggest feature the requisite waterslides, wave pools, and tubing areas, mixed with attractions like miniature golf, arcade games, rides, and food. Hours vary throughout the season, and most offer discounts and passes. The claim to fame of Tempe's **Big Surf** (1500 N. McClintock Dr., 480/994-2297,

COOL CLEAR WATER

To combat summer's triple-digit temperatures, Phoenicians have turned the region's most valuable resource—water—into a diverse range of refreshing retreats and activities. Here's a sampling:

- **Pools:** With more than 50 public pools and thousands more in backyards, finding a sparkling oasis isn't too hard. Most hotels and resorts have at least one pool, and in Scottsdale at **The Phoenician** (6000 E. Camelback Rd., 480/941-8200, www.thephoenician.com), you'll find nine, including the gleaming relaxation pool. It's open only to guests, though you can take a peek if you have dinner or a cocktail at the hotel.

- **Misters:** Experience the magic of misters, simple machines that produce water droplets as fine as the diameter of a human hair. When they make contact with the dry desert air, the droplets "flash evaporate," resulting in a dip in temperature by as much as 25 degrees—and all with just a slight increase in noticeable humidity.

- **Lakes:** Thanks to a series of dams, there are seven large lakes within an easy drive of Phoenix. The most convenient is **Tempe Town Lake** (620 N. Mill Ave., 480/350-8625, www.tempe.gov/lake, free), created by inflatable rubber dams along the Salt River. The man-made lake and its park make a popular gathering spot for festivals, joggers, and rowing clubs. Rent a paddleboat or let the little ones enjoy the monsoon-themed **Splash Playground** (10 A.M.-7 P.M. daily, Apr.-

Sept., free), where water features follow a raindrop's journey to the ocean.

- **Water Parks:** In summer, nothing beats the heat like gliding down a slide into a clear pool of water. There are a half-dozen water parks throughout the Valley, including a few at the larger resorts, but the biggest is **Wet 'n' Wild** (4243 W. Pinnacle Peak Rd., 623/201-2000, http://phoenix.mywetnwild.com, Apr.-mid-Sept., $37 adult, $30 child), $30 million worth of slides, rides, and waves spread out over 25 acres.

- **Rivers:** Many Phoenicians drive 20 minutes northeast of the Valley to float down the mountain-fed Salt River, passing majestic sandstone cliffs, spiraling hawks, wading blue herons, and towering saguaro cacti—as well as beer-soaked partiers on the river and jacked-up trucks blasting classic rock from shore. For $15 per person, **Salt River Recreation** (480/984-3305, www.saltrivertubing.com) will rent you a tube and give you a ride to and from the river.

- **Fountains:** Aptly named Fountain Hills boasts a 560-foot jet of water, one of the world's tallest. Most days, the slender column rises 330 feet from Fountain Lake for 15 minutes at the top of every hour (9 A.M. to 9 P.M.), but on special occasions, it soars to its maximum height of 56 stories. To visit **Fountain Park** (12925 N. Saguaro Blvd., 480/816-5151), which has a splash playground for children, take Shea Boulevard 15 minutes east from central Scottsdale and turn north on Saguaro Boulevard.

http://bigsurffun.com, May–mid-Sept., $27 adult, $20 child) is a wave pool big enough to allow actual surfing. **Golfland Sunsplash** (155 W. Hampton Ave., 480/834-8319, www.golfland.com/mesa, May–Sept., $27 adult, $20 child) in Mesa has a dozen different thrilling waterslides, including Master Blaster Water Coaster and Thrill Falls. In Glendale, **Wet 'n' Wild** (4243 W. Pinnacle Peak Rd., 623/201-2000, http://phoenix.mywetnwild.

com, Apr.–mid-Sept., $37 adult, $30 child), boasts $30 million worth of slides and white-water rafting rides. A favorite of the Travel Channel and *Phoenix New Times,* **Oasis Water Park** (8000 S. Arizona Grand Pkwy., 602/438-9000, www.arizonagrandresort.com, Feb.–Sept.) is a beautifully landscaped seven-acre park open only to guests of the Arizona Grand Resort.

If admission fees to splashy water parks

THE FASTEST UNDER THE SUN

Phoenix lost its shot at hosting the Grand Prix racing team a fourth time, but that doesn't mean this town isn't built for speed. NASCAR races at **Phoenix International Raceway** (www.phoenixraceway.com), **Firebird International Raceway** (www.firebirdraceway.com) hosts the National Hot Rod Association, and several tracks around town let wannabe Vettels and Danicas take the wheel.

Bob Bondurant, the former racer for Carol Shelby and Team Ferrari, coaches thousands of students every year at **The Bob Bondurant School of High Performance Driving** (20000 S. Maricopa Rd., 800/842-7223, www.bondurant.com), his custom-designed, 60-acre facility near Firebird International Raceway. Single-day courses are designed to impart skills ranging from introductory racing techniques to highway survival. Multiday courses cover

all kinds of high-performance driving "experiences," in super sports, open-wheel race cars, and even karts or law enforcement SUVs. Fees start at $400 and rise to well over $5,000.

NASCAR champ Rusty Wallace helped develop the **Rusty Wallace Racing Experience** (508/384-7223, racewithrusty.com), which offers amateurs a chance to drive a NASCAR stock car at Phoenix International Raceway. Ride-alongs start at $100, and you can take the wheel for $300 and up.

A less expensive (and less intense) experience that also involves beer and video games can be had at the **Octane Raceway** (317 S. 48th St., 602/302-7223, www.octaneraceway.com). Their karts can hit speeds upwards of 45 mph, and video cameras and timed clocks keep careful track of who wins and loses for later bragging rights. Fees for single races start at $20.

exceed your budget, check out Chandler's **Desert Oasis Aquatic Center** (1400 W. Summit Place, 480/732-1061, www.chandleraz.gov, mid-May–Labor Day), a bargain at $1 for the kiddos and $2.25 for adults, with three slides, a pool, and playground.

SPECTATOR SPORTS
Auto Racing

Half a dozen times a year, the roar of NASCAR comes to the **Phoenix International Raceway** (7602 S. Avondale Blvd., Avondale, 866/408-7223, www.phoenixraceway.com). On race weekends, luxury lounges and corporate suites go for megabucks, but fans can camp on the grounds in an RV for $60, purchase a pit pass for $50, and root from the stands for as little as $25 per person. The track hosts several bars and restaurants, including SPEED Cantina, and Bashas' operates a grocery store on-site. Live entertainment, gaming, and opportunities to meet NASCAR drivers round out the experience.

Baseball

Chase Field (401 E. Jefferson St., Phoenix, 602/514-8400, http://arizona.diamondbacks.mlb.com) in downtown Phoenix is home to the 2001 World Series champion **Arizona Diamondbacks.** The ballpark has a retractable roof that can be opened on balmy spring and fall days and closed during the heat of summer. The swimming pool in right field gets a lot of attention on the massive high-def LED scoreboard, but other amenities include restaurants over left and right fields, a picnic pavilion above center, and play areas for kids. Outfield seats can be had for $8–16, but prices rise quickly to as much as $150 for box seats. Scalping is legal in Arizona, so check websites and the streets around the field (prices often drop once the game starts) to find deals.

Thanks to Cactus League play, the crack of the bat can be heard in Arizona when the rest of the country is still shoveling snow. More than a dozen teams arrive in late February for their **spring training** (www.cactusleague.

Chase Field is the home of the Arizona Diamondbacks.

com) homes in metro Phoenix, including the D-backs, Chicago Cubs, Chicago White Sox, Cincinnati Reds, Cleveland Indians, Colorado Rockies, Kansas City Royals, Los Angeles Angels of Anaheim, Los Angeles Dodgers, Milwaukee Brewers, Oakland Athletics, San Diego Padres, San Francisco Giants, Seattle Mariners, and Texas Rangers. Games are more casual than in "The Show," and the small fields scattered across the Valley give fans a chance to get a close look at both superstars and up-and-comers.

Basketball

Next door to Chase Field, **US Airways Center** (201 E. Jefferson St., 602/379-2000, www.us-airwayscenter.com) is the home of the NBA's **Phoenix Suns** (602/379-7867, www.nba.com/suns). Tickets for the Suns start around $40 for nosebleed seats and go up to $500 or more for courtside. For about half that, you can watch Olympic gold medalist Diana Taurasi and the

WNBA's **Phoenix Mercury** (602/252-9622, www.wnba.com/mercury). The venue also hosts concerts and the state's arena football team, the **Arizona Rattlers** (800/745-3000, azrattlers.com).

Football

The **Arizona Cardinals** (602/379-0101, www.azcardinals.com) spent years in the National Football League's rankings cellar before making their first Super Bowl appearance ever in 2009, at last sparking an enduring interest among fans. The team's home at **University of Phoenix Stadium** (1 Cardinals Dr.) in Glendale is spectacular. The round silver building seats 63,400 and not only features a retractable roof but also a retractable field that can slide out to catch the sunshine. The 25-acre site has a big footprint (requiring enough concrete to build a sidewalk to San Francisco and enough cooling for 2,300 Valley homes), but stadium officials strive to make it as "green" as possible, recycling

SIGNS OF SPRING

The satisfying crack of a wooden bat. The scent of hot dogs wafting by on a warm breeze. Spring arrives mid-February in Arizona, when 15 **Cactus League** teams (www.cactusleague.com) take the field at 10 ballparks across the Phoenix area. While the league's older parks have a more relaxed, intimate feel, newer, larger venues have made an effort to include areas where fans can have up-close views of players. Bring plenty of sunscreen and a hat, and get to the park early: Players often sign autographs before a game, and most of the time, big-name stars leave the field after a couple of innings. Stadiums and their teams, from west to east:

Take I-10 20 miles west of Phoenix for **Goodyear Ballpark** (1933 S. Ballpark Way, 623/882-3120), where the **Cincinnati Reds** and **Cleveland Indians** play. The stadium's family-friendly vibe makes it a fan favorite, and it feels like home-away-from-home for Ohio natives.

Northwest of Phoenix off Bell Road, **Surprise Stadium** (15960 N. Bullard Ave., 623/222-2222) hosts the **Texas Rangers** and **Kansas City Royals.** The campus includes more than a dozen practice fields and a five-acre lake, making this 10,400-seat stadium a favorite of families.

About 10 miles west of Phoenix, snazzy **Camelback Ranch** (10710 W. Camelback Rd., 623/877-8585) makes fans of the **Los Angeles Dodgers** and **Chicago White Sox** feel at home with replicas of Ebbets Field and Comiskey Park. Opened in 2010, the stadium seats 13,000 and boasts its own citrus grove.

Near Loop 101 at Bell Road, the **Peoria Sports Complex** (16101 N. 83rd Ave., 623/773-8700) is home to the **Seattle Mariners** and **San Diego Padres.** It has room for 12,000 fans, but this well-designed stadium keeps you feeling close to the action.

Just north of the I-10, **Maryvale Stadium** (3600 N. 51st Ave., 602/534-6449) stages the famed sausage race for **Milwaukee Brewers** fans. The 7,000-seat venue has a relaxed, open feel, with a grassy berm for outfield seating.

Southwest of Phoenix, tucked along the I-10 freeway, **Tempe Diablo Stadium** (2200 W. Alameda Dr., 480/350-5205) is home to the **Los Angeles Angels of Anaheim.** The 10,000 seats fill early, thanks to the stadium's location near the heart of the Valley (and ASU).

East of downtown in Papago Park, **Phoenix Municipal "Muni" Stadium** (5999 E. Van Buren, 602/392-0074) hosts the **Oakland Athletics.** It's the granddaddy of the spring training parks, built in 1965, but recent renovations (and great views of Papago Buttes) make this a pleasant spot for 8,000 fans.

In the middle of Scottsdale, with access to downtown shopping and entertainment, you'll find 12,000-seat **Scottsdale Stadium** (7408 E. Osborn Rd., 480/312-2856), home of the **San Francisco Giants.**

Northeast of Phoenix, **Salt River Fields at Talking Stick** (7555 N. Pima Rd., 480/270-5000) hosts the **Arizona Diamondbacks** and **Colorado Rockies.** New in 2011, it's the first Major League park to win LEED gold certification.

Just off Loop 202 in downtown Mesa, **Hohokam Park** (1235 N. Center St., 480/964-4467) is the current spring training locale of the **Chicago Cubs.** Plans are underway for the Cubbies to move in 2014 to a new 15,000-seat stadium at the intersection of Loops 101 and 202.

© GREATER PHOENIX CVB

The Phoenix Municipal Stadium hosts Cactus League games in Papago Park.

FALL BALL

Cactus League ticket prices have been creeping up in recent years, but fans can get great seats for less than $10 when baseball goes into extra innings in October and November. During the six-week **Arizona Fall League** (www.mlb.com), each Major League team sends its six top minor league players to six teams playing in six Phoenix area stadiums: the Peoria Sports Complex, Surprise Stadium, Phoenix Muni, Scottsdale Stadium, Salt River Fields, and Hohokam Park.

Watching a fall game is like traveling forward in time to see a future Major League All-Star game. Maybe you haven't heard of the Mesa Solar Sox or the Phoenix Desert Dogs, but you'll be hearing plenty about their players. Past fall-leaguers have included Derek Jeter, Albert Pujols, Torii Hunter, Roy Halladay, and Ryan Howard.

During AFL games, Major League organizations decide which players and managers are ready for "the Show." Most players don't return to the minors after appearing in the Fall League, so for true baseball fans, it's a chance to play talent scout and preview the upcoming season.

120 tons of trash annually. The stadium hosted Super Bowl XLII and is the annual home of NCAA's annual Fiesta Bowl.

Ice Hockey

To experience a temporary cold snap during Phoenix's not-exactly-frosty winters, either head for the mountains north and east of town or to Jobing.com Arena (9400 W. Maryland Ave., Glendale, www.jobingarena.com) to cheer on the town's National Hockey League team, the **Phoenix Coyotes** (480/563-7825, http://coyotes.nhl.com). Rumors regularly have the Coyotes relocating to northern climes, but in May 2012, as the team was poised to advance to the NHL finals for the first time, local businessman Greg Jamison penned a deal to keep the franchise in Phoenix.

Horse Racing

Five days a week October through May, thoroughbred horses win, place, and show on the mile and a quarter track at **Turf Paradise** (1501 W. Bell Rd., 602/942-1101, www.turfparadise.com). Races generally start shortly after noon or at 1 P.M. in the spring, but the track is open 9 A.M.–7 P.M. daily for horse workouts and simulcast races from tracks around the country. During the season, 2,200 horses call this

1,400 acres and its swath of green paddock their home. The 1,000-seat grandstand is air-conditioned, and two restaurants overlook the track. Reservations are recommended for the tonier Turf Club. The management calls the dress code "country club casual," but this isn't the South, so big hats are optional.

SPAS

Scottsdale may be better known for its world-class spas, but Phoenix knows how to pamper guests too. A handful of old-school resorts have been buffing, soaking, and soothing for decades, and some new hot spots are attracting spa-goers to their spacious surroundings with ever-expanding lists of amenities.

At the **Arizona Biltmore Spa** (2400 E. Missouri Ave., 602/381-7632, www.arizonabiltmore.com/spa, 5:30 A.M.–8:30 P.M. daily), massage therapies extend to shiatsu, ayurveda, quantum biofeedback, and hot stones. Body scrubs, wraps, and a luscious selection of facials are also available. The Biltmore's organic and chemical-free products make treatments a holistic experience. The 22,000-square-foot spa is on the grounds of the renowned Arizona Biltmore, for which Frank Lloyd Wright served as the consulting architect. Spa clients have access to the fitness

Alvadora Spa

© SCOTTSDALE CVB

center, locker room, classes, cascading whirl-pools, and lush gardens.

Just down the street, **Alvadora Spa** at the Royal Palms Resort (5200 E. Camelback Rd., 602/977-6400, www.royalpalmshotel.com, 9 A.M.–6 P.M. Sun.–Thurs., 8 A.M.–8 P.M. Fri.–Sat.) exudes a Mediterranean charm. Alvadora has the distinction of being a SpaFinder "Best for Romance" winner. Classic spa treatments are offered, as well as watsu and other water thera-pies. Skin treatments and massages incorporate signature citrus-scented products. Day spa ser-vices can be combined with lunch or dinner.

Revive Spa at the JW Marriott Desert Ridge Resort (5350 E. Marriott Dr., 480/293-3700, www.spa.jwdesertridgeresort.com, 8 A.M.–7:30 P.M. daily) is designed around the healing element of water. A sky-lit water feature spar-kles beneath the lobby's two-story rotunda, and private cabanas surround a pool sanctuary.

Forty-one treatment rooms and an impressive spa menu include standard therapies and spe-cialties such as table Thai massage, a massage using turquoise and desert sage, or an herb-infused oil massage preceded by a tour of the spa's own herb garden.

Authentic Native American treatments are offered at **Aji Spa** in the Sheraton Wild Horse Pass Resort (5594 West Wild Horse Pass Blvd., Chandler, 602/385-5759, www.wildhorse-passresort.com, 6 A.M.–6 P.M. daily). Elders and healers from the local Gila River Indian Community's Pima and Maricopa tribes de-signed the spa's signature products, as well as services like *Vachk,* a water therapy, and *Ongam Hobin,* a wrap with creosote-infused oil and salt. In addition to classic spa services, Aji also hosts indigenous cultural activities such as sage ceremonies and *Kioho,* a "burden basket" medi-tation for reducing stress.

Accommodations

If you hope to take full advantage of Phoenix's sports and cultural attractions, good hotel choices include downtown's high-rise towers (which offer convenient light-rail access) or one of the popular and quintessentially Arizona resorts in the Camelback Corridor. The resorts tend to be pricier, but they offer manicured grounds, multiple swimming pools, and adjacent golf courses. The lavish amenities and on-site activities are well worth a few extra dollars a night.

It has become a common practice for area properties to add resort fees of $20–40 to room rates. The fees may or may not include parking, Internet, phone calls, fitness center, and other services. However, when the temperature soars, room rates plummet. From May through September, Phoenix hotels offer deep discounts, some slashing their rates by more than half in the thick of summer. Locals often take advantage of these deals for a stay-cation by the pool. The peak season (and highest rates) is from January through April.

DOWNTOWN
$50-100
Finding affordable digs downtown without veering into less-desirable areas can be a challenge. Decades ago, Van Buren Street was the main drag between Phoenix and neighboring Tempe, lined with motor lodges and cocktail lounges. Some of the neon still winks, and a few bargain hotels have staked out claims here, but the area east of downtown has a high concentration of what might be euphemistically called "adult-oriented businesses."

If you simply need cheap and clean, the **Budget Lodge Downtown Phoenix** (402 W. Van Buren St., 602/254-7247, www.budgetlodgedowntownphx.com, $50–60 d) fits the bill. Don't expect much in the way of style, but

for some travelers the decent rooms, large balconies, and spotless bathrooms may outweigh the less-than-stellar neighborhood.

America's Best Value Inn (424 W. Van Buren, 602/257-8331, www.americasbestvalueinn.com, $50–80 d) is three blocks from the light-rail, making it easy to get downtown for a ball game or museum. This chain includes a thoughtful list of amenities, including a continental breakfast, in-room microwaves and refrigerators, free wireless, an on-site laundry, and complimentary airport transportation.

$100-250
Senators, musicians, and movie stars from Mae West to Marilyn Monroe have stayed at the **Hotel San Carlos** (202 N. Central Ave., 602/253-4121, www.hotelsancarlos.com, $145–180 d). When this Italian Renaissance–style

the historic Hotel San Carlos

hotel opened in 1928, it boasted state-of-the-art luxury, with chilled-water taps in every room and the first-ever elevators and air-conditioning in a Phoenix hotel. It's easy to imagine Clark Gable and Carole Lombard canoodling at the elegant bar (his favorite room was 412), or Marilyn moon-bathing alongside the rooftop pool. For history buffs (or ghost hunters), the hotel's charm will outweigh idiosyncrasies like steam radiators, small bathrooms, and restless spirits (yes, there are a few).

If you prefer modern digs, head for the **C Sheraton Phoenix Downtown** (340 N. 3rd St., 602/262-2500, www.sheratonphoenixdowntown.com, $250–300 d). This city-owned, 1,000-room hotel was constructed as part of a massive revitalization of downtown, which includes the new convention center across the street. The 31-story hotel (Arizona's largest) is styled with neutral furnishings, warm dark woods, and modern touches. On the fourth floor you'll find a fitness center and, just outside, a lap pool and sundeck. The hotel's **District American Kitchen** is an award-winning restaurant and wine bar.

The aptly named **Marriot Renaissance** (50 E. Adams St., 800/300-8138 or 602/333-0000, www.phxhotel.com, $160–320 d) underwent a sleek makeover a few years back. The 19-story hotel has large rooms with free wireless Internet, ergonomic Herman Miller Aeron desk chairs, a fitness center, and a rooftop pool. The light-rail is just outside. Next door, the **Hyatt Regency Phoenix** (122 N. 2nd St., 800/492-8804 or 602/252-1234, www.phoenix.hyatt.com, $225–300 d) boasts great views from its 700 hypoallergenic rooms. There's a fitness center and pool or in-room yoga, and the hotel's four restaurants include the only revolving rooftop dining room in Arizona, The Compass. For the price of a drink, you can enjoy a 360-degree panorama of the downtown skyline and the mountain-ringed Valley of the Sun.

Find stylish surroundings only three blocks from the convention center at the **Westin Phoenix Downtown** (333 N. Central, 800/937-8461 or 602/429-3500, www.westinphoenixdowntown.com, $220–490). The hotel's 242 spacious rooms have floor-to-ceiling windows overlooking downtown, as does the hotel's fitness center. The Latin-inspired menu at Province gets high marks from restaurant reviewers.

Hotel Palomar (2 E. Jefferson St., 877/488-1908 or 602/253-6633, www.hotelpalomar-phoenix.com, $270–900) opened in CityScape in 2012, just steps away from downtown's sports arenas and convention center. A Kimpton hotel, it offers amenities like a nightly wine hours, concierge and spa services, a yoga channel, and access to the adjacent Gold's Gym. Rooms are contemporary yet warmly accessorized, with views of the surrounding city and mountains. The dazzling third-floor terrace, with a pool and lounge, is a fine place to enjoy the skyline.

A few blocks from the Heritage Square museums and Chase Field, the **Holiday Inn Express Phoenix Downtown** (620 N. 6th, 602/452-2020 or 888/465-4329, www.ichotelsgroup.com, $150–180 d) is clean, comfortable, and convenient, with a gym and outdoor pool. Rates include breakfast.

Just north of downtown and about 10 minutes from the airport, the **Hilton Suites Phoenix** (10 E. Thomas Rd., 602/222-1111, www.hilton.com, $150–200 d) is well situated, with a light-rail stop just outside the front door that makes commuting to downtown easy, though guests can also take advantage of the complimentary shuttle service. The two-room suites feature large bathrooms, as well as refrigerators and microwaves. An 11-story central atrium has a pleasant garden and small pond, and the indoor swimming pool is lovely.

The well-priced **Holiday Inn Phoenix Downtown North** (212 W. Osborn Rd., 602/595-4444, www.ichotelsgroup.com,

$100–150 d) has comfortable, modern rooms and an outdoor pool. Because it's located only a block from the Central Avenue light-rail, getting to downtown or to nearby museums is a snap.

CENTRAL PHOENIX
$50-100

Near the Piestewa Freeway (State Route 51), **Best Western InnSuites** (1615 E. Northern Ave., 800/842-4242 or 602/997-6285, http:// phoenix.innsuites.com, $90–120 d) is an excellent value, combining a boutique sensibility with such chain amenities as a breakfast buffet, fitness center, in-room refrigerators and microwaves, plentiful parking, and a large outdoor pool. Piestewa Peak's hiking and biking trails are nearby, and so is the Biltmore shopping district.

ZenYard Guest House (830 E. Maryland Ave., 866/594-0242 or 602/845-0830, www. zenyard.com, $70–130 d) is an offbeat alternative to chain hotels and sprawling resorts. Tucked into a north-central Phoenix neighborhood, this mid-20th-century ranch house has been transformed into four guest spaces situated around a saltwater pool, hot tub, and gardens. On-call massage therapy and organic continental breakfasts are part of the relaxed, comfortable experience.

$100-250

Style and service have made the **C Clarendon Hotel** (401 W. Clarendon Ave., 602/252-7363, www.goclarendon.com, $130–270 d) a favorite among locals and visiting celebs, attracting the likes of the Black Eyed Peas, AC/DC, and the Rolling Stones. Rooms feature bold decor and many open onto the Oasis, a hip courtyard pool and 50-person Jacuzzi with colorful tile, giant water walls, and cabana-style furniture. At night, the pool's floor twinkles with 1,000 illuminated starry lights, and the rooftop deck transforms into a popular open-air lounge with impressive views of the downtown skyline.

One of few bed-and-breakfasts in Phoenix, **Maricopa Manor** (15 W. Pasadena Ave., 800/292-6403 or 602/264-9200, www.maricopamanor.com, $190–240 d) is located in the city's gracious Medlock Place historic district. The 1928 hacienda-style inn houses six suites with period furnishings, gas fireplaces, and French doors that open onto a lush courtyard. In the morning, a hot breakfast is delivered to your room for eating en-suite or on your private patio. The pool is unheated, but there is a year-round gazebo hot tub.

The **Embassy Suites Phoenix-Biltmore** (2630 E. Camelback Rd., 602/955-3992, www. embassysuites.com, $170–240 d) is well-situated next door to Biltmore Fashion Park's shops and restaurants. Compared to its posh neighbors, the Ritz-Carlton and Arizona Biltmore Resort, this Camelback Corridor hotel is a relatively inexpensive option, considering its complimentary made-to-order breakfasts, pleasant palm-filled atrium, fitness center, and heated courtyard pool.

Located near the Biltmore neighborhood, **Courtyard Phoenix Camelback** (2101 E. Camelback Rd., 888/236-2427 or 602/955-5200, www.camelbackcourtyard.com, $180–230 d) is within easy reach of numerous restaurants and shops. The four-story hotel has comfortable, modern rooms, many overlooking the pool and landscaped courtyard. The capacious lobby has a bistro, a movie area, and a touch screen information center handy for driving directions, news, and local weather.

Behind the simple exterior of the **Hotel Highland at Biltmore** (2310 E. Highland Ave., 800/956-5221, www.hotelhighlandatbiltmore. com, $150–200 d) are quiet and comfortable rooms, a service-oriented staff, and a patio with a swimming pool, spa, and fire pit. Guests can make the short walk to the Biltmore Fashion

Park's restaurants and shops, though the hotel offers a free shuttle around the neighborhood and to the airport.

Over $250

The Ritz-Carlton (2401 E. Camelback Rd., 800/542-8680 or 602/468-0700, www. ritzcarlton.com, $440–900 d) delivers impeccable service and the opulent old-world style for which the hotel group is famous, including formal marble foyers, chandeliers, and plush linens in its rooms and suites. The pink-stucco tower is the hotel de rigueur for pop stars and athletes passing through town, though less-famous guests will also appreciate the sky-high views of Camelback Mountain and the Phoenix skyline. The second-floor mist-cooled sundeck and pool are surrounded by the neighborhood's glass towers, a distinctly urban experience.

Resorts

The 1929 **☾ Arizona Biltmore Resort & Spa** (2400 E. Missouri Ave., 800/950-0086 or 602/955-6600, www.arizonabiltmore. com, $250–800 d) is a Phoenix landmark, its 39 acres tucked into an upscale residential neighborhood. The Art Deco gem elegantly blends geometric forms and Southwestern touches, a credit to its architect, Albert Chase McArthur, a student of Frank Lloyd Wright. Presidents and movie stars have stayed here. Composer Irving Berlin penned "White Christmas" while sitting poolside. For those who are not content to lounge by one of the resort's eight pools or hit the links at the two adjacent PGA golf courses, the Biltmore offers a full docket of activities that range from life-size lawn chess to salsa tastings to celebrity soirees.

The romantic **☾ Royal Palms Resort and Spa** (5200 E. Camelback Rd., 800/672-6011

The historic Arizona Biltmore Resort is beautifully landscaped.

© KATHLEEN BRYANT

or 602/840-3610, www.royalpalmshotel.com, $350–500 d) is understated, elegant, and intimate. This Mediterranean-style hideaway has stone courtyards with tiled fountains, and its guest rooms, casitas, and villas are decorated with Spanish Colonial furniture, rich colors, and old-world accents. It's the ultimate couple's getaway spot. You won't find better ambience in the city, nor is it easy to top its Alvadora Spa and T. Cook's restaurant. The former private estate sits at the base of Camelback Mountain for an easy 10-minute drive to the Biltmore neighborhood or to Old Town Scottsdale.

The **Pointe Hilton at Squaw Peak** (7677 N. 16th St., 800/947-9784 or 602/997-2626, www.pointehilton.com, $170–300 d) is an enjoyable destination for families, especially in the summer when rates are discounted, and the four-acre Hole-in-the-Wall River Ranch becomes an oasis offering multiple pools, waterfalls, a spiraling 130-foot slide, and a half-mile lazy river for tubing. Coyote Camp keeps young adventurers busy with hands-on activities. There's also an 18-hole miniature putting course, four tennis courts, and the 10,000-square-foot Tocasierra spa and fitness center. Hiking trails lead into the surrounding Phoenix Mountains Preserve.

Like its sister property, the sprawling mountainside **Pointe Hilton Tapatio Cliffs Resort** (11111 N. 7th St., 800/947-9784 or 602/866-7500, www.pointehilton.com, $160–190 d) is a great budget option. Kids will revel in multiple pools, a waterfall-fed lagoon, an enclosed 138-foot waterslide. The Kids Korral has poolside activities. For grown-ups, there's Tocaloma Spa, a fitness center, hiking at the adjacent North Mountain Preserve, and golfing at Lookout Mountain course. The property's restaurants include the sleek Different Pointe of View, which wows diners with breathtaking views of Phoenix.

AWATUKEE AND SOUTH PHOENIX
Resorts

Built on the Gila River Indian Community south of Phoenix, the **Sheraton Wild Horse Pass Resort & Spa** (5594 W. Wild Horse Pass Blvd., 800/325-3535 or 602/225-0100, www.wildhorsepassresort.com, $260–550 d) reflects the architecture, art, and history of the Pima and Maricopa tribes. The beautifully situated resort, with its AAA Four Diamond spa and Five Diamond restaurant, are a 10-minute drive from Chandler and 25 minutes from downtown Phoenix, but you'll find plenty to do, like play golf or tennis, ride horses, or visit the neighboring casino.

The family-friendly **Arizona Grand Resort** (8000 S. Arizona Grand Pkwy., 866/267-1321 or 602/438-9000, www.arizonagrandresort.com, $250–700 d) has amenities found at most resorts—a championship golf course, spa, fitness classes—but it's the Oasis Water Park that has kids and adults buzzing. At the end of a day in the ocean-like wave pool, tubing the lazy river, or plunging down the three eight-story waterslides, the resort's 740 large suites provide plenty of room to relax.

NORTH PHOENIX
Resorts

At Arizona's largest resort, **▮ JW Marriott Desert Ridge Resort & Spa** (5350 E. Marriott Dr., 800/835-6206 or 480/293-3939, www.jwdesertridgeresort.com, $500–700 d), everything is big, from its soaring lobby and 950 rooms to its poolside margaritas. But Desert Ridge carries its size well, with clean, modern lines that give a nod to the Southwest's indigenous architecture. The massive resort frequently hosts multiple conferences and trade shows, but you're just as likely to see leisure travelers and families at the four pools or on the golf courses designed by Jack Nicklaus and

Nick Faldo. The property encompasses 10 restaurants, the elegant Revive Spa, and four acres of pools and water features.

TEMPE AND THE EAST VALLEY
$50-100

Travelers on a budget need only drive a few miles along I-10 or U.S. 60 to find low-priced chain hotels in Tempe, Chandler, or Mesa. For a bit more color (or perhaps too much, depending on your perspective), head for Apache Boulevard, once the main drag between Tempe and Mesa and still home to a handful of inexpensive motels. Close to the light-rail, the **Days Inn** (1221 E. Apache Blvd., 866/539-0036, www.daysinn.com, $65–120 d) may not be distinctive, but it has a pool, spa, and plenty of free parking about a mile from ASU.

$100-250

The conveniently situated **Twin Palms** (225 E. Apache Blvd., 800/367-0835 or 480/967-9431, www.twinpalmshotel.com, $100–180 d) is across the street from Arizona State University's campus and Gammage Auditorium and only 10 minutes from Phoenix Sky Harbor Airport. The seven-story hotel is basic but comfortable, with a small outdoor pool. Guests have access to the mammoth ASU fitness center across the street.

The 270-room **Fiesta Resort Conference Center** (2100 S. Priest Dr., 480/967-1441, www.fiestainnresort.com, $140–200 d) offers an unexpected bit of character in the mid-level price range. The Frank Lloyd Wright–inspired resort is nicely maintained, with stacked concrete blocks, warm woods, and stained-glass accents. There's a spa, restaurant, lounge, and a pleasant courtyard pool surrounded by palm trees.

Tempe Mission Palms Hotel (60 E. 5th St., 800/547-8705 or 480/894-1400, www.missionpalms.com, $180–285 d) is a solid choice

if you're in town to catch a game at Sun Devil Stadium or see a show at Gammage. You can't beat the hotel's Mill Avenue location, which houses dozens of bars and restaurants just outside the front door. The hotel's rooftop terrace pool and tennis court are great places to hang out and survey Tempe and the adjacent ASU campus.

Over $250

The urban-chic, LEED-certified **Aloft** (951 E. Playa Del Norte Dr., 480/621-3300, www.alofttempe.com, $180–375 d) packs a bit of style into its Tempe Town Lake location, with light woods, exposed ducts, and a hip patio with neon-green lounges and trendy lighting. Guests check in at a self-serve kiosk before heading up to rooms equipped with walk-in showers and a plug-and-play connectivity station. The outdoor pool, sleek gym, WXYZ bar, and small lounge add to the urban vibe.

Resorts

Perched on a rugged desert hilltop, **The Buttes** (2000 Westcourt Way, 888/867-7492 or 602/225-9000, www.marriott.com/phxtm, $210–320 d) incorporates rock formations into lobby walls and its two pools. The small resort offers spectacular views of the Valley, especially from its beautifully designed Top of the Rock restaurant. The I-10 freeway runs along the base of the mountain, but thanks to the resort's elevated location, you won't hear a thing. The 25-acre property has a spa, fitness center, tennis and volleyball courts, and waterslide.

An East Valley landmark, the **Crowne Plaza San Marcos Golf Resort** (1 N. San Marcos Pl., 800/528-8071 or 480/812-0900, www.sanmarcosresort.com, $120–195 d) has been welcoming guests since Dr. A. J. Chandler opened the hotel in his namesake town in 1913. Chandler's friend, Frank Lloyd Wright, helped oversee the construction of the California Mission–style resort, and a succession of celebrities have stayed here, including President Herbert Hoover, Fred Astaire, Joan Crawford, and Bing Crosby. The gracious lobby and large rooms are a good value.

WEST VALLEY Resorts

For a taste of old Arizona, try the **Wigwam Golf Resort & Spa** (300 Wigwam Blvd., 800/327-0396 or 623/935-3811, www.wigwamresort.com, $300–400 d) in the West Valley community of Litchfield Park. The Wigwam began as a winter guest ranch in 1929 for Goodyear tire executives and their families. Today, it's a AAA Four Diamond resort with three 18-hole championship golf courses, nine tennis courts, three swimming pools, and an Elizabeth Arden Red Door Spa. The elegant Southwestern property—lushly landscaped with green lawns and tall palms—features casita-style rooms decorated with wood furnishings, Mexican ceramic tile, slate floors, and copper and leather fixtures.

Food

A host of culinary mavericks, along with a burgeoning local food movement, have transformed the city's dining scene from ho-hum to hip. You can tour the world's cuisines at Valley restaurants, travel back in time to classic Western steakhouses, or eat farm-to-table in a grove of pecan or olive trees.

DOWNTOWN
American

The Tuck Shop (2245 N. 12th St., 602/354-2980, www.tuckinphx.com, 5–10 P.M. Tues.–Sat., $8–20) is still one of Phoenix's best-kept secrets, though foodies frequent this Desert Modernist remodel of a 1950s-era building in the Coronado neighborhood. Architect/owner D. J. Fernandes serves up an evolving menu of "neighborhood comfort food" from chicken potpie to skirt steak. Portions are meant for sharing and sampling, so bring your friends and have fun combining small plates like wild mushroom salad with communal-size portions of cannelloni or chicken and waffles. There's a good selection of beer and wine, but the cocktails, some based on house-made ginger ale or tonic, are impressive. For breakfast, lunch, or nibbles, pop into **Astor House** (2243 N. 12th St., 602/687-9775, www.astorinphx.com, 7 A.M.–10 P.M. Tues.–Sat., $5–15), the café and

food shop Fernandes has opened next door. In 2012, Fernandes opened **Vovomeena** (1515 N. 7th Ave., 602/252-2541, www.vovomeena, 6:30 A.M.–1:30 P.M., $5–10), a breakfast-only restaurant in the rapidly gentrifying area north of McDowell along 7th Avenue. Months before the doors opened, foodies tweeted and drooled in anticipation of homemade doughnuts and banana bread pudding French toast.

Durant's (2611 N. Central Ave., 602/264-5967, www.durantsaz.com, 11 A.M.–10 P.M. Mon.–Thurs., 11 A.M.–11 P.M. Fri., 5–11 P.M. Sat., 4:30–10 P.M. Sun., $20–40) is a classic steakhouse, from its ever-so-dry martinis to its deep-red decor. This landmark has changed little since newlyweds Marilyn Monroe and Joe DiMaggio dined here in 1954. Enter like locals through the kitchen in the back, and take a peek at the thick steaks and oysters Rockefeller before heading into the dining room.

Next door, **Switch** (2603 N. Central Ave., 602/264-2295, www.switchofarizona.com, 11 A.M.–11 P.M. Mon.–Thurs., 11 A.M.–midnight Fri., 10 A.M.–midnight Sat., 10 A.M.–11 P.M. Sun., $10–18) is trendy spot for a late breakfast or casual lunch or dinner. The cool blue decor and hip music are backdrop to innovative burgers, salads, and sandwiches. The menu changes seasonally, but flaky, savory galettes are a standby. Eat in at the bar or dining room, or enjoy the long patio.

If your soul yearns for cornbread, fried chicken, collards, and peach cobbler, head for **Mrs. White's Golden Rule Café** (808 E. Jefferson St., 602/262-9256, http://mrswhitesgolenrulecafe.com, 10:30 A.M.–7 P.M. daily, and 9 P.M.–3 A.M. Fri.–Sat., $7–15), a Phoenix soul food favorite operated by Elizabeth White and her family for 45 years. The family dynasty continues south of downtown at White's grandson Larry's popular establishment, **Lo-Lo's** (10 W. Yuma St., 602/340-1304, www.loloschickenandwaffles.com, 10 A.M.–7 P.M. Mon.–Thurs. and Sat., 10 A.M.–10 P.M. Fri., 10 A.M.–4 P.M. Sun., $4–13), specializing in chicken and waffles.

An adventurous couple turned **The Duce** (525 S. Central Ave., 602/866-3823, http://theducephx.com, 11 A.M.–midnight Tues.–Thurs., 10 A.M.–1 A.M. Fri.–Sat., 10 A.M.–4 P.M. Sun., $6–18), a cavernous 1928 warehouse on downtown's abandoned southern edges, into a restaurant/bar/boutique. During Prohibition, this was the site of a bootlegging operation known to insiders as "the Deuce." Today, an old Airstream serves as an outdoor kitchen next to the patio restaurant, serving up baked pancakes, sliders, and ribs. Stripped to bare brick, the warehouse's interior has plenty of room for any vintage finds that catch the owners' fancy, including a 1915 soda fountain, an Art Deco bar that once stood in a Chicago jazz club, and a gym area complete with boxing ring, all operational.

Asian

A historic bungalow provides the setting for ◖ **Nobuo** (622 E. Adams, 602/254-0600, http://nobuofukuda.com, Tues.–Sun., $5–15), a teahouse from 11 A.M.–4 P.M. and, from 5:30 P.M. to closing, an izakaya that serves drinks and small plates. James Beard Award–winning chef Nobuo Fukudu creates classic Japanese dishes with American twists, all exquisitely presented. On Fridays and Saturdays, a special tasting menu ($60 per person) is available with advance reservations.

The beautifully presented dishes at **Wild Thaiger** (2631 N. Central Ave., 602/241-8995, www.wildthaiger.com, 11 A.M.–9 P.M. Mon.–Thurs., 11 A.M.–10 P.M. Fri.–Sat., 5–9 P.M. Sun., $8–17) are as much a feast for the eyes as for the taste buds. Beyond classic noodle dishes and fiery curries, adventurous house specialties include richly spiced wild boar, pork ribs, and seafood dishes.

Breakfast and Lunch

Wallet-friendly **Matt's Big Breakfast** (825 N. 1st St., 602/254-1074, www.mattsbigbreakfast.com, 6:30 A.M.–2:30 P.M. Tues.–Sun., $5–9) is Phoenix's best breakfast joint, hands down. The small, brick café is bright and sunny, and its pleasant orange counter, vintage bar stools, and 1950s decor are the perfect backdrop for hearty diner fare. Owners Matt and Erenia serve simple food with exceptional ingredients, which means the orange juice is squeezed each morning, the eggs come from cage-free chickens, and the burgers are made from Niman Ranch ground chuck. There's usually a queue under the umbrellas outside, but you won't mind the wait once you taste the griddle cakes.

The friendly staff at **Fair Trade Café** (1020 N. 1st Ave., 424 N. Central, 602/253-6912, 7 A.M.–10 P.M. daily, from 6 A.M. weekends) serves inexpensive breakfasts and lunches that are "90 percent organic, 100 percent local, and always vegetarian." The menu changes weekly but usually includes soup, salads, and whole-grain dishes, all $8 or less. The comfortable interior acts as a revolving gallery for local artists. A second downtown location adjacent to Civic Space Park is open on weekdays till 5 P.M. (till 2 P.M. Friday afternoons).

Jobot (918 N. 5th St., 602/228-7373, http://

jobot-coffee.com, 7 A.M.–midnight, $8 or less) pours a great cup of joe, and you can accompany it with one of their delicious crepes in savory or sweet variations. They also offer free wireless Internet.

If trendy urban java joints get your juices flowing, **Lola Coffee** (1001 N. 3rd Ave., 602/252-2265, www.lolacoffeebar.com, 7 A.M.–7 P.M. daily, $2–7) is your kind of place. Its long communal table is more suited to conversation than to serious work, but the coffee is seriously good, as are the pastries.

Unpretentious and charming **Azteca** (416 N. 7th St., 602/253-5864, 7 A.M.–4 P.M. Mon.–Thurs., 7 A.M.–5 P.M. Fri., 8 A.M.–4 P.M. Sat., $3–8) combines a panadería offering a mouthwatering assortment of pastries with a café serving home-style omelets, burritos, tamales, and soups.

The best carne asada in town is on the short menu at **America's Taco Shop** (2041 N. 7th St., 602/682-5627, www.americastacoshop.net, 7:30 A.M.–9 P.M. Mon.–Thurs., 7:30 A.M.–10 P.M. Fri.–Sat., 10 A.M.–9 P.M. Sun., $4–8). The marinated, flame-broiled beef comes wrapped in tacos and burritos or layered on tostadas, quesadillas, and tortas. Non-meat eaters can order the veggie quesadilla or bean-and-cheese burrito. On Fridays and Saturdays, chef/owner America Corrales prepares her zesty ceviche, a combination of diced fresh white shrimp, tomatoes, cucumbers, red onions, serrano chiles, cilantro, and lime. America's food is a refreshing change from the lardy, overcooked offerings you'll find at many "authentic" joints in the Valley. In addition to the bright yellow bungalow are two other locations in the Melrose neighborhood and Tempe.

In Phoenix, TGIF means it's **Food Truck Friday** (14 E. Pierce St., 11 A.M.–1:30 P.M.) at the public market, where you can mix it up

© KATHLEEN BRYANT

On Fridays, food trucks line up near downtown's public market.

with inexpensive selections from a changing circle of vendors, including Short Leash Hot Dogs, Q-Up Barbeque, Jamburritos, and Sweet Republic, all while enjoying live music and a party atmosphere.

The pop-up restaurant phenomenon is just starting to hit Phoenix. Pop-ups are temporary culinary adventures that allow chefs to moonlight or to experiment with a different menu or cuisine without first investing in a property. Consult the blogosphere or the local entertainment weekly, *Phoenix New Times* (www.phoenixnewtimes.com) for the latest scoop. One likely location is the pocket-size **Welcome Diner** (924 E. Roosevelt St., 602/495-1111). Built in Wichita, Kansas, in 1945 as a Valentine Diner, later trucked across the country to serve up burgers and fries on Route 66 in Williams, Arizona, the Welcome Diner made its way to downtown Phoenix in 1980. Today, this slice of Americana is a project of the Martha + Mary foundation, hosting pop-up restaurants and community events.

Desserts

Brides and sugar addicts clamor for the artfully sculpted confections at **Tammie Coe Cakes** (610 E. Roosevelt, Ste. 145, 602/253-0829, www.tammiecoecakes.com, 6:30 A.M.–7 P.M. Mon.–Fri., 8 A.M.–2 P.M. Sat., $2–8). You can satisfy your sweet tooth with one of the signature goodies or, if you're looking for something more substantial, sandwiches are on the menu for breakfast and lunch.

Like moths to a flame (or in this case, a blowtorch), foodies follow **Torched Goodness** (480/296-1609, www.torchedgoodness.com, $2–4). This gourmet food truck shows up at local farmers markets and other events, and fans consult Twitter or Facebook to find out the day's schedule. A Cordon Bleu chef riffs on classic crème brûlée using organic local ingredients, torched to order. Thirty flavors include vanilla, lavender, salted caramel,

pumpkin—and there are teas and other sweet selections, such as angel food cake. For orders of four or more, they will deliver to your door. On Friday afternoons, look for the white truck at the Phoenix Public Market.

Italian

Award-winning (**Pizzeria Bianco** (623 E. Adams St., 602/258-8300, www.pizzeriabianco.com, 11 A.M.–9 P.M. Mon., 11 A.M.–10 P.M. Tues.–Sat., $10–16) has become a culinary legend in Phoenix. Jerry Seinfeld, Oprah, and Martha Stewart are fans, and *Esquire* magazine named owner/chef Chris Bianco's wood-fired pies the best pizza in the country. Bianco uses the freshest ingredients, including herbs cultivated next to the 1929 machine shop the restaurant now inhabits. You'll wish you could try every pie on the menu, from the classic Margherita with homemade mozzarella to the Rosa, a combination of red onion, parmigiano reggiano, rosemary, and Arizona pistachios. The roasted antipasto and fresh salads are also good. Expanded hours and a new location north of downtown have thinned the infamous queue to get in, but be prepared to precede your dinner by heading next door to **Bar Bianco** (609 E. Adams St., 602/528-3699, 4–11 P.M. Tues.–Sat.) to have a beer or glass of wine before being seated.

More than one diner weary of waiting to get into Bianco has traveled a mile west to discover the artisanal pizzas at the family-owned **Cibo** (603 N. 5th Ave., 602/441-2697, www.cibophoenix.com, 11 A.M.–2 P.M. Mon.–Fri., 5–10 P.M. Tues.–Thurs., 5–11 P.M. Fri.–Sat., 10 A.M.–2 P.M. Sun., $9–13). The salads, antipasti, and wood-fired pizzas feature locally grown organic produce and cheeses imported from Italy. The long list of pizzas includes red and white choices, and a new breakfast menu features frittatas and crepes. Dine outside on the large patio or inside the charming 1913 bungalow.

© KATHLEEN BRYANT

Pizzeria Bianco

Mexican and Southwest

There's more to Mexican food than tacos and refried beans, and at **Barrio Café** (2814 N. 16th St., 602/636-0240, www.barriocafe.com, 11 A.M.–10 P.M. Tues.–Thurs., 11 A.M.–10:30 P.M. Fri., 5–10:30 P.M. Sat., and 11 A.M.–9 P.M. Sun., $10–20), Chef Silvana Salcido Esparza proves this with a culinary tour of central and southern Mexico. Start with the pomegranate-seed guacamole, prepared tableside, and sip on one of 250 tequilas as you survey the award-winning menu. Dishes, which change monthly, will likely include a slow-roasted pork from the Yucatán, spinach-seafood enchiladas, or posole verde. Live music, local art, and a Sunday brunch 11 A.M.–3 P.M. add to the atmosphere of this small neighborhood restaurant.

Coronado Café (2201 N. 7th St., 602/258-5149, http://coronadocafe.com, 11 A.M.–2:30 P.M. Mon.–Sat., 5–9 P.M. Tues.–Thurs., 5–10 P.M. Fri.–Sat., 10 A.M.–3 P.M. Sun., $14–18) artfully combines Mediterranean and Southwestern flavors, serving flatbread, seafood, slow-roasted meats, and the occasional comfort dish like the meatloaf with whipped potatoes and Hatch green chile cream. The converted Craftsman-style bungalow's hardwood floors and charming bar provide a romantic atmosphere for a special dinner. Delicious sandwiches, soups, and salads are perfect at lunch.

Don't let the neighborhood dissuade you from trying **La Tolteca** (1205 E. Van Buren, 602/253-1511, http://latoltecamex.com, 9 A.M.–8 P.M. Mon.–Sat., 9 A.M.–7 P.M. Sun., $5–12), which hides a bakery, butcher counter, grocery, and pleasant mural-painted dining room behind its bland exterior. The menu is vast, from the expected burritos and combos, to tortas, moles, grilled dinners, and breakfasts (including all-day chilaquiles). If you're too full for dessert, you can take home some pastries— the panadería offers traditional sweet delights from churros to empanadas.

It doesn't look like much from the outside, but once you step into **San Carlos Bay Seafood Restaurant** (1901 E. McDowell Rd., 602/340-0892, 9 A.M.–9 P.M. daily, $10–18), you'll think you've landed in a small café on Mexico's Sonoran coast. Start with a cold Pacifico beer and the restaurant's signature seven seas cocktail. The spicy seafood stews are extraordinary, but you don't want to miss filling up on fresh tortillas topped with garlic shrimp. This is a place the locals frequent, and the mariachis on the weekends are the real deal, not a touristy production.

CENTRAL AND NORTH PHOENIX
American

◖**Postino** (3939 E. Campbell Ave., 602/852-3939, http://postinowinecafe.com, 11 A.M.–11 P.M. Mon.–Thurs., 11 A.M.–midnight Fri.–Sat., 11 A.M.–10 P.M. Sun., $5–12), housed in a historic building that once served as a post office (hence the name), serves a casual but thoughtful menu of sandwiches, salads, and mix-and-match bruschettas, complemented by a wide selection of wine and beer. Floor-to-ceiling windows and an outdoor patio have been a mainstay since opening in the Arcadia neighborhood back in 2001. Two additional locations have been added in Phoenix's historic Medlock district (5144 N. Central Ave., 602/274-5144) and in the East Valley (302 N. Gilbert Rd., 480/632-6363).

A neighborhood delight, **La Grande Orange** (4410 N. 40th St., 602/840-7777, www.lagrangeorangepizzeria.com, 6:30 A.M.–10 P.M. daily, $9–14) groups a pizzeria, coffee bar, café, and fun retail area all under one roof, a former strip mall that has been utterly transformed into a space that's lively, hip, and colorful. Start with breakfast or lunch, then return after 4 P.M. for some of the finest gourmet pizzas in the city. In between, you can browse the grocery/retail area for unusual gift items, wine, pet products, potted plants, and more.

Part of the local restaurant empire that includes La Grande Orange and Postino, **Chelsea's Kitchen** (5040 N. 40th St., 602/957-2555, www.chelseaskitchenaz.com, 11 A.M.–10 P.M. Mon.–Sat., 9:30 A.M.–9 P.M. Sun., $12–27) is a contemporary take on the roadhouse, a sleek but comfortable spot perfect for meeting friends. The celebrated outdoor patio, located along a canal, offers gorgeous views of the sunset and the city below. A pitcher of Chelsea's signature white sangria is a good accompaniment for the contemporary American menu, featuring fresh, organic ingredients with occasional Southwestern twists like the swordfish taco platter or slow-roasted pork.

Find gourmet burgers, hip hot dogs, and more at the sleek **Delux** (3146 E. Camelback Rd., 602/522-2288, www.deluxburger.com, 11 A.M.–2 A.M. daily, $7–13), a restaurant that keeps nightclub hours to satisfy late-night cravings for Niman Ranch chopped beef topped with gruyère cheese, organic arugula, carmelized onion, or applewood bacon. Regular or sweet potato fries are served "a la carte" in a miniature shopping cart. Soup, salad, and vegetarian selections are also available.

The creative menu at **Tarbell's** (3213 E. Camelback Rd., 602/955-8100, www.tarbells.com, 5–10 P.M. Mon.–Sat., 5–9 P.M. Sun., $15–25) incorporates seasonal produce like scarlet runner beans or heirloom tomatoes from the chef's urban garden. The restaurant has earned 30 awards since it opened in 1994, including a Best Restaurant nod from *Food & Wine* magazine.

True Food Kitchen (2502 E. Camelback Rd., Ste. 135, 602/774-3488, 11 A.M.–9 P.M. Sun.–Thurs., 11 A.M.–10 P.M. Fri.–Sat., $10–22) in Biltmore Fashion Park is a collaboration between holistic-health guru Dr. Andrew Weil and Arizona's über-restaurateur Sam Fox. The menu is centered on organic, seasonal produce and hormone- and antibiotic-free chicken and turkey. The "globally inspired cuisine" includes dishes like Tuscan kale salad, shirataki noodles, gluten-free pizzas, and steak tacos topped with avocado and tomatillo salsa.

The basement bar at **Rokerij** (6335 N. 16th St., 602/287-8900, 11 A.M.–midnight Mon.–Fri., 4 P.M.–midnight Sat.–Sun., $12–32) can be a perfect sanctuary on a hot summer day or a cozy fireside spot for a winter tryst. Roasted and grilled meats, flavorful New Mexico–style sauces, decadent desserts, and superb service make dining here a treat. Siblings next door (Richardson's) and down the street (Dick's Hideaway) venture even further into New Mexican flavors.

Asian

At **SoChu House** (2801 N. Central, 602/340-9777, 11 A.M.–1 A.M. Mon.–Fri., 5 P.M.–1 A.M. Sat.–Sun., $8–14), Chef Johnny Chu has brought his creativity and talent to this modern pan-Asian eatery. Beautifully presented small plates, such as five-spice quail or chicken wings with black pepper–mint sauce, let you sample adventurous spices and ingredients. There are also heartier entrées and noodles, and a bar menu of exotic beers and sakes.

The sushi served at **Hana** (5524 N. 7th Ave., 602/973-1238, http://hanajapaneseeatery.com, 11 A.M.–2:30 P.M., 5–9 P.M. Thurs. and Sun., 5–10 P.M. Fri.–Sat., $5–36) is among Arizona's best, and this family-owned Japanese restaurant also has a full menu that includes bento box lunches, tempura, noodle dishes, and entrées like rib eye prepared teppan style. It's BYOB, and there's no corkage fee.

Cherry Blossom Noodle Café (914 E. Camelback Rd., Ste. 1, 602/248-9090, www.cherryblossom-az.com, 11 A.M.–9:30 P.M. Sun.–Thurs., 11 A.M.–10:30 P.M. Fri.–Sat., $6–15) specializes in Asian noodle dishes—and Italian pasta—as well as salads, sushi, tofu, and homemade soups. And in another quirky twist, the complimentary homemade banana bread is a delicious nosh while you peruse the menu.

Colorful, flavorful, crisp, chewy—the Vietnamese noodles, banh mi sandwiches, rice plates, and soups at **Pho Thanh** (1702 W. Camelback, 602/242-1979, 8:30 A.M.–8:30 P.M. Wed.–Mon., $3–7) are a treat for the senses. The strip-mall atmosphere may be lacking, but with such delicious food at these crazy-low prices, who cares?

Breakfast, Lunch, and Snacks

Simple, fast, good. At **Scramble** (9832 N. 7th St., 602/374-2294, www.azscramble.com, 6 A.M.–2 P.M. daily, $5–12), diners walk up to the counter to order such morning mainstays as buttermilk pancakes, eggs Benedict, and omelets or, for something off the beaten pancake, "brizzas"—pizzas topped with eggs, bacon, chorizo, peppers, and other items. Breakfast is available all day, but after 11 A.M., soups, salad, and sandwiches join the menu. The bright, airy, modern space has free wireless Internet and charging stations.

C La Grande Orange (4410 N. 40th St., 602/840-7777, 6:30 A.M.–10 P.M. daily, $6–12) is one of those magical neighborhood joints where young and old, couples and families, big groups of friends and quiet newspaper readers can all sit down and enjoy themselves. Drop in early in the morning for the trademark fresh-squeezed OJ, and try out the Commuter Sandwich, served on LGO's signature English muffins. Later in the day, pop back in to grab a quick salad or warm Cubano sandwich. The hip market also offers a fun selection of gifts and wine, and its coffee bar is among the best in the city.

From old favorites to contemporary creations from Chef Aaron May, **Over Easy** (4730 E. Indian School Rd., 602/468-3447, www.eatatovereasy.com, 6:30 A.M.–1 P.M. Mon.–Fri., till 2 P.M. Sat.–Sun., $4–10) serves exceptional food in a pleasant atmosphere. The eponymous Over Easy is a toasted brioche topped with an egg, spinach, scallions, and bacon au jus. Waffle dogs, chilaquiles, and caramelized French toast are pure decadence, but the list of healthy choices like smoked salmon and asparagus won't leave you feeling deprived. There's a second location in Scottsdale (9375 E. Bell Rd., 480/270-3447).

Since opening in 1972, **Duck and Decanter** (1651 E. Camelback Rd., 602/274-5429, www.duckanddecanter.com, 7 A.M.–7 P.M. Mon.–Wed., 7 A.M.–9 P.M. Thurs.–Fri., 8 A.M.–8 P.M. Sat.–Sun., $5–9) has grown from a single sandwich shop into three locations, each combining a wine bar with a well-stocked deli and culinary store carrying European imports and Arizona-made products like cactus candies. You can brown bag it or join the neighborhood regulars on the large, shaded patio. Mile-high sandwiches come with a choice of nine breads, but you can also skip the bread and have the fillings tossed into a salad. Breakfast is served all day at "the Duck's" three locations, Camelback, midtown (3111 N. Central Ave., 602/234-3656), and downtown (1 Central Ave. 602/266-6637).

Although its older sibling, Pizzeria Bianco, gets most of the attention, **Pane Bianco** (4404 N. Central Ave., 602/234-2100, www.pizzeriabianco.com, 11 A.M.–3 P.M. Tues.–Sat., $9–10), Chris Bianco's lunchtime sandwich and salad shop, is just as praise-worthy. The menu is limited to a trio of salads and four sandwiches, served on wood-fired focaccia that is kin to Bianco's renowned pizzas. Each day the market sandwich features a different flavorful combination, such as mortadella with date and tomato jam and pecorino Sardo. Bianco is a strong supporter of local growers, and his food reflects this sensibility with its exceptional freshness and flavor.

It's a coffee shop by day and a bar/restaurant at night, but you'll always find a friendly neighborhood vibe at **Lux Central** (4400 N. Central

Ave., 602/696-9976, www.luxcoffee.com, 6 A.M.–midnight, Sun.–Thurs., 6 A.M.–2 A.M. Fri.–Sat., $5–20). The crowd is a mix of local hipsterati and those simply looking for a good cup of joe, and more than a few of either group will wax poetic about the vegan doughnuts and lemon bars.

French

Dining spots don't get much more romantic than **Coup des Tartes** (4626 N. 16th St., 602/212-1082, www.nicetartes.com, 10:30 A.M.–2 P.M. Mon.–Fri., 5:30–9 P.M. Tues.–Sat., $18–36). The bungalow that houses this delightful French bistro looks unassuming from the outside, but its cozy, candlelit interior is pitch-perfect for a cozy meal. The farm-to-table menu changes regularly but almost always includes classic treatments of lamb, duck, and fish. The cheese plate and house-made tarts are swoon-worthy. Don't forget to bring your own wine (or champagne)—the bistro is BYOB.

Christopher's

Sophisticated yet casual, **Christopher's** (2502 E. Camelback Rd., 602/522-2344, 11 A.M.–9 P.M. Mon–Tues., 11 A.M.–10 P.M. Wed.–Sat., noon–8 P.M. Sun., $12–38) is the Biltmore Fashion Park home of James Beard Award–winning chef Christopher Gross. His French bistro–inspired menu runs from burgers and wood-oven pizzas to cote de boeuf and lobster potpie. Foodies might want to hang out at the counter overlooking the open kitchen, or reserve the chef's table, perfect for the specially designed tasting menu. Banquettes line the dining room, and there's an outdoor patio. Cheese platters, small plates, and desserts are served at the restaurant's **Crush Lounge.** During happy hour (3–6 P.M.), half-off specials make culinary adventures possible even on a limited budget.

Italian

The Parlor (1916 E. Camelback Rd., 602/248-2480, http://theparlor.us, 11 A.M.–10 P.M. Mon.–Thurs., 11 A.M.–11 P.M. Fri.–Sat., $8–20) opened in a former beauty parlor in 2009 and quickly won over Phoenicians with its eco-chic look and award-winning, wood-fired, artisanal pizzas. The kitchen also serves Italian sandwiches, salads, and pastas. In summer, special tasting dinners are paired with wines and beers.

For 35 years, **Tomaso's** (3225 E. Camelback Rd. 602/956-0836, www.tomasos.com, 11:30 A.M.–2:30 P.M. Mon.–Fri., 5–10 P.M. Mon.–Sat., 5–9 P.M. Sun., $12–40) has been a Phoenix favorite. The upscale ambience has a Tuscan flair, and so does the menu of pasta, steaks, and seafood.

In the Sunnyslope neighborhood, **Il Posto** (9832 N. 7th Ave., 602/870-4122, 5 –10 P.M. Wed.–Sat., 5–9 P.M. Tues. and Sun., $9–17) pairs a fun, casual setting with classic Italian food. The patio replicates a New York neighborhood scene.

Mediterranean and Middle Eastern

Fast, fresh, and inexpensive, **Pita Jungle** (4340 E. Indian School Rd., 602/955-7482, www.pita-jungle.com, 10:30 A.M.–10 P.M. daily, $7–15) has grown into an Arizona culinary empire. The Arcadia location attracts a busy lunch and dinner crowd thanks to its healthful, Middle Eastern–inspired menu. The eclectic assortment includes salads, burgers, gyros, falafels, and pizza, as well as grilled salmon, tuna, and chicken.

For ambience, it's hard to beat **T. Cook's** (5200 E. Camelback Rd., 602/808-0766, 6 A.M.–2 P.M. and 5:30–10 P.M. daily, $28–55), a romantic hideaway at the Royal Palms Resort. The cozy, Spanish Colonial dining room is complemented by a Southwest-meets-Mediterranean menu, featuring seasonal dishes, fresh fish, and fire-roasted meats. Phoenicians gather at the Sunday morning brunches ($33 pp) for lemon brioche French toast, eggs Benedict, vanilla-scented pancakes, and mimosas.

A successful example of urban reuse, **32 Shea** (10626 N. 32nd St., 602/867-7432, www.32shea.com, 6 A.M.–10 P.M. Mon.–Thurs., 6 A.M.–midnight Fri., 7 A.M.–midnight Sat., 7 A.M.–2 P.M. Sun., $4–11) was transformed from a drive-through photomat into a chic coffee bar cum bistro. The small neighborhood café is difficult to pin down: The patio is a relaxed spot for a breakfast bite, a latte, or lunch, but at night 32 Shea becomes a bistro and wine bar that also mixes excellent cocktails. Diners rave about the OMG sandwich, which layers prosciutto, mascarpone, and figs.

Mexican and Southwest

Richardson's (6335 N. 16th St., 602/287-8900, 11 A.M.–midnight Mon.–Fri., 8 A.M.–midnight Sat.–Sun., $10–30) might just convert you to New Mexico's Southwestern cuisine: roasted chiles, gooey melted cheese, and smoky meats grilled over a pecan wood fire. Traditional favorites such as quesadillas, rellenos, and enchiladas are on the menu with signature dishes like Pasta Heidi, a green chile linguine in a smoky chipotle cream sauce. A pleasant, viga-shaded patio separates Richardson's from its sister restaurant, Rokerij. A third member of the Richardson's family, the compact **Dick's Hideaway** (6008 N. 16th St., 602/265-5886, 8 A.M.–1 A.M. Mon.–Fri., 7 A.M.–1 A.M. Sat.–Sun.) is just down the street, serving the same menu in a Western saloon setting, complete with a polished copper bar. All three restaurants serve fantastic brunches.

Former president George W. Bush ate at the **Tee Pee Mexican Restaurant** (4144 E. Indian School Rd., 602/956-0178, www.tee-peemexicanfood.com, 11 A.M.–10 P.M. Mon.–Sat., 11 A.M.–9 P.M. Sun., $6–13) in 2004, but Phoenicians have been coming to this hole-in-the-wall for authentic Mexican food since

1958. The Tee Pee is known for its chile rellenos, which come to the table as an intimidating, but tasty, mountain of cheese and chile peppers. The menu is affordable and diverse, the booths cozy, so chances are you'll get to know your neighbor.

Chef Vincent Guerithault and his eponymous **Vincent on Camelback** (3930 E. Camelback Rd., Ste. 204, 602/224-0225, www.vincentsoncamelback.com, 11:30 A.M.–2 P.M. and 5–10 P.M. Mon.–Fri., 5–10 P.M. Sat., $30–36) are local classics. The James Beard Award winner combines Southwestern ingredients with French technique. The elegant restaurant is perennially popular for its signature appetizers—like duck tamale with Anaheim chile and raisins—creative entrées, and delicious selection of Grand Marnier, tequila, lemon, and raspberry soufflés.

The casual, hip vibe and deliciously simple menu inspired by Mexican street food have

Gallo Blanco Café and Bar at the Clarendon Hotel

made **Gallo Blanco Café and Bar** (401 W. Clarendon Ave., 602/327-0880, www.galloblancocafe.com, 7:30 A.M.–10 P.M. Sun.–Thurs., 7:30 A.M.–11 P.M. Fri.–Sat., $3–14) a popular choice for locals. Sample some of the small homemade tacos, topped with seasonal veggies or meats, including *cochinita,* pork marinated in achiote, oranges, garlic, and guajillo chiles. Located within the Clarendon Hotel, this small café is also a great spot for an inexpensive but adventurous breakfast, served all day.

Elevated street food is also the theme at **La Condesa** (1919 N. 16th St. 602/254-6330, www.lacondesatacoshop.com, 11 A.M.–9 P.M. Mon.–Sat., 11 A.M.–8 P.M. Sun., $3–10), where tacos approach sublime heights. The colorful Central Phoenix spot also serves quesadillas and burritos and offers an exceptional salsa bar.

If you want to experience a classic neighborhood Mexican restaurant, look no further than **Via de Los Santos Mexican Café** (9120 N. Central Ave., 602/997-6239, www.viadelossantos.net, 11 A.M.–9:30 P.M. Mon.–Thurs. and Sat., 11 A.M.–10:30 P.M. Fri., 11 A.M.–8:30 P.M. Sun., $6–17). This Sunnyslope institution is known for its quality margaritas (which start at $2) and boasts a selection of more than 100 different tequilas. But the food and atmosphere are what makes the family-owned establishment such a gem. The lengthy menu of Sonoran-style Mexican dishes includes standbys, as well as some lighter fare such as salads, grilled seafood, and veggie burritos.

AHWATUKEE AND SOUTH PHOENIX
Breakfast and Lunch

The base of South Mountain, once home to date farms, flower growers, and citrus orchards, has been gobbled up by development, but visitors to **The Farm at South Mountain** (6106 S. 32nd St.) can get a look back into Phoenix's agricultural past. Students, families, the Scottsdale brunching set—well, it seems

like everyone raves about the **Morning Glory Café** (602/276-8804, 8 A.M.–noon Tues.–Fri., 8 A.M.–1 P.M. Sat.–Sun., closed summers, $8–15). The open-air restaurant isn't fancy, but the farm-fresh food is spectacular: cowboy chili and eggs, white truffle scrambled eggs, and rustic French toast, topped with candied walnuts and warm syrup, served in a shady grove of old pecan trees. Also on the property, **The Farm Kitchen** (602/276-7288, 10 A.M.–3 P.M. Tues.–Sun., closed summers, $6–12) features soups, salads, and sandwiches. Head south of Southern on 32nd Street, and pull into the charming farmstead's gravel driveway.

Mexican and Southwest

Kai (5594 W. Wild Horse Pass Blvd., 602/385-5726, 5:30–9 P.M. Tues.–Thurs., 5:30–9:30 P.M. Fri.–Sat., $25–55), which means "seed" in the Pima language, is the brainchild of Tucson restaurateur Janos Wilder. His menu highlights ingredients produced on the Gila River Indian Community or elsewhere in the state. Creative combinations such as tribal buffalo with smoked corn puree and cholla buds, or sea bass with Itoi onion gnocchi and olive tapenade, are a uniquely Arizona experience. Culinary adventurers can embark on an eight-course tasting menu. For this AAA Five Diamond restaurant, located at the Wild Horse Pass Resort, reservations are strongly recommended. You'll also need to turn off your cell phone and wear something more formal than jeans, shorts, or tees.

There are scores of great places to grab good tacos and enchiladas in the Valley, but **Carolina's** (1202 E. Mohave St., 602/252-1503, www.carolinasmex.com, 7 A.M.–7:30 P.M. Mon.–Fri., 7 A.M.–6 P.M. Sat., $3–7) is among the very best, with fresh, made-from-scratch Mexican food. To really experience Carolina Valenzuela's original recipes, order one of the hearty combination platters, which include enchiladas, *machaca,* flautas, and tostadas. You'll see locals taking home red and green tamales by the dozen.

Steakhouse

Best known for its Western kitsch and fun atmosphere, **Rustler's Rooste** (8383 S. 48th St., 602/431-6474, www.rustlersrooste.com, 4–10 P.M. daily, $15–30) also offers splendid views of Phoenix from its perch on South Mountain. There's a two-story waterfall, a longhorn steer, live country music nightly, and hefty servings of steak, ribs, cowboy beans, and corn on the cob. Dinner isn't served until after 5 P.M., but the lounge opens an hour earlier so you can wet your whistle and poke around the general store before riding the slide that descends to the lower floor. (Using the stairs is a perfectly acceptable alternative.)

TEMPE AND THE EAST VALLEY

American

Tucked behind big, leafy trees, **House of Tricks** (114 E. 7th St., 480/968-1114, www.houseoftricks.com, 11 A.M.–10 P.M. Mon.–Sat., $23–36) is one of Tempe's most distinctive restaurants in terms of both food and setting. A 1920s cottage and its older adobe-brick neighbor have been transformed into intimate, elegant dining rooms joined by a shady outdoor patio with a fishpond and resident cats. The eclectic, seasonal menu features sophisticated New American dishes with French, Asian, and Southwestern flavors. If you're watching your budget, lunches are equally inventive and flavorful for $9–13.

Monti's La Casa Vieja (100 S. Mill Ave., 480/967-7594, www.montis.com, 11 A.M.–10 P.M. Sun.–Thurs., 11 A.M.–11 P.M. Fri.–Sat., $12–30) is an Arizona institution. The adobe building was the boyhood home of longtime congressman Carl T. Hayden, whose father ran a ferry across the Salt River before it was dammed in 1911, and it's been a restaurant in one form or another since the 1890s. The focus is on hearty classics like steaks, chops, and ribs, with a good selection of seafood and pasta. Entrées come with Monti's famous Roman bread, a fragrant rosemary focaccia.

Four Peaks Brewing Company (1340 E. 8th St., 480/303-9967, www.fourpeaks.com, 11 A.M.–2 A.M. Mon.–Sat., 10 A.M.–2 A.M. Sun., $5–18) is a regular on local "best of" lists. Set in an 1892 redbrick, Mission-style building just off the beaten path in Tempe, the brewery shows off its floor-to-ceiling steel casks in the back and a chalkboard with the day's brews in the front. The Kilt Lifter, a pleasing Scottish ale, is a three-time medalist at the Great American Beer Festival. The brewpub has long list of appetizers, pizzas, sandwiches, and burgers, and for heartier fare like filet mignon and shrimp carbonara, the menu has pairing suggestions.

Archrivals ASU and U of A can shake hands over the sandwiches at **Bison Witches Bar and Deli** (21 E. 6th St., Ste. 146, 480/894-9104, www.bisonwitches.com, 11 A.M.–2 A.M. daily, $5–9), a Tucson legend that has expanded to Sun Devil territory. This inexpensive, casual spot for lunch or dinner has traditional bar appetizers and a few salads, but regulars know it's all about the Half and Half—a towering half-sandwich paired with one of five soups in a giant bread bowl.

Asian

At **RA Sushi** (411 S. Mill Ave., 480/303-9800, www.rasushi.com, 11 A.M.–11 P.M. daily, $4–20), the fish is fresh, and so is the Mill Avenue vibe. The bar is always packed with revelers, and the sushi bar and dining tables serve up some of the Valley's best sushi, sashimi, noodles, and tempura. The bar serves a large selection of sakes and other libations till 1 A.M. Now part of the Benihana empire, RA has four other locations in Phoenix, Mesa, and Scottsdale.

Since Chandler landed **Lee Lee International Supermarket** (2025 N. Dobson Rd., 480/899-2887), a veritable palace of delights for foodies in search of jackfruit, bitter melon, rice paper, and other hard-to-find ingredients, a number of excellent Asian eateries have opened in the area. Sushi lovers rave about **Shimogamo** (2051 Warner Rd., 480/899-7191, www.shimogamoaz.com, dinner nightly, lunch and dinner Fri., $5–18). At **Takamatsu** (3002 N. Arizona Ave., 480/632-5655, lunch and dinner daily, $7–35), Korean dishes are the house specialty. **Tien Wong** (2330 N. Alma School Rd., 480/802-2525, dinner daily, $10–20) specializes in *shabu shabu,* a traditional Chinese meal in which diners add their selections of meats and vegetables to a simmering broth.

For Vietnamese and pan-Asian cuisine, **Cyclo** (1919 W. Chandler Blvd., 480/963-4490, www.azeats.com/cyclo, 11 A.M.–2:30 P.M. and 5–9 P.M. Tues.–Thurs., 11 A.M.–2:30 P.M. and 5–10 P.M. Fri.–Sat., $6–15) can't be beat. The *goi du du* (green papaya salad) and *pho xe lua* (beef noodle soup) never disappoint. And just for the record, the name (pronounced SEE-klo) is the Vietnamese word for a three-wheeled pedicab.

Desserts

Tempe's Mill Avenue is lined with spots to tempt your sweet tooth, but head a couple miles southwest, and you'll find a gamut of goodies at **Honey Moon Sweets** (606 W. Southern Ave., 480/517-9520, http://honeymoonsweets.com, 7 A.M.–3 P.M. Mon.–Sat., till 5 P.M. Thurs.–Fri.). Breakfast pastries, cupcakes, cake pops, pies, tarts, bars, and cookies are all made from scratch in this 8,000-square-foot bakery. Spend a couple bucks on a treat or leave with a whole pie ($13 and up). You can even make a reservation for a behind-the-scenes tour.

In the tradition of Mexico's *paleterias,* downtown Mesa's **Flor de Michoacan** (734 E. Main, 480/655-7755) blends guava, pineapple, tamarind, coconut, strawberry, and other flavors with chile, then freezes them into pops for a sweet-hot-cold sensation.

Italian

Caffe Boa (398 S. Mill Ave., Ste. 110, 480/968-9112, http://cafeboa.com, 11 A.M.–10 P.M. Mon.–Wed., 11 A.M.–11 P.M. Thurs.–Fri., 10 A.M.–10 P.M. Sat.–Sun., $13–29) has earned numerous dining awards. The exposed brick walls, dark hardwood floors, and modern light fixtures are chic, but the mood is casual. Boa's seasonal menu uses local organic ingredients, with Mediterranean, Slavic, Asian, and Cajun influences. The handmade agnolotti ravioli filled with grilled portobello and cremini mushrooms in a creamy tomato sauce is always a winner, and the wine list is outstanding.

If you like your pizza New York–style, **Slices** (11 E. 6th St., 480/966-4681, http://slicespizzajoint.com, 11 A.M.–10 P.M. Sun.–Wed., 11 A.M.–3 A.M. Thurs.–Sat., $3–20) is there for you—and hordes of hungry college students. This popular joint offers a changing lineup of a dozen pies, including standbys like pepperoni to chipotle veggie or chicken pesto. Order a slice or two at the counter or sit down with an entire pie. Another popular local chain, **Venezia's** (27 E. Southern, 480/858-1660, http://venezias.com, 10:30 A.M.–10 P.M. Sun.–Thurs., 10:30 A.M.–11 P.M. Fri.–Sat., $4–25) delivers to East Valley locations for a small charge.

Mexican

Housed in Tempe's old train station, **Macayo's Depot Cantina** (300 S. Ash Ave., 480/966-6677, www.depotcantina.com, 10 A.M.–midnight daily, $6–14) is a festive Mexican restaurant just west of Mill Avenue's main drag. This local chain has dependably good tacos, tamales, chimichangas, and spicy Baja specialties. The restaurant's large patio is lively during happy hour, particularly on Fridays, when

PHOENIX AND VICINITY

college students and office workers head here to jump-start the weekend.

Another good local chain, **Los Dos Molinos** (260 S. Alma School Rd., 480/969-7475, 11 A.M.–9 P.M.daily, $5–9) offers a spicy departure from the usual Sonoran fare, featuring fiery New Mexican–style enchiladas, burros, and other favorites. Three additional locations are scattered around central and south Phoenix.

Middle Eastern

The first **Pita Jungle** (1250 E. Apache Blvd., 480/804-0234, www.pitajungle.com, 10:30 A.M.–10 P.M. Mon.–Sat., 10:30 A.M.–1 P.M. Sun., $6–15) opened in a funky strip mall near the Arizona State campus with a goal of attracting the burgeoning market of healthful eaters. And it did. Going on 20 years later, the eatery expanded to more than a dozen restaurants across the state and a few in California. The menu is well suited for mixed company—vegetarians and carnivores, that is—because it offers multiple meatless options, including veggie burgers, as well as a selection of beef, chicken, and lamb dishes.

If you like to shop while you eat, **Haji-Baba** (1513 E. Apache Blvd., 480/966-4672, 10 A.M.–8 P.M. Mon.–Sat., 11 A.M.–4:30 P.M. Sun., $5–10) combines a small but mighty Middle-Eastern market with a café, where you can dine on falafel, gyros, dolmades, baba ghanoush, and other Mediterranean standbys. The baklava selection is heavenly (or sinful, depending on your perspective).

Vegetarian

Vegetarians dine well in Tempe, thanks to its large student population and numerous ethnic

eateries. But at **Green** (2240 N. Scottsdale Rd., 480/941-9003, http://greenvegetarian. com, 11 A.M.–9 P.M. Mon.–Sat., $6–10), the menu is 100 percent vegan "comfort food" with a contemporary spin. Choices include burgers, pizzas, and noodle bowls made with mock meat and vegan cheeses. There are also gluten-free options for nearly everything on the menu. The spicy buffalo wings, "steak" po'-boys, and kung pao bowls are tasty enough to please even the most hard-core meat eater. There's a second location in central Phoenix (2202 N. 7th Ave., 602/258-1870).

GLENDALE AND THE WEST VALLEY

American

Fast becoming a Phoenix favorite, **Tryst Café** (21050 N. Tatum Blvd., 480/585-7978, http:// trystcafe.com, 7 A.M.–9 P.M. Mon.–Thurs., 7 A.M.–10 P.M. Fri.–Sat., 7 A.M.–8 P.M. Sun., $6–12), near the Desert Ridge Shopping Center, has a wide-ranging menu with an underlying theme: fresh, organic, and local. Signature dishes include a natural beef burger and house-smoked pork, but vegetarians will find plenty to love here, too.

Mexican

Los Reyes de la Torta (9230 N. 7th St., 602/870-2967, or 4333 W. Indian School Rd., 602/269-3212, http://losreyesdelatortaaz.com, 8 A.M.–9 P.M. Mon.–Thurs., 8 A.M.–11 P.M. Fri.–Sat., 8 A.M.–10 P.M. Sun., $6–12) serves a couple dozen varieties of tortas (hearty Mexican-style sandwiches), along with other home-style Sonoran classics. Be sure to try one of their refreshing fruit drinks.

Information and Services

TOURIST INFORMATION

The **Greater Phoenix Convention & Visitors Bureau** (602/254-6500, www.visitphoenix. com) is a great place to start for additional information about the Valley of the Sun. Its **Downtown Phoenix Visitor Information Center** (125 N. 2nd St., Ste. 120, 8 A.M.–5 P.M. Mon.–Fri.) is conveniently located across from the main entrance of the Hyatt Regency Phoenix.

LIBRARIES

The Phoenix Public Library has 16 branches across the city, including the **Burton Barr Central Library** (1221 N. Central Ave., 602/262-4636, www.phoenixpubliclibrary.org, 9 A.M.–5 P.M. Mon. and Fri.–Sat., 9 A.M.–9 P.M. Tues.–Thurs., 1–5 P.M. Sun.). You'll find computer terminals for easy access to the Internet, as well as an array of resources. The newer branches are almost as architecturally interesting as Burton Barr and worth a mini-tour, particularly **Agave** (23550 N. 36th Ave), **Desert Broom** (29710 N. Cave Creek Rd.), **Palo Verde** (4402 N. 51st Ave.), and **Juniper** (1825 W. Union Hills Dr.). Call the main number with questions or for hours.

HOSPITALS AND EMERGENCY SERVICES

In an emergency, dial 911 for immediate assistance. **St. Joseph's Hospital and Medical Center** (350 W. Thomas Rd., 602/406-3000, www.stjosephs-phx.org) is Phoenix's premier hospital and home of the Barrow Neurological Institute as well as a Level 1 trauma center. Nearby, **Phoenix Children's Hospital** (1919 E. Thomas Rd., 602/546-1000, www.phoenixchildrens.com) is one of the 10 largest children's hospitals in the country, offering a host of pediatric specialties, including neonatology, neurosciences, and Level 1 trauma. **Banner Health** (602/230-2273, www.bannerhealth. com) operates more than a dozen clinics and medical centers around the Valley, ranging from specialized services to general health care.

Getting There and Around

AIR

Phoenix Sky Harbor International Airport (3400 E. Sky Harbor Blvd., 602/273-3300, www.phxskyharbor.com) is a major regional hub for national and international flights. Tempe-based US Airways (800/428-4322, www.usairways.com) is the hometown airline, but more than 20 carriers fly to Sky Harbor's terminals 2, 3, and 4, including British Airways and Hawaiian Airlines. Shuttles connect the three terminals, as well as parking lots, the rental car center, and the light-rail's 44th Street stop.

CAR

Rental Cars

You'll need a vehicle to get around Phoenix, especially if you plan to explore the Valley of the Sun's diverse attractions scattered around the city. Take the free shuttle from any of the terminals to the **Rental Car Center** (1805 E. Sky Harbor Circle, 602/683-3741). You'll find major companies, like **Budget** (602/261-5950, www.budget.com), **Hertz** (602/267-8822, www.hertz.com), and **Enterprise** (602/225-0588, www.enterprise.com), which has convenient drop-off centers around Phoenix and Scottsdale and offers free pickup service. It can

Valley Metro's light-rail system links downtown's attractions, hotels, and restaurants.

© KATHLEEN BRYANT

be hard to find a gas station near the rental car center, so be sure to fill up before returning your vehicle.

Limos, Shuttles, and Taxis

Join a shared-van ride to your resort or hotel with the reliable **SuperShuttle** (602/244-9000 and 800/258-3826, www.supershuttle.com). Its bright blue vans are easy to spot at each of Sky Harbor's terminals.

AAA Sedans (602/454-7433) has a fleet of town cars that can ferry you to downtown Phoenix for about $50, plus tip. **Desert Knights Sedans & Limousines** (480/348-0600, www.desertknights.com) provides taxis, sedans, limos, and luxury minibuses, which can be a practical option for families or groups.

You can grab a taxi at Sky Harbor with one of three contracted companies: **AAA/Yellow Cab** (480/888-8888), **Apache Taxi** (480/557-7000), and **Mayflower** (602/955-1355). And if you want to hit the town at night, try **Courier Cab** (602/232-2222).

PUBLIC TRANSPORTATION
Light-Rail

The Valley's 20-mile light-rail system opened in December 2008, and it has proven to be popular with commuters, bar-hoppers, and visitors alike. Trains wend from 19th Avenue and Bethany Home Road in Phoenix, through downtown and Tempe's Mill Avenue, before ending one mile into Mesa. Its 28 stations include many of the city's most popular attractions such as the Heard Museum and Phoenix Art Museum, the Phoenix Convention Center, and Sun Devil Stadium in Tempe. Trains run daily, every 12 to 20 minutes. The last full trip begins at 11 P.M., and on Friday and Saturday nights, the hours are extended to 2 A.M. Fares start at $1.75 for a one-ride trip, and multi-ride passes are available.

Bus

The **Valley Metro** (602/253-5000, www. valleymetro.org) public transportation network connects the entire Phoenix metropolitan area.In addition to the light-rail line, its buses run throughout the city. Visit the website for a comprehensive schedule, map, and fares.

Apache Trail and Superstition Mountains

East of Phoenix and Mesa, open desert rises to a toothy set of peaks known as the Superstition Mountains, forever associated with Jacob Waltz, the Lost Dutchman, who walked out of the desert one day with a pocketful of nuggets and stories about a hidden mine. The Superstitions encompass 160,000 acres of rugged desert canyons and cliffs, formed 25 million years ago by volcanic activity. Theodore Roosevelt called them "the most sublimely beautiful panorama nature ever created." The area holds the essential ingredients of the legendary West: wide-open spaces, Apache Indians, a lost gold mine, prehistoric ruins, towering saguaros, and all the other creatures and plants we associate with the desert. Hollywood movies have been filmed here, and the surrounding mountains yielded billions in gold, silver, copper, and turquoise.

The area can be explored on a 100-mile loop that begins and ends at the community of Apache Junction, linking historic mining towns, ancient ruins, and dam-created lakes that sparkle like sapphires against the saguaro-studded peaks. The mostly paved route takes in views of the Four Peaks of the Mazatzal Mountains, the Sierra Anchas, and the fabled Superstitions. The highlight is when the loop

Horses wait for their riders near the Superstition Mountains.

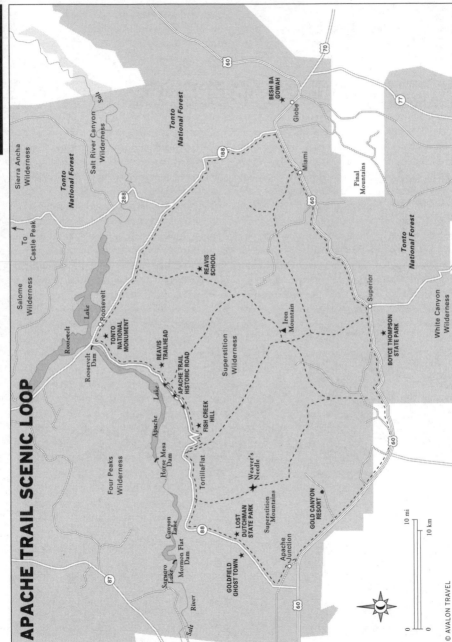

travels over the 40-mile Apache Trail, a former stagecoach route with white-knuckle drop-offs and no barriers, designated an Arizona Scenic Historic Byway.

Pockets of civilization are intermittent on this loop, so fill your gas tank, pack a picnic, or time your drive with a lunch stop in mind. Early morning is best if you plan to hike, though the late afternoon sun burnishes the peaks in gold and copper. The lakes draw a lot of weekend traffic, which you can avoid by traveling on a weekday. In places, the road pinches to a single lane, and the winding 22-mile unpaved section between Tortilla Flat and Roosevelt Dam isn't recommended for RVs or trailers.

Binoculars are handy for wildlife viewing: Desert bighorn sheep frequent the rocky mountainsides, and bald eagles soar above the lakes. Allow at least four hours for the loop, longer if you plan to visit the ruins of Tonto National Monument or wander the shady gardens at Boyce Thompson Arboretum.

SIGHTS

Apache Junction

Once a sleepy haven for retirees, Apache Junction (pop. 36,000) has expanded to serve new subdivisions and the Gold Canyon Golf Resort, making it a convenient place to top off the gas tank. You might find the roads around Apache Junction a bit crowded if you've arrived on a weekend in February or March, when one of the biggest parties in Arizona, the annual **Renaissance Festival** (12601 E. State Route 60, 520/463-2600, www.royalfaires.com, 10 A.M.–6 P.M. Sat.–Sun., $22 adults, $19 seniors, $12 children 5–12), takes place south of town.

Satisfy your curiosity about Jacob Waltz or learn more about area geology at the **Superstition Mountain Museum** (4087 N.

Goldfield, the site of an 1890s boomtown, sits at the base of the Superstition Mountains.

Apache Trail, 480/983-4888, www.superstitionmuseum.org, 9 A.M.–4 P.M. daily, $5 adults, children free), northeast of town on the Apache Trail (State Route 88). A mile farther, State Route 88 passes **Goldfield** (4650 N. Mammoth Mine Rd., 480/983-0333, www.goldfieldghosttown.com, 10 A.M.–5 P.M. daily), the site of an 1890s boomtown gone bust after the $1.5 million gold vein was exhausted and the mine shafts flooded. Reconstructed buildings—not to mention reenacted gunfights—give visitors a taste of the Wild West.

Lost Dutchman State Park

If your timing is right, you'll arrive when the rocky cliffs are blazing with gold...poppies, that is. After a wet winter, this is one of the best places in the Southwest to view wildflowers. In late February or early March, photographers flock here for a spectacular display of Mexican gold poppies and other blooms, backdropped by jagged volcanic cores. "Lost Dutchman" refers to prospector Jacob Waltz's rumored gold mine, never found, though many have tried over the years, and more than a few have died for their efforts.

The 300-acre park has a campground (520/586-2283) and half-dozen easy to moderate hiking trails. The longest and most scenic is the **Siphon Draw Trail** at four miles (round-trip); strong hikers can add another two miles by continuing up Flatiron Peak. The visitor center and gift shop (6109 N. Apache Trail, 480/982-4485, 8 A.M.–4 P.M. daily, summer hours vary, $7 per vehicle) are five miles north of Apache Junction on State Route 88.

Canyon Lake

At milepost 208, Canyon Lake is one of four reservoirs tucked into the Superstition Wilderness Area of Tonto National Forest, and the first of the three you'll encounter along the Apache Trail. The lakes are summer playgrounds for Valley residents hoping to cool off

Canyon Lake

© MESA CONVENTION AND VISITORS BUREAU/GARY JOHNSON

by boating, water-skiing, Jet Skiing, wind-sailing, or fishing. The marina (16802 N. State Route 88, 480/288-9233, www.canyonlakemarina.com) has a campground and hosts the **Dolly** steamboat (480/827-9144, www.dollysteamboat.com), which tours the lake in air-conditioned comfort. If you prefer to pilot yourself, you can rent anything from a kayak to a pontoon from Precision Marine (480/986-0960).

Tortilla Flat

As you continue north on State Route 88, you'll pass **Weaver's Needle,** a distinct rock formation that figures strongly in tales about the Lost Dutchman mine. The 4,553-foot-high volcanic plug juts above the Superstition Wilderness. At milepost 213, the tiny (and privately owned) town of Tortilla Flat welcomes visitors, offering a restaurant, ice cream parlor, and gift shop. In the early 1900s, during the construction of Roosevelt Dam, this was a bustling supply post, but the town's population has plummeted to a half-dozen souls. The small museum (open daily, hours vary seasonally) is packed to the rafters with photographs and memorabilia of the town's heyday. The general store is a good place to pick up an extra bottle of water or snacks.

Apache Trail

At milepost 220, the pavement ends and adventure begins. Though four-wheel-drive is recommended, passenger cars can make this trip—slowly and carefully. RVs are strongly discouraged. In fact, Cruise America forbids drivers to take its rental vehicles on this historic and scenic route. But on weekends you'll see plenty of locals pulling boat trailers, and encountering someone in a big rig is a white-knuckle experience, with one vehicle dangerously close to the steep drop at the edge of the road, the other nearly scraping the mountainside. Keep right, use turnouts, and be aware of blind curves.

Two miles farther, the parking area at the top of **Fish Creek Hill** makes a good place to stop for photos, use the restroom, and gather your courage for the next stretch of winding dirt road, which descends a thousand feet in elevation to Fish Creek Canyon. Between mileposts 227 and 228, Forest Road 212 leads to the **Reavis Ranch Trail,** a nine-mile hike (one way) to the site of a former ranch. In cooler months, the trail is popular with backpackers and horse campers. Day hikers who want to get a taste of the Superstitions' desert terrain can explore for a mile or two along the trail (an old jeep road), before turning around and heading back to their cars.

Theodore Roosevelt once said that the Apache Trail and Superstition Mountains combined "the grandeur of the Alps, the glory of the Rockies, the magnificence of the Grand Canyon, and then adds an indefinable something." If you feel the same, you might consider signing up for a workshop at **Reevis Mountain**

© MESA CONVENTION AND VISITORS BUREAU/APACHE TRAIL TOURS

touring the Apache Trail

School (928/467-2675). Tucked into a canyon 10 miles from the nearest post office or phone line, the school teaches self-reliance at its organic farm and homestead, with classes on foraging, solar cooking, desert survival skills, and other topics. Most classes run $130–240. Camping is free with registration, or you can stay in a cabin ($25–50) or "yurpee" ($10).

Apache Lake

Formed by Horse Mesa Dam, which was completed in 1927, Apache Lake is popular with water-sports enthusiasts. The 17-mile-long lake is surrounded by the Superstition and Four Peaks wilderness areas and the Three Bar wildlife enclosure, and numerous coves and cliffs shelter desert species like javelina, bighorn sheep, deer, as well as eagles and ospreys, who compete with anglers for small- and largemouth bass, walleyes, and other fish. The Apache Lake Vista has paved parking, a picnic ramada, and a short interpretive trail with views of the lake. For food, lodging, and boat rentals, stop by the **Apache Lake Marina and Resort** (20909 E. Apache Trail, 928/467-2511, www.apachelake.com).

Roosevelt Dam and Lake

On either side of Theodore Roosevelt Dam, two overlooks offer views of the dam, reservoirs, and highway bridge. The first (and largest) parking area is on the Apache Lake (downstream) side of the dam, where you'll be able to see the floodgates and powerhouse and marvel at the dam's impressive 357-foot height. Completed in 1911 at a cost of $10 million, it was at that time the world's largest masonry dam. The five-year construction period had a human cost as well, taking the lives of 42 men. The payoff: The dam made it possible to control the flow of the Salt River, opening the way for large-scale agriculture and increased settlement of the Phoenix area.

In 1996, a $430 million upgrade to the dam was completed, increasing its height and, unfortunately, covering up the magnificent rubble-masonry construction of the original Greco-Roman-style dam. Italian stonecutters had carved the blocks from nearby cliffs, part of a cultural mix of workers who included German, Austrian, Swiss, and Scottish masons; American laborers of Chinese, African, Mexican, and European descent; and the crew of Apache Indians who built the road transporting materials and supplies to the dam site. The road became known as the Apache Trail. When the lake is low, remnants of the original masonry can be viewed from the second overlook at Inspiration Point, a half-mile farther along State Route 88, where you can also see the Roosevelt Lake bridge, the longest two-lane steel arch bridge in the United States.

When the dam was completed in 1911, Roosevelt Lake became the largest reservoir in the world. Today, it's still the largest lake located entirely within Arizona. The lake is home to the Tonto Basin district of Tonto National Forest (928/467-3200, www.fs.usda.gov/tonto). Though most recreation is centered on the lake, several hiking and equestrian trails, including the 800-mile-long Arizona Trail, start nearby. Most area trails are too steep and rocky for mountain bikes, but experienced bikers can tackle the seven-mile loop around the Three Bar Wildlife enclosure and cool off in the lake afterward. Stop in at the ranger station for books, maps, and trail information. In winter months, the back patio is a great spot for watching migratory waterfowl.

To continue on the loop, take State Route 188 toward Globe.

Tonto National Monument

This 1,120-acre monument (26260 N. State Route 188, 928/467-2242, www.nps.gov/tont, 8 A.M.–5 P.M. daily, $3 adult, under 16 free) preserves three Salado villages tucked inside rock alcoves high above Roosevelt Lake.

Seven hundred years ago, when the cliff dwellings were inhabited, the scene would have been very different. While the landscape then might have appeared harsh from our point of view, to the Salado people, it was a treasure trove of resources, with the Salt River providing a natural travel corridor and agricultural area. Salado farmers supplemented their diet with wild plants and game. They wove cotton cloth and made striking polychrome pottery.

The Salado constructed their "apartment complexes" from rock, with juniper roof beams cross-laid by saguaro ribs. You can view the 19-room lower cliff dwelling from the visitor center or hike to it on a one-mile (round-trip) trail. The 40-room upper ruin, open November through April, is reached by a three-mile (round-trip) hike, reservations required. Special events include full moon walks, backcountry tours, and cultural demonstrations.

The month of March, when Arizona promotes archaeology awareness, is an especially good time to visit for special programs and wildflower viewing. The turnoff to the monument is 25 miles past Roosevelt Dam on State Route 188 (or 25 miles past Globe, if you are traveling from the other direction).

Globe

At the base of Sleeping Beauty Mountain, about three miles east of the intersection of State Route 188 and U.S. 60 sits the town of Globe (pop. 7,500), established in 1876. Globe got its name from a large, globular chunk of silver found nearby (now displayed in the Smithsonian), and the Old Dominion Copper Company operated here until 1931. The town's proximity to Apache territory and relative isolation meant for a long and colorful Wild West history of lynchings, stage robberies, and Indian raids. Phineas Clanton, who survived the shoot-out at the OK Corral, lived out his days here, and Big Nose Kate, Doc Holliday's common-law wife, was a resident.

Today, Globe is the home of Sleeping Beauty mine, a former silver and copper operation now producing several varieties of turquoise, including the eponymous stone, colored a pure sky-blue without matrix. The mine sells to the public at its **Sleeping Beauty Turquoise store** on U.S. 60 (200 W. Ash, 888/425-7698, 8 A.M.–4 P.M. Mon.–Fri.). Down the street is the **Copper City Rock Shop** (566 Ash, 928/425-7885).

The **Cobre Valley Center for the Arts** (101 N. Broad St., 928/425-0884, www.cvarts.org, 10 A.M.–5 P.M. Mon.–Fri., 10 A.M.–4 P.M. Sat., noon–4 P.M. Sun., gallery is free, event prices vary) is housed in the former Gila County Courthouse, built in 1906, one of several notable buildings in the town's handsome **historic district.** Regional artists display their works in the downstairs gallery, and plays and other performances are staged in the former courtroom. The **Globe-Miami Chamber of Commerce** (1360 N. Broad St., 928/425-4495, www.globemiamichamber.com) has brochures for self-guided walking tours and information about area shopping. Next door is the **Gila County Historical Museum** (1330 N. Broad St., 928/425-7385, 10 A.M.–4 P.M. Mon.–Fri., 11 A.M.–3 P.M. Sun., free), with exhibits ranging from prehistoric pottery to cowboy gear.

The 3,000-square-mile **San Carlos Apache Nation** neighbors Globe, and in mid-October, the town celebrates Apache culture with a day of native crafts, dance and musical performances, and traditional cuisine.

BESH-BA-GOWAH ARCHAEOLOGICAL PARK

During the 13th century, this 300-room pueblo housed more than a thousand Salado villagers. Its location between the Sonoran Desert territory of the Hohokam and the forested uplands inhabited by the Ancestral Puebloans made it a key trading center between cultures. Today, reconstructed rooms help give us a sense of the villagers' daily lives. Two miles south of Globe, the museum (1324 S. Jesse Hayes Rd., 928/425-0320, 9 A.M.–5 P.M. daily, $5 adults, under 12 free) has the largest collection of Salado artifacts in the world, as well as a fascinating ethnobotanical garden describing indigenous uses for local flora.

In mid-December, Besh-Ba-Gowah (Apache for "place of metal") hosts **Noche de las Luminarias,** when the ruins are lit by glowing candles and visitors gather for hot cider, cookies, and live music. Over the last weekend in March, the park hosts a celebration for Arizona's Archaeology and Heritage Awareness Month.

Miami and Superior

Between Miami and Superior, U.S. 60 passes along huge mounds of tailings along the base of Apache Leap Mountain (said to be where a band of Apaches leapt to their death rather than surrender to the U.S. army). Mines in the Miami-Superior area continue to produce copper today. In Superior, three small historic districts include the home of Arizona's sixth governor, preserved as the **Bob Jones Museum** (200 Main St., open weekends Sept–May, free). Superior is also home to the **World's Smallest Museum** (1111 W. U.S. 60, 520/689-5800, open 8 A.M.–1:30 P.M., Wed.–Sun., free, donation appreciated) at 137 square feet. A handful of movies were filmed in the area, including the epic *How the West Was Won* (1962). Miami has a number of antiques stores, and a few shops along Superior's Main Street sell local arts and crafts.

In March, miners compete in the annual **Apache Leap Mining Festival,** a throwback to the days when hard-rock miners demonstrated the feats of strength and skill that were essential to their jobs. The modern version includes live entertainment, food, and a Chihuahua race.

BOYCE THOMPSON ARBORETUM STATE PARK

More than 3,000 desert plants grow in this 1,075-acre outdoor museum located three miles west of Superior. It's also home to 300 species of birds, mammals, reptiles, and amphibians. Founded in 1925 by William Boyce Thompson, it's Arizona's oldest and largest botanical garden, and it continues to function as a research center for the University of Arizona. This shady haven along Queen Creek has a large picnic area and several gardens. The park is busiest in autumn, when Phoenicians make annual pilgrimages to see colorful autumn leaves, and in spring when wildflowers bloom.

A 1.25-mile main trail loops through gardens and natural landscapes, with portions suitable for wheelchairs. A shorter, rockier trail (1 mile round-trip) climbs to views of Weaver's Needle. The **visitor center** (37615 W. U.S. 60, 520/689-2811, 8 A.M.–5 P.M. daily, 6 A.M.–3 P.M. May–Aug., $9 adults, $4.50 children 5–12) houses a gift shop. Special events include guided tours, workshops, and a spring plant sale featuring desert species at bargain prices.

ACCOMMODATIONS AND FOOD
Apache Junction

A hoary Phoenix joke begins "How can you tell when it's fall in the desert?" Answer: "Because the license plates start to change color." Nowhere is this more true than in Apache Junction, at the eastern edge of the Phoenix metro area. Long a favorite destination of "snowbirds," the town has restaurants aplenty, as well as numerous chain motels and RV parks. And though new subdivisions have sprung up in recent years, downtown AJ looks much like it did a half-century ago. **What the Hell Bar and Grill** (10262 E. Apache Trail,

480/986-8974, http://whatthehellbarandgrill. com, all meals daily, $5–15) is a throwback, a neighborhood bar-and-burger joint where bikers and desert rats rub elbows with snowbirds and day-trippers. On Sundays, it becomes a haven for Green Bay Packers fans.

The campground at **Lost Dutchman State Park** (520/586-2283) has 72 sites, 35 with hookups. But if you're looking for cushier digs, **Gold Canyon Golf Resort** (6100 S. Kings Ranch Rd., 800/827-5281 or 480/982-9090, www.gcgr.com, $125–175 d) is a treasure for golfers and travelers hoping to retreat into the desert. Surrounded by the rugged Superstition Mountains, the resort's pueblo-style buildings gleam in the Sonoran Desert setting. The surreal views would cost three times as much in North Scottsdale, but the real highlight is Gold Canyon's two championship desert courses, which *Sports Illustrated* named among the 10 most underrated in the country.

Apache Trail

As you venture farther along the Apache Trail, your options will be limited to a few cafés and motels, and thousands of acres of forest for camping. At Canyon Lake, **Lakeside Restaurant and Cantina** (480/288-8290) is open daily for lunch, plus breakfast and dinner on weekends. Hours vary with the season. The **marina** (16802 N. State Route 88, 480/288-9233, www.canyonlakemarina.com) has a 47-site campground (22 with hookups).

Tortilla Flat is home to a restaurant, ice cream parlor, and general store. **Tonto National Forest** (928/467-3200, www.fs.usda.gov/tonto) operates Tortilla Campground seasonally (Oct. 15–April, 77 sites, 10 available by reservation, 877/444-6777).

Apache Lake Marina and Resort (20909 E. Apache Trail, 928/467-2511, www.apachelake.com) combines a marina, motel, RV campground, and **Jacks Landing** restaurant (all meals daily, year-round). The forest allows dispersed camping in nearby Crabtree Wash.

Dispersed **camping** (with certain restrictions) is also allowed elsewhere in Tonto National Forest (928/467-3200, www.fs.usda.gov/tonto). The forest's Tonto Basin and Globe ranger districts have 11 campgrounds. Most sites are without hookups, available on a first-come, first-served basis.

Globe to Superior

Globe has a few chain restaurants, but the local specialty is Mexican food, with more than a dozen establishments serving up classic Sonoran fare. If you've burned hundreds of calories exploring, you can happily replenish them in one meal at **Libby's El Rey Café** (999 N. Broad St., 928/425-2054, lunch and dinner daily, $5–12), where freshly made tortillas and buttery chips accompany home-style soups, tamales, enchiladas, and burritos. In Superior, the **Buckboard City Café** (1111 U.S. 60, 928/689-5800, breakfast and lunch Wed.–Sun., $5–10) dishes up Western-American fare.

Noftsger Hill Inn (425 North St., 877/780-2479 or 928/425-2260, www.noftsgerhillinn.com, $90–125) once served as Globe's elementary school, attended by Rose Mofford, who remains one of Arizona's best-loved (and least controversial) governors. Spacious and light-filled classrooms now do duty as the B&B's six guest rooms. But be warned: investigators have noted some paranormal activity (i.e., ghosts) wandering the halls. The faint of heart may want to head for the hills southeast of town, where **The Dream Manor Inn** (1 Dream Manor Dr., 928/425-2754, http://dreammanorinn.com, $79–120) offers a hillside retreat on 27 acres of desert, with a pool, waterfall garden, and serene mountain views.

INFORMATION AND SERVICES
Visitor Centers

Lost Dutchman State Park (6109 N. Apache Trail, 480/982-4485, www.azstateparks.com, 8 A.M.–4 P.M. daily, summer hours vary, $7 per vehicle) is a veritable gold mine of information about the Superstition Mountains region. Rangers and volunteers offer programs and lead hikes, even in summer months.

Tonto National Forest's **Roosevelt Lake Visitor Center** (28079 N. State Route 188, 928/467-3200, www.fs.usda.gov/tonto, 7:45 A.M.–4:30 P.M. daily) has stellar views of the lake from its back patio. Indoors you'll find exhibits, videos, and information about trails and other activities. The forest's Globe Ranger Station (7680 S. Six Shooter Canyon Rd., 928/402-6200, 8 A.M.–4:30 P.M. daily), two miles south of town, has maps and information.

The visitor center at **Tonto National Monument** (26260 N. State Route 188, 928/467-2242, www.nps.gov/tont, 8 A.M.–5 P.M. daily, $3 adult, under 16 free) has a small museum and an 18-minute orientation video. Rangers lead guided tours (3–4 hours) to the upper ruins in cooler months; reservations are required.

At **Besh-Ba-Gowah Archaeological Park** (1324 S. Jesse Hayes Rd., 928/425-0320, 9 A.M.–5 P.M. daily, $5 adults, under 12 free), two miles south of Globe, you'll find a fascinating museum with exhibits and artifacts highlighting the Salado culture.

The extensive visitor center at **Boyce Thompson Arboretum State Park** (37615 W. U.S. 60, 520/689-2811, 8 A.M.–5 P.M. daily, 6 A.M.–3 P.M. May–Aug., $9 adults, $4.50 children 5–12) has a gift shop, snacks, picnic area, exhibits, and art gallery. Docents lead tours and offer an impressive lineup of weekend workshops.

For information about businesses, lodging, and events in the towns along the Apache Trail, contact their respective chambers of commerce:

- **Apache Junction Chamber of Commerce** (567 W. Apache Trail, 480/982-3141, www. apachejunctioncoc.com)
- **Globe-Miami Chamber of Commerce** (1360 N. Broad St., 928/425-4495, www.globemiamichamber.com)
- **Superior, Arizona Chamber of Commerce** (230 W. Main St., 520/689-0200, www.superiorazchamber.net)

GETTING THERE AND AROUND

From Phoenix and the East Valley, take the Superstition Freeway (U.S. 60) to Apache Junction. Exit at Idaho Road and turn north on State Route 88, the Apache Trail. (From North Phoenix or Scottsdale, take Loop 101 south to U.S. 60.) You can make the entire 100-mile loop in a passenger car, but if you plan to explore forest roads, you'll need a high-clearance vehicle, preferably with four-wheel-drive, and a good map. No matter what you're driving, be extra cautious on the narrow, unpaved section of the Apache Trail.

Alternatively, you can sign on for a tour and let someone else do the driving. A number of Phoenix tour brokers offer excursions to the Superstition Mountains, many with options for hiking, lake cruises, and other activities. Starting at $120 per adult, **Phoenix Tours** (800/303-5185, www.phoenixtours.us) will collect you at your hotel and transport you via the Apache Trail to Canyon Lake for a steamboat tour. For a few dollars less, **Vaughan's Southwest Tours** (800/513-1381, www.southwesttours.com) features a stop at Goldfield, a re-created ghost town.

SCOTTSDALE AND VICINITY

Are you an art lover or outdoor adventurer? Foodie or scenester? History buff or shopaholic? What's your game? Golf or five-card stud? Whether you want to party all night or be pampered all day—or both—Scottsdale can meet you on your own terms.

One of the desert's most livable cities, Scottsdale's greatest appeal is its unapologetic resort lifestyle. You'll want to spend your time shopping, eating and drinking, browsing art galleries, hitting the links, and hiking desert mountains. Indulge at one of the world-class spas, or time your visit to coincide with one of Scottsdale's signature events, such as January's classic car auctions, the Phoenix Open, or the Great Arizona Picnic.

Valley of the Sun communities flow from one to the next, and Scottsdale is no exception. The city can be roughly delineated into three areas: downtown, central, and north. The compact, southern part of the city, downtown, is where you'll find Old Town and the arts districts of 5th Avenue and Marshall Way, as well as the highest density of shops and nightlife venues. Downtown is bordered by the college town of Tempe to the south and by Phoenix to the west.

Central Scottsdale extends east, along an indistinguishable sprawl of housing developments and strip malls called the Shea Corridor. In this part of the city, you'll also find the community of Paradise Valley, the Valley's answer to

SCOTTSDALE AND VICINITY

HIGHLIGHTS

© AVALON TRAVEL

LOOK FOR ◖ TO FIND RECOMMENDED SIGHTS, ACTIVITIES, DINING, AND LODGING.

◖ **Old Town:** Old West meets New West in Scottsdale's lively town center, where historic sites and performing arts venues share space with nightclubs, restaurants, and galleries. Anchored by a grassy 21-acre mall with an amphitheater, flower gardens, and fountains, Scottsdale's Old Town draws tourists and locals alike (page 117).

◖ **Scottsdale Museum of Contemporary Art (SMoCA):** This intimate museum of modern art, architecture, and design stands out in the capital of cowboy art. The permanent *Knight Rise* installation is an oculus that will change your perception of Arizona's clear skies (page 119).

◖ **Camelback Mountain:** You can't miss the iconic "kneeling camel" profile. The sandstone-and-granite peak rises at the center of the Valley of the Sun and is a top draw for hikers and rock climbers (page 120).

◖ **Musical Instrument Museum:** Combining graceful architecture and state-of-the art exhibits, MIM takes visitors on a cultural tour of the world through music. You can bang a gong, admire iconic rock guitars, or take in a concert or workshop at this first-class museum (page 123).

◖ **Taliesin West:** Frank Lloyd Wright's winter home blends the architect's trademark techniques and design motifs with the desert landscape. Tour the National Landmark, which is still a working architecture school and home to members of the Wright Foundation (page 125).

◖ **Downtown Arts Districts:** Scottsdale commands the country's third-largest art market, with three walkable arts districts along 5th Avenue, Marshall Way, and Main Street. More than a hundred galleries showcase everything from traditional Western bronzes to avant-garde works (page 137).

Beverly Hills and home to big-name celebrities and five-star resorts.

Within the last decade, the northern half of the city has become one of the most sought-after areas in the region and has begun to creep into formerly pristine desert. Fortunately, developers have taken a more enlightened approach to the city's growth, sparing much of the area's indigenous wildlife. While many Valley

of the Sun communities have turned their back on the desert, Scottsdale and its smaller neighbors—Cave Creek, Carefree, and Fountain Hills—embrace their desert setting.

Despite its flashy exterior, Scottsdale is still firmly rooted in its decades-old slogan as "The West's Most Western Town." The city is bordered to the east by the agricultural land of the Salt River Pima–Maricopa Indian Community

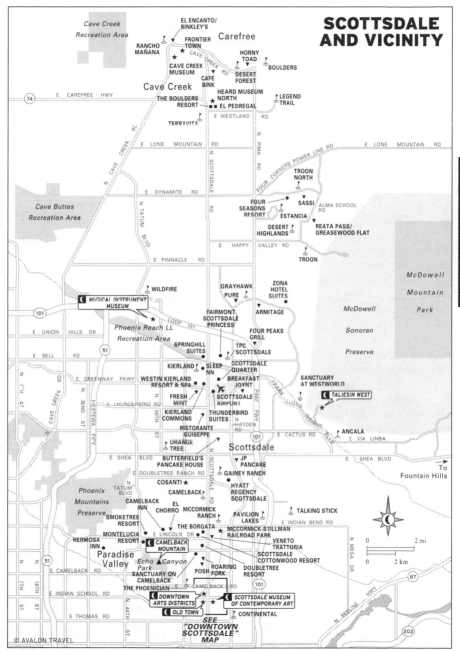

SCOTTSDALE AND VICINITY

SCOTTSDALE AND VICINITY

Cave Creek
Recreation Area

EL ENCANTO/
BINKLEY'S

FRONTIER
TOWN

RANCHO
MAÑANA

Carefree

CAVE CREEK RD

HORNY
TOAD

BOULDERS

CAVE CREEK
MUSEUM

CAFE
BINK

DESERT
FOREST

Cave Creek

HEARD MUSEUM
NORTH

LEGEND
TRAIL

THE BOULDERS
RESORT

EL PEDREGAL

74   E CAREFREE HWY

E WESTLAND   RD

TERRAVITA

E LONE   MOUNTAIN   RD

N PIMA   RD

N SCOTTSDALE   RD

E LONE   MOUNTAIN   RD

Cave Buttes
Recreation Area

E DYNAMITE   RD

N TATUM   BLVD

RD

FOUR CORNERS POWER LINE RD

TROON
NORTH

FOUR
SEASONS
RESORT

SASSI

ALMA SCHOOL
RD

ESTANCIA

DESERT
HIGHLANDS

REATA PASS/
GREASEWOOD FLAT

E HAPPY   VALLEY RD

E PINNACLE   RD

TROON

McDowell

Mountain

WILDFIRE

GRAYHAWK

PURE

ZONA
HOTEL
SUITES

Park

MUSICAL INSTRUMENT
MUSEUM

101

FAIRMONT
SCOTTSDALE
PRINCESS

ARMITAGE

McDowell

Phoenix Reach LL
Recreation Area

LOOP 101

FOUR PEAKS
GRILL

Sonoran

Preserve

E UNION   HILLS DR

E BELL   RD

51

SPRINGHILL
SUITES

TPC
SCOTTSDALE

KIERLAND

SLEEP
INN

SCOTTSDALE
QUARTER

7TH   ST

CAVE CREEK RD

E GREENWAY PKWY

N 32ND

WESTIN KIERLAND
RESORT & SPA

BREAKFAST
JOYNT

SANCTUARY
AT WESTWORLD

E THUNDERBIRD RD

56TH   ST

FRESH
MINT

SCOTTSDALE
AIRPORT

FRANK LLOYD WRIGHT BLVD

TALIESIN WEST

FIESTA FWY

KIERLAND
COMMONS

THUNDERBIRD
SUITES

RISTORANTE
GUISEPPE

N
HAYDEN
RD

101

ANCALA

E CACTUS RD

E VIA LINDA

ORANGE
TREE

Scottsdale

BUTTERFIELD'S
PANCAKE HOUSE

JP
PANCAKE

E SHEA BLVD

E SHEA BLVD

To
Fountain Hills

E DOUBLETREE RANCH RD

GAINEY RANCH

COSANTI

N
TATUM
BLVD

CAMELBACK

HYATT
REGENCY
SCOTTSDALE

Phoenix
Mountains

Preserve

CAMELBACK
INN

EL
CHORRO

McCORMICK
RANCH

PAVILION
LAKES

TALKING STICK

SMOKETREE
RESORT

E INDIAN BEND RD

0   2 mi

THE BORGATA

McCORMICK-STILLMAN
RAILROAD PARK

MONTELUCIA
RESORT

E LINCOLN DR

0   2 km

HERMOSA
INN

CAMELBACK
MOUNTAIN

VENETO
TRATTORIA

N MESA DR

51

Paradise
Valley

Echo
Park

Canyon

SCOTTSDALE
COTTONWOOD RESORT

87

E CAMELBACK RD

SANCTUARY ON
CAMELBACK

POSH

ROARING
FORK

DOUBLETREE
RESORT

N BEELINE HWY

7TH   ST

16TH   ST

THE PHOENICIAN

E CAMELBACK RD

101

E INDIAN SCHOOL RD

DOWNTOWN
ARTS DISTRICTS

SCOTTSDALE MUSEUM
OF CONTEMPORARY ART

202

E THOMAS RD

OLD TOWN

CONTINENTAL

SEE
"DOWNTOWN
SCOTTSDALE"
MAP

© AVALON TRAVEL

and the McDowell Mountains, which have kept its sprawling tendencies in check. It remains one of the few places in metropolitan Phoenix where you can truly feel like you are living in the desert—and this is perhaps Scottsdale's greatest luxury.

PLANNING YOUR TIME

This is the city that invented resort casual—both in terms of attire and attitude. Relax and imagine that your life really consists of endless days of soaking up sunshine, sipping tequila, and dining alfresco at top-notch restaurants that forgo the formality of suits and ties. You could easily spend a week enjoying hours by the pool, playing rounds of golf, browsing in galleries, and getting pampered at one of the city's five-star spas.

If you only have a weekend, though, be sure to see Frank Lloyd Wright's winter home, Taliesin West, before witnessing the clash of civilizations in Old Town. The eclectic mix of expensive galleries, trendy clubs, yuppie biker bars, and boutiques selling Western and Native American kitsch creates some the best people-watching this side of the Rocky Mountains. Bars and restaurants literally slide away their glass walls from November through April, giving you a front-row seat to the streetside spectacle.

Visiting during the summer's triple-digit heat will force you to change your plans—both in terms of what you do and when you do it. But that's not a bad thing. Take a cue from the natives—both wildlife and residents—who switch to a more nocturnal schedule from May well into October. Wake at dawn to take advantage of an early tee time or a sunrise hike to one of Scottsdale's craggy peaks. Then, spend your afternoons in one of the city's air-conditioned oases, like Scottsdale Fashion Square mall. When late afternoon hits, make like a lizard and find some shade for a nap (the thermometer hits its hottest point around 4 P.M.).

Come out to play in the evening when the sun dips below the horizon and the desert's beige tones and blue sky give way to a rich burst of color. Technicolor sunsets are just a preview of the evening's lime-green margaritas, vibrant Southwestern cuisine, and flashy lounges and clubs. And as the temperature drops 20 degrees throughout the night, let the warm, weightless air convince you that living in the desert can be heavenly.

HISTORY

The city of Scottsdale may look new, but its roots date back to the ancient Hohokam civilization, which first inhabited the Salt River Valley circa 300 B.C. When the Hohokam abandoned their villages in the 1400s, their canals served as a foundation for the Pima Indian village known as Vasai Svasoni, or "rotting hay." Although it wasn't the most appealing name, the area proved to be an enduring home for the Pima, who still live in the Salt River Pima–Maricopa Indian Community, which borders Scottsdale's city limits.

In 1888, U.S. army chaplain Winfield Scott bought 640 acres of rocky, desert land northeast of Phoenix. At $2.50 an acre, the purchase may be the Valley's best land deal on record. Scott saw the cheap desert land and its still-functioning canals as rife with opportunity, as well as an ideal climate to recover from wounds he had sustained in the Civil War.

Scott and his wife, Helen, became the first of a succession of New Yorkers who would trade the East Coast's cold, gray winters for desert sunshine—and tell their friends. Scott used his oratory gifts to convince other families to move to his fledgling community of Orangedale. Across from the Scottsdale Center for the Performing Arts (down the center of 2nd Street and Civic Center Boulevard), you can still see the olive trees Scott planted to mark the border of his original 40-acre orange grove. The citrus trees didn't prove to be as hardy, dying in a drought in the late 1890s.

During the next few decades, the small community attracted cowboys, ranchers and miners, as well as Native Americans looking to trade goods and tuberculosis patients seeking the dry desert air to recover from their respiratory ailments.

The mild winter climate and stark landscape even lured famed architect Frank Lloyd Wright, who was in Phoenix to consult on the design of the Arizona Biltmore Resort. Wright was so taken by the Sonoran Desert that he established his "winter camp," Taliesin West, at the base of the McDowell Mountains in 1937. The rocky site would serve as a constant source of inspiration until his death in 1959.

Following World War II, pilots who had trained at Scottsdale Airfield returned to the city, bringing their families. The growing community, which was officially incorporated in 1951, attracted burgeoning high-tech corporations, like Motorola in 1956. Local cartoonist Bil Keane found inspiration in the postwar suburban boom for his comic strip, *Family Circus*. In 1969, Scottsdale became the first city in the nation to enact a sign ordinance restricting the size and height of billboards—a controversial measure that was even challenged at the U.S. Supreme Court.

The availability of air-conditioning increased Scottsdale's popularity. City leaders annexed huge swaths of land in the north, areas once roamed only by cattle and wildlife. Dude ranches gave way to resorts, and developers created large master-planned communities with golf courses and other amenities, attracting retirees and young families. Skyrocketing home prices, along with chichi art galleries and shopping centers, earned the increasingly affluent city the nickname "Snottsdale" among residents of neighboring communities.

Since the 1950s, Scottsdale has grown from 2,000 residents to 220,000, but rapid expansion hasn't diminished its quality of life. The city frequently earns "best of" nods across several categories: for biking and raising kids, and as a travel and arts destination. Once known as a retirement haven, today's Scottsdale has a youthful vibe, and it's been named one of the best cities in the United States for dating. Downtown alone boasts 90 restaurants, 80 art galleries, and 320 shops. Yet only a few miles to the north lies the McDowell Mountain Preserve, where miles of trails lead through pristine desert.

Sights

Many of Scottsdale's historic and cultural attractions center on Old Town, easily toured on foot or by hopping on one of the free trolleys that stop every 15 minutes along 5th Avenue, Marshall Way, and Scottsdale Fashion Square. Two stellar attractions are located in North Scottsdale: the fabulous Musical Instrument Museum and Frank Lloyd Wright's winter home, Taliesin West. Scottsdale's shopping venues and world-class spas are highlights in and of themselves. Even if you're not a guest at a five-star resort, you can stop in for a drink and soak up the ambience—and the desert mountain views, which are among the city's most iconic sights.

DOWNTOWN
◖ Old Town
There's no better place to begin a tour of "The West's Most Western Town." This touristy hodgepodge of restaurants, bars, and Old West–themed boutiques is a little kitschy, but you'll find some historic sites along with the shopping and art. And even if you're not a big

SCOTTSDALE AND VICINITY

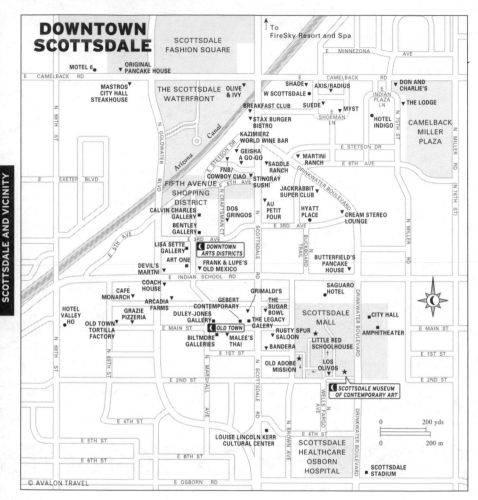

shopper, the live music courtesy of singing cowboys on horseback and Native American performers makes for a fun "only in Arizona" experience.

Start at the beautifully landscaped **Scottsdale Civic Center Mall,** a 21-acre park ringed by chic hotels and restaurants, hole-in-the-wall bars, arts venues, and the city hall and library. The cool fountains and mesquite-shaded walkways attract visitors and residents year-round. You might see friends playing chess

in the sunken garden or a young girl posing for pictures in an elaborate white dress for her *quinceañera* (a Mexican coming-of-age ceremony held on a girl's 15th birthday).

Across from the statue of Winfield and Helen Scott on the western end of the mall, you'll find the **Little Red Schoolhouse** (7333 E. Scottsdale Mall, 480/945-4499, www.scottsdalemuseum.org, 10 A.M.–5 P.M. Wed.–Sat., noon–8 P.M. Sun., closed July–Aug. and holidays, free), the original 1909

© KATHLEEN BRYANT

Scottsdale celebrates its Western heritage in Old Town.

Scottsdale Grammar School that now houses the Scottsdale Historical Society. Inside, artifacts from the Scotts' home and a collection of historic photographs illustrate the city's modest beginnings as a territorial farm community.

Head east to the outdoor **amphitheater,** a popular site for festivals and outdoor concerts. You can see Robert Indiana's iconic *Love* sculpture on the lawn, along with a host of other public artworks.

On the far eastern end of the plaza, you'll see Scottsdale's **City Hall,** designed by native Arizonan Bennie Gonzales, whose Midcentury Modern interpretation of traditional Southwestern design transformed the region's architecture.

SCOTTSDALE MUSEUM OF CONTEMPORARY ART (SMOCA)

Anchoring the southern end of the mall alongside the Scottsdale Center for the Performing Arts is the city's finest example contemporary

architecture, as well as the state's only museum devoted to contemporary art. SMoCA (7374 E. 2nd St., 480/994-2787, www.smoca.org, 10 A.M.–5 P.M. Tues.–Wed. and Fri.–Sat., 10 A.M.–8 P.M. Thurs., noon–5 P.M. Sun., $7 adults, $5 students, kids under 15 free, admission free Thurs.) specializes in modern art, architecture, and design—a refuge for avant-garde art lovers in the land of cowboy paintings. The museum's "eggplant gray" stucco is meant to evoke the McDowell Mountain Range to the east, while the shimmering steel facade reflects the blue Arizona sky. The permanent outdoor installation, *Knight Rise,* is a favorite place to watch a sunset. The oculus in the ceiling distorts your perception of the sky, focusing your attention on the shifting palette of pinks, purples, and velvety blue while you feel like you're floating on air.

Inside, architect Will Bruder deftly reconfigured an old cinema into a series of flexible galleries. The ever-changing lineup of exhibitions

© KATHLEEN BRYANT

The Old Adobe Mission was built by Mexican and Yaqui families in 1933.

has included photography by Aaron Siskind, video works by Peter Sarkisian, and "Strangely Familiar," focusing on design in everyday life. Regular events include the Friday night SMoCA Lounge and a summer program introducing kids to art through hands-on activities.

OLD ADOBE MISSION

Scottsdale's original Catholic church, built by Mexican and Yaqui Indian families who had settled in the area, celebrated its first mass in 1933. Originally called Our Lady of Perpetual Help, the Old Adobe Mission (1st St. and Brown Ave., 480/947-4331, www.olphaz.com, 10 A.M.–4 P.M. daily, Nov.–Apr., free) is being restored to serve as a space for quiet reflection. The brilliant white facade and domed bell tower of the Spanish Colonial Revival church were designed by architect R. T. "Bob" Evans to resemble the Mission of San Xavier del Bac, south of Tucson. Inside, a "truth window" (a small cutaway in the north wall) lets you view the building's original adobe bricks, made by blending local soil, straw, and water, then molded and baked in the sun. The thick adobe moderates the church's temperature in both summer and winter.

CENTRAL SCOTTSDALE AND PARADISE VALLEY
◖ Camelback Mountain

The Valley's most iconic landmark, a ridge in the profile of a kneeling camel, straddles the communities of Phoenix, Scottsdale, and Paradise Valley, luring some 300,000 hikers to its red sandstone and granite cliffs every year. Though the federal government set aside Camelback as an Indian reservation until the late 1800s, it slipped into private hands in the 1940s, and multimillion-dollar homes and posh resorts began to creep up its lower slopes. Finally, in 1968 private citizens, led by Sen. Barry Goldwater, arranged a land exchange which protected the mountain from future

ART SMART

© KATHLEEN BRYANT

Scottsdale's blue and green spire

Scottsdale's commitment to the arts makes living in and traveling around the city feel a bit like exploring an 184-square-mile outdoor gallery. As part of the city's Cultural Improvement Program, large-scale private developments dedicate 1 percent of the project's value to a public art piece, or donate that equivalent to the Downtown Cultural Trust. As a result, more than 70 public works of art now grace the city. Even freeways have an artful flair. Along Loop 101, 60-foot-tall lizards and green-and-pink cacti decorate the overpasses and sound barriers.

Just off the 101, look for the 125-foot-tall spire that Wright proposed in 1957 for Oasis, his rejected Arizona capitol design. Completed in 2004, it's the city's tallest structure. The **blue and green spire** glows at night, marking Scottsdale's western gateway at the intersection of Scottsdale Road and Frank Lloyd

Wright Boulevard. Park in the Promenade shopping center and walk around the base of the spire, where you'll see other public art displays.

You can also drive by the rusted steel fish of the **Tributary Wall** on Goldwater Boulevard between Indian School and Camelback Roads, honoring the nearby Arizona Canal and water, the desert community's most important resource.

For an hour-long stroll that will give you a close look at downtown's best-known art pieces, start at the southwest corner of Scottsdale and Camelback Roads with **The Doors,** a two-story high arrangement of three wooden doors. Step inside, and you'll discover a mirrored installation that muffles traffic noise and acts as a walk-in kaleidoscope.

Walk south to see **Paolo Soleri's steel bridge** spanning the Arizona Canal. The city's largest public art piece, it was completed in 2010 for $3.2 million. The bridge acts as a solar calendar, its brushed steel pylons marking equinox and solstice with a beam of light.

Continue walking south along the canal's west side. At Marshall Way, Herb Mignery's **Passing the Legacy** is a life-size bronze depicting a historic Pony Express rider handing off to the modern Hashknife Pony Express. Continue south on Marshall Way and turn east on Main Street to encounter another half-dozen works of art, finishing up on the grassy Scottsdale Mall with Robert Indiana's iconic **LOVE** sculpture. For a map of all downtown's public art, stop by the Scottsdale Visitors and Convention Bureau at 4343 N. Scottsdale Road, #170, or visit www.scottsdalecvb.com.

The best way to become part of Scottsdale's lively art scene? Join artists, collectors, curators, and Valley residents on the weekly Thursday night **Scottsdale ArtWalk** (www.scottsdalegalleries.com). Almost all the downtown galleries open their doors 7–9 P.M. for this popular event in the country's third-largest art market.

© KATHLEEN BRYANT

Echo Canyon Recreation Area

development. The event was marked by a visit from President Lyndon B. Johnson and Lady Bird Johnson, who walked the mountain in high heels.

The 76-acre park on Camelback's slopes preserves Sonoran Desert and dramatic rock formations where bighorn sheep once roamed. Today, it's an excellent place to see smaller Sonoran critters like spiny lizards, roadrunners, rabbits, and, yes, even rattlesnakes, without leaving the heart of the city.

At the camel's "head," the **Echo Canyon Recreation Area** (5700 N. Echo Canyon Pkwy., 602/256-3220, www.phoenix.gov/recreation/rec/parks/preserves, free) is a popular destination for rock climbers who scale **Praying Monk** rock. From a distance, the free-standing, 80-foot-high rock tower looks like the camel's eyelashes. Neither of the two steep, boulder-choked trails to the 2,704-foot summit are recommended for beginning hikers, but those with more experience will be rewarded

with 360-degree views of the Valley and the surrounding mountain ranges. Trailheads are open daily from sunrise to sunset, but parking is limited. Avoid the congestion by carpooling or catching a ride from the Park n' Hike shuttle (602/696-2883, http://parknhike.com, $5).

Cosanti

In 1947 Paolo Soleri moved from Italy to Scottsdale for a fellowship with Frank Lloyd Wright at Taliesin West. More than a half century later, Soleri is known for an organic style that merges Wright's aesthetics with an ecological focus. Cosanti (6433 E. Doubletree Ranch Rd., 480/948-6145, www.cosanti.com, 9 A.M.–5 P.M. Mon.–Sat., 11 A.M.–5 P.M. Sun., free) serves as Soleri's gallery, studio, and home, and reflects many of his theories on environmentally responsible design.

The small village includes his original subterranean "Earth House," outdoor studios, student dorms, and a performance space, set

© KATHLEEN BRYANT

At Cosanti, visitors can watch Paolo Soleri's students cast bronze windbells.

amidst terraced courtyards and shaded paths. This is also home to the foundry and ceramics studio where the popular Soleri "windbells" are created. The bronze and ceramic bells (most of them $30–60) help fund Arcosanti, an experimental artists' community 70 miles north of Phoenix. The casting process can be viewed weekday mornings.

Southwest of Scottsdale and Camelback Roads, you can walk across the 130-foot-long bridge Paolo Soleri designed to span the Arizona Canal. It's Scottsdale's largest public art piece, completed in 2010 for $3.2 million. The bridge acts as a solar calendar, its brushed steel pylons marking equinox and solstice with a beam of light. The connecting plaza has large cast concrete panels featuring Soleri's designs.

McCormick-Stillman Railroad Park

Children, train buffs, and Americana enthusiasts love McCormick-Stillman Railroad Park (7301 E. Indian Bend Rd., 480/312-2312, www.therailroadpark.com, 11 A.M.–4 P.M. weekdays, summer and weekend hours vary, free general admission, but tickets needed for entry to some attractions), a city park near Paradise Valley that has an air of the Old West about it. Formerly the ranch of Anne and Fowler McCormick (a grandson of John D. Rockefeller), it boasts a scale reproduction of a Colorado narrow-gauge railroad, a beautifully restored carousel, a general store selling hand-dipped ice cream, and an adobe-style playground. The train, donated by Anne's son, Guy Stillman, carries passengers on a one-mile loop through a desert xeriscape arboretum. (Rumor has it Walt Disney tried to buy the railroad for one of his parks.)

Antique engines and train cars dot the property, including a Pullman car that was used by every president from Herbert Hoover to Dwight Eisenhower, and the "Merci Train," one of 49 boxcars donated by France to thank Americans for their aid after World War II. The cars were originally loaded with personal belongings that ranged from wooden shoes and toys to wedding dresses and war medals from dead soldiers. Tickets are required to ride the train and carousel and to visit the museum exhibition ($2 each). The train and carousel schedules vary monthly. The park's shade ramadas make it a popular spot for picnics, concerts, and special events. Check the website for detailed schedules and event listings.

NORTH SCOTTSDALE
◖ Musical Instrument Museum

Combining graceful architecture, state-of-the art exhibits, and an intimate theater, the Musical Instrument Museum (4725 E. Mayo Blvd., 480/478-6000, www.mim.org, 9 A.M.–5 P.M. Mon.–Sat., 10 A.M.–5 P.M. Sun., till 9 P.M. Thurs.–Fri., $18 adults, $14 ages

© KATHLEEN BRYANT

Train enthusiasts will enjoy McCormick-Stillman Railroad Park.

13–19, $10 ages 4–12) is so much more than a mecca for music buffs. It's easy to while away several hours in the light-filled exhibit halls showcasing the spread of musical instruments throughout the world.

MIM's two-story entry lobby has a gallery of iconic electric guitars, as well as examples of outsize instruments hanging from the ceiling. You'll be handed a map and a set of wireless headphones before you set off to explore the geographical exhibits upstairs, where photographs, flat-panel video monitors, colorful clothing, and instruments detail musical history from 200 countries and territories. The growing collection counts 15,000 instruments, many of them works of art as well as historical treasures (such as the Chinese *paigu* drum dating to 5000 B.C.).

As you approach each display, your headphones stream samples of ethnic, folk, and tribal music, from an African village celebration to a Chinese opera or an American big-band jazz performance. Life-size dioramas recreate the process of making Indonesian brass gongs and the interior of the Martin guitar factory. Other displays focus on influential musicians, including John Lennon and the Black Eyed Peas.

Downstairs, MIM's 300-seat theater is an acoustic gem, hosting a full schedule of concerts. Past performers have included Carlos Nakai, Shawn Colvin, Doc Severinson, Junior Brown, the Leipzig Quartet, and the Mariachi Mystery Tour. Other events include lectures and workshops (including many geared to kids) on playing or making instruments like steel drums or African thumb pianos.

Exploring MIM is like traveling around the world, and you'll probably need a break after your cultural adventures. The on-site café (11 A.M.–2 P.M.) is worth a visit by itself, offering an innovative menu and views of the soothing entry courtyard. There's also a coffee shop for quick bites, and a museum store filled with

© MIM / BILL TIMMERMAN

Musical Instrument Museum

books, CDs, and instruments made by global artisans.

◖ Taliesin West

Frank Lloyd Wright's winter home, Taliesin West (12621 N. Frank Lloyd Wright Blvd., 480/860-2700, www.franklloydwright.org, 9 A.M.–4 P.M. daily, closed Tues.–Wed. July–Aug., tours $24–60), is the perfect synthesis of architecture and the desert. Wright's use of local sand, gravel, and stone (what he called "desert masonry") creates the impression that the complex of terraces and walls emerged out of the ground. He masterfully incorporated the environment by integrating indoor and outdoor spaces, diffusing harsh sunlight through canvas ceilings, and creating asymmetrical lines evocative of the surrounding mountains to stunning effect.

Wright first came to Phoenix from his Wisconsin home, Taliesin, to serve as a consultant on the Arizona Biltmore in 1927. He was so captivated by the desert landscape and light that in 1937 he used the money from his Falling Water commission to purchase 600 acres of land in the foothills of the McDowell Mountains.

Wright's "winter camp" evolved into a small cooperative community, where apprentices and students helped build a complex of structures, living on-site in communal sleeping spaces. Wright thought his students should be well-rounded, so in addition to their studies, they helped with chores and performed in the Cabaret Theater and Music Pavilion. Some chose to live in tents around the property, where they could experiment with their own designs and building techniques. This practice grew into a more formalized program of "desert shelters" that continues today, with older structures eventually being razed to make room for the designs of new students.

The insular community resembled a soap opera with its entangled affairs and desire

© RICHARD MAYER

Taliesin West was Frank Lloyd Wright's winter home and workshop.

to create a utopian society. Wright associates, some in their 70s and 80s, still live on the property today. The National Historic Landmark also serves as the headquarters of the Wright Foundation and its accredited school of architecture.

Guided tours range from a one-hour panorama tour to a three-hour behind-the-scenes exclusive. The popular 90-minute Insights tour ($32) showcases Wright's private living quarters and canvas-roofed office, where he designed many of his masterpieces, including the Guggenheim Museum and Tempe's Gammage Auditorium. Discounts are available for students, seniors, and large groups, as well as on Tuesdays and Wednesdays September–June. Call ahead or visit the website for details.

Heard Museum North

For two millennia, indigenous tribes have made their home in and around North Scottsdale's McDowell Mountains, creating a rich and varied culture. Their pottery, kachina carvings, baskets, paintings, sculpture, jewelry, and other treasures are showcased at the Heard Museum North (32633 N. Scottsdale Rd., 480/488-9817, www.heard.org/north, 10 A.M.–5 P.M. Mon.–Sat., 11 A.M.–5 P.M. Sun., summers 10 A.M.–5 P.M. Tues.–Sat., $5 adults, $2 students, children under 6 free), a satellite of Phoenix's outstanding Heard Museum.

Heard North is set in a stunning bit of desert just south of Carefree on Scottsdale Road, among the rounded rock formations that gave the neighboring Boulders Resort its name. Attend a lecture or program, join a free tour of its two galleries, and browse the museum shop featuring artwork from American Indian artisans. Stroll through the sculpture garden or have a bite in the outdoor café, where you might spot javelina, desert cottontails, or quail wandering the lightly developed neighborhood. You can walk next door to the adobe-inspired **El Pedregal** shopping center, where you'll find shops, restaurants, and the occasional festival in its open-air courtyard.

Penske Racing Museum

Car buffs will appreciate the small but very well-designed Penske Racing Museum (7125 E. Chauncey Ln., 480/538-4444, www.penskeracingmuseum.com, 8 A.M.–4 P.M. Mon.–Sat., noon–5 P.M. Sun., free), which showcases 11 of the dynasty's Indy 500 winners, plus stock cars, pace cars, engines, and memorabilia. It's located near the border between Phoenix and North Scottsdale, where luxury car dealers line Scottsdale Road. Turn 4 Café (8 A.M.–3 P.M. Mon.–Fri.), on the museum's second floor, sparkles with trophies and overlooks a test track

and obstacle course. The adjacent gift shop has Penske logo apparel and collectibles.

Scottsdale International Auto Museum

Detroit's finest are the main focus of the Scottsdale International Auto Museum (9119 E. Indian Bend Rd., 480/302-6461, www.scottsdaleinternationalautomuseum.com, 10 A.M.–6 P.M. Mon.–Fri., 10 A.M.–5 P.M. Sat., noon–5 P.M. Sun., $10 adults, kids free), located in North Scottsdale's Pavilions Shopping Center. The collection includes auction items, with exhibition space for about 150 cars, including such oddities as Howard Hughes's 1936 Lincoln Aero Mobile.

Entertainment and Events

Scottsdale's entertainment scene glitters like a gem and is just as multifaceted. Culture mavens can see what's on by checking the local calendar (www.scottsdalecvb.com) for culinary events, film festivals, art tours, and performances. Many of the splashiest events take place during "the season," January through April. But all year long, dozens of nightclubs and lounges lure the Valley's self-indulgent party set, as well as athletes and pop stars who regularly serve as tabloid fodder.

Amidst the glitz and glam, the Old West's saloons and gambling halls continue to live on. Cowboy bars attract boot-wearing regulars to their live shows and honky-tonk dance floors, and signature equestrian events hark back to Scottsdale's roots. A few miles from downtown, neighboring Indian communities host casinos with thousands of slot machines, along with a bit of old-fashioned poker.

NIGHTLIFE

With the exception of Las Vegas, no other city in the Southwest offers a nightlife with as much

glitz as Scottsdale. The downtown area boasts more than 80 after-dark options, encompassing the see-and-be-seen bars, thumping clubs, and trendy lounges. Put on your clubbing finest, as you'll be given the once-over by your fellow patrons (and more than a few bouncers). This is where the Gucci-loving set comes to preen and play.

Bars and Pubs

AZ88 (7353 Scottsdale Mall, 480/994-5576, www.az88.com, 11:30 A.M.–1:30 A.M. Mon.–Fri., 5 P.M.–1:30 A.M. Sat.–Sun.) is a great place to eat, drink, and be seen. The perennial Scottsdale favorite attracts older couples on their way to a show, as well as trendy scenesters who descend on the bar and its all-white patio after 8 P.M. The chic minimalist decor serves as backdrop for great burgers, first-class martinis, and ever-changing art installations.

The neighboring **Old Town Tavern** (7320 E. Scottsdale Mall, 480/945-2882, www.oldtowntavernaz.com, 11 A.M.–midnight Sun.–Thurs. 10 A.M.–1:30 A.M. Fri.–Sat.) is a more laid-back option. This comfortable hideaway, tucked into the grassy lawn of the Scottsdale Mall, has live music on weekends, and the cozy fireplaces on its two patios are perfect for cooler evenings. Drink specials and sociable events create a neighborly ambience.

Old West meets rock and roll at **Saddle Ranch** (4321 N. Scottsdale Rd., 480/429-2263, www.srrestaurants/scottsdale, 11 A.M.–2 A.M. Mon.–Fri., 9 A.M.–2 A.M. Sat.–Sun.). Have a meal, shoot some whiskey, saddle up on the bar's mechanical bull, or head out to the patio to cook up s'mores on the fire pit—not necessarily in that order.

Majerle's Sports Grill (4425 N. Saddlebag Tr., 480/889-9949, www.majerles.com, 11 A.M.–2 A.M. daily), the fourth Valley location owned by Phoenix Suns great Dan Majerle, is a good spot to catch a game or gear up for a night on the town. Dozens of flat-screen TVs, dazzling purple and orange neon, and a first-class menu of drinks and pub food give this downtown hangout an uptown vibe.

Like a lone cabin in the woods, **The Lodge** (4422 N. 75th St., 480/945-0828, www.scottsdalelodge.com, 11 A.M.–2 A.M. Mon.–Sat., 10:30 A.M.–2 A.M. Sun.) provides a warm retreat in the cold, glitzy forest of downtown's nightclub district. Look for the pair of hand-carved Sasquatches at the entrance, and head into the cozy watering hole to order a drink at the honey-colored "log" bar. Don't be fooled by the pool table, small arcade, and wood-paneled walls—this is still Scottsdale, so expect an upscale crowd and a respectable menu, even on Tequila Tuesdays and Fish Fry Fridays.

The latest in a string of establishments to open in this spot, **Smashboxx** (7419 E. Indian Plaza, 480/946-3510, www.smashboxxaz.com, 9 P.M.–2 A.M. Tues.–Sat.) discovered the magic formula of success—DJs, dancing, trendy drinks, beautiful people, and a video booth where clubbers can immortalize

their revelry (but probably shouldn't) on social media sites.

Sushi and karaoke are on the menu at **Geisha A Go-Go** (7150 E. 6th Ave., 480/699-0055, www.geishaagogo.com, 5 P.M.–2 A.M. Tues.–Sun.), a rock-and-roll Japanese bistro. Order Japanese beer or fruity Hello Kitty cocktails in the dark, wood-paneled bar aka "rock" garden, complete with bonsai tree and portraits of Jimi Hendrix and Jim Morrison. Groups can rent private karaoke rooms by the hour ($75 per hour for a 10-person room), and reservations are recommended.

Scottsdale's oldest tavern attracts an impressively diverse mix of club-goers, Cactus Leaguers, and old regulars. **Coach House** (7011 E. Indian School Rd., 480/990-3433, www.coachhousescottsdale.com, 6 A.M.–2 A.M. Mon.–Sat., 10 A.M.–2 A.M. Sun.) is a down-to-earth establishment, where a serious drinker can end a long night (or start the next morning) with a Bloody Mary to greet the sunrise. Don't miss it from Halloween to New Year's, when thousands of festive twinkle lights cover the walls and ceiling.

With three patio bars, **Dos Gringos** (4209 N. Craftsman Ct., 480/423-3800, www.dosgringosaz.com, 11 A.M.–2 A.M. daily) aims to replicate Mexico's casual beachside cantinas. A young crowd, cheap drinks, and tacos served till closing time lend to the spring break atmosphere. (Three additional locations in the East Valley are proof this formula works.)

On Scottsdale's Waterfront, **Olive & Ivy** (7135 E. Camelback Rd., 480/751-2200, 11 A.M.–midnight Sun.–Thurs., 11 A.M.–1 A.M. Fri.–Sat.) is part of the Fox restaurant empire. With a Cali-Med menu, chic decor, and a large outdoor lounge overlooking the Arizona Canal, this is the place to see Scottsdale's professional set at play. The people-watching hits its prime at 10 P.M., when a steady stream of styled 30- and 40-somethings sidle up to the bar for specialty margaritas and martinis.

Lounges and Wine Bars

Head for Paradise Valley's **Jade Bar** (5700 E. McDonald Dr., 480/948-2100, 10 A.M.–2 A.M. daily) early in the evening, when you can order delicious small plates and signature cocktails at happy hour prices while watching sunset colors bathe Mummy Mountain. Sanctuary Camelback Mountain Resort & Spa hosts this sleek and sexy alternative to the gaudy lounges of Old Town.

If you're looking for great wine and a more adult crowd, **Kazimierz World Wine Bar** (7137 E. Stetson Dr., 480/946-3004, http://kazbar. net, 6 P.M.–2 A.M. daily) provides an unpretentious retreat for friends or a romantic date. Oenophiles will appreciate the list of more than 2,000 wines from around the world, which has earned regular recognition from *Wine Spectator* magazine for its depth and value. Curl up on one of the plush sofas and pair an Arizona varietal with one of the Egyptian flatbreads or imported cheeses. Be forewarned: "Kazbar" isn't easy to find. Walk down the outdoor corridor beneath the Stetson Plaza sign; the entrance is in back of the building.

The shady, hidden patio at **5th and Wine** (7051 E. 5th Ave., 480/699-8001, www.5thandwine.com, 11 A.M.–11 P.M. daily, till 9 P.M. Sun.) is a relaxed, casual spot for sipping something red or white. Located in the heart of Old Town and frequented by locals as well as visitors, this restaurant and wine bar offers a lengthy list of wines and daily specials, with live music on weekends.

Shade (7277 E. Camelback Rd., 602/405-0099, 11 A.M.–midnight daily, later on weekends) is Scottsdale at its $15 martini–loving, Louis Vuitton handbag–carrying trendiest. On any given evening at this über-glam lounge at the W Scottsdale Hotel, you could be crashing some Hollywood celebrity's birthday party or the debut of a Valley resident on a reality TV show. If you can get past the bouncers, you'll be treated to some prime people-watching. Step

outside to experience Shade's poolside sibling **Sunset Beach,** a rooftop "beach bar" with a stretch of white sand, cabanas, fire pits, and spectacular views of the city.

Don't let the name scare you: **Terroir** (7001 N. Scottsdale Rd., 480/922-3470, www.terroirwinepub.com, 11 A.M.–10 P.M. Mon.–Thurs., 11 A.M.–11 P.M. Fri.–Sat., 3–10 P.M. Sun.) is a bike-friendly, dog-friendly, and people-friendly wine pub near Paradise Valley's McCormick-Stillman Railroad Park. In wine-speak, *terroir* refers to regional uniqueness, from the French *terre,* for earth. This down-to-earth neighborhood pub has a rotating wine list and a serious approach to wine.

Dance Clubs and Live Music

Less pompous than some of Scottsdale's other nightclubs, downtown's **Martini Ranch** (7295 E. Stetson Dr., 480/970-0500, http://martinranchaz.net, 8 P.M.–2 A.M. Thurs.–Sun.) has become a solid venue for national acts looking for an intimate place to perform. With two bars downstairs, a patio, and an upscale dance lounge upstairs, Martini Ranch attracts a diverse crowd. Hours vary for special events and concerts; call or check the website for tickets or to reserve VIP seating in the Shaker Lounge.

Downtown's **Red Revolver Lounge** (7316 E. Stetson Dr., 480/946-2005, http://redrevolverlounge.com, 8 P.M.–2 A.M. Thurs.–Sat.) adds a touch of steampunk flair to Scottsdale high style. The roomy wood-floored dancehall, packed on weekends, features DJs remixing Top 40, electronica, and 1980s rock.

You'll find the beating, cologne-scented heart of the city's nightlife scene at **Axis/Radius** (7340 E. Indian Plaza, 480/970-1112, www.axis-radius.com, 10 P.M.–2 A.M. Thurs.–Fri., 9 P.M.–2 A.M. Sat.). These Siamese twin clubs share beautiful young people, large patios, and expensive drinks. A glass catwalk connects Axis, featuring Top 40 and dance music, with Radius, where DJs spin hip-hop and other sounds.

A lack of liquor doesn't keep the patrons of **Afterlife** (4282 N. Drinkwater Blvd., 480/264-8300, 10 P.M.–4 A.M. Fri.–Sat.) from having a wild time; it just means that the party can last longer. This all-ages, after-hours club has go-go girls, a hookah lounge, a patio arcade, two dance floors with Top 40 tunes and DJs, and energy drinks to help you keep up with all the action.

Listen for the strumming guitars and clacking castanets on the Scottsdale Mall. **Pepin** (7363 E. Scottsdale Mall, 480/990-9026, www.pepinrestaurant.com, 4 P.M.–2 A.M. Tues.–Sun.) presents live flamenco shows Friday and Saturday evenings during dinner, then clears space for open Latin dancing, which begins at 10 P.M. on Fridays and Saturdays, and at 9 P.M. on Sundays.

The burlesque craze hit Scottsdale a few years ago with the opening of **Jackrabbit Lounge** (4280 N. Drinkwater Blvd., 480/429-4494, www.jackrabbitaz.com, 9 P.M.–2 A.M. Thurs.–Sat.). Today, the spray-on-tan crowd still enjoys the nightly—and quite tame—strip-tease shows and musical acts. Should things get a little too warm inside, head out to the patio, which has hosted the likes of Britney Spears and Arizona Cardinal Matt Leinart.

Three times a week, **Roxy Lounge** (7443 E. Sixth Ave., 480/970-1222, www.roxyaz.com, variable hours) hosts live shows by local and national bands, with ticket prices ranging from $5 to $30, depending on who's taking the stage. All shows are 21 and over, and doors usually open at 8 P.M. Check the website for tickets and information.

You don't have to wear skinny jeans, retro-hip glasses, or punk threads to appreciate **The Rogue** (423 N. Scottsdale Rd., 480/947-3580, 8 A.M.–2 A.M. Mon.–Thurs., 6 A.M.–2 A.M. Fri.–Sat., 10 A.M.–2 A.M. Sun.). This low-key bar in South Scottsdale attracts indie-rock fans

for live performances. When there's no band, DJs spin the likes of The Cure, Pat Benatar, and The Smiths. Booths surround a small dance floor for ease of people-watching, and the graffiti-covered bathrooms are infamous.

Cowboy Bars and Saloons

An original stagecoach stop between Fort McDowell and Phoenix, **Greasewood Flat** (27375 N. Alma School Pkwy., 480/585-9430, http://greasewoodflat.net, 11 A.M.–11 P.M. Sun.–Thurs., 11 A.M.–midnight Fri.–Sat.) is a North Scottsdale landmark, serving up cold beers and barbecue grub for years. The popular open-air bar is the perfect place to grab a drink and chat at the picnic tables with bikers, real-life cowboys, and well-to-do locals. Dance to live music under the stars on the weekend, or bundle up next to one of the campfires on cool evenings.

You'll find live country music every night, a busy dance floor, and a superb patio at the **Handlebar-J Restaurant and Saloon** (7116 E. Becker Lane, 480/948-0110, www.handlebarj.com, 4 P.M.–2 A.M. Mon.–Sat., 5 P.M.–2 A.M. Sun.). Loretta Lynn and Lyle Lovett have been known to pop in, and there are free dance lessons on Tuesday and Wednesday nights.

Scottsdale's oldest saloon is tucked into a landmarked historic building in Old Town. The **Rusty Spur Saloon** (7245 E. Main St., 480/425-7787, http://rustyspursaloon.com, 11 A.M.–2 A.M. daily) hosts live entertainment midday through evening, encompassing country, rockabilly, blues, and roots music. The saloon was once a bank—the original vault now stores alcohol.

CASINOS

Neighbored by two Indian reservations, Scottsdale is within easy access of three big casinos, offering gaming 24 hours a day, along with entertainment and dining options and resort accommodations.

Operated by the Salt River Pima–Maricopa Indian Community, **Casino Arizona** (480/850-7777, www.casinoaz.com) has two locations just off Highway 101 (Loop 101). **Casino Arizona at Salt River** (Highway 101 and McKellips Rd.) has more than a thousand slot machines in addition to two blackjack rooms and a keno parlor. For a break from the din of the casino, the 250-seat theater regularly books national acts, and its Showstoppers Live event/show features impersonations of classic music acts like Elvis, Madonna, and The Four Tops.

Follow Lady Luck less than 10 minutes up the road for the casino's sister property **Talking Stick Resort** (Highway 101 and Indian Bend Rd.). Its 240,000-square-foot casino boasts more than 700 slots, 50-plus table games, keno, and a poker room with 47 nonsmoking tables. Live entertainment, lounges, and a half-dozen restaurants round out this four-star golf resort and spa. The resort's elegant **Orange Sky** restaurant, located 15 stories up, has knockout views.

The **Fort McDowell Casino** (10424 N. Fort McDowell Rd., 480/837-1424, www.fortmcdowellcasino.com), operated by the Fort McDowell Yavapai Nation, is a little bit farther out of town. Take Shea Boulevard 20 minutes east to State Route 87 (Beeline Highway) toward the town of Fountain Hills, and turn left on Fort McDowell Road. More than 800 gaming machines, 55 table and poker games, live keno, and a 1,700-seat bingo hall will keep gamblers busy.

PERFORMING ARTS

The **Scottsdale Center for the Performing Arts** (7380 E. 2nd St., 480/994-2787, www.scottsdaleperformingarts.org) showcases a host of live events, from theater and comedy to music and dancing. The SCA's white Modernist pavilion and its stages have featured a diverse roster of touring acts, like Ravi Shankar, Clint Black, and the Capitol Steps. Larger shows are held at its **Virginia G. Piper Theater** (7380 E. 2nd St., 480/994-2787), but you'll also find touring acts and local performers at **Stage 2.**

The open-air **amphitheater** (75th St. and Main St., 480/994-ARTS, www.scottsdaleperformingarts.org), just outside SCA on Scottsdale Mall's grassy lawn, provides a lovely setting for concerts. Be sure to catch **Native Trails,** free performances by Native American musicians, singers, and dancers, held at noon Thursdays and Saturdays, mid-January through mid-April.

For an evening of easygoing entertainment, take in a popular musical or comedy at **Desert Stages Theater** (4720 N. Scottsdale Rd., 480/483-1664, desertstages.org). Recent productions have included *The Odd Couple, Rent, Footloose,* and *Joseph and the Amazing Technicolor Dreamcoat.* Three stages mean productions can alternate, and performances often include students from Desert Stages' theater academy and summer camp. Buy tickets in advance to avoid disappointment; shows by this award-winning company often sell out quickly.

For 50 years, the **Louise Lincoln Kerr Cultural Center** (6110 N. Scottsdale Rd., 480/596-2660, www.asukerr.com) has served as an artist colony for emerging musicians, artists, and writers. Kerr's beautifully maintained adobe home and guesthouses, listed on the National Register of Historic Places, provide an intimate setting for jazz, blues, classical, and world music, as well as storytelling and theater.

FESTIVALS AND EVENTS

The near-perfect weather from autumn through spring makes it easy to find a fun outdoor festival. The hard part is choosing which one.

January

The **Barrett-Jackson Auto Auction** (16601 N. Pima Rd., 480/663-6255, www.barrett-jackson.com, day passes at gate $10–55 with

SCOTTSDALE AND VICINITY

SCOTTSDALE AND VICINITY

© KATHLEEN BRYANT

Car shows and auctions cruise into town in January.

discounts on advance purchase), one of the finest car collector events in the world, kicks off the social calendar. The weeklong extravaganza at the WestWorld complex in North Scottsdale showcases extraordinary cars, as well as art, fashion, and jewelry, drawing nearly a quarter-million attendees and, in 2012, generating a stunning $92 million in sales...and it's only one of a half-dozen auctions taking place during Scottsdale's "car month," a tradition for more than 40 years.

The annual **Celebration of Fine Art** (southeast corner of Scottsdale Rd. and Mayo Blvd., 480/443-7695, www.celebrateart.com, $10 adult, children under 12 free) runs January through March, when big white tents dot the desert near Hayden Road and Loop 101, sheltering an extensive collection of Western and contemporary paintings, sculptures, glass, ceramics, and jewelry. Some 100 artists set up temporary studios, inviting browsers and buyers to watch them work.

February

February is marked by Scottsdale's most distinctive equestrian traditions, stretching back for 60 years. The **Parada del Sol Rodeo** (various venues, 480/990-3179, www.paradadelsol. us) celebrates Western culture with a Hashknife Pony Express ride, rodeo and bull-riding, and the "World's Largest Horsedrawn Parade" in Old Town, a monthlong series of colorful events that benefit local charities.

Mid-month, the **Scottsdale Arabian Horse Show** (16601 N. Pima Rd., 480/515-1500, www.scottsdaleshow.com, $7–25) gathers some 2,000 Arabian horses at WestWorld for 10 days of competitions, demonstrations, and seminars.

March

Named one of the nation's top art festivals by *American Style* magazine, the three-day **Scottsdale Arts Festival** (3939 N. Drinkwater Blvd., 480/499-8587, www.scottsdaleartsfestival.org, $5–12, children under 12 free) in early

March invites 200 jury-selected artists to the Scottsdale Mall for entertainment, artist demonstrations, live music, and exhibitions galore.

Formerly a popular fall event drawing emerging and national designers, **Scottsdale Fashion Week** (www.scottsdalefashionweek.com) is moving to spring after a hiatus to refashion its lineup of glamorous exhibitors, lounges, and shows. The multi-day event includes a community night showcasing local talent. General admission runs around $20, with individual shows priced separately.

April

Burger battles, epicurean expos, chocolate and wine tastings, and a brew fest are a few of the events that draw celebrity chefs and 40,000 hungry visitors to the **Scottsdale Culinary Festival** (3939 N. Drinkwater Blvd., 480/945-7193, www.scottsdalefest.org). Events take place at various venues around town over five days, culminating with the **Great Arizona Picnic** held on the grassy lawns of the Scottsdale Mall.

The **McDowell Mountain Music Festival** (602/343-0453, www.mmmf.net, $25–150) brings a weekend lineup of indie, folk, and world music to North Scottsdale in mid-April. Past performers have included Big Head Todd and the Monsters, Los Lonely Boys, and Burning Spear.

May-September

Spring ends, at least unofficially, with the Valley's first 100-degree day, usually sometime in late April or early May. Snowbirds return to the Midwest or East, large festivals dwindle, and galleries and arts organizations tighten their schedules. Events become more hometown-focused, and many are family-friendly. It's a great time to get out and meet the locals while enjoying the soft warmth of a summer evening.

Free outdoor concerts are staged at **McCormick-Stillman Railroad Park** (7301 E. Indian Bend Rd., 480/312-2312, www.therailroadpark.com), **Kierland Commons** (15205 N. Kierland Blvd., 480/348-1577, www.kierlandcommons.com), the **Promenade** (Frank Lloyd Wright Blvd. and Scottsdale Rd. 480/385-2820, http://scottsdalepromenade.com), and other locations, while the cool interiors of the **Musical Instrument Museum** (480/478-6000, www.mim.org) host an impressive concert lineup throughout summer months.

"Dive-in" movies are popular at local resorts, such as **Montelucia** (888/627-3010, www.montelucia.com) and the **Four Seasons** (480/515-5700, www.fourseasons.com/scottsdale). The **Hotel Valley Ho** (480/248-2000, www.hotelvalleyho.com) and **Saguaro Scottsdale** (480/308-1100, www.jvdhotels.com) host summertime pool parties.

On Saturday mornings, the **farmers market** (623/848-1234) continues in Old Town, with local growers offering everything from fresh organic produce to tamales, preserves, and picadillo (a savory and sometimes sweet filling for tacos, empanadas, etc.).

Scottsdale's free Thursday night **ArtWalk** (www.scottsdalegalleries.com) also extends through summer, with one "spectacular" evening in July featuring live music, wine tasting, and prizes. Another midsummer art event is the annual **Family Night** at the Scottsdale Contemporary Museum of Art (480/874-4642, www.smoca.org, reservation required), which combines an art tour, hands-on activities, and live music, followed by a splash in the fountain.

On the weekend of the Fourth, Salt River Fields at Talking Stick (7555 N. Pima Rd., 480/270-5000, www.saltriverfields.com) hosts the **Independence Day Music Festival** ($25–90) featuring an evening of performances (past headliners have included Blake Shelton and Darius Rucker), followed by fireworks.

Marking the beginning and end of summer, **Arizona Restaurant Week** (602/307-9134, www.arizonarestaurantweek.com) is especially popular with locals on the lookout for the next foodster favorite. In late May and mid-September, dozens of Valley restaurants offer three-course, prix fixe dinners for $30 or $40 per person, including some of Scottsdale's finest, such as Cowboy Ciao, Pure, and Zinc Bistro.

October–December

Cooler weather in October marks a return to the busy social calendar. The small but good **Scottsdale International Film Festival** (866/811-4111, www.scottsdalefilmfestival.com, single ticket $10) attracts audiences to Harkins Shea 14 Theater (7453 E. Shea Blvd.,

800/948-6555), for five days of global dramas, comedies, and documentaries.

At the end of October, Thunderbird Artists (480/837-5637, www.thunderbirdartists.com) launch their season of **fine art and wine festivals** at various locations, including the Scottsdale Waterfront, Fountain Hills, and Carefree. The last two weekends in November, the delightful **Hidden in the Hills Studio Tour** (480/575-6624, www.sonoranartsleague.com) takes you through some of the area's most secluded neighborhoods in North Scottsdale, Carefree, and Cave Creek as you drive to 45 artists' home studios to view their work.

Shopping

In Scottsdale, shopping approaches an art form. Luxury brands, Native American crafts and jewelry, authentic cowboy boots and hats—find it all in this city's cool boutiques and palatial malls. Also home to the country's third-largest art market, Scottsdale has more than 100 galleries featuring traditional Southwestern pieces as well as cutting-edge, contemporary installations that blend painting, sculpture, glass, and ceramics.

To find those only-in-Arizona souvenirs, spend some time browsing downtown shops and galleries. If you're in need of an air-conditioned getaway in the summer, the colossal Scottsdale Fashion Square mall has 250 stores to keep your credit cards busy. The majority of the city's retail options are found at malls and open-air shopping centers along Scottsdale Road.

SHOPPING CENTERS AND DISTRICTS
Old Town

Park your car at the old hitching posts and make your way down the covered sidewalks.

Next to the Scottsdale Civic Center Mall, **Bischoff's at the Park** (3925 N. Brown Ave., 480/946-6155, www.bischoffsouthwestart.com, 10 A.M.–5:30 P.M. daily) is a terrific place to pick up Southwestern souvenirs, including books, rugs, Hopi kachina dolls, and Pima baskets and pottery. The store's brick walls and high ceilings originally housed a bank, which explains why Bischoff's doesn't feel as touristy as some of the other shopping options in Old Town. Pick up a few postcards inside, and head out to the charming shaded courtyard to jot down a few notes to friends.

The larger **Bischoff's Shades of the West** (7247 E. Main St., 480/945-3289, http://shadesofthewest.com, 9 A.M.–9 P.M. Mon.–Fri., 9 A.M.–8 P.M. Sat., 9 A.M.–7 P.M. Sun.) offers "everything needed to transform a bunkhouse into a Southwestern palace," from Mexican glasses and blankets to bronze hardware.

You can smell the leather when you walk through the door of **Saba's** (7254 E. Main St., 480/949-7404, www.sabas.com, 10 A.M.–7 P.M. Mon.–Fri., 10 A.M.–6 P.M. Sat., noon–5 P.M. Sun.). "Arizona's Original Western Store"

STRIP SEARCH

Travelers to Phoenix and Scottsdale at some point will visit the ubiquitous strip shopping centers that line streets throughout the Valley. Like many cities in the West, Phoenix came of age after the birth of the automobile and, as a result, the city's postwar building boom created a city tailor-made to serve cars and drivers.

Belying their bland facades, strip malls are frequently home to some of the city's most noteworthy mom-and-pop businesses, from ethnic restaurants to yoga studios and vintage shops.

Hilton Village (6149 N. Scottsdale Rd.), near Paradise Valley, for example, features popular restaurants, trendy boutiques and salons, and even a gourmet cupcake shop. The delightful Terroir wine pub is tucked inside **Seville Center** (7001 N. Scottsdale Rd.). And you'll find delicious vegetarian Vietnamese dishes at **Fresh Mint** in Thunderbird Square (13802 N. Scottsdale Rd.). Looking behind plain-Jane wrappers to uncover hidden gems like these is part of the fun of exploring this sprawling metro area.

has grown considerably since David Saba, a Lebanese immigrant, opened his first trading post in 1927. You'll still find Saba family members behind the counters selling belt buckles and hats to longtime customers. Check out the wall of boots and children's fringe leather vests at the sister store across the street at (3965 N. Brown Ave., 480/947-7664, same hours). The Saba family operates six additional stores around the Valley, including ones in Cave Creek and the Shea Corridor (7231 E. Shea, 480/948-9201).

It seems like you can't turn a corner in Old Town without bumping into one of the **Gilbert Ortega Galleries,** mammoth emporiums filled with Navajo rugs, pottery, and equestrian art in a range of prices. If you're looking for the perfect Southwestern souvenir, you'll find something at **Gilbert Ortega Gallery & Museum** (3925 N. Scottsdale Rd., 480/990-1808, 10 A.M.–6 P.M. Sun.–Tues., 10 A.M.–9 P.M. Wed.–Sat.). For native silver and turquoise, browse the wide selection at **Gilbert Ortega Gallery of Fine Jewelry** (7237 E. Main, 480/990-0788).

Civil War buffs and Old West admirers should stop in at **Guidon Books** (7109 E. 2nd St., 480/945-8811, www.guidon.com, 10 A.M.–5 P.M. Mon.–Sat.). This tiny bookstore with new and out-of-print specialty titles about

Western America and the Civil War. Peruse the shelves, where you'll find categories that range from women of the West and Union generals to Indian crafts and Southwest furniture.

Between its Scottsdale store, catalog, and website, **The Poisoned Pen** (4014 N. Goldwater Blvd., 480/947-2974, http://poisonedpen.com, 10 A.M.–7 P.M. Mon.–Fri., 10 A.M.–6 P.M. Sat., noon–5 P.M. Sun.) is the world's largest bookstore specializing in mysteries, crime, and espionage. Owner Barbara Peters says it comes down to one simple tenet: "You have to know your customers." In addition to the dozens of signed and first edition mysteries, the bookstore hosts some 200 events a year.

Scottsdale Fashion Square

Shoppers, welcome to your temple. The nearly two-million-square-foot Scottsdale Fashion Square (Camelback Rd. and Scottsdale Rd., downtown, 480/941-2140, 10 A.M.–9 P.M. Mon.–Sat., 11 A.M.–6 P.M. Sun.) is one of the country's best shopping centers. High-end department stores like Nordstrom, Neiman Marcus, and a new Barneys New York anchor the vast air-conditioned mega-mall, and the impressive list of luxe boutiques should send any fashionista's heart racing: Burberry, Kate Spade, Gucci, Louis Vuitton, Tiffany and Co., Cartier, and Bottega Veneta, just to name-drop a few. Shoppers will also find the mall standbys like Banana Republic and Anthropologie, along with local shops like HUB Clothing, a hipster favorite selling trendy jeans, cool jackets, and one-of-a-kind tees.

SouthBridge

This new complex of "mix-and-mingle-style" shops and restaurants along the Arizona Canal brought an ambitious concept to Scottsdale: a chain-free, walkable "urban village." SouthBridge's retail shops, collectively known as **The Mix** (5th Ave. and Stetson Dr., downtown), blend into a dozen interconnected boutiques that neatly fall into four concepts: Nest (home furnishings), Live (fashion), Cherish and Treasure (beauty and treats), and Play (sporting goods and memorabilia).

Stop in at **Studio Joy Li** (480/970-1043, www.joyli.net) to see this Scottsdale designer's latest collections, which incorporate high-quality fabrics in sleek, comfortable styles that bridge trendy and timeless. For the fashionable little one, **Garage: A Body Shop & Filling Station** (480/556-6900, 10 A.M.–7 P.M. Mon.–Fri., 10 A.M.–8 P.M. Sat., 11 A.M.–4 P.M. Sun.) mixes rock-and-roll style with high-end designers like Little Marc by Marc Jacobs and Sonia Rykiel. **Nestldown** (480/941-5599, www.nestledownlinens.com, 10 A.M.–6 P.M. Mon.–Sat., noon–5 P.M. Sun.) stocks luxury European linens that can be monogrammed, as well as bath accessories, baby items, and garden products.

Pampered doggies that ride in designer handbags go to **Oh My Dog! Boutique + Spa** (480/874-1200, www.ohmydogboutique.com, 10 A.M.–6 P.M. Mon.–Sat.) for organic treats or something couture from lines such as Kwigy-bo or Poochie Beverly Hills dog furniture. OMD's spa has a glass window that allows pet owners to watch their fur-babies get deep conditioning massages and custom hairstyles.

The Borgata and Hilton Village

The turrets and cobblestone walkways of The Borgata (6166 N. Scottsdale Rd., 602/953-6538, www.borgata.com, 10 A.M.–7 P.M. Mon.–Sat., noon–6 P.M. Sun.), located a couple miles north of Old Town, are inspired by a Tuscan hillside town. The open-air mall is home to 30 upscale shops, galleries, and restaurants. It's a convenient option for visitors staying in Paradise Valley, and one less overwhelming than bustling Fashion Square.

The ecofriendly Twig & Twill Boutique showcases organic maternity wear, children's apparel, and linens, many of which support environmental causes, while small resort-wear boutiques like Fresh Produce, The Beach House Swimwear, and Lilly Pulitzer's Pink Paradise round out the retail offerings. There's live jazz on Friday evenings and occasional weekend events. Across Scottsdale Road, the Hilton Village shops include several eateries, services, and boutiques, such as Gotta Have It! and Mackie's Parlour for pets.

Kierland Commons

The perfectly manicured Kierland Commons (Greenway Pkwy. and Scottsdale Rd., North Scottsdale, 480/348-1577, www.kierland-commons.com, 10 A.M.–9 P.M. Mon.–Sat., noon–6 P.M. Sun.) was the first mall in the Valley to kick off the "urban village" concept, updating the idea of small-town Main Street. Park streetside and stroll the complex's sidewalks, small gardens, and water fountains, where you'll see children playing on warm afternoons.

Restaurants, bars, and big-name chains like J. Crew, Juicy Couture, and French Connection set up shop on the ground floor, while residents live upstairs in steel-and-glass condos. Pop into Hemingway's Cigar Boutique for a quality smoke or sample something at Oils & Olives, featuring local products from the Queen Creek Olive Mill.

El Pedregal

The Moroccan-style El Pedregal (Scottsdale Rd. and Carefree Hwy., North Scottsdale, 480/488-1072, www.elpedregal.com, 10 A.M.–5:30 P.M. Mon.–Sat., noon–5 P.M. Sun.) fits nicely into the beautiful desert surroundings near Carefree. The open-air shopping center features 30 upscale restaurants, galleries, and stores, including boutiques for men's and women's resort wear, leather goods, lingerie, and jewelry. The plaza's outdoor amphitheater serves as a frequent venue for concerts, live theater, dances, and charity events.

Scottsdale's downtown shopping districts include more than 100 galleries.

Scottsdale Quarter

North Scottsdale's newest village shopping experience is Scottsdale Quarter (15279 N. Scottsdale Rd. 480/270-8123, www.scottsdalequarter.com, 10 A.M.–8 P.M. Mon.–Thurs., 10 A.M.–9 P.M. Fri.–Sat., noon–6 P.M. Sun.), located across Scottsdale Road from Kierland Commons. The vibe here is a bit more sleek, but the idea is the same: gathering upscale shopping and dining options in a walkable village-within-a-city. With 45 shops, from the Apple Store to the Republic of Couture, as well as a dozen restaurants, a yoga studio, and a multiplex, there's something here for everyone. Resort-wear shoppers will find lululemon and Beach Bunny Swimwear among such retail powerhouses as Nike, Gap, H&M, and Sephora. Local favorite **Elan** (480/941-5575, http://azelanstyle.com) specializes in new designers from around the world, and offers an in-house jewelry line.

◖ Downtown Arts Districts

Scottsdale's 100-plus art galleries are among the city's biggest attractions and an important economic force. (Only New York and Santa Fe can tout larger art markets.) Western and Native American art once dominated the scene, but now a host of contemporary galleries showcase some of the art world's biggest names as well as emerging talent. Most of the city's galleries are clustered in the Marshall Way, 5th Avenue, and Main Street arts districts, located just west of Scottsdale Road in downtown. You can expect shorter hours at galleries in the summer, so be sure to call ahead for times.

The best way to become a part of the local art scene—at least for an evening—is to join the weekly Thursday night **Scottsdale ArtWalk** (www.scottsdalegalleries.com). Socialize with artists, collectors, curators, and Valley residents 7–9 P.M., when almost all downtown galleries open their doors for the popular event.

You can also join **Ultimate Art and Cultural Tours** (6646 E. Monterosa, 480/634-6850, www.ultimatearttours.com) for a two-hour guided trolley tour of Scottsdale's arts district (free, reservations required). Or ask owner Ace Bailey to design a custom itinerary that may include artist studio visits, demonstrations by Native American artisans, backstage theater tours, or architectural icons (prices vary).

© KATHLEEN BRYANT

SCOTTSDALE AND VICINITY

CONTEMPORARY GALLERIES

The beautifully curated paintings, sculptures, photographs, and drawings at **Bentley Gallery** (4161 N. Marshall Way, 480/946-6060, www. bentleygallery.com, 9:30 A.M.–5:30 P.M. Tues.– Sat.) make it one of Scottsdale's best contemporary art galleries. Bentley's impressive roster of established artists includes Richard Serra, Dominique Blain, and Daniel Brice.

The polished concrete floors, high ceilings, and natural light make **Calvin Charles Gallery** (4201 N. Marshall Way, 480/421-1818, www. calvincharlesgallery.com, 10 A.M.–6 P.M. Mon.– Sat.) a terrific spot to view contemporary works by mid-career and emerging artists. Collectors will find modern works from China, Vietnam, and Japan, as well as Europe and the Americas. A smattering of Asian antiques rounds out the gallery, and the rooftop sculpture terrace offers a nice view of Camelback Mountain.

Bonner David (7040 Main St., 480/941-8500, www.bonnerdavid.com, 10 A.M.–5:30 P.M. Mon.–Sat.), one of Scottsdale's largest galleries, has a children's studio where kids can play while adults browse a collection of figurative, contemporary, and romantic sculpture and paintings, including Ron Burns's whimsical animal portraits and the Nyanhongo family's sculptures, inspired by their Shona heritage.

Gebert Contemporary (7160 E. Main St., 480/429-0711, www.gebertartaz.com, 10 A.M.–5 P.M. Mon.–Fri., 11 A.M.–5 P.M. Sat.) specializes in abstract painting and sculpture by contemporary artists, gracefully displayed in the gallery's minimalist spaces.

Lisa Sette Gallery (4142 N. Marshall Way, 480/990-7342, www.lisasettegallery.com, 10 A.M.–5 P.M. Tues.–Fri., noon–5 P.M. Sat.) always puts on a good show, with more than a half-dozen featured exhibits each year. The thoughtful artworks, often with a political or social commentary, include painting, sculpture, photography, and mixed-media installation. Be sure to check out Matthew Moore's photographs of suburban sprawl, James Turrell's fascination with Roden Crater, and William Wegman's quirky dog portraits.

If you don't have the deep pockets to invest in a piece of art, **Art One** (4130 N. Marshall Way, 480/946-5076, www.artonegalleryinc. com, 10 A.M.–5:30 P.M. Mon.–Sat.) showcases reasonably priced paintings and sculpture by young and emerging artists, including local students. The regularly changing lineup can be a fun way to dip your toes into the art world.

Another place to hunt for art bargains is in North Scottsdale's **Work of Artists** (7000 E. Mayo Blvd., 480/596-0304, www. workofartists.com, 10 A.M.–6 P.M. Mon.–Sat., 11 A.M.–5 P.M. Sun.), a 6,000-square-foot gallery showcasing mostly local work, in various styles and media, from oils and sculptures to kaleidoscopes and clocks.

At Kierland Commons, the **Rock Star Gallery** (15220 N. Scottsdale Rd., 480/275-4501, http://rockstargallery.net, 10 A.M.–9 P.M. Mon.–Sat., noon–5 P.M. Sun.) features paintings and drawings by Paul McCartney, Janis Joplin, Jimi Hendrix, and other musicians, as well as memorabilia from signed guitars to album art.

COWBOY, NATIVE AMERICAN, AND SOUTHWESTERN GALLERIES

Representing more than 100 artists, **The Legacy Gallery** (7178 Main St., 480/945-1113, www.legacygallery.com, 10 A.M.–5:30 P.M. Mon.–Sat., 11 A.M.–5 P.M. Sun.) is one of Scottsdale's largest Southwestern art galleries. The Native American portraits, Western landscapes, romantic pastels, and life-size bronze sculptures include works by Taos Art Colony painters of the early 20th century and Cowboy Artists of America founding member Joe Beeler.

Trailside Galleries (7330 Scottsdale Mall, 480/945-7751, www.trailsidegalleries.com, 10 A.M.–5:30 P.M. Mon.–Sat.) offers classic Western art, with colorful paintings of wildlife, traditional scenes of the Old West, and expansive landscapes, as well as an extensive collection of bronze sculpture. Prix de West winner Curt Walters's impressionistic landscapes are a highlight.

See the work of Contemporary American Realists and Russian Impressionists at **Overland Gallery** (7155 E. Main St., 480/947-1934, www.overlandgallery.com, 10 A.M.–5 P.M. Mon.–Sat.). Ed Mell's bold paintings and sculptures portray traditional subjects in an angular, contemporary style, and Gary Ernest Smith's minimalist landscapes convey the peacefulness of the West's vast spaces.

The oldest major fine art gallery in the West, **Biltmore Galleries** (7113 E. Main St., 480/947-5975, www.biltmoregalleries.com, 10 A.M.–5 P.M. Mon.–Sat.) specializes in 19th- and 20th-century American artists. The impressionistic cowboy paintings, blazing sunsets, and barren landscapes are evocative of another era, and Western art aficionados may spot a small block print by Gustave Baumann or oils by Albert Bierstadt among the changing inventory.

Sports and Recreation

Urban delights aren't all Scottsdale has to offer. Its spectacular desert setting makes it an ideal place to get out and explore nature. Though the Sonoran Desert receives an average of only seven inches of rain per year, its various plants and animals make it one of the most diverse ecosystems on Earth. The best way to truly appreciate the city's sweeping desert landscapes and color-saturated sunsets is by experiencing them firsthand—whether on bike, on foot, on a raft, or on the links. Just be sure to drink lots of water, especially in the summer. Many visitors are easily caught off-guard by the heat and arid climate.

ADVENTURE TOURS

When summertime temperatures soar, most animals in the Sonoran Desert go nocturnal. Catch a glimpse of this secret world by donning night-vision goggles with **Stellar Adventures** (877/878-3552, www.stellaradventures.com). This company offers a variety of ways to get out in the desert, from ATV rentals ($170 for three hours) and Blazer tours ($100 adult, $80 child)

of mining ghost towns and ancient Native American ruins to "advanced" Hummer tours ($170) that show off the rock-hopping, wall-climbing capabilities of these military vehicles. Stargazing, target shooting, and team-building round out the options.

Thanks to the Southwest's minimal "light pollution," Arizona's skies twinkle with some of the best stargazing in the country. Venture into the desert with astronomers to survey the heavens with the aid of state-of-the-art telescopes and constellation charts. **Sky Jewels** (602/294-6775, www.gemland.com) features one- and two-hour astronomy tours, with some Scottsdale resorts (including The Boulders, Camelback Inn, and The Four Seasons) offering the course for guests.

For the next step in Jeep safaris, try driving your own TOMCAR off-road vehicle with **Desert Wolf Tours** (877/613-9653, www.desertwolftours.com, $145 adult, $87 child). A cross between an ATV and a baby Hummer, the golf cart–size vehicles were originally developed for the Israeli Defense Forces, but they'll take you

MEET THE DESERT AFTER DARK

Humans can learn a lot by observing the desert's creatures. Many are nocturnal or crepuscular—active at the cooler hours around dawn and twilight. Those who visit the Valley of the Sun during one of its infamous summers, when daytime temperatures soar into the hundred-teens, can make like a lizard to beat the heat:

Hike or golf in the early morning. Spend the hot afternoons exploring museums, shopping at Fashion Square, or taking a poolside siesta at a resort spa. Venture out again at golden hour, that magical time before sunset when the desert and mountains are awash in rich oranges and lavenders.

Watch the shifting colors through *Knight Rise*, the oculus at the **Scottsdale Museum of Contemporary Art** (7374 E. 2nd St., 480/994-2787, www.smoca.org). Or enjoy a cold drink on the patio at **El Chorro Lodge** (5550 E. Lincoln Dr., 480/948-5170, www. elchorrolodge.com) as the slopes of Mummy Mountain turn pink.

Meet the desert's wildlife when it comes out to play: Twice weekly at the **Desert Botanical Garden** (1201 N. Galvin Pkwy., 480/941-1225, www.dbg.org) it's BYOF—bring your own flashlight—to explore the sights, sounds, and scents of the desert's summer nights. The **Phoenix Zoo** (455 N. Galvin Pkwy., 602/273-1341, www. phoenixzoo.org) hosts a monthly "prowl and play" night when kids can cool off in the zoo's lagoon, join a squirt-gun battle, and visit animals active after dark.

Make a twilight visit to **Taliesin West** (12621 N. Frank Lloyd Wright Blvd., 480/860-2700, www.franklloydwright.org). The two-hour Night Lights tour ($25-35), offered once or twice weekly, gives visitors the opportunity to see Frank Lloyd Wright's home illuminated from within.

Arizona's clear, dry air means skies twinkle with some of the best stargazing in the country. **Sky Jewels** (602/294-6775, www.gemland. com) features one- and two-hour astronomy tours, with some Scottsdale resorts offering their guests the course free of charge. Guests at the **Four Seasons Resort Scottsdale at Troon North** (10600 E. Crescent Moon Dr., 480/515-5700, www.fourseasons.com/scottsdale) can picnic under the stars.

Find your moon shadow at **McDowell Mountain Regional Park** (480/471-0173, www.maricopa.gov/parks/mcdowell) east of Scottsdale, where rangers lead guided full-moon hikes, often near a pond hopping with critters. If you'd rather pedal, the park opens up the Pemberton Trail to mountain bikers a few nights each summer.

over rocky roads and through desert washes on a guided half-day tour that brings new meaning to the word convoy.

Check out a range of possible desert encounters with one stop at the **Scottsdale Adventure Center** (7014 E. Camelback Rd., www.scottsdaleadventurecenter.com, 10 A.M.–6 P.M. Mon.–Sat., 10 A.M.–4 P.M. Sun.) located near the food court in Fashion Square. The Scottsdale Convention and Visitors Bureau (800/782-1117, www.scottsdalecvb.com) staffs the adventure center.

BALLOONING

There are few better ways to get a new perspective on the desert than by gliding silently above it in a hot-air balloon. On calm days, the sky might be dotted with dozens of the colorful balloons, but inside the basket, the world feels like it's all yours.

A Balloon Experience by Hot Air Expeditions (480/502-6999, www.hotairexpeditions.com) floats 400 feet above the desert floor, low enough to see critters like jackrabbits, roadrunners, and coyotes. After landing, a red-carpet welcome includes either a champagne breakfast or full dinner catered by award-winning Arizona chef Vincent Guerithault's restaurant, Vincent's ($175). The company is FAA-certified and offers free hotel transfers.

Fliers on **A Great American Balloon Co.** (877/933-6359, www.wedoflyscottsdale.com)

celebrate every flight with a champagne toast, with prices starting at $170 an hour. The company is FAA-certified and has 30 years of experience flying.

Anyone short on time or transportation can combine a Jeep tour and balloon flight with **Adventures Out West** (480/991-3666, www.advoutwest.com, $275 adult, $235 child). Jeeps pick you up at most hotels in Scottsdale, and guides pass the time en route to the balloon-launch site by telling tales of Arizona's Old West past. Following the flight, guides lead extended desert tours focused on plants, wildlife, and survival skills. You can also sign up for just the balloon flight (starting at $139).

BIKING
Mountain Biking

Some of the finest mountain-biking trails in the United States snake their way up the rocky peaks and through the desert washes in and around Scottsdale. **The Pemberton Trail** (15.4-miles round-trip), located just north of Scottsdale in the scenic **McDowell Mountain Regional Park** (www.maricopa.gov/parks/mcdowell), shoots riders up and down rolling hills along a loop that alternately narrows to single-track and widens to open speed-runs. It's easy enough for novice riders to navigate but varied enough to keep even the hard-core adventurer interested.

Another good destination for the intrepid mountain biker is the maze of trails beneath the power lines running north of **Pima and Dynamite Roads.** Pedal northeast of the parking area along a Jeep road. After a mile or so, single-track trails start to branch off to the right and left. Most go up and down the rocky hills nearby and eventually return to the access road under the power lines, so pick your favorite and let it rip.

For a more organized experience—not to

© GREATER PHOENIX CVB

biking in McDowell Mountain Regional Park

SCOTTSDALE AND VICINITY

mention transportation and bike rentals—call **Arizona Outback Adventures** (480/945-2881, www.aoa-adventures.com). The company charges $125 per person for a half-day outing that includes gear, guide, and hotel transportation. Multiday tours are also available.

Road Biking

Road bikers shouldn't feel left out. *Sunset* magazine recently named Scottsdale one of the West's "best burbs for biking," noting that 75 percent of the city's residences are within a half-mile of a bike path or lane. The skinny-tire crowd enjoys speeding along **Pima Road to Bartlett Lake** (starting anywhere north of Frank Lloyd Wright Boulevard). The ride passes through stunning high desert and quite a few tony neighborhoods. The full distance from Frank Lloyd Wright to the dam is about 60 miles; park farther north along Pima for a quicker out-and-back.

Find out about other good trips from local bike shops, including **Rage Cycles** (2724 N. Scottsdale Rd., 480/968-8116, www.ragecycles.com), or from the **Phoenix Metro Bicycle Club** (www.pmbcaz.org), which schedules regular group rides.

GOLF

Golf may have been born in Scotland, but it has been transformed into a way of life in Scottsdale. The natural, rocky terrain and lack of rainfall may seem like an odd match for acre after acre of thirsty greens. Courses in the Valley are limited to less than 5 acre feet of water per acre per year, which translates to about 80–90 acres of turf. This challenge, though, has only pushed the creativity of designers further, with new courses showcasing the stunning contrast between verdant green fairways and golden desert washes.

The city's nearly 50 courses span the gamut from municipal executive greens to PGA tournament stops. And though you'll find far more affordable options in Phoenix and its suburbs, none of them will match Scottsdale's premier courses. Greens fees tumble as the heat rises, with even the best courses charging a fraction of their winter prices in the summer. Call ahead for current fees.

National magazines regularly rank the 36-hole **Boulders Golf Club** (34631 N. Tom Darlington Rd., 480/488-9028, www.theboulders.com) as one of the best golf resorts in the country. It's a true desert course, so don't be surprised to see rabbits, coyotes, or javelina scurrying across the fairway as you tee off. The scenic South Course is a highlight of the property, with its greens nestled along the resort's signature rock formations. The acclaimed golf academy offers personalized 30-minute tune-ups, multiday immersions, even family packages.

Camelback Golf Club (7847 N. Mockingbird Ln., 480/596-7050, www.camelbackinn.com) tees up 36 holes of championship golf. Try the par-72 Padre Course, which is known for its challenging water holes, including the infamous 18th. The Indian Bend Course is scheduled to reopen in autumn 2013 with a new Hurdzan Fry environmental design. (The majestic mountain backdrop will stay the same.)

Who says you can't find an affordable golf course in Scottsdale? The executive-style **Continental Golf Club** (7920 E. Osborn Rd., 480/941-1585, www.continentalgc.com) is a fun, par-60 course just a few blocks from Old Town. The long tees and narrow greens give the Continental a little character. Play a full 18 holes or hit the executive nine before your kids wake up. Be sure to call the pro shop to ask about any specials.

Don't let the laid-back vibe at **Grayhawk Golf Club** (8620 E. Thompson Peak Pkwy., 480/502-1800, www.grayhawkgolf.com) fool you. The two 18-hole courses, Talon and the Tom Fazio–designed Raptor, are among the best in the Valley. This desert course in North

THE GREATEST SHOW ON GRASS

© GREATER PHOENIX CVB

TPC Scottsdale, the home of the Phoenix Open

The **Phoenix Open** (www.phoenixopen.com) is the biggest party in town—and the largest event on the PGA Tour, luring nearly a half million people to TPC Scottsdale over the course of a week.

The infamous annual event, usually held in late January or early February, is not your traditional, polite-applause tournament. In fact, it's more like a nightclub on the fairway. You're as likely to see seniors with scorecards as 20-somethings in tube tops and heels, barhopping from beer gardens to VIP skyboxes. The plentiful bars and young crowds fuel a raucous party atmosphere, so much so that Tiger Woods, who sunk a legendary hole-in-one on the 16th hole, has vowed not to return.

TPC Scottsdale's Stadium Course was specifically designed to accommodate an "unlimited number of people." And by the final day,

that can mean as many as 50,000 fans gathered around the 18th hole to watch pros like Phil Mickelson and Vijay Singh sink a tournament-winning putt.

Golf is only part of the draw, though, with half the crowd arriving when the sun sets and the putting is over. These latecomers flock to the Birds Nest, a party tent where big-name bands entertain thousands of carousers with drinks.

The Thunderbirds, a group of the Valley's leading businesspeople, have hosted the event since 1939, making it one of the five oldest events on the tour. It's the philanthropic group's biggest fundraiser, netting more than $50 million for Arizona charities. Admission begins at $25 per day, though there are additional fees for skyboxes and entrance to the after-hours Birds Nest.

© KATHLEEN BRYANT

The Boulders Golf Club is a desert course where cacti edge the greens.

Scottsdale blasts classic rock tunes in the practice areas and offers live music and drink specials in the evenings as golfers wrap up their games.

The **Kierland Golf Club** (15636 N. Clubgate Dr., 480/922-9283, www.kierlandgolf.com) was the first course in Arizona to roll out the Segway GT (Golf Transporter) to carry a golfer and bag around the 27-hole desert course, which has more than 300 bunkers. Three 9-hole courses—Ironwood, Acacia, and Mesquite—are played in three different 18-hole combinations. (Mesquite is the hardest.) If you'd like some help with your game, individual lessons and daily clinics are offered.

McCormick Ranch Golf Club (7505 E. McCormick Pkwy., 480/948-0260, www. mccormickranchgolf.com) is another reasonably affordable option, conveniently located near downtown Scottsdale and Paradise Valley. *Golf Illustrated* named its Palm Course's ninth hole as one of the top water holes in the country, and its practice facility has one of the Southwest's largest putting greens. Best of all, parents can bring their children to the Junior Golf Academy to learn golf rules and etiquette, as well as technique and strategy.

It's hard to believe this 27-hole, luxury golf sanctuary sits in the middle of a metropolitan area. **The Phoenician** (6000 E. Camelback Rd., 480/423-2449, www.thephoenician.com) has three USGA championship golf courses that sprawl below the red-hued Camelback Mountain. The course is a fantastic splurge and a popular choice for golfers of all skill levels, thanks in part to its slightly shorter fairways.

TPC Scottsdale (17020 N. Hayden Rd., 480/585-4334, www.tpc.com/scottsdale) lives up to its hype as one of the country's best courses. Tee off at the Phoenix Open's Stadium Course, designed by Tom Weiskopf and Jay Morrish, or head out to the recently renovated Champions course. It's hard to beat the thrill of sinking a putt on the Stadium's famed 16th hole, but on either course, you'll be rewarded with spectacular views of the McDowell Mountains. Private instruction and two-, three-, and five-day classes at the Tour Academy are available.

Tom Weiskopf and Jay Morrish teamed up again at **Troon North Golf Club** (10320 E. Dynamite Blvd., 480/585-7700, www. troonnorthgolf.com), and its two courses have emerged as the pinnacle of desert golf course design. Rolling greens meander seamlessly through the natural ravines and unspoiled terrain. The state-of-the-art Callaway Performance Center and chic clubhouse attract serious players and North Scottsdale's most affluent residents.

Troon also manages **Talking Stick Golf Club** (9998 E. Indian Bend, 480/860-2221, www. takingstickgolfclub.com) on the Salt River Pima–Maricopa Indian Reservation north of Scottsdale. It's a good option for those who miss flat, grassy, tree-lined expanses, though the mountain backdrop will remind you that you're in the West.

A fair piece from downtown Scottsdale but considered a must-play course by many golfers, **We-Ko-Pa Golf Club** (18200 E. Toh Vee Circle, 480/836-9000, http://wekopa.com) sits on tribal land at the Fort McDowell Yavapai Nation. The name is the Yavapai word for Four Peaks Mountain, which towers over the public 36-hole course. Isolated by thick Sonoran Desert, the stunning Saguaro and Cholla courses run through canyons, over ridges, and down mountainsides.

HIKING AND ROCK CLIMBING

Even if you're new to hiking, don't pass up the chance to explore the Sonoran Desert on foot. You'll be surprised by the quantity and variety of desert life and all its adaptations. The key to desert hiking is preparation. Even for a short excursion, bring water and sun protection, and wear comfortable, sturdy shoes to protect your feet from rocks and cactus.

If you prefer to leave the planning to someone else, a guided hiking, biking, or rock-climbing excursion is a great option. Contact **360 Adventures** (602/795-1877, www.360-adventures.com) for a range of possibilities, from informative wildflower walks to all-day rock-climbing adventures.

Camelback Mountain

The challenging Camelback Mountain (www. phoenix.gov/parks/hikecmlb.html) is a must-climb destination for hikers, with two summit trails scaling the 1,200-foot slopes in a little more than a mile. The popular **Echo Canyon Summit Trail** starts at the "camel's head" in the **Echo Canyon Recreation Area** (5700 N. Echo Canyon Pkwy., 602/256-3220, www.phoenix. gov/recreation/rec/parks/preserves). Expect rough terrain and loose rocks as you climb the trail, but the hidden caves and rock formations like the 80-foot-tall **Praying Monk** make the effort worthwhile. For an easier trek, try the quarter-mile **Ramada Loop Trail.**

The less popular **Cholla Trail** at the "camel's hump" offers a manageable ascent to Camelback's summit and views of the Eden-like Phoenician Resort. The trailhead is on Cholla Lane, but parking is restricted to Invergordon Street.

Trailheads are open daily from sunrise to sunset, but parking is limited. Avoid the congestion by carpooling or catching a ride from the Park n' Hike shuttle (602/696-2883, http:// parknhike.com, $5).

McDowell Sonoran Preserve

Hikers, mountain bikers, climbers, and horseback riders of all skill levels can trek through the McDowell Sonoran Preserve (480/312-7013, www.scottsdaleaz.gov/preserve) on the eastern edge of Scottsdale. The protected park serves as a wildlife corridor for the McDowell

© GREATER PHOENIX CVB

the distinctive outline of Camelback Mountain

Mountains and Tonto National Forest, making it an important habitat for a host of desert plants and animals. The reserve is a transition zone between the low deserts and uplands, and its higher elevation and greater rainfall make it lusher and more diverse than the Valley.

The 16,000-acre preserve has eight access areas, including **Lost Dog Wash Trailhead** (on 124th St., just north of Shea Blvd.). The **Gateway Access Area** (on Thompson Peak Pkwy., west of Bell Rd.) has desert exhibitions, an amphitheater, lots of parking, and an accessible, ADA-approved trail. Most trailheads open about 30 minutes before sunrise and close at sundown.

Hikers can pick up maps at trailheads or download them from the City of Scottsdale website (www.scottsdaleaz.gov/preserve) for exploring trails on their own. For a more educational experience, join a guided tour with the McDowell Sonoran Conservancy (16435 N. Scottsdale Rd., Ste. 110, 480/998-7971, www.mcdowellsonoran.org). Climbers wanting to scale one of the preserve's rock formations should contact the **Arizona Mountaineering Club** (www.amcaz.org) for information about choice locales or to book one of its beginner classes.

Ten miles north of Fountain Hills, bordering the Fort McDowell Yavapai Nation and the McDowell Sonoran Preserve, **McDowell Mountain Regional Park** (16300 McDowell Mountain Park Dr., 480/471-0173, www.maricopa.gov/parks/mcdowell, $6/vehicle) offers camping, picnicking, and 50 miles of multiuse trails ranging from half-mile strolls to challenging 15-mile trails. Check with the visitor center (8 A.M.–4 P.M.) for scheduled programs, which include kids' activities, nature talks, guided hikes, and astronomy nights.

HORSEBACK RIDING

Scottsdale's desert-mountain setting and Old West past might have you hankering to explore on horseback. With **Windwalker Expeditions, Inc.** (888/785-3382, www.windwalkerexpeditions.com), riders from beginners to experts can head down a trail atop guide-owned Arabian or quarter horses. For experienced riders, the company also organizes multiday pack trips through the backcountry lasting 2–10 days.

For those who'd like to add roping, herding, and other skills to equitation, **Arizona Cowboy College** (30208 N. 152nd St., 480/471-3151, www.cowboycollege.com) offers honest-to-goodness, "no frills" lessons in cowboyin'. From three days ($1,250) to six ($2,250), you'll have the experience of a lifetime, taking meals in the main house, sleeping in the bunkhouse, and learning the trade of a real working cowhand. One-day sessions ($450) are also offered.

RAFTING

See another side of the Sonoran Desert by traveling through one of its treasured riparian areas. Paddle down the Salt or Verde River with **Cimarron Adventures & River Company** (480/994-1199, www.cimarrontours.com) on one of its rafting or kayaking expeditions. Tours start 30 minutes east of Scottsdale. The Class I rapids (no white water) are pretty tame, but don't be surprised if a splash fight breaks out on a hot day.

Grab a paddle with **Desert Voyagers** (480/998-7238, www.desertvoyagers.com) on a guided raft or kayak tour, traveling the lower Salt River, where you'll spot a surprising mix of wildlife, including otters, wild mustangs, and the most-active bald eagle nesting areas in Arizona. Tours start at $90 per person. In addition to tours, Desert Voyagers outfits self-guided trips, renting boats, backpacks, and other gear, and arranging shuttle transportation.

SPECTATOR SPORTS

Most of the Valley's sports action takes place in Phoenix, but every spring Cactus Leaguers descend on Scottsdale for spring training. Baseball fans can catch the San Francisco Giants at **Scottsdale Stadium** (7408 E. Osborn Rd., 480/312-2586, www.scottsdaleaz.gov/stadium), battling one of 13 other MLB teams on the field, including the Chicago Cubs, Seattle Mariners, Los Angeles Dodgers, and hometown Arizona Diamondbacks. You can also watch the Scottsdale Scorpions take the field in October during the Arizona Fall League, which showcases the MLB's top minor league prospects.

The biggest sport in town is golf, and the PGA tour's largest event, the **Phoenix Open,** comes to TPC Scottsdale (17020 N. Hayden Rd., 480/585-4334, www.tpc.com/scottsdale) in January or February. Thousands of fans gather around the 18th hole of TPC's aptly named Stadium course, creating a party atmosphere.

SPAS

Scottsdale is one of the spa capitals of the world, boasting some of the largest and most lavish facilities that you'll find anywhere. Whether you're in the mood for a deep-tissue massage or Native American–inspired treatments, you'll find the perfect spa in Scottsdale to get scrubbed, rubbed, and buffed.

Although there are a host of day spas throughout the city, none offer the amenities of the big resorts. Many locals book a facial or massage at a resort so that they can spend the entire day taking advantage of the spa's pool, fitness classes, on-site gym, and amenities like steam rooms and saunas. It's a great way to experience a five-star resort without having to pay to stay there. Basic hour-long massages begin at $125, and multi-treatment packages are available.

The Centre for Well-Being at The Phoenician Resort & Spa (6000 E. Camelback Rd., 480/423-2452, www.thephoenician.com, 7 A.M.–7 P.M. daily) takes a holistic approach. In addition to

FIND YOUR BLISS

If you've never experienced a spa treatment before, you've come to the right place. According to a 2005 study, Arizona has more destination spas per capita than any other state. A few tips to make your first spa visit blissful:

Make reservations. Call ahead for the best times and largest selection of treatment options. Let the spa know if you are pregnant or have any health-related issues. Check the spa's cancellation policy.

Arrive early. Check in a half-hour or more before your scheduled appointment so that you have a chance to orient yourself, relax, shower, soak, or steam. You'll make the most of your treatment if you unwind first.

Slip into something comfortable. Most spas provide robes and slippers. Bring a swimsuit if you plan to use the pool before or after your appointment. Your therapist will drape you in a sheet during your treatment (but you can leave your undergarments on if you're modest).

Embrace the quiet. Spas are oases of tranquility. Turn off your cell phone. Stash the iPod in your assigned locker. (Better yet, leave them both in your room or car.) Keep your voice down. You can enjoy silence during your treatment or chat with the therapist. Feel free to ask questions or give feedback about temperature, pressure, etc.

Share the love. Spas may include an 18-20 percent gratuity on your credit card slip when you check in, which you can modify when you sign and leave. Others have a cash-only tipping policy; you can leave a tip in an envelope at the

© GREATER PHOENIX CVB

Sanctuary Spa

reception desk. If the spa's policy isn't clear, inquire when you make your appointment or at check-in.

Soak up the ambience. Many larger resorts invite spa clients to spend a few hours enjoying luxurious on-site amenities, which may include pools and whirlpools, peaceful gardens, and state-of-the-art fitness equipment.

---

the usual whirlpools, saunas, and Swiss showers, the Centre is one of the first spas in the country to offer homeopathic and wellness consultations with a naturopathic physician. Massages and treatments, such as the Well-Being Hot Stone Ritual or the hydrating Desert Serenity Scrub, Wrap, and Massage, start at $150. For a New Age-y experience, a "circle of intuitive guides" offers personalized meditation, astrology, hypnotherapy, and sports-guided imagery sessions.

The Moroccan-inspired **Joya Spa** at the Montelucia Resort (4949 E. Lincoln Dr., 480/627-3020, www.joyaspa.com, 8:30 A.M.–8 P.M. daily) has set the bar in Scottsdale for an over-the-top spa experience. You'll want to spend the day (and evening) at this sprawling complex to take advantage of the hammam-style bathing facilities, which include a warming room, sauna, steam room, cold deluge shower, and whirlpool. In between treatments, enjoy the rooftop pool terrace with views of Camelback Mountain and the whisper lounges, a serene place to relax, or try one of the suites, which feature private terraces and outdoor showers. Massages start at $154.

The **Spa at Camelback Inn** (5402 E. Lincoln Dr., 800/922-2635, www.camelback-spa.com, 6:15 A.M.–7:30 P.M. daily) is an excellent value, with a lot of amenities included for the price of a treatment. Soothing massages and wraps start at $135. The saunas, steam rooms, whirlpools, and cold plunge pools are beautifully bathed in natural light, and the outdoor sundecks provide a private retreat before and after treatments. Savor a healthy meal from Sprouts, the spa's own poolside restaurant, while you enjoy uninterrupted views of the desert and mountains.

Spa Avania at the Scottsdale Hyatt Regency Resort & Spa at Gainey Ranch (7500 E. Doubletree Ranch Rd., 480/444-1234, www.scottsdale.hyatt.com, 8:30 A.M.–8 P.M. daily) seamlessly blends indoors and out. Glass walls slide open onto terraces with outdoor showers, comfy lounge chairs, and hot and cold plunge pools. The facility incorporates elegant stonework, garden treatment rooms, and a coed French-Celtic mineral pool and lotus pond. Avania's "science of time" philosophy takes a holistic approach to relaxation, syncing treatments to the body's natural biorhythms and subtly incorporating herbal medicine and traditional Thai therapies into treatments. Massages start at $165.

Chic design and a beautiful mountainside setting helped earn **Sanctuary Spa** at Sanctuary Camelback Mountain Resort & Spa (5700 E. McDonald Dr., 480/607-2326, www.sanctuaryoncamelback.com, 6 A.M.–8:30 P.M. daily) four-star status from Forbes Travel. Restyled as a Modernist Zen retreat, the spa has a meditation garden and reflecting pond. The Asian-inspired treatments, which start at $170, are available in one of 12 indoor and outdoor treatment rooms, including the Sanctum, a private stone-walled outdoor suite for one or two.

One of the finest spas in the world, **Willow Stream Spa** at the Fairmont Scottsdale (7575 E. Princess Dr., 480/585-4848, www.willowstream.com, 6 A.M.–10 P.M. daily) pays homage to Havasu Canyon, a hidden oasis of waterfalls and pools near the Grand Canyon. The spa's special spaces include the red-stone Canyon Oasis with its outdoor waterfall treatment and the rooftop Mesa Oasis Pool and cabanas, which provide views of the McDowell Mountains. The menu includes massages beginning at $160, as well as signature packages, like the two-hour Havasupai Falls Rejuvenation ($309), which includes an exfoliation with desert salts, an herbal bath, a hot stone massage, a body wrap and oil treatment, and a scalp massage.

The intimate **Spa at the Four Seasons Scottsdale** (10600 E. Crescent Moon Dr., 480/513-5145, www.fourseasons.com/Scottsdale, 6 A.M.–9 P.M. daily) doesn't offer the sprawling amenities of its competitors, but its desert-inspired treatments make it a worthwhile option. Try the Jojoba and Prickly Pear Body Polish or cool off after a day in the sun with an aloe vera and cucumber wrap. Massages start at $95 for 25 minutes.

Younger spa-goers looking for hipper crowds may want to check out the **VH Spa** at the Hotel Valley Ho (6850 E. Main St., 480/421-7777, www.hotelvalleyho.com, 8 A.M.–8 P.M. daily). Although a bit small, its mod decor, wild-harvested products, and poolside setting will appeal to 20-somethings looking to splurge. Massages here start at $125.

A local favorite, **Jurlique Spa** at the FireSky Resort (4925 N. Scottsdale Blvd., 480/424-6072, www.fireskyresort.com, 9 A.M.–7 P.M. daily) is an oasis of calm in Old

Town Scottsdale. Massages start at $75, and though this small spa doesn't have as many options as you'll encounter in large resort spas, the outdoor pools and lagoon are peaceful, and products are formulated from organic and biodynamic herbs grown on-site.

Accommodations

You'll find a broad spectrum of options, prices, and styles when you're looking for places to be your temporary home in Scottsdale. The city doesn't offer much in the way of historic hotels or bed-and-breakfasts, though you'll find many retro-cool and newly renovated 1960s properties that were first built when Scottsdale came of age as a resort destination.

If you'd like to experience the city's best shopping and nightlife without the hassle of a car, stay downtown, where most hotels offer a free shuttle within a three-mile radius. However, if you're dreaming of escaping to a desert playground, try one of the city's megaresorts, an Arizona specialty. Enjoy mornings on the tee, afternoons in the pool, and evenings under the stars.

Fortunately, even the most luxurious resorts become affordable in the summer, when the temperatures soar into the triple digits and visitors become a bit wary of making a trip to the Valley of the Sun. Locals, though, take advantage of these hometown oases, spending a "staycation" at the four- and five-star resorts, which often offer spa and food vouchers. Don't dismiss them as out of your price range until you give them a call or check their websites.

DOWNTOWN
$50-100
Finding an inexpensive hotel in Scottsdale is challenging, though not impossible. **Best Western Papago Inn & Resort** (7017 E. McDowell Road, 480/947-7335, www.bestwesternarizona.com, $60–100 d) offers a bit of personality and rooms that overlook a grassy, flower-filled courtyard and swimming pool. Its

location near Tempe, Papago Park, and the airport makes it a handy option if you plan to explore the rest of the Valley of the Sun.

There's nothing like clean and functional when you're on a budget. **Motel 6 Scottsdale** (6848 E. Camelback Rd., 480/946-2280, www.motel6.com, $50–100 d) is downtown's cheapest hotel, and its location next to Scottsdale Fashion Square can't be beat.

$100-250
Hotel Indigo (4415 N. Civic Center Plaza, 480/941-9400, www.scottsdalehiphotel.com, $150–250 d) packs a lot of style into a converted motel. Younger guests will love its location near Scottsdale's best bars and clubs, not to mention the boldly decorated rooms that were clearly inspired by more expensive boutique hotels. Guests can take advantage of the gym and outdoor swimming pool, or head out to the second-story terrace for cocktails by the fire pit on cool evenings.

Hyatt Place (7300 E. 3rd Ave., 480/423-9944, http://scottsdaleoldtown.place.hyatt.com, $160–290 d) is conveniently located within walking distance of Scottsdale Stadium and Old Town's shops, restaurants, and nightlife. Comfy, modern rooms feature a fridge, free Wireless Internet, and a 42-inch flat-screen TV. Rates include parking, fitness center access, and a complimentary hot breakfast.

Dressed in the desert's spiciest colors, **The Saguaro Scottsdale** (4000 N. Drinkwater Blvd., 480/308-1100, www.jvdhotels.com, $140–230), a Joie de Vivre hotel, has a spa and two pools to give it a resort feel. Guest rooms blend contemporary furnishings with

© KATHLEEN BRYANT

The Saguaro Scottsdale

handcrafted Mexican pieces. The property's two restaurants were created by a James Beard Award–winning chef, and its location next to the Civic Center Mall in Old Town is perfect for taking in the city's cultural events.

The budget-boutique **3 Palms** (7707 E. McDowell Rd., 480/941-1202, www.scottsdale-resort-hotels.com, $150–230 d) is a terrific value, with contemporary guest rooms, an inviting poolside bar, an on-site restaurant, and neighboring El Dorado park. The in-room DVD player, refrigerator, and microwave make it practical for families. A 10-minute drive from Old Town, its location near Tempe attracts parents and friends visiting students at Arizona State University.

Over $250

Classic Midcentury Modern architecture and a chic decor make C **Hotel Valley Ho** (6850 E. Main St., 480/248-2000, www.hotelvalleyho.com, $250–300 d) a swank place to hang your fedora. Restored to its glory days, when Hollywood celebrities like Tony Curtis and Janet Leigh lounged by the pool, the hotel has translucent walls, cabana guest rooms, and a hip bar that appeal to a younger crowd, though everyone will dig the large patios, designer touches, and retro Café ZuZu.

W Scottsdale (7277 E. Camelback Rd., 480/970-2100, www.starwoodhotels.com, $260–1,000) combines high style with a touch of Zen, especially in the large rooms, which have "culturally aware" media libraries, shoji-style doors, and frosted-glass showers. The infinity pool, Bliss Spa, and the hip Sushi Roku draw a youthful clientele.

CENTRAL SCOTTSDALE AND PARADISE VALLEY $100-250

The family-owned **SmokeTree Resort and Bungalows** (7101 E. Lincoln Dr., 480/948-7660, www.smoketreeresort.com, $150–220 d) is the longest-running independent hotel in Paradise Valley, and it's no wonder. The charming Arizona decor of the 26 recently remodeled private bungalows make it feel like you are staying in a friend's cozy guesthouse or at an exclusive retreat. There are one- and two-bedroom villas, some with small, full-service kitchens.

For more amenities, consider the Frank Lloyd Wright–inspired **DoubleTree Paradise Valley Resort** (5401 N. Scottsdale Rd., 480/947-5400, www.doubletree.com, $190–265 d), a Hilton property. The two large pools with whirlpools, racquetball and tennis courts, health club, and nine-hole putting green are fun for families and business travelers who would like a few distractions between meetings. Spacious rooms are contemporary with a Southwestern flair, and have private balconies or patios.

The **Scottsdale Cottonwood Resort and Suites** (6160 N. Scottsdale Rd., 480/991-1414, www.scottsdalecottonwoods.com, $160–220

d) offers a lot for its relatively modest price: a huge pool, on-site dining, and sprawling, well-maintained grounds with a putting green, tennis courts, and paths for walking and jogging. Suites are comfortable and spacious, and the location next to the shops at the Borgata and Hilton Village is a plus.

Thunderbird Suites (7515 E. Butherus Dr., 480/951-4000, www.thunderbirdsuiteshotel.com, $130–190 d) has large comfortable rooms, a courtyard pool, and a can't-be-beat location for shoppers, only two blocks from Kierland Commons and Scottsdale Quarter. It's also convenient to the Scottsdale Airport (but soundproofed with a concrete Outinard system), and WWII aviation photographs grace the downstairs lounge. Accommodations include a hot breakfast at the property's Silver Wings Restaurant.

Over $250

The lovely **Hermosa Inn** (5532 N. Palo Cristi, 602/955-8614, www.hermosainn.com, $300–600 d) exudes old Arizona. Cowboy artist Lon Megargee built the hacienda as his home and studio, and it was a converted into a small inn in the 1930s. Recently undergoing a $2 million remodel, the intimate 35-room inn features luxurious casita accommodations with fireplaces and private patios. The meticulously landscaped grounds have stunning views of Camelback Mountain, and the dining room regularly lands on "best of" lists.

Resorts

Since its opening in 1936, celebrities from Jimmy Stewart and Bette Davis to Oprah Winfrey have decamped to Paradise Valley's **Camelback Inn** (5402 E. Lincoln Dr., 480/948-1700, www.camelbackinn.com, $360–750 d). The five-star hacienda-style resort pays homage to the past but highlights modern comfort with well-appointed suites and casitas and a world-class spa. Guests can relax by the pools, play

golf at Camelback Golf Club's 36-hole course, or hike Mummy Mountain's desert terrain.

The inviting 🄲 **FireSky Resort and Spa** (4925 N. Scottsdale Rd., 480/945-7666, www.fireskyresort.com, $225–305 d), just north of Scottsdale Fashion Square, has friendly service and amenities similar to those at the five-star resorts up the road. Gorgeous stonework, lush landscaping, a torch-lit pool, and the Jurlique Spa make this an especially soothing retreat after a day of exploring. "Tall rooms" with extra-long beds are available.

The Spanish-themed **Montelucia Resort and Spa** (4949 E. Lincoln Dr., 480/627-3200, www.montelucia.com, $370–500) makes an aesthetic tie between the Sonoran Desert and Andalucia's arid landscape, setting an elegant mix of dark woods, Moroccan screens, and Moorish geometric patterns among extraordinary views of the red-hued Camelback Mountain. Rooms feature sunken tubs, walk-in showers, and high-tech hookups to link your laptop and iPod to the room's flat-screen TV and sound system. On the property are three beautiful pools, the highly regarded Joya Spa, and Prado restaurant.

The Phoenician Resort & Spa (6000 E. Camelback Rd., 480/941-8200, www.thephoenician.com, $490–600 d) is the grande dame of Valley resorts, hosting royalty, heads of state, A-list actors, and rock stars. The 250-acre property sprawls across the base of Camelback Mountain, with a 27-hole championship golf course, its renowned Centre for Well-Being spa, and a 12-court "tennis garden." The resort's nine swimming pools include a 165-foot waterslide and a pool inlaid with handcrafted mother-of-pearl tiles. For stunning Valley views, enjoy a cocktail on the lobby terrace or dinner at Chef Jean-Georges Vongerichten's J&G Steakhouse.

When Hollywood types come to Scottsdale in search of style and discretion, they often hide away at 🄲 **Sanctuary Camelback Mountain**

Resort & Spa (5700 E. McDonald Dr., 480/948-2100, www.sanctuaryaz.com, $500–600 d). Once a 1960s "tennis ranch," the chic resort preserves many architectural details, sleekly updated with subtle Asian touches that carry through to the innovative Elements restaurant and destination spa. The resort's 105 luxury casitas—many with outdoor balconies, fireplaces, and private outdoor soaking tubs—climb the side of Camelback, giving guests cliffside views of Paradise Valley and Mummy Mountain.

Secluded in the elegant neighborhood of Gainey Ranch, the **Hyatt Regency Scottsdale** (7500 E. Doubletree Ranch Rd., 480/444-1234, www.scottsdale.hyatt.com, $300–400 d) is a blissful retreat 10 minutes from Old Town Scottsdale. Most days, the lobby's glass walls slide open to views of the turquoise pools, golf courses, and McDowell Mountains. Spend your day getting pampered at the alfresco spa or lounging by one of the 10 interconnected pools, which feature sandy beaches, a three-story waterslide, Jacuzzis, and a swim-through temple. In the evening, have dinner at one of the four on-site restaurants before taking a romantic gondola ride around the lagoon or enjoying the nightly live musical performances.

NORTH SCOTTSDALE
$100-250

Visitors who want to stay near Scottsdale WestWorld or the FBR Open's TPC golf course will find a few affordable options in North Scottsdale. **SpringHill Suites** (17020 N. Scottsdale Rd., 480/922-8700, www.marriott.com, $130–300 d) has practical, large rooms and a clean, contemporary style. The neighboring **Sleep Inn** (16630 N. Scottsdale Rd., 480/998-9211, www.sleepinn.com, $150–200 d) can help arrange golf packages. Both hotels are within walking distance of the TPC golf course and a host of restaurants and bars. They

offer free daily breakfast, pleasant pools, and Wireless Internet access.

A former high-end apartment complex, the **Zona Hotel & Suites** (7677 E. Princess Blvd., 888/222-1059, http://zonascottsdale.com, $200–300 d) offers loads of space in North Scottsdale. Families and groups will appreciate the large living rooms, full kitchens, and one- to four-bedroom suites—not to mention the four pools and generous balconies.

Resorts

The Boulders Resort (34631 N. Tom Darlington Dr., 480/488-9009, www.theboulders.com, $360–400 d) nestles at the foot of a 12-million-year-old rock formation on 1,300 acres where you're likely to come across quail, jackrabbits, lizards, and even javelina. Yet this surreal Sonoran setting offers all the amenities of Scottsdale: shimmering pools, two championship golf courses, tennis courts, and the Golden Door Spa, one of the finest in the world. Casitas have a masculine ambience, with overstuffed leather chairs and fireplaces. Rock-climbing clinics are available for those who want to conquer the impressive boulders.

The **Fairmont Scottsdale Princess** (7575 E. Princess Dr., 480/585-4848, www.fairmont.com/scottsdale, $350–480 d) marries luxury service with a relaxed, fun atmosphere. Kids can join in the activities at Bobcat Billy's Clubhouse or splash around the resort's pools and waterslide, while adults can take on the two 18-hole championship golf courses (home to the Phoenix Open) or spend the day blissing out at the exquisite Willow Stream Spa. Evening options include dining at Chef Michael Mina's fashionable Bourbon Steak or having drinks at the chic Stone Rose Lounge. The resort, which recently underwent a $55 million makeover, has received AAA's Five Diamond award every year since 1990.

The **◖ Four Seasons Resort Scottsdale at Troon North** (10600 E. Crescent Moon Dr.,

480/515-5700, www.fourseasons.com/scotts-dale, $425–500 d) overlooks the city from its stunning perch at Pinnacle Peak, a 20-minute drive north of Old Town. Adobe-inspired casitas have fireplaces and private patios or balconies with views of the desert or mountains. The resort's 40 acres include two pools, a spa, and tennis courts. After a day on the links at Troon North, guests can attend stargazing programs, weekly wine tastings, or relax on the terrace with a prickly pear margarita and stunning sunset views.

If you're hoping for a vacation destination where your golf bag doesn't leave your side, **The Westin Kierland Resort & Spa** (6902 E. Greenway Pkwy., 480/624-1000, www.kierlandresort.com, $300–550 d) delivers. But there's more here than Kierland Golf Club. The informal resort's monstrous waterslide and lazy river are popular with kids, and neighboring Kierland Commons mall offers a multitude of shopping and dining options without having to get into a car. Rooms have private balconies or patios, and many have mountain or golf course views.

Food

Foodies know: Scottsdale is a mecca for great eating. First-time visitors will discover the outposts of New York's best-known chefs, as well as homegrown talents who infuse their cooking with the indigenous flavors of the Southwest. And though some of the best restaurants can be a little pricey, it's worth loosening the purse strings for a culinary adventure.

DOWNTOWN
American
If you make one culinary splurge in Scottsdale, **Cowboy Ciao** (7133 E. Stetson Dr., 480/946-3111, www.cowboyciao.com, 11:30 A.M.–2:30 P.M. daily, 5:30–10 P.M. Sun.–Thurs., 5:30–11 P.M. Fri.–Sat., $15–32) should be your stop. The New American menu has a global twist, with bold flavors and unpredictable combinations of fresh ingredients. The Stetson Chop Salad is the stuff of culinary legend in the Valley, and the exotic mushroom panfry and Berkshire pork rib eye are equally good. Few restaurants can compete with the list of 1,800 wines, making Cowboy Ciao's a 10-time *Wine Spectator* award winner.

Three of the Valley's top culinary forces teamed up in 2009 to open **FnB** (7133 E. Stetson Dr., 480/425-9463, http://fnbrestaurant.com, 5–10 P.M. Wed.–Sun., $13–32). The award-winning gastropub features a seasonal, farm-focused menu with decidedly global influences, ranging from Mediterranean to Southwestern. Start with one of the fresh salads and sample from the hearty, roasted meats or fresh seafood. Wine lovers will not be disappointed by the extensive wine list, and you don't have to have a sweet tooth to appreciate the innovative desserts.

A couple blocks south, look for FnB's "little sister" **Baratin** (7125 E. 5th Ave., Ste. 31, 480/284-4777, 11 A.M.–8 P.M. Tues.–Sun., till 10 P.M. Fri.–Sat., $9–10), an intimate wine bar café. With only 11 tables and 5 featured dishes, this is a jewel. The atmosphere is decidedly European, the menu market-fresh American. The wine list highlights local vineyards but includes wines from around the world. A couple doors down, the owners of FnB and Baratin have opened **Bodega** (Ste. 16A, also 480/284-4777, 11 A.M.–7 P.M. Tues.–Sun.), a green grocer and market where you can pick up fresh bread, locally sourced cheeses, and other delectables, and **AZ Wine Merchants** (480/588-7489, 11 A.M.–7 P.M. Tues.–Sun.), which has a wide selection of half-bottles, perfect for picnics and intimate dinners.

Lunching at the small but stylish **Café Monarch** (6934 E. 1st Ave., 480/970-4682, 11 A.M.–2 P.M. Thurs.–Sun., dinner by reservation, closed summers, $13–35) is like going to a friend's house—if your friend is an accomplished chef, interior designer, and raconteur. Take a seat on the delightful butterfly-frequented patio or near the open kitchen to watch owner-chef Christopher Van Arsdale create a changing menu of American comfort food. It's BYOB, with a corkage fee of $10.

The slider craze has hit Arizona at **Stax Burger Bistro** (4400 N. Scottsdale Rd., 480/946-4222, www.staxburgerbistro.com, 11 A.M.–10 P.M. Mon.–Fri., till midnight Sat.–Sun., $5–20), which serves up mini-hamburgers and hearty sides in a host of mix-and-match options. Select your protein(s)—beef, turkey, lamb, ostrich, buffalo, salmon, or veggie—and top it with your choice of bun, cheese, and condiments, including crispy bacon, fresh guacamole, and fancy aiolis. If you have room, add a salad, tater tots, mac-n-jack, or other sides. Wild meats—such as boar with Asian slaw and coconut curry sauce—are available seasonally.

There is no menu at **Posh** (7167 E. Rancho Vista Dr., 480/663-7674, www.poshscottsdale.com, 5–11 P.M. Tues.–Sat., $50–80). Instead, you fill out a checklist of preferences, allergies, number of courses, and requests for wine pairings. The chef takes over from there. Each person at your table gets something different, which means an epic meal that's as memorable as it is surprising. Grab a seat at the bar that overlooks the open kitchen, or have a plate or two, along with a swank cocktail, in the glass-walled lounge.

Salt Cellar (550 N. Hayden Rd., 480/947-1963, www.saltcellarrestaurant.com, 5–11 P.M. Sun.–Thurs., 5 P.M.–midnight Fri.–Sat., $25–75) is the place to go for fresh seafood in the desert. Enter the blue-canopied doorway and descend the antique wooden staircase to the dining area. Lobster is the house specialty, complemented by mussels, mahimahi, scallops, and monkfish—all flown in fresh from across the country. This subterranean venue maintains a casual vibe with tasty cuisine.

Asian

Malee's Thai on Main (7131 E. Main St., 480/947-6042, www.maleesthaibistro.com, 11 A.M.–9 P.M. Mon.–Thurs., 11 A.M.–10 P.M. Fri.–Sat., 4:30–9 P.M. Sun., $10–19) attracts a devoted following of diners, who praise its comfy atmosphere, warm service, and reasonable prices. The Thai-inspired cuisine ranges from classic spring rolls, curries, and pad thai to the "Tropical Pineapple," a spicy mix of shrimp, scallops, and minced chicken in coconut curry sauce.

The lively **Stingray Sushi** (4302 N. Scottsdale Rd., 480/941-4460, www.stingraysushi.com, 11:30 A.M.–midnight daily, $10–25) lures the trendy set into its sleek dining room in Old Town. When you walk in the door, check out the koi pond under the glass floor. On the menu, you'll find classic udon bowls and tempura, along with an interesting lobster ceviche and seasoned calamari steak. Dive into the sushi list with wild abandon, as you're guaranteed a fresh, tasty selection. Stingray Sushi has two additional locations in Scottsdale Quarter (15027 N. Scottsdale Rd., 480/427-2011) and at Biltmore Fashion Park (2502 E. Camelback, 602/955-2008).

At swank **Sushi Roku** (7277 E. Camelback Rd., 480/970-2121, all meals daily, $8–34), located inside the W Hotel, a lengthy list of choices—soups, salad, steaks, chicken, tempura—include plenty of options for those who don't fancy sushi. A special three-course sunset menu ($23) is a good value, or you can indulge in the chef's omakase tasting menu ($80), lingering over multiple courses while you enjoy the stylish crowd.

Breakfast, Lunch, and Snacks

The charming, cottage setting at **Arcadia Farms** (7014 E. 1st Ave., 480/941-5665, www.arcadiafarmscafe.com, 8 A.M.–3 P.M. daily, $8–16) provides a pleasant backdrop for breakfast, brunch, lunch, or dinner. The fresh and organic omelets, sandwiches, and soups never disappoint, and the warm goat cheese salad with fresh raspberries is legendary.

The Breakfast Club and Barrista Bar (4400 N. Scottsdale Road, 480/222-2582, www.breakfastclub.us, 6 A.M.–3 P.M. Mon.–Fri., 7 A.M.–3 P.M. Sat.–Sun., $5–15) calls breakfast "the new happy hour," and the polished concrete floors and contemporary decor are as fresh as the market list of ingredients. Build your own omelet or try the Southwest-inspired breakfast burrito with eggs, refried black beans, chorizo, and pepper jack cheese. Dishes are inexpensive and hearty, drawing a diverse mix of patrons. A second location has opened in Phoenix's new CityScape (2 E. Jefferson, 602/354-7284).

You can't beat a good breakfast joint. **The Orange Table** (7373 E. Scottsdale Mall, http://scottsdalebreakfast.com, 480/424-6819, 7 A.M.–4 P.M. daily, $5–15) is tucked into a nondescript, white-stucco plaza on the Scottsdale Mall, but its bright orange tables make it easy to find. The large menu will appeal to most, including vegetarians. Someone at your table should order the strawberry pancakes or corned beef hash—no exceptions.

The throwback **Original Pancake House** (6840 E. Camelback Rd., 480/946-4902, www.orginalpancakehouse.com, 7 A.M.–2 P.M. daily, $7–12) is the kind of place where you find fluffy sky-high pancakes, slabs of crispy bacon, and freshly squeezed orange juice, along with surprising treats like lingonberry crepes and the oven-baked Dutch Baby, served with whipped butter, lemon, and powdered sugar. Bring some cash, as credit cards are not accepted.

A Scottsdale icon for more than a half-century, the **Sugar Bowl** (4005 N. Scottsdale Rd., 480/946-0051, www.sugarbowlscottsdale.com, 11 A.M.–10 P.M. Sun.–Thurs., till midnight Fri.–Sat., $2–11) has been featured in cartoonist Bil Keane's *Family Circus*. This old-fashioned ice cream parlor whips up shakes, malts, floats, sundaes, and splits, and it's a local favorite for birthday parties and other sweet celebrations. The menu also includes soups, salads, and sandwiches... but, be honest, you know you're here for dessert.

Farmers Market

On Saturday mornings, a small parking lot at the corner of Brown and 1st Street transforms into the **Old Town Farmers Market** (8:30 A.M.–1 P.M., earlier in the summer). The market has become a popular shopping destination for locals year-round. Make a picnic from the seasonal specialties like local cheeses, fresh tamales, artisan breads, jams, and organic vegetables.

French

For joie de vivre, try the delightful **Au Petit Four** (7217 E. 4th Ave., 480/946-3834, www.aupetitfour.com, 8 A.M.–3 P.M. Mon.–Sat., 5–9 P.M. Fri.–Sat., 9 A.M.–2 P.M. Sun., $16–26). This charming café makes irresistible pastries, plus omelets, quiches, and baguette sandwiches for breakfast and lunch. The weekend dinner menu includes *vol-au-vent* chicken, *boeuf bourguignon*, and other classics.

Italian

Stop in at **DeFalco's Italian Eatery** (2334 N. Scottsdale Rd., 480/990-8660, http://defalcos-deli.com, 9 A.M.–10 P.M. Mon.–Sat., 11 A.M.–9 P.M. Sun., $6–12) for deli takeout or a casual meal at the in-store café, and chances are you won't be able to leave without a bagful of pantry items from the well-stocked grocery. The menu includes the classics—hearty sandwiches, pastas, pizza, and calzone—and if you didn't

COOL BREWS AND ICY CONCOCTIONS

Valley bars and restaurants know how to chill, so whether you're thirsting for a tall glass of basil lemonade or a G&T sparkling with ice cubes, you're guaranteed to find an air-conditioned haven or mist-cooled patio where you can enjoy something liquid or frozen.

Start with an iced cup of Joe. The freshly roasted beans at **Cartel Coffee Lab** (225 W. University, Tempe, 480/225-3899; 7124 E. 5th Ave., Scottsdale, 480/712-0675; and 1 N. 1st St., Phoenix, 480/299-8951; www.cartelcoffeelab.com) make a rich, nutty base for cool coffee drinks.

Find some of the best *aguas frescas* and *cremosas* this side of the border at **Los Reyes de la Torta** (9230 N. 7th St., Phoenix, 602/870-2967, or 4333 W. Indian School Rd., Phoenix, 602/269-3212; http://losreyesdelatortaaz.com). The lightly sweetened selections include classic watermelon and *jamaica* (hibiscus) flavors. They also whip up smoothies and fresh fruit juices.

In the tradition of Mexico's *paleterias*, downtown Mesa's **Flor de Michoacan** (734 E. Main, 480/655-7755) blends guava, pineapple, tamarind, coconut, strawberry, and other flavors with chile, then freezes them into pops for a sweet-hot-cold sensation.

Scottsdale's iconic ice cream parlor, the **Sugar Bowl** (4005 N. Scottsdale Rd., 480/946-0051, www.sugarbowlscottsdale. com) has been scooping up floats, sundaes, splits, shakes, and malts for over fifty years.

Try an adults-only version of ice cream at **Lee's Cream Liqueur** (7137 E. Stetson Dr.,

Scottsdale, 480/429-5337, http://leescream-liqueur.com). Are you brave enough for the Almond Habanero with Jack Daniels? If not, stick to the familiar comfort of Brandy Alexander or Fudge Mint flavored with peppermint schnapps.

Cool down twice over at the **Main Ingredient Ale House** (2337 N. 7th St., Phoenix, 602/843-6246, www.tmialehouse.com), where you can order a tall frosty mug filled with Sonoran Brewing Company's Inebriator Stout and a scoop of ice cream.

Head for the **Muddle Bar** at Kierland Resort (6902 E. Greenway Pkwy., Scottsdale, 480/624-1030) for an iced concoction of fresh fruits and herbs, with or without your favorite spirit.

At Old Town Scottsdale's **AZ88** (7353 Scottsdale Mall, 480/994-5576, www.az88.com), you can select from an extensive list of cocktails, including the cucumber-flavored Pimm's Cup, which is served in a chilled brass mug.

It's easier to chill out when you're surrounded by water. The second-story hotel pool at **W Scottsdale** (7277 E. Camelback Rd., 480/970-2100, www.starwoodhotels.com) has a sizzling nightlife scene with cool drinks from the poolside bar.

Ask 10 locals where to find the best margarita, and you'll get 10 different answers. But at **Cien Agaves** (7228 E. 1st Ave., Scottsdale, 480/970-9002, www.cienagaves.com), they use fresh-squeezed lime, simple syrup, and your choice of 100 tequilas. *¡Salud!*

leave room for cannoli, you can always add a couple to your shopping bag for later.

Fans of ultra thin and crispy crust head for **Oregano's Pizza Bistro** (3102 N. Scottsdale Rd., 480/970-1860, www.oreganos.com, 11 A.M.–10 P.M. daily, $8–20), an Arizona chain that launched right here in Scottsdale. The friendly staff, out-of-the-attic decor, and piped-in jump jazz create a fun family atmosphere. It's hard to pass up the pizza, but salads, pastas, and sandwiches are also on the menu.

Mexican and Southwest

A timeless atmosphere awaits at the █ **Old Town Tortilla Factory** (6910 E. Main St., 480/945-4567, www.oldtowntortillafactory. com, 5–9 P.M. Sun.–Thurs., 5–10 P.M. Fri.–Sat., $13–33). Enjoy a margarita on the large flagstone patio shaded by citrus and pecan trees, or choose from one of 80 premium tequilas in the gazebo bar. Move inside the 75-year-old adobe home to sample the homemade tortillas and savory specialties like the tangy *achiote* ribs or Pollo Margarita, stuffed with cheese and roasted peppers.

Casual, contemporary, and lively **Bandera** (3821 N. Scottsdale Rd., 480/994-3524, www.hillstone.com, 4:30–10 P.M. daily, till 11 P.M. Fri.–Sat., $12–33) features a contemporary Western menu with wood-fire-roasted chicken and ribs, as well as steaks, burgers, and grilled fish. Try the Kobe steak and enchilada platter with Mexican cucumber salad, but save room for the banana cream pie or the homemade Oreo ice cream sandwich with créme de cocoa and fresh whipped cream.

Frank and Lupe's Old Mexico (4121 N. Marshall Way, 480/990-9844, www.frankandlupes.com, 11 A.M.–10 P.M. daily, $7–15) has been serving up delicious chicken enchiladas for more than 25 years. It's hard to beat the casual atmosphere and colorful patio, not to mention the reasonable prices in the middle of downtown. Order a Mexican beer or a prickly pear margarita, and dig into the green corn tamales, shredded beef tacos, or Lupe's enchilada plate.

If you're ready to explore beyond the usual Sonoran fare, **Los Sombreros Café & Cantina** (2534 N. Scottsdale Rd., 480/994-1799, www.lossombreros.com, noon–3 P.M. and 4–9 P.M. daily, till 10 P.M. Fri.–Sat., $10–22) serves up dishes from southern, central, and northern Mexico. Owner Azucena Tovar's *queso fundido* with crab and crepes with goat and blue cheese in pomegranate sauce are inspired, especially when paired with a margarita made with fresh lime juice. Dine outside on the homey patio, and learn how Mexican food is more than just *frijoles y tacos.*

❰ The Mission (3815 N. Brown Ave., 480/636-5005, www.themissionaz.com, 11 A.M.–10 P.M. daily, till 11 P.M. Fri.–Sat., $12–32) is a perfect Scottsdale combination of Latin flavors and chic style. The neighboring Old Adobe Mission served as the inspiration for the restaurant's modern-colonial decor. Start

with one of the house cocktails and an appetizer like *almejas al vapor,* steamed clams with rock shrimp, chorizo, and yucca. Main dishes and sides include grilled street corn, pork shoulder tacos, diver scallops, and butternut squash stuffed with black beans.

The Corral family started **Los Olivos** (7328 E. 2nd St., 480/946-2256, www.losolivosrestaurants.com, 11 A.M.–10 P.M. Mon.–Thurs., till 11 P.M. Fri.–Sat., $10–15) more than 50 years ago and named it for the old olive trees along 2nd Street. This affordable Old Town Scottsdale favorite features the Sonoran-style Mexican food that Arizona natives grew up on. Enjoy your carne asada and steak picado (served with homemade flour tortillas hot off the griddle) while being serenaded, on weekends, by mariachis. The family has added a second restaurant in North Scottsdale (15544 N. Pima, 480/596-9787).

❰ Roaring Fork (4800 N. Scottsdale Rd., 480/947-0795, www.roaringfork.com, 4–10 P.M. Mon.–Sat., 4–9 P.M. Sun., $13–26) serves hearty cowboy grub fit for the most finicky foodies. Share a kettle of green chile pork stew, then order the Roaring Fork "Big Ass" Burger, New Mexico fondue pot with little lamb chops, or grilled grouper fish tacos. Happy hour is a huge draw here; arrive early if you plan to have a drink on the patio, or make reservations for the dining room.

Pizza

Grazie Pizzeria & Wine Bar (6952 E. Main St., 480/663-9797, www.grazie.us, 11 A.M.– 10 P.M. daily, $13–16) has a delicious selection of thin-crust pies, prepared with hand-tossed dough and house-made mozzarella, topped with simple ingredients like prosciutto, arugula, shaved parmigiano reggiano, and kalamata olives. Select a bottle of sangiovese or chianti from the extensive wine list, and start thinking about how you're going to make room for the panna cotta.

Grimaldi's (4000 N. Scottsdale Road, 480/994-1100, www.grimaldispizzeria.com, 11 A.M.–11 P.M. Mon.–Thurs., 11 A.M.–midnight Fri.–Sat., $10–16) brings a Brooklyn tradition to the Valley of the Sun with its coal-fired brick ovens and famous "secret" sauce. The simple menu offers salads, calzones, and pizzas built from a list of fresh toppings. This growing chain has added several Valley locations, including two in North Scottsdale near DC Ranch (20715 N. Pima Rd., 480/515-5588) and another in Scottsdale Quarter (15147 N. Scottsdale Rd., 480/596-4070).

Steakhouses

An old-Scottsdale gem, **Don and Charlie's Steakhouse** (7501 E. Camelback Rd., 480/990-0900, www.donandcharlies.com, 5–9:30 P.M. Mon.–Sat., 5–9 P.M. Sun., closed Mon. in summer, $15–42) woos sports-history buffs and carnivores alike. The upscale eatery is adorned with rich, dark woods and enough sports memorabilia and autographs to make Bob Costas's head spin. After a round of golf, rebuild your protein stores with the chicken schnitzel sandwich or the bone-in rib eye, accompanied by something cool from the full bar.

Mastro's City Hall Steakhouse (6991 E. Camelback Rd., 480/941-4700, www.mastrosrestaurants.com, 5–10 P.M. Sun.–Thurs., 5–11 P.M. Fri.–Sat., $30–75) serves all the classics you'd expect at a high-end steakhouse: lobster cocktails, oysters Rockefeller, and a host of fillets, porterhouses, rib eyes, and chops. Side dishes—sautéed asparagus, creamed spinach, au gratin potatoes—are ordered family style. The popular bar often has live music in the evenings. The original **Mastro's Steakhouse** (8852 E. Pinnacle Peak Rd., 480/585-9500) and **Mastro's Ocean Club** (15045 N. Kierland Blvd. 480/443-8555) are located farther north.

CENTRAL SCOTTSDALE AND PARADISE VALLEY
Breakfast

Where to begin at **Butterfield's Pancake House & Restaurant** (7388 E. Shea Blvd., 480/951-6002, http://butterfieldsrestaurant.com, 6:30 A.M.–2:30 P.M. daily, $9–12)? The menu is an epic breakfast journey, with a dozen kinds of pancakes, and omelets that range from Denver to Jambalaya, not to mention French toast and crepes, Belgian waffles, Spanish frittatas, or the Dutch oven-baked pancakes. Order a cup of coffee while you ponder the possibilities. Lunch adds salads, sandwiches, and wraps. A sister restaurant, **Butters Café** (8390 E. Via de Ventura, 480/629-4333), has opened near McCormick Ranch, a couple miles farther south.

Italian

Veneto Trattoria Italiana (6137 N. Scottsdale Rd., 480/948-9928, www.venetotrattoria.com, 11:30 A.M.–2:30 P.M. and 5–10 P.M. Mon.–Sat., 4:30–9 P.M. Sun., $15–26) specializes in cuisine from Venice and northern Italy. Dine alfresco on the patio, enjoying dishes like *risotto dell' Adriatico* (rice with clams, scallops, and shrimp) or garlicky pork sausages with grilled polenta. But save room for *crema cotta* (the house interpretation of *crème brûlée*), or *affogato*, vanilla ice cream with white chocolate chips and a shot of Scotch-flavored espresso.

New American

Originally a private school for girls, now newly renovated and LEED-certified, **El Chorro Lodge** (5550 E. Lincoln Dr., 480/948-5170, www.elchorrolodge.com, 5–10 P.M. Tues.–Sat., 9 A.M.–3 P.M. Sun., $15–38) has been serving trout, beef stroganoff, and mesquite-broiled steaks since the 1930s. The updated menu highlights organic and local items, but all entrées include El Chorro's famous sticky buns, a 65-year-old tradition. For a romantic evening, have a drink in the garden lounge while watching sunset colors wash over Mummy Mountain, then dine on the chateaubriand for two.

From its perch at the Sanctuary Camelback, **Elements** (5700 E. McDonald Dr., Paradise Valley, 480/607-2300, www.elementsrestaurant.com, all meals daily, $17–42) offers stunning views. The mod decor is stylish, and the simple and natural menu by *Iron Chef*–winner Beau McMillan, the friendliest chef you're likely to meet, makes Elements special. His innovative seasonal menu has a farm-fresh American flavor with Asian accents. Reservations are recommended.

Lon's at the Hermosa Inn (5532 N. Palo Cristi Rd., 602/955-7878, www.lons.com, 7–10 A.M. and 5:30–10 P.M. daily, 11:30 A.M.–2 P.M. Mon.–Fri., brunch 10 A.M.–2 P.M. Sat.–Sun., $15–40) prides itself on being the most authentic hacienda in Arizona. Once the home of cowboy artist Lon Megargee, the adobe-and-wood interior captures the desert's allure. Elegant meals are prepared from the one-acre organic garden just outside the kitchen, and the multicourse tasting menu is a culinary adventure.

Slow food chef Chrysa Robertson's **Rancho Pinot** (6208 N. Scottsdale Rd., 480/367-8030, www.ranchopinot.com, 5:30–9 P.M. Mon.–Sat., $15–35) relies on the simple delights of fresh, seasonal food. The frequently changing menu may include stuffed squash blossoms, diver scallops with corn fritters or risotto, roast chicken, or handmade pasta with whatever local growers have available at the moment. The modern comfort food has an Arizona flair, as does the cowboy-chic decor.

Spanish

Dining at award-winning **Prado** (4949 E. Lincoln Dr., 480/627-3010, www.montelucia.com, all meals daily, $25–42), located within the elegant Montelucia Resort, is like traveling to Spain. The menu draws its inspiration from traditional Andalusian cooking, featuring smoky wood-grilled meats, paella, rich cheeses. Savor the ambience and nightly tapas in the restaurant's lounge, especially on weekends, when there's live jazz.

Steakhouse

Chef Laurent Tourondel's modern American steakhouse, **BLT Steak** (5402 E. Lincoln Dr., 480/905-7979, www.bltscottsdale.com, 5–10 P.M. Sun.–Thurs., 5–11 P.M. Fri.–Sat., $15–50) serves a an impressive lineup of certified Black Angus, Kobe, and Wagyu steaks, as well as fish and chicken. Located in Paradise Valley's Camelback Inn, the restaurant has New York style with a hint of France that shows up in rich sauces, sides, and desserts, such as the gruyère popovers and bittersweet chocolate tart. Each month, five-course wine dinners spotlight a different vineyard.

NORTH SCOTTSDALE
Asian

At **Pure** (20567 N. Hayden Rd., 480/355-0999, www.puresushibar.com, 11:30 A.M.–12:30 A.M. daily, $15–25), elegant decor provides the perfect setting for some of the best sushi in Scottsdale. While the tuna and yellowtail nigiri shouldn't be missed, try a few of the innovative house-specialty rolls, like the potato spicy tuna roll. Dinner selections include steaks, chicken, and fish as well as noodle dishes and teriyaki. The extensive drink menu features regional sakes from Japan and signature cocktails, like the Lychee Lemon Drop.

The food at **Fresh Mint** (13802 N. Scottsdale Rd., 480/443-2556, www.freshmint.us.com, 11 A.M.–9 P.M. Mon.–Sat., $8–14) is vegetarian, vegan, and certified kosher, but most of all, it's fresh and flavorful. The Vietnamese-inspired dishes at this cheerful café include curries, noodles, rolls, and scrumptious salads and soups, like the green papaya salad with fresh basil and peanuts, and the spicy lemongrass noodle soup. Faux-meat is used in a handful of entrées, such as the citrus "spareribs" and clay pot "fish." Fresh Mint has earned "best of" nods from vegetarians and nonvegetarians alike.

Breakfast, Lunch, and Snacks

The bright and airy **Breakfast Joynt** (14891 N. Northsight Blvd., 480/443-5324, www.thebreakfastjoynt.com, 6:30 A.M.–2:30 P.M. daily, $6–10) serves up Texas French toast, chocolate-chip pancakes, home-style biscuits with sausage gravy, and other crowd-pleasers. Added to this at lunchtime are salads, burgers, and classic sandwiches like BLTs, Reubens, and the Monte Cristo.

The hipster diner and market **Chloe's Corner** (15215 N. Kierland Blvd., 480/998-0202, www.chloescorneraz.com, 7 A.M.–6 P.M. Mon.–Fri., 8 A.M.–6 P.M. Sat., 8 A.M.–4 P.M. Sun., $5–8) is a fun place to get a quick and inexpensive meal at Kierland Commons. Grab an egg sandwich and 50-cent coffee in the morning, or plop down at the lunch counter for the albacore tuna on cranberry-walnut bread. The hand-dipped milk shakes make a perfect midafternoon pick-me-up.

At **JP Pancake** (9619 N. Hayden Rd., 480/596-9369, www.jppancake.com, 7:30 A.M.–1 P.M. Tues.–Sun., $8–10) you'll find light and golden flapjacks topped with mounds of fruit, nuts, and chocolate, all made to order. Try the oven-baked pancakes (the house special) or branch out to waffles, French toast, eggs, or omelets. There's also an East Valley location in Gilbert (3641 E. Baseline, 480/539-4435).

Burgers and Sandwiches

Four Peaks Grill & Tap (15730 N. Pima Rd., 480/991-1795, www.fourpeaks.com, 11 A.M.–2 A.M. Mon.–Sat., 10 A.M.–2 A.M. Sun., $15–25) showcases its Tempe-brewed beers at this North Scottsdale location. The Kiltlifter

and 8th Street ales are local favorites, but serious hopheads will enjoy the Hop Knot IPA. If you're hungry, the Tap Room Tenderloin with beer-battered fries is especially good when upgraded from the hoagie to "beer bread." And for those limiting their red meat intake, the veggie burger is one of the best in town.

French

Chef Matt Carter's onion soup, on the menu of **Zinc Bistro** (15034 N. Scottsdale Rd., 480/603-0922, www.zincbistroaz.com, 11 A.M.–10 P.M. daily, $15–36), has been highlighted on the Food Network's *The Best Thing I Ever Ate*. It makes this Kierland Commons restaurant feel like a Parisian café. (The mosaic-tiled floor, red leather banquettes, mirrored walls, and 25-foot zinc bar add to the illusion.) Order the cheese board and sit at a sidewalk table for a little people-watching or, for a romantic dinner, pair a bordeaux with the braised lamb shank and dine on the candle-lit garden patio.

Italian

North (15024 N. Scottsdale Road, 480/948-2055, www.foxrc.com, 11 A.M.–9:30 P.M. Sun.–Thurs., 11 A.M.–10:30 P.M. Fri.–Sat., $9–20) at Kierland Commons offers light, modern northern Italian dishes in an urban, loft-like space. At this Fox Concept restaurant, diners can enjoy traditional antipasti and thin-crust pizzas or select from a variety of "plates of the day." Entrées such as chicken parmesan or braised shortribs are served alongside fresh, organic vegetables. The wine-savvy servers can suggest a bottle of vino to round out your meal.

Ristorante Giuseppe (13610 N. Scottsdale Rd., 480/991-4792, www.giuseppescottsdale. com, 11 A.M.–8:30 P.M. Mon.–Fri., 5–9 P.M. Sat., 5–8 P.M. Sun. $8–16) is a family-owned classic, where you'll feel welcomed by the entire staff. House specialties are named after family members, one of whom could very likely be your server. Order one of the famous meatballs, or dine on a Sunday, when homemade ravioli is on the menu. The cash-only restaurant is BYOB, but there isn't a corkage fee.

AAA Four Diamond award-winner **Sassi** (10455 Pinnacle Peak Pkwy., 480/502-9095, www.sassi.biz, 5:30–10 P.M. Tues.–Sun., $15–36) earns high praise from foodies for its updated and reimagined southern Italian cuisine. Sharing dishes with your companions is the best approach for sampling delicious antipasti, followed by *primi* like the orrecchiate with housemade sausage, and such *secondi* as a wood-grilled pork chop or yellowfin tuna with olives, capers, and arugula. Separate dining rooms lend an Italian villa ambience, and the terrace is lovely at sunset. Sassi means "rocks" in Italian, a reference to the Pinnacle Peak location.

Latin American and Mexican

Deseo (6902 E. Greenway Pkwy., 480/624-1030, www.kierlandresort.com, 6–10 P.M. Wed.–Sun., $12–35) is the finest of the many dining options at The Westin Kierland. The Nuevo Latino cuisine spans Latin, Mexican, Caribbean, and Native American flavors, with options like ceviche, goat cheese empanadas, shrimp chicharron, Kobe meatballs, and brie potato mash. Start with a cocktail from the Muddle Bar, where fresh fruits and herbs get a kick from an assortment of premium liquors. (Call ahead for summer hours.)

New American

In Scottsdale Quarter, **Eddie V's** (15323 N. Scottsdale Rd., 480/730-4800, www.eddiev. com, 4–11 P.M. Sun.–Thurs., 4 P.M.–midnight Fri.–Sat., $30–45) prepares some of the best seafood in town, with new deliveries of lobster, shrimp, and scallops arriving every morning. Start with the tower of iced shellfish before

trying out the Chilean sea bass or a Black Angus steak. A sister restaurant, **Wildfish** (7135 E. Camelback Rd., 480/994-4040), is located at downtown's Waterfront.

Armitage (20751 N. Pima Rd., 480/502-1641, www.armitagewine.com, 4 P.M.–midnight Mon.–Thurs., noon–1 A.M. Fri.–Sat., 10 A.M.–midnight Sun., $9–17), located in North Scottsdale's DC Ranch Marketplace, is a wine bar and bistro with light fare perfect for pairing, from tasty bruschetta and cheese boards to burgers, sliders, butternut ravioli, and bourbon-glazed ribs. On Sundays, a hearty brunch menu lures neighbors from their million-dollar homes with the promise of bellinis and Bloody Marys, and the live music in the evening keeps the party going.

Steakhouses

Chef Michael Mina's chic-and-sleek **Bourbon Steak** (7575 E. Princess Dr., 480/513-6002, www.michaelmina.net, 5–10 P.M. Tues.–Sat., $34–85) at the Fairmont Scottsdale Princess is decidedly upscale, with steaks, poultry, and fish all slow-poached in butter, then finished over mesquite-wood flames. An extensive list of side dishes includes truffled mac and cheese, roasted sweet potato puree, and soy-glazed shiitake mushrooms. Classic, handcrafted cocktails complement the reimagined comfort food and stunning Desert Modernist architecture.

Established the 1880s as a stagecoach stop, **Reata Pass** (27500 N. Alma School Pkwy., 480/585-7277, www.reatapass.com, 11 A.M.–9 P.M. Tues.–Thurs., 11 A.M.–11 P.M. Fri.–Sat., noon–9 P.M. Sun., $7–33) has been serving meals to hungry travelers in one way or another for over a century. The cowboy steakhouse radiates Western atmosphere, even attracting Hollywood's attention as a movie backdrop. Grab a beer at the saloon, and take your grub to one of the indoor or outdoor picnic tables. The restaurant is closed summers, but you can head down the road to the owners' other establishment, **Greasewood Flat** (27375 N. Alma School Pkwy., 480/585-9430, http:// greasewoodflat.net, 11 A.M.–11 P.M. Sun.– Thurs., 11 A.M.–midnight Fri.–Sat.) for live country music and dancing under the stars year-round.

Information and Services

TOURIST INFORMATION

The **Scottsdale Convention and Visitors Bureau** (800/782-1117, www.scottsdalecvb. com) excels at distributing useful information to help you plan a trip to the city. Visit the extensive website or stop by the main office at the **Galleria Corporate Centre** (4343 N. Scottsdale Rd., Ste. 170, 8 A.M.–5 P.M. Mon.– Fri.). You also can pick up materials from the concierge desk at **Scottsdale Fashion Square** (7014 E. Camelback Rd., 10 A.M.–6 P.M. Mon.–Sat., 11 A.M.–4 P.M. Sun., 11 A.M.–4 P.M. daily June–Sept.) or the **Scottsdale Downtown** office (4248 N. Craftsman Ct., www.scottsdaledowntown.com, 8 A.M.–5 P.M. Mon.–Fri., plus 10 A.M.–5 P.M. Sat. Oct.–June).

LIBRARIES

The four branches of the **Scottsdale Public Library** (480/312-7323, http://library.scottsdaleaz.gov) can be handy resources for visitors. The **Civic Center Library** (3839 N. Drinkwater Blvd., 9 A.M.–9 P.M. Mon.–Thurs., 10 A.M.–6 P.M. Fri.–Sat., 1–5 P.M. Sun.) is a popular destination because of its free Wireless Internet, frequent events, and large children's section. The architecturally stunning **Arabian Library** (10215 E. McDowell Mountain Ranch Rd., 9 A.M.–8 P.M. Mon.–Thurs., 10 A.M.–6 P.M. Fri.–Sat., 1–5 P.M. Sun.) brings

Desert Modernism to North Scottsdale. Its rusted, metal facade seems to emerge like a small mountain from its rocky site, and the glass walls allow natural light to bathe the reading rooms.

HOSPITALS AND EMERGENCY SERVICES

The renowned **Mayo Clinic** (13400 E. Shea Blvd., 480/301-8000) in North Scottsdale serves as an important medical center in the Valley. In fact, the large complex attracts patients from around the world because of its respected doctors, high-tech equipment, and clinical trials. The 244-bed **Mayo Clinic Hospital** (5777 E. Mayo Blvd., 480/515-6296, www.mayoclinic.org/arizona) provides in-patient care to support the clinic's programs.

Scottsdale Heathcare (www.shc.org) has three hospitals scattered around the city, each with emergency rooms and a spectrum of services. **Scottsdale Healthcare Osborn** (7400 E. Osborn Rd., 480/882-4000) is conveniently located in Old Town, while the **Scottsdale Healthcare Shea** (9003 E. Shea Blvd., 480/323-3000) and **Scottsdale Healthcare Thompson Peak** (7400 E. Thompson Peak Pkwy., 480/324-7000) are located farther north.

Getting There and Around

AIR

Phoenix Sky Harbor International Airport (3400 E. Sky Harbor Blvd., 602/273-3300, www.phxskyharbor.com) is a 15-minute ride from downtown Scottsdale's restaurants, bar, and hotels. The airport serves as an important regional hub for national and international flights, including direct flights to and from New York, London, and Mexico.

If you're able to fly by private plane, **Scottsdale Airport** (15000 N. Airport Dr., 480/312-2321, www.scottsdaleaz.gov/airport) is a handy, headache-free option. The North

Scottsdale airpark (sometimes referred to by its WWII designation, Thunderbird Field #2), is a frequent choice of celebrities and one of the busiest single-runway airports in the country.

CAR

Rental Cars

You'll need a vehicle to get around Scottsdale, especially if you want to explore both Old Town and North Scottsdale's attractions. Take the free shuttle from any of Sky Harbor Airport's terminals to the **Rental Car Center** (1805 E.

PLANES, TRAINS, AND AUTOMOBILES

Every family has one—the guy or gal who loves all things related to rapid forward momentum. If that's you, head for one of the Valley's many transportation-related attractions or get behind the wheel yourself.

In Peoria, the **Challenger Space Center** (211870 N. 83rd Ave., 623/322-2001, www.azchallenger.org) has exhibits and activities relating to space travel, including a two-hour simulated mission ($23) that transports you to Mars or takes you on a scientific probe of the comet Encke.

Hop on board a reproduction of a Colorado narrow-gauge train at the **McCormick-Stillman Railroad Park** (7301 E. Indian Bend Rd., 480/312-2312, www.therailroadpark.com) near Paradise Valley. Antique engines and train cars dot this former ranch, including a presidential Pullman car and a boxcar from the "Merci Train," donated by France to thank Americans for their aid after World War II. Admission is free, but there's a small fee to ride the train or the park's antique carousel.

Auto racing buffs love the **Penske Racing Museum** (7125 E. Chauncey Ln., 480/538-4444, www.penskeracingmuseum.com, free) in North Scottsdale. The well-designed museum showcases 11 of the dynasty's Indy 500 winners, along with other cars and memorabilia.

If you prefer to take the wheel yourself, check out the classes at the **Bob Bondurant School of High Performance Driving** (20000 S. Maricopa Rd., Phoenix, 800/842-7223, www.bondurant.com, $400 and up) near Firebird International Raceway. Or go on a ride-along with the **Rusty Wallace Racing Experience** (508/384-7223, racewithrusty.com, $100) at Phoenix International Raceway in Avondale. If your fantasy is to be a fighter pilot, **Fighter Combat International** (5865 S. Sossaman Rd., Mesa, 866/359-4273, www.fightercombat.com, $800 and up) teaches in-the-air training, including air-to-air combats.

For automobile collectors, there's no better time to visit the Valley than in January, when Scottsdale hosts more than a half-dozen glamorous **car auctions,** including those managed by Barrett-Jackson, RM, and Gooding.

Almost any time of year, you're likely to stumble onto a car show or see a well-preserved classic rolling down Valley highways, especially in April, when the Men's Arts Council hosts the **Copperstate 1000** (www.mensartscouncil.org), a four-day road rally for vintage autos that covers 1,000 miles of scenic Arizona terrain.

Sky Harbor Circle, 602/683-3741). You'll find major companies, like **Budget** (602/261-5950, www.budget.com), **Hertz** (602/267-8822, www.hertz.com), and **Enterprise** (602/225-0588, www.enterprise.com), which has convenient drop-off centers around Phoenix and Scottsdale and offers free pickup service. It can be hard to find a gas station near the rental car center, so be sure to fill up before returning your vehicle. Alamo, Enterprise, Hertz, and National rental car agencies also serve the Scottsdale Airport.

Limos, Shuttles, and Taxis

From Sky Harbor, you can join a shared-van ride to your resort or hotel with the reliable **SuperShuttle** (602/232-4610 and 800/258-3826, www.supershuttle.com). Its bright blue vans are easy to spot at all terminals.

You can grab a taxi at Sky Harbor with one of three contracted companies: **Apache Taxi** (480/557-7000), **Mayflower** (602/955-1355), and **Yellow Cab** (480/888-8888, www.aaayellowaz.com), which has vans in addition to cars. A practical option for families or groups, **Desert Knights Sedans & Limousines** (480/348-0600, www.desertknights.com) provides taxis, sedans, limos, and luxury minibuses.

PUBLIC TRANSPORTATION
Trolley

If you're tired of driving or walking around downtown, the free **Scottsdale Trolley** (480/421-1004, www.scottsdaleaz.gov/trolley, 11 A.M.–6 P.M. daily) shuttles visitors throughout the area on three different routes. Trolleys on the **downtown route** stop every 15 minutes along 5th Avenue, Marshall Way, and Scottsdale Fashion Square. During the Thursday night ArtWalk, the trolley runs till 9 P.M. The downtown route has two transfer stops, linking to the **Miller Road route** (which travels to the Civic Center, Scottsdale Stadium, and other locations) and the **neighborhood route** (which stops at Scottsdale Healthcare, schools, and other local destinations).

Bus

Scottsdale is a part of the **Valley Metro** (602/253-5000, www.valleymetro.org) public transportation network, which connects the Phoenix metropolitan area. Its buses run throughout the city, and fares start at $1.75 for a single ride. Multiday passes are available. Visit the website for a comprehensive schedule and map. (The new light-rail system, which links the communities of Mesa, Tempe, and Central Phoenix, doesn't extend to Scottsdale.)

Vicinity of Scottsdale

North and east of Scottsdale, the city melts into the Sonoran Desert. Houses are tucked into gently rolling hills, and many side streets are unpaved, edged by saguaros, chollas, and other desert vegetation. Here, on the far edges of the city, golf courses and resorts like the Boulders offer long views and natural quiet.

The small communities of Cave Creek and Carefree are home to artists and others who are inspired by the desert surroundings and mountain backdrops. Fountain Hills, which

has the feel of a detached suburb, acts as a gateway to the wide-open spaces of Tonto National Forest, McDowell Mountain Regional Park, and the Fort McDowell Indian Community. Despite being part of a larger metro area, these towns offer a relaxed pace and a small-town sensibility. Urban delights are never very far away, but neither are desert trails. It may be the countless attractions of downtown Scottsdale and Phoenix that draw visitors to the Valley of the Sun, but it's often a peek at the laid-back lifestyle here on the edges that will tempt visitors into becoming residents.

CAVE CREEK

These days, you're more likely to find yuppie bikers and artist studios than ranchers in Cave Creek (pop. 5,000), but the town manages to retain more of its Old West character than any other Valley community. First settled by miners and ranchers in the 1870s as a hardscrabble outpost, Cave Creek has changed with the times. In the 1920s, "lunger camps" promised clear, dry desert air to those suffering from tuberculosis and other lung ailments. In the 1930s, the WPA established quarters for workers building Bartlett Lake and Horseshoe Dams. By the 1940s and 1950s, old homesteads converted to dude ranches, and visitors have been coming ever since.

Sights

You can get a sense of Cave Creek's Old West past at **Frontier Town** (6245 E. Cave Creek Rd., 480/488-3317, www.frontiertownaz.com), an "1880s-style theme town." Sure, it's a little hokey, but where else can you stroll down wooden boardwalks, dodging hitching posts and antique wagons on your way to grab a beer? Frontier Town is home to gift shops, a saloon, and even a wedding chapel. The **Cave Creek Smokehouse** (11 A.M.–10 P.M. daily) serves American-style food and on weekends hosts live music on its fountain patio.

Just down the street, the **Cave Creek Museum** (6140 E. Skyline Dr., 480/488-2764, http://cavecreekmuseum.com, 1–4:30 P.M. Wed.–Sun. Oct.–May) preserves a slice of the town's mining and ranching past. The last remaining tuberculosis cabin in the state of Arizona is here, along with an *arrastre,* a revolving mill used to crush ore.

Recreation

The par-70 **Rancho Mañana Golf Club** (5734

E. Rancho Manana Blvd., 480/488-0398, www.ranchomanana.com) in Cave Creek will definitely wow you with its dramatic elevation changes and pristine desert surroundings. The rolling course's green lawns, sculptural cacti, and sweeping mountain views make it the most scenic course in the Valley. As a bonus, the high Sonoran Desert setting outside of the city means slightly cooler temperatures on warmer days.

Cave Creek's **Spur Cross Stables** (44029 N. Spur Cross Rd., 480/488-9117, www.horsebackarizona.com) can get even the newest cowpokes into the saddle. The ranch, located on the site of an 1870s gold mine, offers spectacular rides through the desert and mountain passes of Tonto National Forest, with rates beginning at $25 for a half-hour. Customize your horseback adventure, or select the Native American Ruin, Stagecoach Stop, or Sunset trail ride. Children age six and older can sign up for one- to six-hour rides, and younger tykes can ride guided ponies in the ranch arena.

Shopping

Whether you arrive by car or motorcycle, the shops at **Cave Creek's Frontier Town** (6245 E. Cave Creek Rd., North Scottsdale, 480/488-9129, www.frontiertownaz.com) will seem like another world compared to Scottsdale's high-end shopping centers. You can join the "Creekers" and bikers who frequent the saloon or amble down the touristy wooden sidewalks to pick up a few Arizona souvenirs at Glory Bee's, the Totem Pole, or Debra Ortega Traders. Leather Outpost sells jackets, chaps, and other biker apparel.

Just down the street, **The Town Dump** (6820 E. Cave Creek Rd., 480/488-9047, www.towndump.net, 10 A.M.–6 P.M. daily) is packed with indoor/outdoor furniture, old light fixtures, giant metal lizards, rusted gates, and brightly painted Mexican pottery. The shop's offerings range from practical to whimsical to purely eccentric.

Food

Cave Creek's **El Encanto** (6248 E. Cave Creek Rd., 480/488-1752, www.elencantorestaurants.com, 11 A.M.–10 P.M. Mon.–Sat., 9 A.M.–10 P.M. Sun., $9–17) serves Mexican cuisine in a casual, romantic setting next to a lagoon shaded by palm trees and frequented by ducks and turtles. The chef, who hails from coastal Mazatlán, has perfected the art of preparing seafood, but there's also chicken mole enchiladas and slow-roasted pork served with tomatillo-chipotle sauce. In fall, the restaurant hosts a Saturday farmers market with live music. Sister restaurants include **El Encanto Dos** (1112 E. Carefree Hwy., 623/780-5948) and **El Encanto de la Fuente** (11044 N. Saguaro Blvd.,480/837-1070) in Fountain Hills.

Considered one of the top restaurants in the state, **Binkley's** (6920 E. Cave Creek Rd., 480/437-1072, www.binkleysrestaurant.com, 5–10:30 P.M. Tues.–Sat., $25–46) showcases fresh, seasonal ingredients on a menu that changes daily. For culinary adventurers, Chef Kevin Binkley offers a four-, five- or six-course tasting menu. Selections such as short rib stuffed squash blossoms or charred halibut are punctuated by a series of eye-catching *amuse-bouche* presentations.

The Horny Toad (6738 E. Cave Creek Rd., 480/488-9542, www.thehornytoad.com, 11 A.M.–10 P.M. Sun.–Thurs., 11 A.M.–11 P.M. Fri.–Sat., $9–26) is one of the few restaurants within riding distance of North Scottsdale where the cowboy boots aren't for show. Come on Monday, when the barbecue beef ribs are all-you-can-eat, or just come hungry for burgers, steaks, prime rib, fried chicken, grilled salmon, strawberry shortcake, and other down-home classics.

Getting There

From downtown Scottsdale, head north on Scottsdale Road, which becomes Tom Darlington Drive after it passes El Pedregal and edges the Boulders Resort. Continue on Tom Darlington Drive to downtown Carefree, turning left (west) on Cave Creek Road to reach the town of Cave Creek. From the I-17 freeway, you can get to Cave Creek by turning east on the Carefree Highway (State Route 74) at exit 224.

CAREFREE

If you guessed by its name that neighboring Carefree (pop. 4,000) started as a retirement community, you'd be right. Today, Carefree is home to artists and families seeking a haven from the Valley's busy metro areas.

Carefree is a short drive from Scottsdale.

© KATHLEEN BRYANT

Sights

Stroll along Easy Street to see the **Carefree Desert Gardens,** a four-acre botanical garden incorporating the world's second-largest sundial, a playground, public art, and an amphitheater. A handful of boutiques, art galleries, and restaurants also line Easy Street.

Spa

The 33,000-square-foot **Golden Door Spa** at The Boulders Resort (34631 N. Tom Darlington Dr., 480/595-3500, www.theboulders.com, 8 A.M.–8 P.M. daily, varies seasonally) is set against Carefree's craggy desert landscape. Before and after your session, you can walk the meditative labyrinth, which overlooks the resort's namesake boulder formation. Services include ayurvedic treatments, watsu, and tui na massage, and you can select a trio of treatments for $450, including lunch. The spa also offers rockclimbing and bouldering adventures if you like a little excitement with your pampering.

Events

The town rolls out the welcome mat each spring and fall for several large events that focus on art, culture, and food. One of the most intriguing is the **Hidden in the Hills Studio Tour** (480/575-6624, www.sonoranartsleague.com), held the last two weekends in November, when you can visit artists in their home studios. Late in January, Carefree joins its more rough-and-tumble neighbor to host the **Carefree-Cave Creek Balloon Festival** (www.carefreeballoonfestival.com).

Food

At **English Rose Tea Room** (201 Easy Street, 480/488-4812, www.carefreetea.com, 10 A.M.–5 P.M. Mon.–Sat., 11 A.M.–4 P.M. Sun. and summers), you can share a pot of Earl Grey, Darjeeling, and other blends over a light lunch or enjoy traditional afternoon tea selections, such as scones with Devon cream.

For New American cuisine, try **Café Bink** (36899 N. Tom Darlington Dr., 480/488-9796, www.cafebink.com, 11 A.M.–9 P.M. Tues.–Sat. June 1–Sept. 30 or daily Oct. 1–May 31 with brunch 10 A.M.–2 P.M. Sat.–Sun., $9–24), which features superb mountain views, a cozy patio, and bistro-inspired fare. At lunch, you'll find quiche, salads, and a selection of delicious sandwiches, along with steak, trout, and polenta bolognese. The expanded dinner lineup includes meatloaf, bouillabaisse, pork osso bucco, buttermilk fried chicken, and other entrées.

Getting There

From downtown Scottsdale, head north on Scottsdale Road, which becomes Tom Darlington Drive after it passes El Pedregal and edges the Boulders Resort. Continue on Tom Darlington Drive to downtown Carefree. From the I-17 freeway, you can get to Carefree by turning east on the Carefree Highway (State Route 74) at exit 224.

FOUNTAIN HILLS

Fountain Hills (pop. 22,500), a planned community started on a former ranch in 1969, acts as a gateway to McDowell Mountain Park, the Fort McDowell Indian Community and, via the Beeline Highway (State Route 87), Arizona's Rim Country. The namesake fountain at the town's center shoots 560 feet (three times the height of Old Faithful) into the air every daylight hour. The fountain and its surrounding park are the center of the town's family-oriented Fourth of July celebration. Over the second weekend in November, 500 artists gather in the park for the annual **Fountain Festival of Arts and Crafts,** one of the Valley's largest outdoor art celebrations.

Sights

The **River of Time Museum** (12901 E. La Montana, 480/837-2612, www.riveroftimemuseum.org, 1–4 P.M. Tues.–Sat., Fri.–Sat. in summer, $3) focuses on the lower Verde River and its geological and human history, with exhibits on the ancients, the historic Yavapai and Apache tribes, Spanish explorers, prospectors and mountain men, and early ranchers and townspeople. The small but well-designed museum also has dazzling specimens from the Four Peaks amethyst mine.

Getting There

To get to Fountain Hills from central Scottsdale or Loop 101, take Shea Boulevard east. Turn left (north) on Fountain Hills Boulevard. From south Scottsdale and Loop 202, take the Beeline Highway (State Route 87) north. Turn left (northwest) on Shea Boulevard, and then right (northeast) on Saguaro Boulevard, which curves north and leads to the town's namesake fountain, with its surrounding lake and park.

SCOTTSDALE AND VICINITY

SEDONA AND RED ROCK COUNTRY

Locals like to quip, "God created the Grand Canyon, but He lives in Sedona." Named "the most beautiful place in America" by *USA Today,* Sedona encompasses crimson spires and mesas, evergreen woodlands, and sparkling Oak Creek. The landscape is simply stunning, especially when the stone monoliths and sheer cliffs are burnished by the setting sun.

Sedona's red- and buff-colored rocks mark the southern rim of the Colorado Plateau, a massive expanse of land that rises 2,000 feet from the high-desert floor and stretches into Utah, Colorado, and New Mexico. The colorful stone layers underlying the plateau are revealed here, shaped by geological forces into blocky formations and delicate spires that seem to defy gravity.

The evocative terrain attracts an eclectic following of visitors and residents. Hikers, climbers, and mountain bikers of all skill levels come to scale the colossal buttes, while photographers and painters hope to be inspired by their beauty. Spiritual pilgrims, too, are drawn by the landscape; many believe it is marked by centers of spiraling energy, called vortexes. For others, the scenery merely serves as a magnificent backdrop for golf games, Southwestern cuisine, and rejuvenating spa treatments.

Sedona's fame as a travel destination belies its relatively small size. Situated about 90

© KATHLEEN BRYANT

© KATHLEEN BRYANT

Red Rock Scenic Byway

minutes north of Phoenix, the 19-square-mile community can be divided into three distinct areas: the Village of Oak Creek, Uptown, and West Sedona. Just north is Oak Creek Canyon, a shady retreat with campgrounds, picnic areas, swimming holes, and Slide Rock State Park. To the southwest lies the Verde Valley and Jerome.

Visitors driving from Phoenix on State Route 179 will arrive first in the Village of Oak Creek, an unincorporated area of golf resorts, shopping centers, hotels, and restaurants. The village or VOC, as it's often known, is a handy option for exploring the red rocks and feels pleasantly less congested than the rest of Sedona.

Continue north on State Route 179, known as Red Rock Scenic Byway, and you'll see prominent formations like Bell Rock, Courthouse Butte, and The Nuns. Once you cross over the leafy banks of Oak Creek, you'll arrive at "the Y," a three-pronged intersection that splits West Sedona and Uptown. Touristy Uptown commands impressive views and caters to visitors by offering a diverse selection of accommodations, restaurants, galleries, and shops. You'll find locals, as well as less-expensive hotels and popular bars and bistros, in West Sedona.

Though it can be hard at times to look beyond the hordes of shoppers, convoys of brightly painted tour Jeeps, and storefronts hawking time-shares or psychic readings, none of these can distract from the magical landscape. After all, no matter where you go or what you do in Sedona, the red rocks are a constant presence, reminding you that everything else is a mere blip on the grand geological scale that resulted in this very special place.

PLANNING YOUR TIME

Sedona makes a terrific getaway, whether you have a day or a week, offering scenic beauty and interesting sites within a relatively compact area. The city has developed to accommodate legions of tourists, and its pedestrian-friendly

HIGHLIGHTS

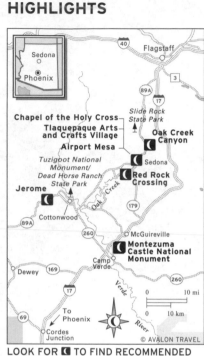

© AVALON TRAVEL

LOOK FOR 【 TO FIND RECOMMENDED SIGHTS, ACTIVITIES, DINING, AND LODGING.

【 Chapel of the Holy Cross: Admire this iconic church, which appears to rise from the red rocks in a brilliant union of art, nature, and God. Its quiet interior is the perfect place to contemplate Sedona's majestic landscape (page 176).

【 Airport Mesa: Enjoy a bird's-eye view of the red rocks from the top of Airport Mesa, and see if you can recognize Chimney Rock, Capitol Butte, Steamboat, and other colorfully eroded formations (page 177).

【 Red Rock Crossing: Behold what's said to be the most photographed view in Arizona: the majestic spires of Cathedral Rock rising above Oak Creek at Crescent Moon Ranch Picnic Area. Find the right spot, and you'll see them reflecting in the creek's clear waters (page 178).

【 Tlaquepaque Arts and Crafts Village: Visit Sedona's charming art-focused shopping village, inspired by Colonial Mexico. It boasts some of the city's best shops, galleries, and restaurants (page 186).

【 Oak Creek Canyon: Drive the scenic highway through this leafy refuge north of Sedona. The quiet, wooded setting is an ideal place to take a hike. Kids will want to slip down the natural chute at Slide Rock State Park (page 212).

【 Jerome: Explore this hillside mining town perched above the Verde Valley, which locals like to say is haunted. The narrow streets that were once home to saloons and brothels now feature small restaurants, galleries, and shops (page 217).

【 Montezuma Castle National Monument: Discover one of the best-preserved cliff dwellings in the country. The five-story, 20-room pueblo, which clings to side of a limestone wall 75 feet above the ground, is an impressive testament to the ingenuity of the prehistoric Sinagua culture (page 229).

shopping areas, varied restaurants, and intriguing galleries—backdropped by gorgeous red rocks—make getting around easy and fun.

Couples yearning for a romantic weekend can easily pop up from Phoenix for an overnight stay at one of Sedona's charming resorts or inns. More adventurous travelers, though, may want to stay longer in order to explore the natural beauty and historic sites throughout the Verde Valley. Sedona is a convenient home base for scenic drives to fascinating archaeological sites or the mining town of Jerome. Outdoor lovers could easily spend days hiking and biking forest trails, playing golf or tennis, investigating vortex sites, or kayaking down Oak Creek to a wine-tasting room.

No matter what time of year you visit, Sedona's landscape is enchanting. When

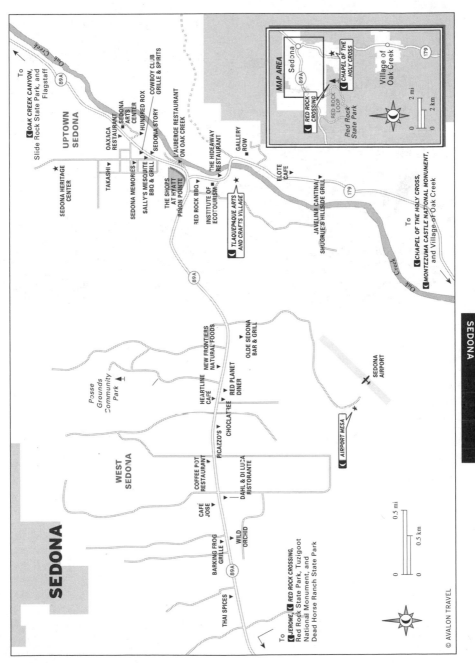

SEDONA

© AVALON TRAVEL

Uptown Sedona's shops and galleries, with Snoopy Rock in the background

SEDONA

temperatures are mild, spring wildflowers or autumn leaves are added incentives. Summer, on the other hand, is hot, with highs in the mid- to high-90s, though it cools off considerably at night. The occasional dusting of snow—along with annual holiday lights and hotel bargains—make a winter trip an intriguing option.

HISTORY

To first-time visitors, Sedona may appear to be a newly inhabited boomtown. Sure, its red buttes are millions of years old, but the freshly stuccoed shopping centers and recently constructed housing developments don't inspire a sense of history. The truth is, though, people have been coming to Sedona and the Verde Valley for thousands of years, lured by the dramatic surroundings, rich natural resources, and mild climate.

The Sinagua were the first to leave a lasting mark on the area. Sometime during the first millennium, they began raising crops. They built pit houses dating to A.D. 650, and later moved to cliff dwellings and hilltop pueblos. Sinagua ruins can be found throughout Red Rock Country and the Verde Valley, including the stunning Montezuma Castle, all abandoned by 1400. Archaeologists believe many Sinagua families joined other Ancestral Puebloans to the north, while some stayed behind and joined the seminomadic Yavapai bands who entered the area around A.D. 1300.

In 1876, after Yavapais and Apaches were forced onto reservations by the U.S. government, J. J. Thompson arrived in Oak Creek Canyon, settling on a piece of land where Indian crops still grew and calling it Indian Gardens. Additional ranching and farming families moved into the area, including T. C. Schnebly, an entrepreneurial settler who built a two-story wood-frame house where Tlaquepaque and the Los Abrigados Resort now stand. Schnebly ran a general store, lodged

THE MOVIES COME TO SEDONA

In 1923 five army trucks loaded with equipment slowly made their way down the switchbacks of Oak Creek Canyon to West Fork. Hollywood had arrived.

Call of the Canyon, based on a Zane Grey novel, was the first of more than 80 movies that would be made in the Sedona area, many filmed during the golden age of westerns. Among the finest are Angel and the Badman (1946), Broken Arrow (1950), and The Rounders (1965). The latter is notable not only for being a good flick, but also because it was the first film in which Sedona played itself. Until then, Sedona stood in for Canada (Pony Soldier, 1952), Bisbee (3:10 to Yuma, 1957), southeastern Arizona's Apache country (Broken Arrow, 1950), and other locales.

Hosting Hollywood often required the cooperation and ingenuity of locals (who ironically didn't have a movie theater of their own until 1975). A town set was constructed in Grasshopper Flat (now West Sedona), and a soundstage once stood where a hotel is located today. For Pony Soldier, workers added ponderosa pines to make convincing backdrops for Canadian Mounties. Wax saguaros decorated the set of Broken Arrow, one of many films that lives on in Sedona's place-names, which include streets called Gun Fury, Fabulous Texan, and Johnny Guitar.

Among the actors who worked in the red rocks: William Boyd (Hopalong Cassidy), Errol Flynn, John Wayne, Robert Mitchum, Hedy Lamarr, Jane Russell, James Stewart, Glenn Ford, Henry Fonda, Joan Crawford, Rock Hudson, Yvonne DeCarlo, Richard Widmark, Elvis Presley, Woody Harrelson, Robert De Niro, and Johnny Depp. A local history buff with plans to establish a film museum has put together a list of movies made in the Sedona area (www.arizonaslittleholly-wood.com).

You can also learn more about the local film résumé at the **Sedona Heritage Museum,** and your hotel room might have a few DVDs for loan. If you're a true-blue movie buff, check out the **Yavapai College film school** (928/649-4276, www.yc.edu), or visit in February for the annual film festival (www.sedonafilmfestival.com). During the weeklong event, more than 150 films are screened, from student shorts to indie flicks to Hollywood features.

guests, and established the area's first post office in 1902, which required him to submit a name for the burgeoning community. After the postmaster general in Washington rejected Schnebly Station and Oak Creek Crossing as being too long for a cancellation stamp, Schnebly followed his brother's advice and submitted his wife's name, Sedona.

In the early 1900s, more settlers began to stream into the Verde Valley, where they found work as farmers or in Jerome's ore-rich mines. However, it was another industry that would make Sedona famous: the movies. Hollywood filmed many of its classic westerns against the backdrop of Sedona's massive rock formations, beginning with Zane Grey's Call of the Canyon in 1923. Since then, stars from John Wayne to Johnny Depp have shot nearly a hundred movies and TV episodes in the area, and the rugged terrain continues to attract filmmakers.

Sedona's tourism industry took off as Americans began to explore the country by car after WWII. In the 1980s and 1990s, Sedona boomed as a retirement and vacation destination. More than half of the land around Sedona has been protected by state parks and national forest, driving up real estate values and pushing many new residents into neighboring areas, such as the Village of Oak Creek and Cottonwood. Still, some 11,000 people live in Sedona today—outnumbered by 3.5 million visitors every year—and the community manages to retain plenty of small-town character.

SEDONA

Sights

Sedona's main attraction is its awe-inspiring landscape. Reddish sandstone buttes, blue skies, and evergreen junipers and piñons dominate the horizon, while refreshing Oak Creek cuts through town, creating a peaceful, leafy axis. Make driving scenic byways and hiking the numerous trails your top priorities, but set aside some time to visit Chapel of the Holy Cross or other attractions before losing yourself in the plethora of shops and galleries.

UPTOWN AND HIGHWAY 179
◖ Chapel of the Holy Cross

In a region of such natural beauty, it's hard for a man-made structure not to compete or detract, which is why the Chapel of the Holy Cross (780 Chapel Rd., 928/282-4069, www.chapeloftheholycross.com, 9 A.M.–5 P.M. Mon.–Sat., 10 A.M.–5 P.M. Sun., free) is such a treasure. Perched above neighborhood and forest, the Modernist chapel has a structural support that doubles as its central motif, a 90-foot-tall cross rising between two red sandstone outcroppings. Set amid a deep red layer of stone, a spiraling ramp gives visitors time to appreciate the site's very special ambience and panoramic views before entering the chapel.

The interior is embellished only by floor-to-ceiling windows framing red rocks and blue skies. The chapel's designer, Marguerite Brunswig Staude, wanted it to be a place of prayer, and an aura of peace permeates the simple interior, lit by flickering votives. Spend some quiet time here before visiting the small gift shop downstairs.

Staude's design was inspired by a 1932 trip to New York City, where she saw a cross in the steel-and-glass facade of the recently constructed Empire State Building. Early sketches of her glass cathedral impressed Lloyd Wright, son of architect Frank Lloyd Wright, but the archbishop of Los Angeles ultimately rejected them for a proposed cathedral. When Staude and her husband bought a ranch in Sedona in 1941, she found the perfect setting for her vision. The small chapel was completed in 1956.

Schnebly Hill Road

At the roundabout intersection on the south side of Oak Creek Bridge, you'll see a turn-off for Schnebly Hill Road, one of the most scenic—and rockiest—drives in Sedona. Take the time to travel the first mile, which is paved all the way to the **Schnebly Hill Trailhead,** where you'll find lots of parking and a few shaded picnic tables with postcard-pretty views of Uptown. Look across the road to see **Snoopy Rock** and **Camel Head.**

Linger to soak up the views or, if you have time and a high-clearance, four-wheel-drive vehicle,

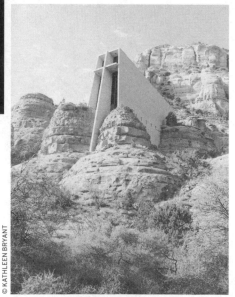

Chapel of the Holy Cross

continue up Schnebly Hill Road. It's another bone-rattling five miles to Schnebly Hill Vista, a dirt parking area that makes a good turnaround point. En route you'll pass the softly rounded red sandstone buttes known as **The Cowpies** and **The Merry-Go-Round,** a red sandstone formation circled by blocks of gray limestone that make up the carousel "horses." (If you'd prefer not to risk your oil pan or suspension, you can make this trip on a guided Jeep tour.)

Institute of Ecotourism

Located next to the Tlaquepaque Arts and Crafts Village, the Institute of Ecotourism (91 Portal Ln., 928/282-2720, www.ioet.org, 10 A.M.–6 P.M. Mon.–Fri., free) introduces the region's natural history and indigenous cultures through interactive exhibits highlighting geology, astronomy, and Arizona's fragile ecosystem. The modest grounds showcase native plants, and weekly classes range from geology talks to botanical walks. More than a museum, this nonprofit serves as a think tank for environmentally sensitive travel and tourism.

Sedona Heritage Museum

Get a glimpse of how Sedona's pioneers lived at the Sedona Heritage Museum and Jordan Park (735 Jordan Rd., 928/282-7038, www.sedonamuseum.org, 11 A.M.–3 P.M. daily, $7 adults, $2 children), the former home and orchards of Walter and Ruth Jordan. The Jordans' original one-room cabin, built in 1930 from red rock, was expanded over the years to accommodate a growing family and business. Rooms are filled with photos and artifacts showing life in early Sedona, from the rough work of real cowboys to the Hollywood version. More than 80 movies were filmed in the area, many shot during Hollywood's golden age of westerns. Be sure to enjoy the grounds of the museum, encompassing a botanical walk, heritage apple trees, and the shed that houses vintage machinery, including Walter Jordan's apple sorter.

Sedona Arts Center

Launched in 1958 as a place for local artists to teach and share ideas, the Sedona Arts Center (15 Art Barn Rd., 928/282-3809, www.sedonaartscenter.com, 10 A.M.–5 P.M. daily) helped establish Sedona's reputation as an art town. SAC's galleries feature rotating exhibitions of work by local and regional artists, and the gift shop has an excellent selection of reasonably priced work, including fine art, jewelry, sculpture, pottery, textiles, and photography. An integral part of the community since its beginnings in George Jordan's old apple barn (now a gallery), SAC hosts receptions and events, including **First Friday Art Walks** and the annual **Plein Air Festival** held in October. Its Nassan Gobran School of the Arts offers more than a hundred art classes every year, including three- to five-day intensive art workshops and field expeditions.

WEST SEDONA
◖ Airport Mesa

For a breathtaking bird's-eye view of the city, drive Airport Road to the top of the mesa and **Airport Vista.** Walk across the road from the large parking area to the vista's paved overlook for sweeping views from Cockscomb on the west to Wilson Mountain on the east. See if you can identify Chimney Rock, Lizard Head, Capitol Butte, Sugar Loaf, Coffeepot Rock, and other formations by their shapes. As you might guess, this is a popular spot to watch a sunset. Past the vista, the airport and its mile-long landing strip host a number of plane and helicopter touring companies. You'll also find a hotel and restaurant.

As you drove up the mesa, you likely noticed a small pullout with room for a half-dozen cars on the left side of Airport Road. This is the start of a short scramble up to a rocky saddle, said to be the location of the **Airport vortex.** The saddle has beautiful views eastward to the cliffs that mark the edge of Munds Mountain.

Amitabha Stupa and Peace Park

Designed and constructed by the Buddhist group Kunzang Palyul Chöling (KPC), the 36-foot-tall Amitabha Stupa (2650 Pueblo Dr., 877/788-7229, www.stupas.org, dusk to dawn daily, free) graces 14 acres of piñon-juniper woodland below Chimney Rock. Tucked into a West Sedona neighborhood, this peaceful sanctuary receives about 20,000 visitors a year. Stupa architecture incorporates sacred symbols and numbers, and this stupa (dedicated to the Buddha of Compassion) was filled with thousands of prayers and offerings during its construction. Along winding footpaths, you will also see fluttering prayer flags, a smaller White Tara stupa, and a large carved wooden Buddha. Circumambulate the stupas, find a quiet spot for contemplation or meditation, or simply enjoy the views. KPC has continued to welcome the public to the stupa park, despite financial setbacks that may affect its future. To get to the stupa park from State Route 89A, turn north on Andante Drive (at the Circle K) and continue for about a mile to Pueblo Drive. Turn left and proceed about 50 yards to the entrance, parking on the shoulder. Be respectful of private property as you walk the gently sloping path to the stupa.

◖ Red Rock Crossing

The view of **Cathedral Rock** from Oak Creek's Red Rock Crossing is said to be one of the most-photographed scenes in Arizona. Find it by taking State Route 89A west of town and turning left (south) on Upper Red Rock Loop Road. On its winding descent, the narrow paved road delivers tantalizing views of your destination. Turn left again at Chavez Ranch Road, then follow signs for Red Rock Crossing and **Crescent Moon Recreation Area** (928/203-2900, www.fs.fed.us/r3/Coconino, 8 A.M.–8 P.M. daily Memorial Day–Labor Day, otherwise closing at dusk, $9 per vehicle). This is a popular spot for weddings, picnics, and especially for photographers, thanks to the cool waters of Oak Creek and postcard views of Cathedral Rock's spires, perhaps the loveliest of Sedona's famed vortex sites. Informal paths meander along the creek to swimming holes like Buddha Beach, where visitants pile improbable stacks of rocks. You can also arrive at this lovely spot on foot or mountain bike via the Templeton Trail, which starts at the Back O' Beyond trailhead (off State Route 179). Or, from the Village of Oak Creek, drive to the end of the Verde Valley School Road and cross the creek on foot. (If the simple plank bridge has washed away, you'll find plenty of stepping stones.)

Red Rock State Park

Oak Creek flows through 286-acre Red Rock State Park (4050 Red Rock Loop Rd., 928/282-6907, http://azstateparks.com/parks/rero, 8 A.M.–5 P.M. daily, $6 per vehicle), the

© KATHLEEN BRYANT

The Amitabha Stupa and Peace Park are situated below Chimney Rock.

SEEING RED

The red rocks' famous color is just one small chapter in a complex geological story. The dramatic and vibrant landscape was created over eons, as this part of Arizona has been submerged by seas, alternated between muddy coastal plain and Sahara-like dunes, and endured volcanic eruptions, leaving behind colorful layers of limestone, sandstone, and basalt.

These layers are exposed at the edge of the massive, uplifted Colorado Plateau, which extends well into the Four Corners region. The plateau's exposed southern edge—known as the Mogollon Rim—has eroded into fantastically sculpted buttes and tall, slender spires. From the ground up, you'll see deep red Hermit shale; the 700-foot-thick horizontally banded Schnebly Hill formation; the aeolian (wind-deposited) light-gold Coconino sandstone; and on the highest peaks, the almost-white Kaibab limestone. In places, a cap of hard basalt (cooled lava), protects the softer layers underneath.

And the varying shades of red? Dissolved, oxidized iron—more prosaically known as rust—has permeated the sedimentary sandstone layers. Those who want to learn more about Sedona's geological history will find intriguing interpretive displays at Red Rock State Park and the forest service's Red Rock Visitor Center.

© KATHLEEN BRYANT

Sandstone rock layers have eroded into fantastic forms.

site of some of the area's earliest homesteads. Opened in 1991, the park serves as a protected riparian habitat for native wildlife and plants, as well as hosting an environmental education center (9 A.M.–5 P.M. daily) with interactive exhibits and a small theater. Architectural features include a viewing patio and a geology wall made up of the various layers of sandstone, limestone, and basalt from Sedona's famed rock formations. Volunteers and naturalists lead bird walks and nature hikes, including monthly full moon walks. The park's half-dozen short trails can be linked for longer hikes. To get to the park, take Upper or Lower Red Rock Loop Road off State Route 89A and follow the signs.

Prehistoric Ruins and Rock Art

About 15 miles northwest of town, **Palatki** (928/282-3854, 9 A.M.–3 P.M. daily, $5 per vehicle, reservations recommended) is a red-rock cliff dwelling occupied by Sinagua villagers eight hundred years ago. A short trail leads to **Red Cliffs,** a series of alcoves holding more than 5,000 pictographs and petroglyphs. To get here, take State Route 89A eight miles west of the Y intersection. Just past mile marker 365, turn right on Forest Road 525, a good dirt road suitable for most passenger cars when conditions are dry. Drive five miles to a fork; stay right, continuing on Forest Road 795 to the parking lot. After touring Palatki, you can make a scenic loop back to Sedona by turning left (east) on the Boynton Pass Road (Forest Road 152C), which changes from a rough dirt road to pavement after a couple miles. Continue to a "T," where you'll turn right, and then right again at the next "T" onto Dry Creek Road, which will return you to West Sedona.

If you have a sturdy vehicle, you can venture even farther into the cliffs and canyons to visit **Honanki** (10 A.M.–6 P.M. daily, weather permitting). This prehistoric village and rock art site tucked below Loy Butte is four miles away from Palatki via Forest Road 525. It's a good idea to check first with the forest service (928/203-7500) or the rangers at Palatki (928/282-3854) for directions and current road conditions, and your parking pass for Palatki is good for Honanki as well. Alternatively, you can travel to Honanki via a Pink Jeep tour.

VILLAGE OF OAK CREEK
Ranger Station and Visitor Center

The Red Rock Ranger District's **Visitor Center** (8375 State Route 179, 928/203-7500, 8 A.M.–5 P.M. daily), located just south of the Village of Oak Creek, has exhibits and a small retail area with fun nature-themed gifts, as well as books and maps. The expansive veranda out front is a great spot to snap a panoramic shot of Bell Rock and Courthouse Butte. You can ask for information about trails and scenic drives, and pick up a **Red Rock Pass** ($5 day, $15/week), required for parking at some forest service trailheads.

Scenic Red Rock Byway

Much of State Route 179 is designated as the Scenic Red Rock Byway, and it's easy to understand why. Rocky monuments line both sides of the road, luring you deeper into Red Rock Country. Paved pullouts and parking areas provide a safe place to stop and admire the views or take photos. After passing through VOC's main drag, look right (east) for the **Bell Rock Vista** parking area, a picnic spot and hub for biking and hiking trails. You'll easily recognize **Bell Rock.** Just east of the bell-shaped butte, is blocky **Courthouse Butte** and, across the highway to the west, **Castle Rock.**

As you continue toward Sedona on State Route 179, you'll pass **Cathedral Rock** (which from this side looks a little like a natural reddish Stonehenge), the **Little Horse** trailhead and parking area, and the Chapel of the Holy Cross, rising out of the red rocks near the spires known as **The Nuns** and the **Madonna and Child.** The scenic road designation ends at milepost 310, but the stunning views continue.

V-Bar-V Heritage Site

Archaeology buffs will be intrigued by the large rock art panel at V-Bar-V (9:30 A.M.–3 P.M. Fri.–Mon.), a former ranch along Beaver Creek. Now a heritage site under the protection of the forest service, it boasts the densest concentration of petroglyphs (rock art pecked into stone) in the area, including a possible solar calendar. To get here, take State Route 179 south of the Village of Oak Creek toward I-17. Continue under the freeway, where the road becomes Forest Road 618. It's three paved miles to the parking lot and a short (0.3 mile) stroll to the site, where docents share their knowledge of the Sinagua culture.

SEDONA

Entertainment and Events

Sedona hosts a handful of notable festivals and events, most crowding the calendar in spring and fall. Yet, despite the millions of tourists who visit annually, this is still a small town, with a slow pace and relaxed atmosphere that mean you won't discover a buzzing club scene. A number of local restaurants host local musicians during evening hours, and there are live performances around town most every weekend. But you may find that a quiet night under the stars is just the right way to cap a full day of hiking and exploring the red rocks.

NIGHTLIFE

Couples will find plenty of romantic restaurants in which to enjoy a glass of wine, and the big resorts expertly set the mood with cozy fireplaces and leafy patios. Make the 15-minute drive to **Enchantment Resort** (525 Boynton Canyon Rd., 928/282-2900, http://enchantmentresort.com), which is nestled in the horseshoe-shaped Boynton Canyon. The red-rock walls glow at sunset and provide a memorable backdrop for a drink in the lounge, where glass walls unfold to take in the view. The creekside bar at **L'Auberge de Sedona** (301 L'Auberge Ln., 928/282-1661, www.lauberge.com) in Uptown Sedona is an intimate, alfresco spot to share a bottle of wine.

If you want to catch a game on TV, **Stakes and Sticks Sports Bar and Grill** (160 Portal Ln., 928/204-7849, 11 A.M.–11 P.M. daily) at Los Abrigados Resort has two dozen screens broadcasting the wide world of sports. True to its promise of "pilsner, pool, and ponies," here you can wager on horse races at the automated betting stations inside the billiards room or enjoy a beer on the more subdued patio.

The **Rooftop Cantina** (321 N. State Route 89A, 928/282-4179, 11 A.M.–9 P.M. daily) at Oaxaca Restaurant has a menu of 50 tequilas

that can be mixed into some tasty margaritas. The views of Snoopy Rock are as much fun as the atmosphere at this Uptown Mexican restaurant.

Live music is on the menu most nights at **Sound Bites Grill** (101 N. State Route 89A, 928/282-2713, www.soundbitesgrille.com, 11 A.M.–11 P.M. Tues.–Sun., till midnight Fri.–Sat.) in Uptown's Piñon Pointe shops. The owners have a sister establishment in the VOC, the **Marketplace Café** (6645 State Route 179, 928/284-5478, www.mpcsedona. com, 11 A.M.–9 P.M. Sun.–Thurs., till 10 P.M. Fri.–Sat.), where you're likely to find live music on weekends.

Join the friendly crowd and casual vibe at **Full Moon Saloon** (7000 State Route 179, 928/284-1872, www.thefullmoonsaloon.com, 11 A.M.–2 A.M. daily) at Tequa Marketplace in the Village of Oak Creek. Depending on when you drop by, you might find a pool tournament, karaoke, open mic, or the occasional live band.

PJ's Village Pub & Sports Lounge (40 W. Cortez Dr., 928/284-2250, www.pjsvillagepub. com, 10 A.M.–2 A.M. daily) is another laid-back watering hole in the Village of Oak Creek that packs in locals with live music on Saturday nights. You'll find regulars playing darts and video games, as well as three pool tables that are free on Sunday evenings.

Olde Sedona Bar & Grill (1405 W. State Route 89A, 928/282-5670, www.oldsedona. com, 11 A.M.–2 A.M. daily) in West Sedona offers live entertainment most nights. The second-story patio has a view of the red rocks, or head downstairs to the bar, where you can dance, shoot pool, or shoot the breeze with new friends.

During temperate months, musicians take to the outdoor stage next to the **Martini Bar**

SEDONA

(1350 W. State Route 89A, 928/282-9288, 3 P.M.–2 A.M. daily). The pond-centered patio makes a pleasant gathering spot in West Sedona, with entertainment most nights between 7 and 10 P.M.

West Sedona's **Oak Creek Brewing Company** (2050 Yavapai Rd., 928/203-9441, www.oakcreekbrew.com, 4–11 P.M. Mon.–Thurs., noon–1 A.M. Fri.–Sun.) serves up award-winning craft beers, like its popular amber ale and refreshing hefeweizen. Take a seat near the fermentation tanks or head out to the patio to listen to live music, which ranges from Celtic and rockabilly to a weekly drumming circle. You can soak up your brew with a hot dog, but if you're hungry for a full meal, the brewery's more upscale grill is located in Tlaquepaque.

You never know what you'll find at **Relics Restaurant & Lounge at Rainbow's End** (3235 W. State Route 89A, 928/282-1593, www.relicsrestaurant.com, 4 P.M.–2 A.M. daily), a former homestead, USO club, and roller rink. The dancehall retains much of its rustic ambience, boasting northern Arizona's largest wooden dance floor and hosting weekly events, including 1950s revues, Latino nights, and DJ dance parties that range from Motown to country. If the barroom looks a little familiar, you may have seen it in *The Rounders* (1965), a Western comedy starring Henry Fonda and Glenn Ford.

PERFORMING ARTS

Canyon Moon Theatre Company (6601 State Route 179, 928/282-6212, www.canyonmoontheatre.org) stages a mix of dramas, comedies, and musicals at its theater in the Village of Oak Creek. **Shakespeare Sedona** (602/535-1202, www.swshakespeare.org) performs on select summer evenings in the courtyards of Tlaquepaque.

Chamber Music Sedona (928/204-2415, www.chambermusicsedona.org) presents an eclectic series of artists year-round at venues throughout Sedona, from pianists and string quartets to Latin guitar and small jazz bands. Check the website for performance dates and locations.

In West Sedona, **Studio Live** and **the Backyard** (215 Coffeepot Dr., 928/282-0549, www.studiolivesedona.com) host weekly performances by indie musicians, with recent appearances by Patty Larkin, Maria Muldaur, and Stanley Jordan. Home to the Sedona Performing Arts Alliance, this is also a great place to catch community events like theme nights and songwriter showcases.

The **Mary D. Fisher Theater** (2030 W. State Route 89A, 928/282-1177, www.sedonafilmfestival.com) is a small jewel, screening independent and foreign films every week, with occasional treats like big-screen, hi-def performances from London's National Theater or programs such as *Live from NY's 92nd Street Y*.

"New Age" is a convenient and somewhat inaccurate label for a host of performances, lectures, and events appealing to local residents, spiritual pilgrims, travel gypsies, and global music fans, held at various venues around town. You might, for example, watch a belly dance troupe at a local restaurant, attend an astrology lecture at the Unity church (65 Deertail Dr., 928/282-7181, www.unityofsedona.com), or sing along with a touring kirtan musician at 7 Centers Yoga Arts (2115 Mountain Rd., 928/203-4400, www.7centers.com). Self-improvement gurus and spiritual leaders like Deepak Chopra, Wayne Dyer, Ram Dass, Don Miguel Ruiz, Julia Cameron have visited Sedona, many of them appearing at the **Sedona Creative Life Center** (333 Schnebly Hill Rd., 928/282-9300, www.sedonacreativelifecenter.com), situated on a lovely 15-acre site near Oak Creek. Large community events and concerts are held in Posse Grounds Park or the Performing Arts Center at Red Rock High School.

For information about current happenings, stop by the Chamber of Commerce Visitor Center (1 Forest Rd., 928/282-7722 or 800/288-7336, www.visitsedona.com, 8:30 A.M.–5 P.M. Mon.–Sat., 8 A.M.–3 P.M. Sun.) or look for flyers at community bulletin boards in local bookstores and restaurants. Or pick up a free copy of *Kudos,* a weekly newspaper with the latest entertainment listings.

FESTIVALS AND EVENTS

Sedona's cultural calendar encompasses everything from intimate studio tours to grand galas. Most large outdoor events are scheduled for fall, when the weather is at its finest. To find out more about upcoming events, check

---

SEDONA'S ARTISTIC TRADITION

© KATHLEEN BRYANT

See an exhibit, take a class, or shop at the gallery at Sedona Arts Center.

It's no surprise why so many artists follow their muse to Sedona. The sculptural rock forms and bold color palette are powerful inspiration. Over the decades, a growing artistic community has helped shape the town and define its identity. Among the first to arrive were surrealist Max Ernst, who lived here briefly in the 1940s; painter Stephen Juharos, who opened Treasure Art Gallery; and Egyptian émigré and sculptor Nassan Gobran, who arrived to teach at Verde Valley School. The burgeoning art scene really began to

take hold in 1958, when Gobran and other artists established an art school at the Jordans' apple and peach packing barn in Uptown Sedona. This studio/exhibition space evolved into the **Sedona Arts Center (SAC).** Today SAC continues its mission to serve as a resource for local artists, providing gallery and classroom space, and hosting festivals and events.

One of SAC's founding members, jeweler and sculptor Marguerite Brunswig Staude, gave Sedona its most iconic landmark in 1956, the Chapel of the Holy Cross. SAC also displays work by member Joe Beeler, a painter and sculptor who moved to Sedona in the early 1960s. In 1965, Beeler met with Charlie Dye, George Phippen, and John Hampton at the Oak Creek Tavern (now the Cowboy Club Grille & Spirits), where they formed the Cowboy Artists of America. Beeler died in 2006, after seeing CAA grow into a respected organization whose members' works are prized by collectors.

As you explore Sedona's artistic side, you'll find numerous public sculptures, dozens of galleries, and top-notch events like the **Sedona Arts Festival** (www.sedonaartsfestival.org) and the **Plein Air Festival** (www.sedonapleinairfestival. com). Little wonder Sedona was named one of America's best small art towns by *American Style* magazine.

To immerse yourself in the local art scene, join the **First Friday** art walk, when galleries host receptions and artist demonstrations from 5 to 8 P.M. The Sedona Trolley offers free transportation between galleries. For more information, contact the **Sedona Gallery Association** (928/282-7390, www.sedonagalleryassociation.com).

SEDONA

the Sedona Events Alliance calendar (www.sedonaeventsalliance.org).

Spring

March is Arizona's Archaeology and Heritage Awareness Month, with dozens of events throughout the state. One, V-Bar-V Ranch's **Archaeology Discovery Days** (www.azstateparks.com, 928/203-2909), showcases prehistoric technologies like flint-knapping. Traditional foods are available for sampling, and visitors can try their hand at throwing an atlatl (hunting spear) or weaving yucca fiber sandals.

Late in April, the **Verde Valley Birding and Nature Festival** (www.birdyverde.org) celebrates the region's diverse natural habitats. Affectionately dubbed the "Birdy Verde," the multiday event hosted by Cottonwood's Dead Horse Ranch State Park includes expert speakers, field trips, and workshops. Past programs have featured lectures about Sedona geology, river trips, guided bird walks, and kid-centric games and activities.

Tlaquepaque (www.tlaq.com) hosts events throughout the year, but one of the most colorful occurs on **Cinco de Mayo** weekend, when folklorico dancers, mariachi musicians, and a chili contest lend a street party atmosphere to the shopping village.

Summer

On first weekend in June, the Chamber Music Sedona strikes a different note with its **Bluegrass Festival** (www.chambermusicsedona.org), featuring two days of finger-pickin' music, including workshops, a free community program, and an outdoor concert and barbecue.

The **Red Rock Music Festival** (877/733-7257, www.redrocksmusicfestival.com) in late August and early September attracts classical musical lovers for a vibrant showcase of chamber and orchestral music, as well as performances by flamenco and Native American performers. Concerts and events are held at venues throughout Sedona.

A long list of small-town celebrations (including the National Day of the Cowboy in July and the Moonlight Madness street festival marking Labor Day) are scheduled throughout summer, which is also the season for **open studio tours** hosted by members of the Sedona Visual Artists Coalition (http://sedonaartistscoalition.org).

Autumn

The answer to Sedona's increasingly commercial art scene is **Gumption Fest** (www.gumptionfest.org), when local and regional artists gather for a weekend of music, dance, art, and poetry, including the Haiku Death Match Poetry Slam. The free festival takes over a slice of West Sedona along Coffeepot Drive in mid-September.

In late September, the venerable **Sedona Jazz on the Rocks** (928/282-0590, www.sedonajazz.com) showcases live outdoor jazz performances. Spyro Gyra, Herbie Hancock, Diane Krall, and Poncho Sanchez have all taken the stage under the red rocks. In recent years, venues and dates have shifted; call or check the website for the current schedule.

In October, look for the sea of white tents near Red Rock High School marking the **Sedona Arts Festival** (995 Upper Red Rock Loop Rd., 928/204-9456, www.sedonaartsfestival.org), when more than 100 artists gather to show their work. There's also live music, food booths, and the Kid Zone, where children can create their own masterpieces.

The **Sedona Plein Air Festival** (928/282-3809, www.sedonapleinairfestival.com) in late October attracts artists from around the United States to paint "in the open air," a technique made famous by the French Impressionists. The weeklong event—at trailheads, creeks, and parks throughout town—includes demonstrations and workshops for painters hoping to develop their technical abilities, as well for art lovers who like to "brush up" their observation skills.

Winter

When the weather turns chilly in late November, more than a million lights go up at Los Abrigados Resort & Spa for **Red Rock Fantasy** (1090 W. State Route 89A, 928/282-1777, www.rcdrockfantasy.com). Participants compete by creating traditional and quirky nighttime displays that twinkle through the holiday season. In early December, neighboring Tlaquepaque hosts a Southwestern holiday tradition, the **Festival of Lights** (336 State Route 179, 928/282-4838, www.tlaq.com). Some 6,000 luminarias—small paper bags filled with sand and a single lit candle—glow in the shopping village's charming courtyards and stairways.

Runners converge the first week of February for the **Sedona Marathon** (800/775-7671, www.sedonamarathon.com). The challenging course, some of it on dirt forest roads, offers spectacular views and a few wildlife sightings as it wends its way from West Sedona to Boynton Pass. The full- and half-marathon runs, as well as the more manageable 5K option, are open to runners of all levels.

The last week of February, the **Sedona International Film Festival** (2030 W. State Route 89A, 928/282-1177, www.sedonafilm-festival.com) presents more than 100 movies from around the world, including big-budget features, documentaries, shorts, and student films. Workshops and parties round out the schedule, with directors, producers, and stars frequently in attendance.

Shopping

After admiring the red rocks, shopping is probably Sedona's most popular activity, with the vast majority of stores targeting the out-of-state visitors who flock here for a taste of Arizona—or to experience the New Age vibe. Specialty stores sell cactus jellies, cowboy boots and hats, colorful pottery, and mystical gemstones. You'll also find Native American arts and crafts from tiny carved fetishes to room-size Navajo rugs, and a thriving gallery scene that attracts serious collectors as well as first-time buyers.

UPTOWN AND HIGHWAY 179

Uptown boasts the greatest concentration of souvenir shops, clothing boutiques, and Western-themed galleries. Just south of Uptown along State Route 179, there's a pedestrian-friendly stretch of galleries ranging from mammoth, light-filled spaces selling large-format bronzes and canvases to intimate studios

specializing in handcrafted furniture, pottery, glass, or jewelry. On the **First Friday** of every month, galleries host receptions and stay open till 8 P.M.

Jewelry and Fashion

Looking for a piece of turquoise jewelry? Find this classic Southwestern stone at the **Turquoise Buffalo** (252 N. State Route 89A, 928/282-2994, www.turquoisebuffalo.com, 9 A.M.–6 P.M. Tues.–Wed., 9 A.M.–7:30 P.M. Thurs.–Mon.), which stocks more than 1,700 unique pieces. The helpful staff guides buyers and browsers through dozens of varieties of turquoise, from the green-veined Lone Mountain and the copper-flecked Morenci to the creamy white variations.

Also in Uptown, **Blue-Eyed Bear** (450 Jordan Rd., 928/282-9081, www.blueeyed-bear.com, 9 A.M.–5:30 P.M. daily) specializes

SEDONA

in handmade pieces in sterling silver, gold, and semiprecious stones, all designed by Native American and Southwestern artists. The necklaces, bracelets, and earrings evoke Arizona's indigenous roots while the clean lines and bold colors give the work a modern feel.

A handful of shops sell fashions from local designers. At **Looking West** (242 N. State Route 89A, 928/282-4877, daily) you'll find clothing designed and made in Sedona—flowing "broomstick" skirts, comfortable jackets, and accessories. **Victorian Cowgirl** (181 State Route 179, 877/232-3455 or 928/282-0778, www.victoriancowgirl.com, 10 A.M.–6 P.M. daily) has become a popular choice for brides and other romantics, though steampunks would also fall for the beautifully tailored garments with turn-of-the-20th-century flair. Gentlemen, don't feel left out: Head for **Cowboy Corral** (219 N. State Route 89A, 928/282-2040, www.cowboycorral.com, 10 A.M.–6 P.M. daily) where wannabe desperados outfit themselves with dusters, vests, and handmade hats. Leather fashions are the specialty at **UpWest** (470 N. State Route 89A, 928/204-1341, www.upwestleather.com, 10 A.M.–5 P.M. daily), housed in the historic Jordan sales building, where Sedona's Depression-era farmers sold fruit.

For a well-dressed home and a peek at old Sedona, stop by the landmarked **Hummingbird House** (100 Brewer Rd., 928/282-0705, 10 A.M.–5 P.M. Mon.–Sat., 11:30 A.M.–3:30 P.M. Sun.). Tucked behind a white picket fence and shaded by large sycamore trees, the 1920s general store has been lovingly refurbished, complete with an old waterwheel that churns outside. It now sells collectible Americana and reproductions, furniture and garden decor, and exquisitely curated toiletries and gifts.

The Shops at Hyatt Piñon Pointe

On a small bluff overlooking the Y intersection of State Routes 179 and 89A, The Shops at Hyatt Piñon Pointe (101 N. State Route 89A, 928/254-1006, www.theshopsathyattpinonpointe.com) include some interesting independent boutiques along with a few chains, which are creeping into Sedona. **Marchesa's Fine Shoe Salon** (928/282-3212, 10 A.M.–6 P.M. daily) stocks heels, boots, and sandals by high-end designers like Marc Jacobs, Betsey Johnson, Christian LaCroix, and Stuart Weitzman, as well as more affordable options. **George Kelly Fine Jewelers** (928/282-8884, www.sedonafinejewelry.com, 10 A.M.–6 P.M. daily) carries imaginative and contemporary necklaces and rings. And for a tasty souvenir or gift, pick up a bottle of Arizona vino at **The Art of Wine** (877/903-9463, www.artowine.com, 10 A.M.–6 P.M. Mon.–Wed., 10 A.M.–8 P.M. Thurs.–Sun.).

◖ Tlaquepaque Arts and Crafts Village

Rarely does a shopping center become an attraction in its own right, but the charming Tlaquepaque (336 State Route 179, 928/282-4838, www.tlaq.com, shops open 10 A.M.–5 P.M. daily) is a beloved Sedona landmark. Even if you're not a shopper, come for one of Tlaquepaque's lively weekend festivals, or simply to enjoy the fountains and lushly landscaped courtyards. Its creator, Abe Miller, purchased a 4.5-acre garden business on the banks of Oak Creek in the early 1970s, promising the owners that he would do his best to preserve the site's sycamore trees. He envisioned an artists' enclave where visitors could see craftspeople at work. For inspiration, he visited Mexican towns and villages, including the original Tlaquepaque, an elegant colonial retreat outside of Guadalajara.

Miller replicated the colonial town's tile-embellished buildings, stairways, and courtyards, wrapping them around the old sycamore and catalpa trees, and incorporating truckloads of ironwork, carved doors, and other details he shipped north from Mexico. He was particularly proud of the chapel, a romanticized confection of stained-glass windows, hand-carved leather pews, and adobe walls. And though Miller's vision of a live-work artists' village proved unviable, Tlaquepaque (pronounced tuh-LAH-kuh-PAH-kee) is home to dozens of boutiques, galleries, cafés, and restaurants, including a few of the original tenants. Recent additions making room for larger enterprises were given a patina of age, so that old and new are almost indistinguishable.

Under the clock tower, **Rowe Gallery** (928/282-8877, www.rowegallery.com) displays distinguished Western bronzes and paintings. Sculptor and owner Ken Rowe is often on hand answering questions or demonstrating technique. (Rowe and Kim Kori, whose works are also in the gallery, created the large bronze ravens and eagle that grace the double roundabout at the Sedona's Y intersection.)

For a colorful collection of handblown glass art, visit **Kuivato Glass Gallery** (928/282-1212, www.kuivato.com). The delicate glass sculptures, fountains, and chandeliers sparkle in the light, tempting many buyers to ship one of the fragile pieces home. **Isadora** (928/282-6232) stocks hand-loomed coats and vests in bold patterns, as well as Native American–inspired shawls and scarves.

One of Tlaquepaque's original tenants, **Cocopah** (928/282-4928, www.beadofthemonthclub.com) bills itself the "oldest bead store in Arizona," and also carries an impressive array of Art Nouveau and Art Deco estate jewelry, antique Tibetan beads, and Native American jewelry and accessories. **Hyde Out Fine Leathers** (928/282-1292) sells handbags, jackets, luggage, and belts in buttery tans and browns, deep reds, and rich blacks.

The Garland Building

At the foot of Schnebly Hill Road, the red-rock Garland Building (411 State Route 179, 10 A.M.–5 P.M. Mon.–Sat., 11 A.M.–5 P.M. Sun.) is home to a handful of shops, including Mary Margaret's delightful **Sedona Pottery** (928/282-1192, http://sedonapotter.com); **Kopavi** (928/282-4774, http://kopaviinternational.com), specializing in Hopi jewelry; and **Garland's Navajo Rugs** (928/282-4070, www.garlandsrugs.com). For more than 30 years, the Garland family has purchased directly from Indian artists, amassing a vast selection of Navajo weavings, including antique pieces and hard-to-find large floor rugs. You'll also see tastefully displayed Navajo sand paintings, hand-carved Hopi kachina dolls, Pueblo pottery, and handwoven baskets.

Hozho

Santa Fe–style Hozho (431 State Route 179, 10 A.M.–5:30 P.M. Mon.–Sat., 11 A.M.–5 P.M. Sun.) hosts a diverse lineup. **Turquoise Tortoise Gallery** (928/282-2262, www.turqtortsedona.com) has sculpture, jewelry, and contemporary paintings by Tony Abeyta, David Johns, and other artists. **Lanning Gallery** (928/282-6865, www.lanninggallery.com) features classic and contemporary paintings, as well as ceramics, glass, and handmade furniture. You could say that **The Hike House** (928/282-5820, http://thehikehouse.com) specializes in the art of hiking—it's a great stop for picking up maps and gear or learning more about trails.

Hillside

Farther south on State Route 179, **Hillside Sedona** (671 State Route 179, 928/282-4500, www.hillsidesedona.net, 10 A.M.–6 P.M. daily) is home to restaurants, specialty shops, and galleries, including the long-running **James Ratliff Gallery** (928/282-1404, www.jamesratliffgallery.com, 10 A.M.–5 P.M. Mon.–Sat., 11 A.M.–5 P.M. Sun.), selling high-end bronzes and strikingly modern Southwestern canvases. **El Prado** (928/282-7309,

SEDONA

www.elpradogalleries.com) showcases contemporary and Western paintings (including John Cogan's Grand Canyon scenes), but it's perhaps best known for large metal sculptures that twist and revolve in the wind.

WEST SEDONA

West of the Y along State Route 89A, mostly residential West Sedona is home to service businesses like grocers and hardware stores, though newer hotels have spurred more shops catering to visitors. The interests of locals and visitors intersect at the plethora of metaphysical shops selling books, crystals, and gifts.

New Age

Explore Sedona's New Age side at **Crystal Magic** (2978 W. State Route 89A, 928/282-1622, www.crystalmagicsedona.com, 9 A.M.–9 P.M. Mon.–Sat., 9 A.M.–8 P.M. Sun.), "a resource center for discovery and personal growth." Take home some healing crystals or stock up on aromatherapy oils and candles, feng shui supplies, incense, books, or music. The store also serves as an unofficial chamber of commerce where you can find information about metaphysical events and services like psychic readings or reflexology. Next door, the staff at **Magic Clothing** (2970 W. State Route 89A, 928/203-0053) can help you put together the gypsy goddess look popular in Sedona.

Mystical Bazaar (1449 W. State Route 89A, 928/204-5615, www.mysticalbazaar. com, 9 A.M.–8 P.M. Sun.–Wed., 9 A.M.–9 P.M. Thurs.–Sat.) sells jewelry made in Sedona, as well as a host of metaphysical items, including books, music, tarot cards, and crystals. The shop also offers aura photographs, which come with a 23-page report, and "facilitated spiritual tours" ranging from treks to Sedona's vortex spots to personalized shamanic journeys and starlight fire ceremonies.

Books

Owned by mystery author Kris Neri, the **Well Red Coyote** (3190 W. State Route 89A, 928/282-2284, www.wellredcoyote.com, 10 A.M.–6 P.M. Mon.–Sat.) stocks general interest books as well as regional titles, and often hosts weekend author events, poetry readings, and live musical performances.

Arts and Crafts

Raven's Nest (1145 W. State Route 89A, 928/204-2728, www.ravensnest-silversmith. com, 10 A.M.–5 P.M. Mon.–Sat., 1–5 P.M. Sun.), housed in a circular building at the corner of Airport Road, is a treasure trove of old pawn (items that were pawned for cash and not redeemed, once a common practice on Southwest reservations). Owner and silversmith Bob Colony is usually on hand for advice and repairs. The store also sells contemporary Native American jewelry, photographic art, and a selection of handmade gift items.

Mexidona (1670 W. State Route 89A, 928/282-0858, www.mexidona.com, 10 A.M.–5 P.M. daily) imports furniture, architectural embellishments, and handcrafted decor from Mexico, including Talavera, Mata Ortiz, and Oaxacan pottery.

Kachina House (2920 Hopi Dr., 928/204-9750, www.kachinahouse.com, 8:30 A.M.–4:30 P.M. Mon.–Fri., 8:30 A.M.–2:30 P.M. Sat., 10 A.M.–2 P.M. Sun.) is Arizona's largest distributor of Native American arts and crafts—many for reasonable prices. The 5,000-square-foot showroom sells hundreds of kachina dolls, ceremonial masks, horsehair pottery pieces, Hopi baskets, and sand paintings.

At the **Art Mart of Sedona** (2081 W. State Route 89A, 928/203-4576), located next to the Harkins movie theater, you'll find booth spaces offering a variety of arts and crafts, from inexpensive imported clothing to exquisite kachina figures carved and painted by local artist Gerald Quotskuyua.

VILLAGE OF OAK CREEK

Wonderfully unique shops have a habit of popping up in the Village, then fading away. Several of the big retail chains that were once a staple at the **Factory Outlet Mall** (6645 State Route 179, 10 A.M.–6 P.M. daily) have bowed out, but that's made room for interesting local shops like **The Worm** (928/282-3471, www.

sedonaworm.com), which has the area's best selection of Southwestern books, as well as general titles, music, and gifts.

Buddha's Dream (51 Bell Rock Plaza, 928/554-4677, www.buddhasdreamllc.com, 10 A.M.–7 P.M. daily) is a must-stop for tea-drinkers. Not only does the shop carry a wide selection of organic teas, it also hosts free daily tastings and tea ceremony classes. Shop for books and handmade silk clothing, or inquire about the owner's traditional Chinese wedding-planning services.

Sports and Recreation

If you're not content viewing Sedona's majestic red rocks from the comfort of a hotel balcony or a restaurant patio, you'll find plenty of ways to get outside and get a little dirty. Hikers and bikers could spend weeks, if not months, exploring the miles and miles of trails that wind through the national forest, three wilderness areas, and two state parks. The diversity of topography and wildlife frequently surprises visitors.

Jeep tours over rugged forest roads hint at how the pioneers who arrived by stagecoach more than a century ago must have felt. Of course, there are more refined ways to sneak in your time outdoors: a round of golf, an alfresco massage at a four-star spa, or a hot-air balloon trip. No matter what you choose—guided hikes, biplane tours, river floats—be sure to wear sturdy shoes, a hat, and sunscreen when you venture outside. Also bring water—lots of it—as it's not uncommon to dehydrate quickly in this arid climate and moderate elevation.

TOURS
Jeep Tours

Taking a ride with iconic **Pink Jeep Tours** (204 N. State Route 89A, 928/282-5000, www.pinkjeep.com) is a popular way to romp over Sedona's red rocks. Entertaining guides

describe the geology and ecosystem surrounding Sedona as they drive beefed-up Jeep Wranglers over steep boulders and occasionally treacherous passes. The popular Broken Arrow Tour ($75 adults, $56.25 children) explores Submarine Rock and scouts out postcard-perfect views from Chicken Point. The three-hour Ancient Ruins Tour ($72 adults, $54 children) stops at the ancient Sinagua cliff dwelling of Honanki and tracks down prehistoric rock art. Plush motorcoach tours to the Grand Canyon are also available ($125 adults, $115 children). Advanced reservations are recommended, though walk-ins can frequently get same-day seats.

Red Rock Western Jeep Tours (270 N. State Route 89A, Ste. 2, 928/282-6826, www.redrockjeep.com) offers four-wheeling excursions and much more. The cowboy guides may look like movie set extras, but these local experts enrich a traveler's understanding of Sedona's complex geology and wildlife. Red Rock's various outings range from romps with wine tasting to romantic private tours *à deux* to Western-themed treks that trace Apache and cowboy trails. The company also provides horseback riding, ranch cookouts, and sunset trips to the Grand Canyon. Basic Jeep tours

© KATHLEEN BRYANT

Jeep tours explore forest roads, vortex sites, and prehistoric ruins.

SEDONA

start around $50 per person. Parties of 10 or more may qualify for group rates.

If you're looking for a Jeep tour with a metaphysical approach, the guides at **Earth Wisdom Tours** (293 N. State Route 89A, 928/282-4714, www.earthwisdomtours.com) specialize in journeys that foster a deeper connection to the landscape and an appreciation for Native American spirituality. They'll take you on your choice of vortex tours, scenic drives, or hikes, all while imparting fascinating cultural and natural history. Two-hour tours start at $50 for adults; $25 for children under 12.

Adventure Tours

If you're not content letting the scenery pass you by from the seat of a Jeep, **Sedona Adventure Tours** (877/673-3661, www.sedonaadventure-tours.com) leads trips that highlight the area's diverse outdoor activities, including hiking, kayaking, and water tubing. The Water to Wine Tour ($130 adults) combines a four-mile

guided kayaking trip down the Verde River with a tour to Alcantara Vineyard for a pleasant afternoon of wine-tasting.

Adventures Out West (441 Forest Rd., 928/282-4611, www.advoutwest.com) offers Segway tours through Uptown or to the Chapel of the Holy Cross, starting at $65 and lasting 1–2 hours. Timing depends primarily on how expertly you handle the battery-powered, two-wheeled transport.

Mr. Sedona Private Guides (928/204-2201, http://mrsedona.com) lead half- and full-day tours geared to your abilities and interests, from gentle strolls and vortex adventures to downright challenging hikes. **Sedona Vortex Tours** (150 State Route 179, 928/282-2733, www.sedonaretreats.com) can customize a trip to visit a medicine wheel or include a Native American ceremony.

You can also opt for yoga hikes, botanical walks, shamanic journeys, or fly-fishing expeditions—if you need help making a selection, stop in at the Chamber of Commerce Visitor Center (1 Forest Rd., 928/282-7722 or 800/288-7336, www.visitsedona.com, 8:30 A.M.–5 P.M. Mon.–Sat., 8 A.M.–3 P.M. Sun.), or ask local hotels or stores for recommendations.

Air Tours

Arizona Helicopter Adventures (235 Air Terminal Dr., 928/282-0904, www.azheli.com) skims massive buttes and green forests on routes like the Red Rock Roundup ($65 per person), which surveys the area's best-known formations, incuding Bell and Snoopy Rocks, as well as the Chapel of the Holy Cross.

Take to the skies in a helicopter or Red Waco biplane with **Sedona Air Tours** (1225 Airport Rd., 928/204-5939, www.sedonaairtours.com). Biplane flights can accommodate two passengers at a time, while a pilot provides commentary about the landscape. Tours range from the 20-minute Classic Tour ($99 per person)—which soars past Bell Rock, the Chapel of the Holy Cross, and other landmarks—to an hour-long flight through Sedona and Oak Creek ($489 per person). Combination trips that incorporate Jeep tours, fishing, white-water rafting, and flights to the Grand Canyon and Monument Valley are available.

THE VORTEX BUZZ

© KATHLEEN BRYANT

Cathedral Rock's spires are said to be an energy vortex.

Sedona's vortexes embody much of the city's New Age culture: an ever-present phenomenon

that earns curiosity from locals and visitors alike. You may be familiar with more mundane vortexes, like the desert's spiraling dust devils or water going down a drain. Sedona's vortexes are centers of energy—invisible and immeasurable by practical means—that believers say lead to heightened self-awareness and spiritual experiences.

Depending on whom you ask, numerous sites are scattered around town, but there are four well-known and easy-to-reach vortexes: the saddle of Airport Mesa, Boynton Canyon, Bell Rock, and Cathedral Rock. Some are associated with masculine energy, improving strength and self-confidence, while others are more feminine, boosting patience and kindness. But don't take anyone's word for it: See for yourself where your inner journey leads.

If you're a nonbeliever, you might try thinking of vortexes as beautiful natural spots that offer an opportunity for reflection. You could also view them as an introduction to Sedona's metaphysical side, because if you've ever wanted to experience a psychic reading or explore alternative healing techniques, you're in the right place. The local chamber of commerce even has an affinity group for member businesses that focus on the metaphysical (www.sedonaspiritual.com).

SEDONA

Astronomy Tour

Sedona's clean air, low humidity, and dark skies provide the perfect backdrop for shimmering planets, galaxies, and thousands upon thousands of stars. **Sedona Stargazing Tours** (928/853-9778, www.eveningskytours.com, $60 adults, $35 ages 6–12) survey the nighttime canopy with custom-built telescopes that offer so-close-you-can-touch-it views of the moon, meteor showers, and even Saturn's rings. Professional astronomers act as guides, beginning with an overview of the night's celestial display before turning telescopes over to guests.

BALLOONING

Though several ballooning companies advertise tours, only two are permitted by the Coconino National Forest to fly in the red-rock area, so be sure to verify routes when booking with other companies. Tours begin at sunrise, when the air is still and sunlight reaches across the landscape. Your reward for the early start is seeing the red rocks emerge from purple shadows to be burnished in gold.

Northern Light Balloon Expeditions (800/230-6222 or 928/282-2274, www.northernlightballoon.com, $195 per person) has been floating over the red rocks since 1974. Their balloons carry no more than seven passengers, for a personalized feel. (Groups of up to 35 are accommodated in separate balloons.) Flights, approximately an hour long, are followed by a champagne picnic and include transportation to your hotel. Day-before reservations are usually available.

Red Rock Balloon Adventures (800/258-3754, www.redrockballoons.com, $195 person) also offers 60- to 90-minute sunrise tours, concluding with a mimosa picnic. Brides and grooms may want to consider the Wedding Package ($2,500), which can accommodate up to six people on a private flight and includes a "commemorative picnic" with wedding cake.

HIKING

Hikers, welcome to a paradise of spectacular scenery, massive geological formations, and acres upon acres of protected land. It's easy to use a succession of clichés to describe the views from Sedona's trails (breathtaking, heart-stopping, etc.), but it's hard to convey the riches of experiences you'll find when you enter the landscape on foot. Even if you're not a hiker, you can't help but enjoy a stroll among red-rock monuments or along the lush banks of Oak Creek. With more than 200 miles of trails to choose from, you're sure to find one that matches your skill level and schedule. For maps and advice, stop by an official visitor center or contact the forest service's Red Rock Ranger District (8375 State Route 179, 928/203-7500, www.redrockcountry.org, 8 A.M.–5 P.M. daily).

The **Courthouse Loop** (four-mile loop) is a fine introductory trail. Beginning on the Bell Rock Pathway just north of the Village of Oak Creek on State Route 179. The trail is often busy, and for good reason: it's beautiful. The leisurely route circles Bell Rock (considered a vortex) and Courthouse Butte, making it a can't-miss trek for families and first-time hikers.

About a mile north on State Route 179, turn onto Back O' Beyond Road and proceed to the parking lot for the **Cathedral Rock Trail** (1.5 miles round-trip). The short but steep hike to the heart of Cathedral Rock (another vortex) is challenging, especially for acrophobes, but the views from the formation's central spires are a big reward. Follow the cairns (rock markers), and be prepared to use toeholds carved into the rock to ascend a particularly steep section.

In West Sedona, the **Airport Mesa Trail** (4.5-mile loop) provides a series of camera-ready vistas of Sedona and its red-rock buttes. It's best to hit this trail early in the morning before the parking lot—about halfway up Airport Road—fills up.

From State Route 89A, turn north on

Soldiers Pass Road and follow the brown signs marking a small parking area for the **Soldier Pass Trail** (four miles round-trip). Highlights include Devil's Kitchen (a large sinkhole) and Seven Sacred Pools, a series of natural basins eroded into the bedrock of Soldier Wash. Just after the trail crosses the boundary of the Red Rock–Secret Mountain Wilderness, a challenging quarter-mile spur heads right, up to a series of arches.

The **Devil's Bridge Trail** (two miles round-trip) leads to the area's largest natural stone arch. To get to the trailhead from West Sedona, take Dry Creek Road north to Forest Road 152, where you'll need a four-wheel-drive vehicle to continue another 1.5 miles to the parking area. At about three-quarters of a mile into the moderate hike, the trail splits, the right fork going to the end of the arch, the left winding below it. Be prepared to climb stone-slab stairs, which do not have handrails, and do heed the forest service's warning not to stand atop the arch. (Geology happens, sometimes over eons, sometimes suddenly.)

Park just outside Enchantment Resort to trek the **Boynton Canyon Trail** (five miles round-trip) an easy to moderate hike that traverses several different terrains, from cactus-dotted desert to pine-shaded forest. As you make your way up the canyon, pause to look up at shady alcoves in the cliffs: Many shelter prehistoric Sinagua dwellings. The cocooning box canyon is said to be imbued with vortex energy, and for the Yavapai people, it is an important location in tribal history. The canyon's entrance is guarded by the tall, elegant spire referred to as **Kachina Woman,** accessible from the intersecting Vista Trail (0.5 mile round-trip).

Just west of the resort on Boynton Pass Road, a large paved parking area marks the start of the **Fay Canyon Trail** (2.5 miles round-trip). Scrub oak and ponderosa pines shade much of this relatively level trail. Less than a mile into the trek, look for an easy-to-miss side trail,

The Fay Canyon Trail's sandstone cliffs are streaked with mineral deposits.

© KATHLEEN BRYANT

which leads to a natural stone arch. A bit farther down the main trail, look midway up the canyon walls for a red sandstone spire that resembles a goblet or mace.

BIKING

Mountain bikers will find some of the best off-roading in the country, across a terrain every bit as diverse and challenging as meccas in Moab, Utah, and Durango, Colorado—though far less crowded. The single-track trails lure die-hards and beginners alike, thanks to challenging combinations of dirt, sand, and slickrock.

Many of Sedona's hiking trails accommodate bikers, the most notable exceptions being designated wilderness trails where bikes are strictly forbidden. Consult maps or trailhead signage before setting out or, better yet, stop by one of the local bike shops for friendly advice. Always exercise caution on rock formations and near cliff edges.

© KATHLEEN BRYANT

Teapot Rock near Schnebly Hill

The **Jim Thompson Trail** (five miles round-trip) can be accessed from the end of Jordan Road in Uptown Sedona or a couple of miles north at the Wilson Canyon Trailhead at the Midgley Bridge on State Route 89A. Thompson built this rocky trail in the 1880s as a wagon road to his cabin. The wide route passes beneath the "sail" of Ship Rock and neighboring Steamboat Rock, offering views of Uptown and the colorful Schnebly Hill rock formations.

For a moderately challenging half-day trek, try the **Submarine Loop** (10 miles), beginning on the Broken Arrow hiking trail at the end of Morgan Road, which lies east of State Route 179 south of Sedona. The trail changes from dirt single-track to slickrock at Submarine Rock and Chicken Point. Make this a loop by circling around the west side of Twin Buttes on the Little Horse trail to the Bell Rock Pathway, then using neighborhood streets to pick up the Mystic trail and return to Morgan Road.

Starting at the high school west of Sedona,

the **Red Rock Pathways Multi-Use Trail** gives bikers a safer alternative to State Route 89A for accessing a network of trails and forest roads along **Lower Red Rock Loop Road.** Options include traveling through **Red Rock State Park** and crossing Oak Creek to the Turkey Creek Road, which intersects with Verde Valley School Road. From here, you can return to the loop road via Red Rock Crossing. Or you might take the challenging trail across Scheurman Mountain, which connects the Upper and Lower Red Rock Loops.

If you need to rent some wheels, **Sedona Bike & Bean** (6020 State Route 179, 928/284-0210, www.bike-bean.com, 8 A.M.–5 P.M. daily) in the Village of Oak Creek offers convenient access to trails near Bell, Courthouse, and Cathedral Rocks. The laid-back shop rents mountain and road bikes starting at $25 for two hours, and same-day reservations are welcome on any bike for any length of time. The coffee's pretty darn good, too. Inquire about the Bean's tours, which include family-friendly mountain biking and road tours to wineries and galleries. A new location near Uptown (671 State Route 179, 928/204-5666, 8 A.M.–5 P.M. daily) specializes in road bikes.

Over the Edge Sports (1695 W. State Route 89A, 928/282-1106, http://otesports. com, 9 A.M.–6 P.M. daily) caters to the fat-tire crowd, though they also rent spiffy Italian road bikes. Prices start at $30 per day and rise to $80 for premium-suspension bikes. You'll find maps and trail advice here, along with custom Sedona jerseys and other gear. They host group rides; stop in and chat with the friendly staff to find out what's on the calendar.

BIRDING

More than 300 bird species flock to the Verde Valley's lush riparian areas, woodlands, and forests, making the region a prime spot for bird-watching. Throughout the year, it's not uncommon to see ravens, eagles, great blue herons, orioles, canyon wrens, and several species of hawks. Canada geese, kingfishers, mergansers, ducks, and other waterfowl winter in Oak Creek Canyon and the wetlands created by the treatment ponds west of Sedona. A good place to see black hawks (a threatened species) is along the creek in **Red Rock State Park** (4050 Red Rock Loop Rd., 928/282-6907, http://az-stateparks.com/parks/rero, 8 A.M.–5 P.M. daily, $6 per vehicle), where volunteers lead daily bird walks.

Serious birders should consider timing a visit with the **Verde Valley Birding and Nature Festival** (www.birdyverde.org) held each April, featuring field trips led by local experts. An excellent guide, *Birding in Sedona and the Verde Valley,* is available from the Northern Arizona chapter of the **Audobon Society** (www.northernarizonaaudobon.org). If you forgot your binoculars, stop by **Jay's Bird Barn** (2370 W. State Route 89A, 928/203-5700, www.jaysbird-barn.com, 8:30 A.M.–5:30 P.M. Mon.–Sat.) in

the Safeway shopping center. They host bird walks on Wednesday mornings.

GOLF

For those who appreciate the pleasure of a golf course's design as much as the thrill of a challenging game, Sedona won't disappoint. Lush fairways provide a brilliant contrast to the crimson buttes that surround the area's courses. Sedona is "land-locked" by Coconino National Forest, keeping real estate at a premium: Thus, you can expect slightly shorter drives and imaginatively designed tees and greens.

If the scenery looks familiar at the **Sedona Golf Resort** (35 Ridge Trail Dr., 877/733-6630 or 928/284-2093, www.sedonagolfresort.com), you may recognize it from one of the classic westerns that were filmed here long before the carefully manicured greens and sandy bunkers arrived. The championship course in the Village of Oak Creek features long, rolling fairways and scenic vistas—including the view of Cathedral Rock from the signature tenth hole. *Golf Digest* regularly bestows the 6,646-yard, par-71 course with a well-deserved four-star rating. The clubhouse offers clinics, private and group lessons, and even a club-fitting analysis.

Purists who prefer a traditional layout will appreciate the **Oak Creek Country Club** (690 Bell Rock Blvd., 888/284-1660 or 928/284-1660, www.oakcreekcountryclub.com), also in the VOC. Robert Trent Jones Sr. and Robert Trent Jones Jr. designed the par-72, 18-hole championship golf course to be a tough play, with tree-lined fairways that dogleg, slightly elevated greens, and lakes that pose the occasional hazard. The signature fourth hole, which is complemented by terrific views of the red rocks, will push most golfers to earn a par 3.

Northwest of Sedona, incongruously tucked among wilderness canyons, **Seven Canyons** (755 Golf Club Way, 928/203-3001, www. sevencanyons.com) has earned accolades from golfers, including being named one of the Top

100 Modern Courses by *Golfweek* magazine. Tom Weiskopf designed the par-70 course to emphasize the natural topography of the landscape, with tees that take advantage of changes in elevation, naturally rolling fairways, and small, quick greens. Rock walls, water features, bridges, and high-desert landscaping are backdropped by red sandstone buttes and Maroon Mountain.

The par-3 executive course at the **Poco Diablo Resort** (1752 S. State Route 179, 928/282-7333, www.pocodiablo.com) provides an excellent opportunity to work on your short game while taking in some impressive views along Oak Creek. The duck ponds, willow and pine trees, and low-key atmosphere offer a refreshing break from Uptown's crowds. The water hazards and fast greens can be challenging, but the real draw to this nine-hole course is its manageable size, offering a quick and affordable way to fit in a game of golf on a short trip to Sedona.

SPAS

One of the finest spas in the world, **Mii Amo** (525 Boynton Canyon Rd., 888/749-2137, www.miiamo.com, 6 A.M.–10 P.M. daily) regularly tops "best of" lists for its comprehensive treatments, sleek decor, and incredible setting in Boynton Canyon. The luxury spa is only open to guests of Mii Amo or its sister resort, Enchantment, so consider splurging on a stay here—you won't be disappointed. You'll want to spend days relaxing by indoor and outdoor pools, enjoying a yoga class on the lawn, or taking a moment for quiet contemplation in the Crystal Grotto, which perfectly aligns with the sun's light during the summer solstice. Day packages for Enchantment guests start at $415, and prices for an all-inclusive three-night journey begin at $2,400.

Hilton Sedona Spa (10 Ridge View Dr., 928/284-6900, www.hiltonsedonaspa.com, 5:30 A.M.–8 P.M. Mon.–Fri., 7 A.M.–8 P.M.

Sat.–Sun.) boasts a devoted local membership who frequent the 25,000-square-foot facility for its gym, three tennis courts, outdoor heated lap pool, and fitness classes that range from basic cardio to tai chi, yoga, zumba, and qi gong. Hour-long massages, scrubs, and other treatments start at $140, and you can make a day of it by taking advantage of the separate men's and women's steam rooms, saunas, and rooftop sundecks.

The chic boutique **Spa at Sedona Rouge** (2250 W. State Route 89A, 928/340-5331, www.sedonarouge.com/spa, 10 A.M.–7 P.M. daily) offers substance along with style, as therapists are trained in a host of techniques, including ayurvedic treatments, Thai massage, Lomi Lomi, cranial sacral therapy, reflexology, and cupping massage. In addition to gender-specific steam rooms and alfresco whirlpools, guests can enjoy the coed tranquility room and garden. Massages here start at $120.

Amara Spa (100 Amara Ln., 800/891-0105 or 928/282-6088, www.amararesort.com, 10 A.M.–7 P.M. daily) is another mod boutique-resort option, with a decidedly luxe atmosphere. Guests can create a custom-tailored massage (starting at $120) or select from a menu of full-body treatments, like the Chakra-Balancing Scrub and Wrap ($180). Daily yoga classes and private fitness sessions are available.

Sedona Spa (160 Portal Ln., 928/282-5108, www.sedonaspa.com, 6 A.M.–9 P.M. Mon.–Sat., 8 A.M.–6 P.M. Sun.) at Los Abrigados Resort offers an impressive selection of therapeutic massages that begin at $95, as well as acupuncture and full-body polishes, herbal wraps, and soothing mud masks. Get to the spa early to relax in the eucalyptus steam room, sauna, and whirlpool, or to fit in a game of tennis or a Pilates class.

Therapy on the Rocks (676 N. State Route 89 A, 928/282-3002, www.therapyontherocks.org, 9 A.M.–5:30 P.M. Mon.–Sat.), housed in a cottage just north of Uptown on Oak Creek, specializes in myofascial release, a massage technique practitioners say relieves pain and increases range of motion. There are half-hour, hour, and half-day sessions, as well as comprehensive two-week programs for people with chronic pain conditions. If it's warm enough, you can enjoy a creekside treatment or the outdoor whirlpool on the sundeck. Customized treatments vary from person to person; call ahead for prices.

In West Sedona, **New Day Spa** (1449 W. State Route 89A, 928/282-7502, www.sedonanewdayspa.com, 9 A.M.–7 P.M. Mon.–Sat., 10 A.M.–7 P.M. Sun.) may not have resort surroundings, but it offers a full menu of massages and treatments that start at $115. Many of the spa products are formulated in Sedona from essential oils and native herbs.

Sedona is known for its alternative therapies, and even at larger resorts the lines between spa treatments and healing modalities tend to blur. Skilled local practitioners of acupuncture, reflexology, ayurveda, hypnotherapy, or other integrative modalities might work in a hotel spa, a small studio, or both. In the Village of Oak Creek, **Ayurveda Sedona** (70 Navajo Rd., 928/284-1114, http://ayurvedasedona.com) adds treatments like shirodhara or marma point therapy to massage. At **Lovejoy's Enchanted Cottage** (235 Birch Blvd., 928/301-1903, deblovejoy.com) in West Sedona, a pampering pedicure can be combined with reflexology, aromatherapy, reiki, and other energy work. West Sedona's **Thunder Mountain Wellness** (2940 Southwest Dr., 928/202-2273, www.tmwc.org) offers yoga therapy and somatic bodywork in addition to massage.

Accommodations

More than a century ago, T. C. and Sedona Schnebly rented rooms to guests in their wood-frame house along Oak Creek, where Tlaquepaque now stands. Sedona's tradition of hospitality continues today. Though a few chain hotels have popped up among the mom-and-pop motels and luxury resorts, the town's specialty is the romantic getaway—charming inns, B&Bs, and lodges. Rates peak in the fall and spring, though you'll be able to find discounts if you stay midweek, or visit during summer or winter months. Lively and walkable Uptown has a village feel, while West Sedona offers the convenience of nearby service businesses. A few miles south, the Village of Oak Creek has budget options (and half the sales tax), with some motels mere blocks from golf courses. No matter where you stay, everything is within a few minutes' drive, and even if your room doesn't have a view, red-rock panoramas are never very far away.

UPTOWN AND HIGHWAY 179
$50-100

Star Motel (295 Jordan Rd., 928/282-3641, starmotelsedona.com, $80–90 d) is an ideal spot for budget travelers looking for affordability with a little character. The motel was built in the 1950s, and its 11 units are bright and clean. The hospitable owners, Marcelle and Anne, couldn't be sweeter. Families will love the second-floor suite's two queen beds, full kitchen, and private patio with views of the red rocks.

The Sedona Motel (218 State Route 179, 928/282-7187, www.thesedonamotel.com, $90–110 d) is a good value. The motel's terraced patio has commanding views of the red rocks, and the central location just south of the 89A/179 intersection is within walking distance of Tlaquepaque or Uptown.

© KATHLEEN BRYANT

SEDONA

It's easy to find a room with a view in Uptown Sedona.

$100-250

Along the banks of Oak Creek below Uptown's shops and galleries, **Amara Hotel, Restaurant & Spa** (100 Amara Ln., 928/282-4828, www.amararesort.com, $185–215 d) brings a bit of big-city chic to Red Rock Country. The posh boutique hotel stands out among Sedona's ubiquitous Southwestern style, though its minimalist design doesn't try to overshadow its natural setting among giant sycamore trees and spectacular views. You'll find all the usual luxury amenities—300-thread-count linens, oversize soaking tubs, private balconies, elegantly manicured grounds—but Amara ups the game with a heated saltwater pool and the Hundred Rox restaurant.

You can't beat the location of ◖ **The Orchards Inn** (254 N. State Route 89A, 800/474-7719 or 928/282-2405, www.orchardsinn.com, $200–240 d). A block from Uptown's main drag, the inn's contemporary

Southwestern rooms have patios and decks with views of Snoopy Rock and the surrounding buttes. If a "room with a view" is a priority, this may be an ideal place to hang your hat, and the recently renovated hotel includes welcome amenities for the price. Uptown's shops, restaurants, and bars are just outside your front door, and the on-site **Taos Cantina** serves lunch and dinner.

The **Matterhorn Inn** (230 Apple Ave., 800/372-8207 or 928/282-7176, www.matterhorninn.com, $160–180 d) is only steps from Uptown Sedona's shops, galleries, and restaurants. Thanks to its hillside location, each of the hotel's 23 rooms has a private balcony or terrace with panoramic views of Snoopy Rock, Camel's Head, and Teapot Rock. The hotel has a hot tub and a seasonal pool, making it a favorite choice for families.

Next to the Sedona Arts Center, **Best Western Arroyo Roble Hotel & Creekside Villas** (400 N. State Route 89A, 800/773-3662 or 928/282-4001, www.bestwesternsedona.com, $225–265 d) has a host of amenities you typically would find at a large resort: tennis and racquetball courts, a fully equipped exercise room, and an indoor/outdoor heated swimming pool. Some rooms in the five-story hotel even have fireplaces and whirlpool tubs, and roomy two-bedroom villas along the creek are just steps away from shady paths.

Los Abrigados Resort & Spa (160 Portal Ln., 928/282-1777, www.ilxresorts.com, $180–280 d), operated by Diamond Resorts, sits on a historical property at the heart of Sedona, where T. C. and Sedona Schnebly built a two-story frame home in the early 1900s. Walking the 22-acre, beautifully landscaped resort next to Tlaquepaque and Oak Creek, you'll find plenty of diversions: two swimming pools, a whirlpool spa, tennis and basketball courts, a fitness center, and a creekside miniature golf course. Plus, the on-site Sedona Spa features some fine treatments for guests looking for a little R&R.

A classic B&B, the **Creekside Inn at Sedona** (99 Copper Cliffs Dr., 800/390-8621 or 928/282-4992, www.creeksideinn.net, $200–270 d) is decorated with period antiques, and its six cheerful rooms and suites are bright and clean. The Creekview Suite has a mammoth, ceiling-high walnut bed and French doors leading to a private deck, ideal for a romantic getaway. Guests can pass the time by fishing in the creek on the three-acre property, relaxing on the porch with a glass of wine, or taking a short stroll along Gallery Row.

On the site of a former CCC camp and movie soundstage, the **Kings Ransom Motel** (771 State Route 179, 800/846-6164 or 928/282-7151, www.kingsransomsedona.com, $80–150 d) and neighboring **Kings Ransom Inn** (725 State Route 179, 877/480-0044 or 928/282-3132, http://kingsransominn.com, $115–180 d) sit at the end of Gallery Row, a short walk from shops and forest service trails. Rooms at the motel have balconies or patio access, some with views of the lovely courtyard pool or the red rocks. Views are also included with the free continental breakfast, which you can enjoy in the dining room or on the courtyard deck.

About halfway between Uptown and the Village of Oak Creek, **Radisson Poco Diablo Resort** (1752 State Route 179, 877/282-5755 or 928/282-7333, www.pocodiablo.com, $200–240 d) offers a peaceful, creekside setting with red-rock views and nearby hiking, as well as the amenities of a larger resort, including a fitness center, a swimming pool, a nine-hole golf course, and tennis courts. Select rooms have a fireplace and private whirlpool bath. The on-site restaurant, **T. Carl's,** serves breakfast, lunch, and dinner.

Over $250

◖ L'Auberge de Sedona (301 L'Auberge Ln., 855/905-5745, www.lauberge.com, $400–650 d) seduces guests with its warm, friendly atmosphere, thoughtful service, and romantic setting along the banks of Oak Creek. The intimate resort feels hidden away under giant sycamores, and the morning duck feedings and relaxing spa feel a world away from the congestion and crowds just up the hill in Uptown. Cozy rooms are available in the main lodge, though the creekside cabins are worth the splurge. The new hillside cottages are refreshingly modern, boasting outdoor showers and large observation decks. Be sure to savor at least one meal at the property's award-winning restaurant along the creek.

One of Arizona's finest hotels, **◖ El Portal Sedona** (95 Portal Ln., 800/313-0017 or 928/203-9405, www.elportalsedona.com, $260–400 d) blends Arts-and-Crafts design with Southwestern touches and hacienda-style hospitality. Owners Connie and Steve Segner have created a luxurious, intimate inn with a commitment to even the smallest details. Each of the 12 unique rooms and suites echoes El Portal's eclectic historical style—stained-glass doors, cozy fireplaces, antique furnishings, thick adobe walls, and private gardens. Situated next to Tlaquepaque, the inn is only a short stroll from some of Sedona's best restaurants and galleries, but you may not want to leave this elegant hideaway. (If you're on a budget, don't despair: Midweek rates, last-minute deals, and summer specials can make this dream stay a reality.)

WEST SEDONA
$50-100

Cheap, clean, and convenient, **Sugar Loaf Lodge** (1870 W. State Route 89A, 928/282-9451, www.sedonasugarloaf.com, $60–90 d) provides the basics just off of State Route 89A and even throws in a few frills like a pool, free wireless Internet, and in-room refrigerators. The motel isn't fancy, but its low price is hard

SEDONA

to beat, as is the convenient access to neighboring hiking and mountain biking trails.

Recently refurbished, the **Baby Quail Inn** (50 Willow Way, 866/977-8245 or 928/282-2835, $85–95) has clean rooms and welcome amenities like free wireless Internet, in-room refrigerators and microwaves, and a complimentary breakfast. The tidy little property makes the most of its space with a quiet patio and outdoor hot tub, tucked into in a residential neighborhood just off State Route 89A.

$100-250

Sky Ranch Lodge (1105 Airport Rd., 888/708-6400 or 928/282-6400, www.skyranchlodge.com, $105–180 d) is a pleasant throwback to a 1970s ranch or vacation home. Rooms are plain-Jane, but chances are you'll spend most of your time enjoying the property and its views, especially if you've requested a private deck or rim-view cottage. Small ponds, bridges, and grassy lawns dot the six-acre property, with quaint stone paths leading to quiet gardens and a secluded swimming pool. Best of all, the inn is perched on Airport Mesa, 500 feet above Sedona, providing elevated views of the town and its red-rock formations. When you're ready to venture from this mesa-top haven, a five-minute drive will drop you back in the heart of West Sedona.

Perched on a hillside, the **Best Western Inn of Sedona** (1200 W. State Route 89A, 800/292-6344 or 928/282-3072, www.innofsedona.com, $150–180 d) has a sensitive, slope-hugging design with four terraced balconies that boast 360-degree views of the red rocks. The rooms are clean and comfortable—with surprising touches like glass-bowl sinks in the bathroom—and the hotel throws in a long list of amenities, including an outdoor pool, a breakfast buffet, an in-town shuttle, free wireless Internet, and concierge services, as well as a free shuttle to/from Uptown.

The Lodge at Sedona (125 Kallof Pl.,

800/619-4467 or 928/204-1942, www.lodgeatsedona.com, $210–300 d) is a surprisingly secluded retreat in the midst of West Sedona. The lodge is decorated in gracious Mission style, with cozy, fireside seating areas and a handsome dining room that serves as a gathering spot for gourmet breakfasts and sunset treats. Second-story guest rooms offer red-rock views, and king suites on the main level have private decks. The lodge's soothing gardens incorporate water features and a labyrinth for meditative walks.

The Santa Fe–style **Southwest Inn at Sedona** (3250 W. State Route 89A, 800/483-7422 or 928/282-3344, www.swinn.com, $140–170 d) is a comfortable place to sleep, with excellent bedding, gas fireplaces, roomy baths, and other resort-worthy amenities in a welcoming B&B atmosphere. It's located near Dry Creek Road, with convenient access to the library and trailheads. Be sure to ask for a room with a view.

Sedona Rouge Hotel & Spa (2250 W. State Route 89A, 866/312-4111 or 928/203-4111, www.sedonarouge.com, $240–310 d) combines clean, contemporary lines with Mediterranean flair, accented in deep reds. The comfortable, well-appointed rooms on the second and third levels feature generous walk-in showers with dual heads. This hotel has a more urban vibe than some of its competitors, while still honoring the natural setting, particularly from the Observation Terrace, open at night for stargazing. Plus, you'll find other amenities, like a large outdoor seating area with fireplace, a heated swimming pool and Jacuzzi, a top-notch spa, and the on-site restaurant **Reds.**

The name **Boots and Saddles** (2900 Hopi Dr., 800/201-1944 or 928/282-1944, www.oldwestbb.com, $250–295 d) suggests plenty of Western style, and you'll get it at this popular bed-and-breakfast. Innkeepers Irith and Sam Raz have earned a loyal following, thanks to their warm hospitality and sumptuous breakfasts. Each of the inn's six rooms is theme-decorated, with amenities that vary from fireplaces and outdoor air-jet tubs to telescopes for stargazing. The 600-square-foot City Slickers suite boasts lots of rich leather and a sunny breakfast nook.

The **Alma De Sedona Inn** (50 Hozoni Dr., 800/923-2282 or 928/282-2737, www.almadesedona.com, $190–260 d) is a lovely bed-and-breakfast for those who appreciate a little privacy with their red-rock views. The 12 large rooms have king-size beds, gas fireplaces, and two-person tubs. The grounds are well maintained and feature a host of desert cacti and agave, along with shady sycamores. Plenty of poolside seating means you can breakfast alfresco.

Somewhat ordinary on the outside, **Sedona Real Inn & Suites** (95 Arroyo Piñon Dr., 800/353-1239 or 928/282-1414, www.sedonareal.com, $155–235 d) has clean, comfortable, spacious rooms and suites, making it a good option for families and groups. This family-owned hotel offers perks not found at budget competitors: free high-speed Internet, an outdoor pool and spa, complimentary breakfast, room service, private balconies, and outstanding concierge service.

Cathedral Rock Lodge & Retreat Center (61 W. Los Amigos Lane, 928/282 5560, www.cathedralrocklodge.com, $150–300) isn't fancy, but its views of Cathedral Rock are unmatched. Situated near Red Rock Crossing, about 15 minutes from Uptown, the lodge's three secluded cabins are surrounded by green lawns and wooded grounds. The largest, Homestead House, sleeps up to six people, offering a roomy kitchen, two bedrooms, two bathrooms, and a collection of westerns filmed in Sedona ready to pop into the DVD player.

Over $250

You won't find a hotel in Sedona with a more stunning backdrop than **Enchantment Resort** (525 Boynton Canyon Rd., 800/826-4180 or 928/282-2900, www.enchantmentresort.com, $425–825 d). Situated 10 minutes outside of town, the resort's 70 acres are nestled within the soaring cliffs of Boynton Canyon, creating a sense of seclusion and protection. A recent $25 million makeover gave the resort and its casitas a sophisticated yet earthy flair. Guests have exclusive access to swimming pools, tennis courts, lawn games, pitch-and-putt golf, resort trails, and the adjacent Mii Amo spa, one of the finest in the world. Kids will enjoy spending time at Camp Coyote, with its focus on Native American culture and the Southwestern environment.

◖ **Mii Amo** (525 Boynton Canyon Rd., 928/282-2900, www.miiamo.com) sets the bar for spa retreats, blending holistic treatments, Native American traditions, and luxury pampering. Mii Amo's seamless indoor/outdoor design blends chic, modern style with Boynton Canyon's soaring red cliffs, a soothing yet stimulating backdrop for three-, four-, and seven-night "personal journeys" tailored to each guest's goals: de-stress, spiritual exploration, etc. Rates begin at $1,600/night for a three-night package, which includes accommodations in one of 16 spa casitas and suites, three meals a day, and two spa treatments every day, as well as fitness classes, spa amenities, and activities like tennis, hiking, and mountain biking. The small, communal setting is perfect for solo travelers who want to balance personal time and socializing.

Subtle isn't the word for **Adobe Grand Villas** (35 Hozoni Dr., 800/900-7616 or 928/203-7616, www.adobegrandvillas.com, $399–699 d), where themed "mansion-style" suites start at 850 square feet, each with at least one king-size bed and two fireplaces. (One suite has lantern chandeliers and a canopy bed designed to look like a Conestoga wagon.) Some rooms feature steam showers and tubs for two, while others offer red-rock views, private patios, and wood-beam ceilings.

VILLAGE OF OAK CREEK
$50-150

Tucked into a corner of Bell Rock Plaza, **Sedona Village Lodge** (105 Bell Rock Plaza, 800/890-0521 or 928/284-3626, www.sedonalodge.com, $50–90) offers basic accommodation at budget prices. The standard rooms include wireless Internet, and for another $30, the suites have microwaves, refrigerators, and gas fireplaces.

Wildflower Inn (6086 State Route 179, 928/284-3937, www.sedonawildflowerinn.com, $99–210 d) is nicer than your standard chain motel fare, with superb views of Bell Rock from some rooms. Expect a few pleasant perks like flat-screen TVs, an in-room fridge, and continental breakfast. Be sure to call the motel directly for any late-breaking deals.

$150-300

Bordering the national forest, ◖**Adobe Village Graham Inn** (150 Canyon Circle Dr., 800/228-1425 or 928/284-1425, www.adobevillagegrahaminn.com, $180–360 d) promises a bit of "rustic luxury" and doesn't disappoint. The boutique inn's unique rooms and villas have an earthy but romantic ambience. The Sundance offers a fireplace, wood-plank flooring, king-size canopy bed, and large bathroom with a rainforest shower and jet tub. The Wilderness Villa has peeled pine walls, a charming periwinkle-blue sleigh bed, and a river-rock fireplace that connects the bedroom with a two-person tub. The small gardens and incomparable views of Bell, Cathedral, and Courthouse Rocks make this bed-and-breakfast a real gem.

Adobe Hacienda Bed & Breakfast (10 Rojo Dr., 800/454-7191, www.adobe-hacienda.com, $210–300 d) has four guest rooms and a casita, each decorated with traditional Southwestern touches, like lodgepole beams, Saltillo tile floors, Native American rugs, hand-painted Mexican sinks, and cozy Pendleton blankets. Owners Pauline and Brad Staub are consummate hosts, happy to point you in the direction of an easy hiking trail or to serve up a hearty breakfast on the flagstone patio that overlooks the adjacent golf course and the red rocks. Call for last-minute discounts or to request a specific room.

Families will appreciate the **Hilton Sedona Resort & Spa** (90 Ridge Trail Dr., 928/284-4040, www.hiltonsedona.com, $260–310 d), which provides an impressively diverse assortment of amenities, including a championship golf course, a fitness center, a full-service spa, and multiple pools. Guest rooms and one-bedroom suites—which can accommodate up to five—are tastefully decorated and boast gas fireplaces and small balconies overlooking the fairways or red rocks. Perched on a ridge above the Village of Oak Creek, the hotel's location far from the crowds of Uptown can provide a nice change of pace.

If you are planning to spend more than a few days in Sedona, **Las Posadas of Sedona** (26 Avenida De Piedras, 928/284-5288, www.lasposadasofsedona.com, $180–220 d) will make you feel at home with roomy, amenity-rich suites featuring private entrances, desks, double-sided fireplaces, and kitchenettes. The boutique inn's French-trained chef goes above and beyond every morning to create a three-course Southwestern-style breakfast.

Food

As in many tourist towns, Sedona's dining options can be hit or miss—a divine meal one night, followed the next night by a so-so offering from the same restaurant. The inconsistency can be maddening, but your options are many: Mom-and-pop cafés, ethnic eateries, casual bistros, Western steakhouses, and elegant resort dining rooms. Many have picture-window views or charming patios, and a fair number are accommodating to vegetarians, who can dine well in Sedona. The food may be a bit pricier than you're used to, but go ahead and splurge at least once at one of the romantic dining spots that make a stay in Red Rock Country such a treat. If you're a night owl, be warned: Most Sedona restaurants stop serving before 9 P.M.

UPTOWN AND HIGHWAY 179
American
Dine inside the glam contemporary **Hundred Rox** (100 Amara Ln., 928/340-8859, www. amararesort.com/dining, 7 A.M.–9 P.M. daily, $20–30) in Uptown's Amara Resort or under the stars on the restaurant's patio. The innovative menu runs from updated American comfort food to global flavors, such as fresh spring rolls, duck schnitzel, and chicken piccata. Most weekends and a few weeknights, the lounge hosts local musicians.

One of the few spots in town where you can dine relatively late, **Sound Bites Grill** (101 N. State Route 89A, 928/282-2713, www.soundbitesgrille.com, 11 A.M.–11 P.M. Tues.–Sun., till midnight Fri.–Sat., $12–45), located in the Piñon Pointe shops has a wide-ranging menu and live entertainment most nights.

Ken's Creekside (251 State Route 179, 928/282-1705, www.kenscreekside.com, 7:30 A.M.–10 P.M. daily, $14–33) has a pleasant and shady second-story patio and a varied menu that has a little bit of everything from seafood and steak to creative vegetarian entrées. The lounge features infusion drinks, and on busy weekends, a late-night menu may be available.

Enjoy Sedona's award-winning microbrew at **Oak Creek Brewery & Grill** (336 State Route 179, 928/282-3300, www.oakcreekpub.com, 11:30 A.M.–8:30 P.M. daily, $12–26). The comfortable second-story pub at Tlaquepaque serves sandwiches, salads, pastas, burgers, and "fire-kissed" pizzas, like the feta-olive-and-artichoke Oak Creek Greek. Check out the refreshing ales and pilsners brewing in copper tanks behind the bar before heading out to the patio, where you'll have tree-house views of Snoopy Rock.

"Peak views" are also on the menu at **Shugrue's Hillside Grill** (671 State Route 179, 928/282-5300, http://shugrueshillside. com, 11:30 A.M.–3 P.M. and 5–8:30 P.M. daily, $14–36). Seafood—such as lemon-seared scallops or the signature flame-broiled shrimp scampi—is the house specialty, but in addition you'll find a wide selection of pastas, salads, and steaks, along with a few vegetarian options.

Asian
Thoughtful details like paper lanterns, handmade pottery, and rustic wooden furnishings give **☪ Takashi** (465 Jordan Rd., 928/282-2334, www.takashisedona.com, 4–9 P.M. Tues.–Sun., plus lunch Tues. and Fri., $20–25) an air of traditional Japan. The tree-shaded patio is a peaceful oasis a block from Uptown's busy strip, and the classic menu includes sukiyaki, teppanyaki, sushi, teriyaki, and tempura. Save some room for the green tea ice cream.

Tucked behind the shops along Uptown's main drag, **Thai Palace** (260 Van Deren Rd., 928/282-8424, www.thaipalacesedona.com, 11 A.M.–9 P.M. Tues.–Sun., $13–16) has a delightful patio and a cozy but elegant dining

SEDONA

room. The menu includes classic curry and noodle dishes, spiced to your preference.

Breakfast and Lunch

The sandwiches and salads at **Sedona Memories** (321 Jordan Rd., 928/282-0032, 10 A.M.–2 P.M. Mon.–Fri., $5–10) won't bust your budget (though you may have to loosen your belt a couple notches). This cash-only, mom-and-pop shop has a few tables outside, or you can head for one of Red Rock Country's plentiful picnic spots. Hint: Whether you plan to eat here or on the trail, if you call in your order ahead of time, you'll get a free cookie.

Located in the Hyatt Piñon Pointe shops, **Wildflower Bread Company** (101 N. State Route 89A, 928/204-2223, www.wildflowerbread.com, 6 A.M.–9 P.M. Mon.–Fri., 7 A.M.–9 P.M. Sat., 7 A.M.–8 P.M. Sun., $5–9) has pastries, soups, salads, pastas, and sandwiches made with fresh, hearty bread. (It's part of the ever-expanding Fox restaurant chain that has staked out many locations in Arizona.)

The **Secret Garden Café at Tlaquepaque** (336 State Route 179, 928/203-9564, www.sedonasecretgardencafe.com, 9 A.M.–5 P.M. daily, $7–13) is a pleasant place to enjoy breakfast, especially in the shady, flower-filled garden. Try the French toast dipped in Grand Marnier or a hearty breakfast burrito. In the afternoon, the café serves salads, sandwiches, burgers, and their signature deep-dish quiche.

A favorite with locals, **Señor Bob's** (841 State Route 179, 928/282-0131, www.senorbobshotdogs.com, 10:30 A.M.–5 P.M. daily, under $10) is a convenient place to grab a cup of coffee and a bratwurst or hot dog. (Yes, even a veggie dog.) Layer on the condiments and get back on the trail...or look for a seat on the small porch and watch the rest of the world drive past on their way to Uptown.

Desserts

If your taste buds are screaming for something sweet, you won't have to walk far to find relief in Uptown. A handful of confectionaries dot both sides of the highway, including the **Black Cow Café** (229 N. State Route 89A, 928/203-9868, daily, hours vary), an old-fashioned ice cream parlor where you can order a house-made waffle cone with a scoop or two of prickly pear, malted vanilla, espresso, and other flavors.

How Sweet It Is (336 State Route 179, 928/282-5455, 10 A.M.–6 P.M. daily) sells fudge, chocolates, lollipops, and an assortment of unique licorices, jelly beans, and other confections. This small sweetshop in Tlaquepaque also whips up fresh fruit smoothies, shakes, sundaes, and floats.

French

For a memorable setting, it's hard to top **L'Auberge Restaurant on Oak Creek** (301 L'Auberge Ln., 928/282-1661, www.lauberge.com, 7 A.M.–8 P.M. Mon.–Thurs., till 9 P.M. Fri.–Sat., $15–85). The restaurant's flagstone patio edges the banks of Oak Creek, and you can watch ducks glide past under a shady canopy of sycamores. A seasonal menu incorporates wild game and hearty soups in winter, shifting to fresh salads and creamy cheeses in summer. For dinner, three to five courses are available prix fixe. The champagne brunch, served Sundays 9 A.M.–2 P.M., is a special treat. Oenophiles will appreciate the wine menu, which has earned *Wine Spectator* magazine's "Award of Excellence" for more than 20 years.

A beloved Sedona landmark, **René at Tlaquepaque** (336 State Route 179, 928/282-9225, www.rene-sedona.com, 11:30 A.M.–2:30 P.M. and 5–8:30 P.M. daily, $15–45) draws locals and visitors celebrating weddings, anniversaries, and birthdays. The menu includes classics like French onion soup and roasted duck, as well as entrées with a Southwestern twist, like the antelope tenderloin with a whiskey-juniper berry sauce.

Italian

The Hideaway Restaurant (251 State Route 179, 928/282-4204, http://sedonahideawayrestaurant.com, 11 A.M.–9 P.M. daily, $7–20) is tucked into a small shopping center uphill from Tlaquepaque. This is where locals go for tasty subs, pastas, and pizzas, piled high with toppings like homemade sausage. You'll find plenty of kid-friendly choices—and a long deck above tree-lined Oak Creek, where you can enjoy views of Snoopy Rock and watch hummingbirds battling over feeders.

Mexican and Southwest

You might have to stand in line for the delicious and diverse Mexican cuisine at **Elote Café** (771 State Route 179, 928/203-0105, www.elotecafe.com, 5–9 P.M. Tues.–Sat., $17–25) because reservations aren't accepted at this popular spot. Chef Jeff Smedstad traveled through Mexico for more than 15 years, exploring regional flavors that he has combined for a menu of savory, slow-roasted meats and intriguing moles. Vegetarian selections are limited, but meat eaters will dine well on lamb adobo, braised buffalo ribs, smoked chicken enchiladas, and other flavorful creations.

The Mexican village atmosphere of Tlaquepaque provides a fitting backdrop for **El Rincon** (336 State Route 179, 928/282-4648, www.elrinconrestaurant.com, 11 A.M.–9 P.M. Tues.–Sat., 11 A.M.–8 P.M. Sun., 11 A.M.–4 P.M. Mon., $5–15), serving the classic Sonoran-style cuisine that most Americans recognize, including shredded-beef burritos, cheese enchiladas, and green corn tamales.

In the Hillside shops, **Javelina Cantina** (671 State Route 179, 928/282-1313, http://javelinacantinasedona.com, 11:30 A.M.–8:30 P.M. daily, $7–16) serves up the usual crowd-pleasers plus some fine fajitas—grilled beef, chicken, fish, or shrimp with sautéed onions, peppers, warm tortillas, guacamole, and crème fraîche. The large dining room and patio (with great views) are especially lively around dinnertime.

In Uptown, **Oaxaca Restaurant** (321 N. State Route 89A, 928/282-4179, http://oaxacarestaurant.com, 10 A.M.–9 P.M. daily, $12–20) offers stunning views of Sedona's red rocks, as well as great people-watching along the city's main drag. The menu includes familiar classics, plus lighter dishes and traditional ingredients like blue corn and nopales (cactus pads).

Steakhouses and Barbecue

If you have a hankering for cactus fries, buffalo burgers, or rattlesnake, settle into one of the big booths at **Cowboy Club Grille & Spirits** (241 N. State Route 89A, 928/282-4200, www.cowboyclub.com, 11 A.M.–10 P.M. daily, $10–37). Formerly the Oak Creek Tavern, where Joe Beeler and his artist friends founded the Cowboy Artists of America in 1965, this is now the place to go for cowboy-worthy steaks and ribs. You'll also find seafood, roast chicken or duck, barbecue, and even a few vegetarian options. Next door, the more upscale sibling, **Silver Saddle Room** (5–9 P.M. daily, $10–37), offers a similar menu in a more refined atmosphere.

Every town needs a hole-in-the-wall barbecue joint. Drop into **Sally's Mesquite BBQ & Grill** (250 Jordan Rd., 928/282-6533, www.sallysbbq.com, 11 A.M.–7 P.M. daily, $8–15) for a pulled pork sandwich, smoked beef brisket, or St. Louis–style ribs. The relaxed lunch and dinner spot has been serving up barbecue and classic sides like fresh-cut fries and homemade baked beans for more than 25 years.

At **Red Rock BBQ** (150 State Route 179, 928/204-5975, www.redrockbbq.com, 11 A.M.–9 P.M. Sun.–Thurs., 11 A.M.–10 P.M. Fri.–Sat., $9–15), you can dive into the hickory-smoked pork sandwiches, cornmeal-crusted catfish, and juicy hamburgers, or keep it light with one of the specialty salads. Sampler platters are great for sharing with family and friends, while you kick back on the patio and take in the views.

WINE NOT?

The **Verde Valley Wine Trail** (www.vvwine-trail.com) travels from the banks of Oak Creek in Page Springs to the mountainside town of Jerome. En route you'll discover an astonishing number of varietals, including charbono, Grenache, marsanne, merlot, mourvedre, petite sirah, pinot noir, sauvignon blanc, tempranillo, viognier, and zinfandel. Though the landscape is arid, many vineyards retain pioneering water rights granting them access to Oak Creek, the Verde River, or deep underground aquifers. Harvests run between late August and the end of September, but any time of year, you can stop by a tasting room to sample a flight for $5-10. Call a cab for transportation, or check out wine tours from **Sedona Adventure Tours** (877/673-3661, www.sedonaadventuretours.com).

PAGE SPRINGS ROAD

- **Javelina Leap Vineyards**
  (1565 Page Springs Rd., 928/649-2681, www.javelinaleapwinery.com, 11 A.M.-5 P.M. daily, cellar tours 11 A.M.-3 P.M. Fri. and Sat.)

- **Oak Creek Vineyards**
  (1555 Page Springs Rd., 928/649-0290, www.oakcreekvineyards.net, 10 A.M.-6 P.M. daily)

- **Page Springs Cellars**
  (1500 N. Page Springs Rd., 928/639-3004, www.pagespringscellars.com, 11 A.M.-6 P.M. Sun.-Thurs., till 9 P.M. Fri.-Sat.)

OLD TOWN COTTONWOOD

- **Arizona Stronghold**
  (1023 N. Main St., 928/639-2789, www.azstronghold.com, noon-7 P.M. daily, till 9 P.M. Fri.-Sat.)

- **Burning Tree Cellars**
  (1040 N. Main St., 928/649-8733, noon-9 P.M. daily)

- **Pillsbury**
  (1012 N. Main St., 928/639-0646, www.pillsburywine.com, 11 A.M.-6 P.M. Mon.-Thurs., 11 A.M.-9 P.M. Fri.-Sat., noon-6 P.M. Sun.)

- **The Vineyard Wine Bar and Shop**
  (1001 N. Main St., 928/634-2440, www.thevineyardbistro.com, 11 A.M.-11 P.M. Tues.-Sun., later on weekends)

- **The Wine Cellar**
  (1029 N. Main St., 928/649-0444, noon-9 P.M. daily)

JEROME

- **Bitter Creek Winery**
  (240 Hull Ave., 928/634-7033, bittercreekwinery.com, 11 A.M.-5 P.M. Sun.-Fri., 10 A.M.-6 P.M. Sat., hours vary seasonally)

- **Caduceus Cellars**
  (158 Main St., 928/634-3444, www.caduceus.org, 11 A.M.-6 P.M. Sun.-Thurs., 11 A.M.-8 P.M. Fri.-Sat.)

- **Jerome Winery**
  (403 Clark St., 928/639-9067, www.jeromewinery.com, noon-5 P.M. Sun.-Thurs., noon-6 P.M. Fri., 11 A.M.-6 P.M. Sat.)

BETWEEN COTTONWOOD AND CAMP VERDE

- **Alcantara Vineyard**
  (3445 S. Grapevine Way, 928/649-8463, www.alcantaravineyard.com, 11 A.M.-5 P.M. daily)

SEDONA

- **The Art of Wine**
  (101 N. State Route 89A, #B-9, 877/903-9463, www.artowine.com, 10 A.M.-6 P.M. Mon.-Wed., 10 A.M.-8 P.M. Thurs.-Sun.)

WEST SEDONA

American

Follow Airport Road to its end at the very top of the mesa, where you'll see red-rock panoramas and the soaring roofline of the contemporary **Mesa Grill** (1185 Airport Rd. 928/282-2400, http://mesagrillsedona.com, 7 A.M.–9 P.M. daily, $15–30). Plane buffs can keep an eye on the runway while dining on gourmet burgers, pasta, steak, or seafood.

The seasonal menu at **(Heartline Café** (1610 W. State Route 89A, 928/282-0785, http://heartlinecafe.com, 4:30–10 P.M. daily, $15–32) combines Southwestern flavors and Asian touches with a dash of continental flair. Small plates and entrées at this longtime local favorite include sweet potato–corn chowder, tea-smoked chicken dumplings, and daily pasta and fish specials. The dining room has a casual elegance, and the trellised patio is especially lovely. For breakfast or lunch, head next door to **Heartline Gourmet Express** (928/282-3365, 8 A.M.–4 P.M. daily, $15–32), where choices include crab Benedict, lemon-crème stuffed French toast, and a Southwestern wrap, as well as a selection of salads and sandwiches.

To find the **Red Planet Diner** (1655 W. State Route 89A, 928/282-6070, www.redplanetdiner.net, 10 A.M.–11 P.M. daily, $8–18), just look for the UFO out front. Inside you'll find a 1950s-diner-meets-outer-space motif complete with burgers, fries, and old-fashioned malts and shakes. The menu also includes hearty breakfasts and salads, and dinner entrées like steak or vegetarian lasagna.

It's easy to guess the most popular menu item at **Bodacious Burgers** (1950 State Route 89A, 928/282-2255, 11 A.M.–9 P.M. daily, $7–20), but you'll also find an extensive soup-and-salad bar, sandwiches, and other comfort-food classics from meatloaf to prime rib.

If you're looking for a classic small-town diner, head for **Café Jose** (2370 W. State Route 89A, 928/282-0299, http://sedonacafejose.com, breakfast, lunch, and dinner, daily, $5–12) in the Safeway shopping center. Check the whiteboard near the entry for daily specials like chicken and dumplings or pot roast, or order from the varied menu of sandwiches, salads, pastas, and Southwestern entrées. The service is always friendly and, if you're counting pennies, one of the hearty Mexican-style breakfasts is enough to fuel an all-day hike.

Asian

The **Szechuan Restaurant** (1350 W. State Route 89A, 928/282-9288, http://szechuansedona.net, lunch and dinner daily, $11–20) combines Chinese dishes with sushi selections and the popular Martini Bar. Dine in, enjoy the beautiful patio and nightly entertainment, or call ahead for takeout.

For inexpensive sushi, look for **Hiro's** (1730 W. State Route 89A, 928/226-8030, lunch and dinner daily, $5–20), tucked into a small storefront along the highway. Fresh and tasty bento boxes, teriyaki, tempura, and other traditional Japanese favorites round out the menu.

Wild Orchid (2611 W. State Route 89A, 928/282-4422, http://thewildorchidrestaurant.com, lunch and dinner Mon.–Sat., $23–41) features a pan-Asian menu, with choices that include roti, salads, curries, noodles, and teriyaki.

At **Thai Spices** (2986 W. State Route 89A, 928/282-0599, www.thaispices.com, 11:30 A.M.–9 P.M. Mon.–Sat., $10–14), a favorite among local vegetarians, meat eaters can add chicken, beef, or shrimp to most entrées, which include hot noodle dishes, sautées, and flavorful soups and curries. The inexpensive lunch specials are a big hit, and for guests who reserve a day ahead, owner Pearl Black will prepare a platter of macrobiotic selections.

Breakfast and Lunch

In a building once owned by actress Jane Russell, who filmed *Outlaw* in Sedona, **Coffee Pot Restaurant** (2050 W. State Route 89A,

SEDONA

928/282-6626, www.coffeepotsedona.com, 6 A.M.–2 P.M. daily, $5–10) boasts 101 omelets. (But does anyone ever really order the PB&J omelet?) You'll find all-day breakfast favorites, including fluffy pancakes and waffles, and hearty Western-style Mexican fare from huevos rancheros to chimichangas. The dining room is lively and friendly, and when weather permits, you can sit in the spacious enclosed patio in back.

New Frontiers Natural Foods (1420 W. State Route 89A, 928/282-6311, http://newfrontiersmarket.com, 8 A.M.–9 P.M. Mon.–Sat., 8 A.M.–8 P.M. Sun.) is a good spot to pick up supplies for a picnic. The deli offers lots of choices, with seating indoors or on the patio, where you can watch Sedona's health-conscious crowd come to shop, network, or get a chair massage. The grocery side has an impressive selection of organic produce, naturally raised meats, fresh breads, and gourmet cheeses.

Indian

For a touch of the exotic, head for **India Palace** (1910 W. State Route 89A, 928/204-2300, lunch and dinner daily, $5–10). The plentiful lunch buffet is a great value, served with delightfully tender-crisp *naan* (bread) hot from the tandoori oven. Or order from the menu of tandoori-roasted meats, seafood, and curries that can be prepared spicy or not, to your taste. Colorful wall murals provide a rich backdrop for the richly flavored cuisine.

Italian

Dahl & Di Luca Ristorante (2321 W. State Route 89A, 928/282-5219, http://dahlanddiluca.com, 5–10 P.M. daily, $13–33) is always packed with appreciative diners, locals and visitors alike. Start with the extensive antipasti menu, which includes classic bruschetta, polenta parmigiana, or crisp calamari, but leave room for the decadent pastas and grilled meats. If the dining room's over-the-top Tuscan decor isn't your thing, you'll find live music and a lively atmosphere in the bar.

Modern-but-casual **Picazzo's** (1855 W. State Route 89A, 928/282-4140, http://picazzos.com, 11 A.M.–9 P.M. Sun.–Thurs., 11 A.M.–10 P.M. Fri.–Sat., $11–26) epic menu ranges from the meaty (sausage, pepperoni, Canadian bacon) to the cheesy (ricotta, parmesan, mozzarella) to the spicy (chipotle sauce, chorizo, fresh jalapeños) to the gourmet (applewood-smoked bacon, Thai chicken, goat cheese). Crusts include whole grain and gluten-free options, with salads and pastas rounding out the menu.

One of the most delightful (and hidden) patios in Sedona is tucked behind **Apizza Heaven** (2675 W. State Route 89A, 928/282-0519, www.apizzaheavenaz.com, lunch and dinner daily, $10–30), where you can linger over a glass of wine or beer and listen to live music under the stars. It's hard to look beyond the delicious pizza selections, but pastas, calzones, and sandwiches are also on the menu. The hours can be erratic, and it's a bit challenging to find (look for the red sign south of the highway), but once you're here, you'll feel instantly at home.

Mexican and Southwestern

The tiny **Tortas de Fuego** (1630 W. State Route 89A, 928/282-0226, lunch and dinner daily, less than $10) serves salads, tacos, menudo, and the eponymous tortas—hearty Norteño-style sandwiches. The salsa bar has an array of fresh, flavorful concoctions from pico de gallo to pineapple. Don't be discouraged by the lack of parking spaces in front—pull around back where there's room for a few cars.

Barking Frog Grille (2620 W. State Route 89A, 928/204-2000, www.barkingfroggrille.com, 5–10 P.M. daily, $14–30) serves Southwestern favorites that don't seem tired or dated. Kick off happy hour with a prickly pear mojito and stay for dinner to enjoy the crab tacos, pork-belly carnitas, or baby back ribs. Conclude the night with the tequila-laced crème brûlée.

Vegetarian

Raw foodists, here's your Eden. **ChocolaTree** (1595 W. State Route 89A, 928/282-2997, http://chocolatree.com, 9 A.M.–9 P.M. daily) is a confectionery and restaurant serving a mostly raw, 100 percent organic, and all-vegetarian menu. Vibrant soups, spring rolls, sandwiches, and wraps are beautifully prepared, incorporating ingredients grown in the on-site garden. There's also an extensive list of teas, smoothies, wheatgrass shakes, and healing herbal concoctions, as well as the signature handmade chocolates sweetened with agave syrup or honey.

VILLAGE OF OAK CREEK

American

For delicious, no-fuss steak sandwiches and Reubens, join the locals at **PJ's Village Pub & Sports Lounge** (40 W. Cortez Dr., 928/284-2250, www.pjsvillagepub.com, 10 A.M.–2 A.M. daily, $8–14). You'll see bikers, hikers, and golfers huddled around the closely packed tables or at the bar. The tavern is known for its nightly specials like Taco Tuesdays and Baby Back Rib Wednesdays, and the Friday night fish fry has become a weekly VOC ritual.

At the **Marketplace Café** (6645 State Route 179, 928/284-5478, www.mpcsedona.com, 11 A.M.–9 P.M. Sun.–Thurs., till 10 P.M. Fri.–Sat., $8–26), you're likely to find live music, along with a wide-ranging menu of appetizers, hearty salads, seafood, steak, pasta, and pizza. Nightly happy hour specials and a Sunday jazz brunch help keep things lively.

Breakfast and Lunch

Breakfast is served all day at **Miley's Café** (7000 State Route 179, 928/284-4123, 7 A.M.–8 P.M. daily, $6–15) in the Tequa shopping center. This cross between a small-town dinner and a Mexican restaurant serves healthful omelets, huevos rancheros, short stacks and waffles, as well as a diverse lunch and dinner lineup: fish

and chips, burgers, and vegetarian dishes, along with burritos, enchiladas, and carne asada.

Hidden away in a small strip center, the down-home **Blue Moon Café** (6101 State Route 179, 928/284-1831, http://bluemooncafe.us, 7 A.M.–9 P.M. daily, $6–10) is a great way to fuel up before a hike or round of golf or refuel afterward on hearty Philly sandwiches, subs, burgers, and hand-tossed pizzas. You'll also find a few Southwestern specialties and a decent beer and wine list.

For coffee drinks, granola, and delectable pastries, look to **Desert Flour** (6446 State Route 179, 928/284-4633, 7 A.M.–3 P.M. Mon., 7 A.M.–8 P.M. Tues.–Sat., 8 A.M.–2 P.M. Sun., $5–12). Heartier breakfasts are also available, and the lunch and dinner menus include wood-fired pizza and generous sandwiches, perfect for a picnic on the red rocks.

It may be a bit off the beaten track, but the **Red Rock Café** (100 Verde Valley School Rd., 928/284-1441, 6:30 A.M.–3 P.M. daily, $6–13) gets praise for its "eggs-ceptional" breakfast menu. For lunch, there's a long list of sandwiches and refreshing salads.

Italian

Award-winning ◀ **Cucina Rustica Dahl & Di Luca** (7000 State Route 179, 928/284-3010, http://cucinarustica.com, 5–11 P.M. daily, $13–30) offers an elegant, romantic ambience. The salads, soups, and meat dishes are delicious, but it's the fresh, homemade pasta that has made the restaurant a hit with Sedona diners. Eat on the patio or have a seat in the dining room, which features a twinkling, starry sky mural.

Grab a sub or a slice and wash it down with a microbrew at **Famous Pizza** (25 Bell Rock Plaza, 928/284-3805, www.azfamouspizza.com, 11 A.M.–9 P.M. Sun.–Thurs., till 10 P.M. Fri.–Sat., $3–15). The hole-in-the-wall joint serves pies with flaky thin crust, and adds a few pasta dishes for dinner.

SEDONA

Information and Services

TOURIST INFORMATION

Be wary of signs offering travel information. Many are fronts for local time-share companies, and as a trade-off for picking up a handful of brochures, you may be subjected to a hard-sell spiel. (Conversely, you can also land some genuine lodging bargains with coupons for local restaurants and tours if you are willing to sign up for a sales presentation.)

The main official visitor center is staffed by Coconino National Forest and the **Sedona Chamber of Commerce** (1 Forest Rd., 928/282-7722 or 800/288-7336, www.visitsedona.com, 8:30 A.M.–5 P.M. Mon.–Sat., 8 A.M.–3 P.M. Sun.). The convenient Uptown office supplies visitors with maps, directions, and suggestions for choosing the best trail or making the most of your time.

The forest service's **Red Rock Visitor Center** (8375 State Route 179, 928/203-7500, www.redrockcountry.org, 8 A.M.–5 P.M. daily), located just south of the Village of Oak Creek, has exhibits and a small retail area with fun nature-themed gifts, as well as books and maps. The expansive veranda out front is a great spot to snap a panorama of Bell Rock and Courthouse Butte. Two smaller contact stations are staffed seasonally in Oak Creek Canyon. At any of these locations (as well as at businesses in town and a few trailhead vending machines), you can pick up a **Red Rock Pass** ($5 day, $15/week), required for parking at some forest service trailheads.

LIBRARIES

The **Sedona Public Library** (3250 White Bear Rd., 928/282-7714, www.sedonalibrary.org, 10 A.M.–6 P.M. Mon.–Thurs., 10 A.M.–5 P.M. Fri.–Sat.) is a pleasant, light-filled space (by the local architectural firm Design Group) with computers for public use. A smaller branch, **SPL In the Village** (56 W. Cortez Dr., 928/284-1603, www.sedonalibrary.org, 1–5 P.M. Mon.–Fri., 9 A.M.–1 P.M. Sat.), serves the Village of Oak Creek.

HOSPITALS AND EMERGENCY SERVICES

The **Verde Valley Medical Center's Sedona Campus** (3700 W. Highway 89A, 928/204-4100, www.verdevalleymedicalcenter.com) offers 24-hour emergency services in West Sedona, as well as specialty health care. It's a part of Northern Arizona Healthcare, the nonprofit group that includes Cottonwood's Verde Valley Medical Center and Flagstaff Medical Center, the nearest sizable hospitals. Nonemergencies can be handled at **Sedona Urgent Care** (2530 W. State Route 89A, 928/203-4813).

Getting There and Around

Sedona is about two hours north of Phoenix via I-17. You can exit the freeway for State Route 260 (exit 289) or State Route 179 (exit 311). The former route passes through Cottonwood and joins State Route 89A for the Dry Creek Scenic Road. The latter follows the Scenic Red Rock Byway between the Village of Oak Creek and Sedona. Whichever route you choose, the views are inspiring.

Sedona is roughly divided into three areas along State Routes 89A and 179: Uptown, the bustling strip of shops along State Route 89A north of its intersection with State Route 179; West Sedona, a quieter, mostly residential section west of the intersection; and the Village of Oak Creek, an unincorporated area of residences, resorts, and shops approximately seven miles south of the intersection en route to I-17.

Almost all of the area's natural attractions, cultural sights, and restaurants can be reached within a 10-minute drive of Uptown. And with so much neck-craning scenery, you won't mind your time behind the wheel, though the weekend traffic, especially during holidays, can test your patience. Use pullouts to let faster traffic pass or to take photos of the monumental rock formations. If you stop to ask for directions, keep in mind that locals call the 89A/179 intersection "the Y" and use it as a reference point.

Having a car will make Sedona sightseeing easier.

© NATALIA BRATSLAVSKY/123RF.COM

AIR

Most likely, you'll fly into **Phoenix Sky Harbor International Airport** (3400 E. Sky Harbor Blvd., 602/273-3300, www.phxsky-harbor.com) and drive the 90 minutes north to Sedona on I-17, exiting on State Route 179. If you don't want to rent a car, the **Sedona-Phoenix Shuttle** (800/448-7988 or 928/282-2066, www.sedona-phoenix-shuttle.com) has van service from Sky Harbor to the Village of Oak Creek and West Sedona for $50 one-way and $90 round-trip.

US Airways flies into Flagstaff's Pulliam Field. The **Sedona Airport** (235 Terminal Dr., 928/282-1046, www.sedonaairport.org) hosts five fixed-wing and helicopter tour companies, charter air services, and a restaurant.

CAR

Rental Cars

To explore Sedona, Red Rock Country, and the Verde Valley, you'll need a car. Pick up a rental at Phoenix's Sky Harbor Airport or in Sedona. **Hertz** (3009 W. State Route 89, 928/774-4452, www.hertz.com) and **Enterprise** (2090 W. State Route 89A,

928/282-2052, www.enterprise,com) have rental centers in West Sedona. At the Sedona airport terminal, **Discount Rent-a-Car** (877/467-8578) offers hourly rentals in addition to standard rates.

To reach remote trailheads or explore along rocky forest roads, you may want to consider renting a vehicle with four-wheel drive. Jeep rental companies like **Barlow's** (3009 W. State Route 89A, 928/282-4344 or 888/928-5337), located next to Hertz, will provide maps and information about 4WD trails.

Other Transportation

Though it's easy to get around town in your own vehicle, if you prefer to have someone else introduce you to the sights, the **Sedona Trolley** (276 State Route 89A, 928/282-4211, www.sedonatrolley.com, $12 adults, children under 12 free) has two routes that give riders a narrated overview of the town's layout and vistas. The **Verde Lynx** (928/282-0938, $2) connects

SEDONA

© KATHLEEN BRYANT

The Sedona Trolley offers both transportation and tours.

Sedona to the Verde Valley community of Cottonwood, making several in-town stops and running until early evening. If you're out late, you can call **Bob's Taxi** (928/282-1234) or hire **White Tie Transportation** (928/203-4500) to usher you around in a limo or luxury SUV.

Vicinity of Sedona

The red rocks are captivating, but there's plenty of notable natural attractions and historic sites outside of Sedona. Within a few minutes of Uptown, you enter leafy Oak Creek Canyon on Arizona's first officially designated scenic highway.

◖ OAK CREEK CANYON

Drive north from Uptown Sedona on State Route 89A to discover one of Arizona's most picturesque byways. The lush green oasis of Oak Creek Canyon makes a pleasant contrast to the red rocks, and the sparkling creek brings out the Huck Finn in everyone. The scenic highway meanders from Sedona to

Flagstaff for 23 miles, taking about an hour to trace the 12-mile-long canyon and climb the steep switchbacks up to the ponderosa forests of "Flag."

Oak Creek Canyon was formed by a geological fault, creating sheer walls that range from 800 to 2,000 feet tall. Numerous springs feed cool, clear Oak Creek, which nurtures riparian species like Arizona sycamores, blackberries, golden columbine, great blue herons, and raccoons. Trailheads, picnic areas, campgrounds, cabins, and lodges help visitors make the most of this delightful recreation area.

J. J. Thompson was the first to settle in the canyon, arriving on the spot he named Indian

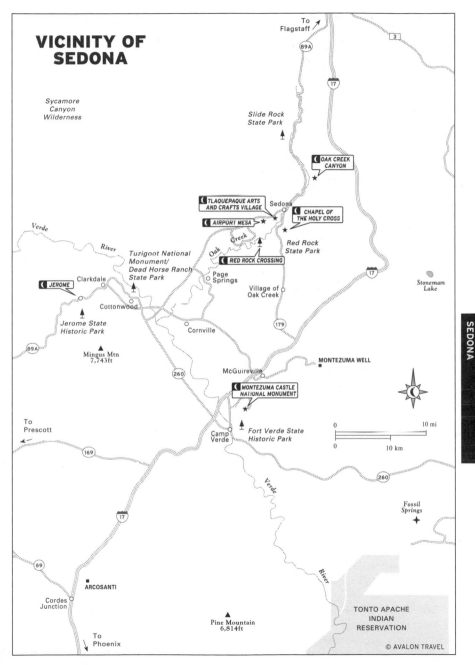

VICINITY OF SEDONA

To Flagstaff

89A

3

17

Sycamore
Canyon
Wilderness

Slide Rock
State Park

OAK CREEK
CANYON

89A

TLAQUEPAQUE ARTS
AND CRAFTS VILLAGE   Sedona

AIRPORT MESA   CHAPEL OF
THE HOLY CROSS

Verde

River

Oak Creek

Red Rock
State Park

Tuzigoot National
Monument/
Dead Horse Ranch
State Park   RED ROCK CROSSING

JEROME   Clarkdale   Page
Springs   Village of
Oak Creek   Stoneman
Lake

Cottonwood

Jerome State
Historic Park

17

89A

Cornville

179

Mingus Mtn
7,743ft

260

MONTEZUMA WELL

McGuireville

MONTEZUMA CASTLE
NATIONAL MONUMENT

To
Prescott

Camp
Verde   Fort Verde State
Historic Park

169   0   10 mi

0   10 km

260

Verde

Fossil
Springs

17

69

River

ARCOSANTI

Cordes
Junction

TONTO APACHE
INDIAN
RESERVATION

To
Phoenix   Pine Mountain
6,814ft

© AVALON TRAVEL

SEDONA

© KATHLEEN BRYANT

Oak Creek's spring-fed waters attract swimmers and anglers.

SEDONA

Gardens in 1876. Hollywood came in 1923 to film Zane Grey's popular tale, *Call of the Canyon*. The romantic setting can be visited at Call of the Canyon Day-Use Area, the site of the former Mayhew's Lodge (where some say Grey got his inspiration), and the iconic West Fork Trail. Through the intervening decades, the canyon was a shady sanctuary of motor lodges and camps, and the retreat atmosphere lingers today.

Oak Creek Canyon continues to be a place of rest and relaxation—though you won't escape the crowds, especially in summer when a parade of vehicles cruise the highway looking for campsites or parking spots near popular swimming holes. Fall attracts leaf-peepers when the creek becomes a golden band of sycamores and cottonwoods, punctuated by red splashes of bigtooth maples and set off by evergreen oaks, junipers, and ponderosa pines. No matter the time of year, it's possible to find a quiet

spot for a picnic or a splash in the creek. Be respectful of private property, as homeowners share space with Coconino National Forest and Slide Rock State Park.

Oak Creek Vista

For an overview of Oak Creek Canyon, stop at the vista (8:30 A.M.–4:30 P.M. daily) located at the top of the switchbacks roughly halfway between Sedona and Flagstaff. This pretty spot in the ponderosa forest is one of the oldest roadside rest areas in the united States. There's a forest service contact station here, where you can pick up books and maps. Most days, weather permitting, Navajo artisans and their families sell items at an arts-and-crafts market.

Slide Rock State Park

When the temperatures start to climb in late spring, the cool waters of Oak Creek beckon. Take the plunge at Slide Rock State Park (6871 N. State Route 89A, 928/282-3034, www.az-stateparks.com, 8 A.M.–7 P.M. daily May–Sept., 8 A.M.–5 P.M. daily Oct.–April, $20 per vehicle), situated seven miles north of Sedona and home to an 80-foot-long natural rock slide, carved into sandstone and basalt bedrock by Oak Creek. The spring-fed water can be a little brisk, and the ride can be a little rough, so be sure to bring water shoes or old sneakers. For a more relaxed experience, wade and splash in an eroded basin or sunbathe like a lizard on a slickrock "beach." The **Slide Rock Market** sells snacks and water, though you may want to bring a picnic and cooler if you plan to stay the day.

Like any well-loved attraction, Slide Rock has become too popular for its own good in recent years. Families from Phoenix and across Arizona descend upon the park on weekends and during holidays in the summer, causing temporary closings when the parking lots fill up or when daily water tests reveals high levels of *E. coli* bacteria. In the fall and winter, the park can be blissfully quiet, providing a nice opportunity to go on a ranger-led nature walk or explore the historic buildings and apple orchard that once belonged to the Pendley family.

Hiking

There are plenty of good hiking trails in Oak Creek Canyon, but the **West Fork Trail** is by far the most popular, and for good reason. The trail follows a tributary canyon for an enchanting Eden of golden columbine, red and yellow monkey flowers, canyon wrens, and redstarts. Tall trees and high canyon walls provide lots of shade—blissful relief during the hot summer. Even first-time hikers will enjoy the easy trail. The canyon's small stream braids over bedrock or collects in reflective pools, easy to wade through or walk around. Most visitors turn around at the three-mile point or sooner for a delightful day hike.

Serious explorers, though, can penetrate even farther into the deep, forested canyon, where they'll need to wade into the creek—and even swim in some spots. The vegetation gets thicker and the trail less defined. It takes a full day to make the additional 11 miles; overnight camping is allowed beyond the first six miles. You must notify rangers if you are planning to backpack overnight.

To get to the trailhead, take State Route 89A past milepost 385 to the **Call of the Canyon Recreation Area** (8 A.M.–8 P.M. Memorial Day–Labor Day, till dusk otherwise, $9), named after Zane Grey's classic Western novel. The trail begins in a small meadow along Oak Creek, passing by the ruins of historic Mayhew's Lodge as it slices into the tributary slot formed by West Fork. You'll find a half-dozen picnic tables near the parking area, which also provides access to the Thomas Point Trail (two miles round-trip), a less-trafficked alternative that climbs the opposite side of Oak Creek Canyon.

Shopping

Two venerable trading posts are located in Oak Creek Canyon. Four miles north of Uptown Sedona, at **Garland's Indian Jewelry** (3953 N. State Route 89A, 928/282-6632, www.garlandsjewelry.com, 10 A.M.–5 P.M. daily), you'll see walls of silver-and-leather concho belts, baskets, kachina carvings, and jewelry. The store sells traditional pieces as well as stunningly modern designs by emerging artisans from Hopi, Navajo, and Zuni tribes.

For more than 60 years, **Hoel's Indian Shop** (9589 N. State Route 89A, 928/282-3925, www.hoelsindianshop.com, 9:30 A.M.–5 P.M. daily) has bought directly from Native artisans, and their first-rate inventory is a testament to this tradition, encompassing jewelry, kachina carvings, pottery, baskets, intricate beadwork, fetishes, and Navajo rugs and blankets. The store is located about 10 miles north of Sedona, and it's a good idea to call first to make sure the doors will be open.

Accommodations

Tucked into the forest along the creek, **Briar Patch Inn** (3190 N. State Route 89A, 928/282-2342, www.briarpatchinn.com, $220–295 d) has 19 cabin-like rooms furnished with rustic wood tables, big beds, old rocking chairs, and brightly colored Native American blankets and rugs, all lovingly cared for by the incredibly friendly and hardworking staff. The accommodations range from quaint one-room hideaways to the sprawling four-bedroom Ponderosa cabin, which is large enough to accommodate 20 people. There are only three TVs on the property, but you can fish for trout, jump into the private swimming hole during the summer, or take a creekside yoga class in the morning before enjoying the buffet breakfast.

Small and pleasantly rustic, **Canyon Wren Cabins** (6425 N. State Route 89A, 928/282-6900, www.canyonwrencabins.com, $155–175 d) has three chalet-styled cedar cabins designed to accommodate two people comfortably, with a small living room, kitchen, bath, and wood-burning fireplace downstairs, and an open loft bedroom with queen bed upstairs.

Garland's Oak Creek Lodge (8067 N. State Route 89A, 928/282-3343, www.garlandslodge.com, $255–305 d) blends the romance of a cabin in the woods with all the style of a small resort. The 1908 homestead is a well-kept Arizona secret, though you may have a hard time getting a reservation for one of the 16 cabins. And as at any good summer hideaway, the lodge's on-site restaurant—simply called The Dining Room—will keep you coming back night after night. Breakfast and dinner are included with your stay. The resort is open early April through mid-November and closed on Sunday. If possible, try to book one of the large cabins with a fireplace.

Forest Houses Resort (9275 N. State Route 89A, 928/282-2999, www.foresthousesresort.com, $120–160 d) offers a quirky woodsy escape. The 15 cabins, A-frame homes, and stone cottages are scattered on 20 acres and range in size to accommodate 2–10 people. Try to reserve one of the creekside cottages, the charming Rock House, or the arty Studio, a former sculpting workshop that overlooks a grassy meadow.

Within the shelter of Oak Creek Canyon are three **forest service campgrounds** (www.fs.usda.gov/coconino, $18/night). Only the smallest is open year-round; the others close for the winter. Amenities are limited to fire rings or grills, tables, toilets, and drinking water (no hookups), but the pluses are shade, easy creek access, and nearby trails and fishing holes. Cave Springs has coin-operated showers that are open to guests from other campgrounds. Some sites can be reserved in advance (877/444-6777, www.recreation.gov).

Food

For an impromptu creekside picnic, pop into

Garland's Indian Gardens (3951 N. State Route 89A, 928/282-7702, 10 A.M.–5 P.M. daily). The small deli and market prepares fresh sandwiches, salads, and baked goods, and from the grocery you can add lunchtime essentials like water, soda, and chips, as well as locally grown apples and fresh juice. Take your selections to the lovely shady patio in back, or sit out front and watch traffic parade by.

The elegant dining room at **Garland's Oak Creek Lodge** (8067 N. State Route 89A, 928/282-3343, $40 per person) serves up a shared culinary experience. A prix fixe menu of seasonal gourmet delights is presented nightly. Lodge guests and other diners sit at communal tables for a convivial atmosphere. Cocktails are served at 6 P.M. by the fire or out on the lawn, depending on weather, and the dinner bell rings at 7 P.M. The restaurant is open early April through mid-November and closed on Sundays; reservations are required.

PICNIC AREAS

Just north of Sedona on the other side of **Midgely Bridge,** you'll spot a paved parking area. You can walk underneath the bridge for views of Oak Creek Canyon or hike the Huckaby Trail (five miles round-trip) or Wilson Canyon Trail (three miles round-trip). The challenging Wilson Mountain Trail (11 miles round-trip) also begins here.

Two miles north of Uptown, you'll find **Grasshopper Point** (928/203-2900, 8 A.M.–8 P.M. Memorial Day–Labor Day, till dusk otherwise, $8/vehicle), a popular swimming hole and picnic area. In the summer, be sure to arrive early, as the deep pool attracts crowds of cliff-jumpers on weekends. If you're seeking a little solitude, you can stroll along the pleasant Allen's Bend Trail (one mile round-trip).

The heart of Oak Creek Canyon shelters numerous forest service campgrounds and picnic areas. Most day-use sites are open from

8 A.M.–8 P.M. Memorial Day–Labor Day, and till dusk the rest of the year. All require a Red Rock Pass ($5/day, $15/week), available in Sedona, at the contact station near Indian Gardens, or from on-site vending machines.

Encinoso Picnic Area, five miles north of Uptown, has a dozen picnic tables, cooking grills, and lots of elbow room. The North Wilson Trail (11 miles round-trip, strenuous) begins here.

About seven miles north of Uptown, the shady **Halfway Picnic Site** has parking for eight cars and picnic sites above sparkling Oak Creek.

Just a bit farther up the canyon you'll find **Banjo Bill Picnic Area,** a delightful spot with 12 picnic tables and grills.

Bootlegger Picnic Area is a creekside haven nine miles north of Uptown, with a popular fishing hole in addition to picnic tables and grills. The steep and challenging A.B. Young Trail (six miles round-trip) leaves from the south end of the picnic grounds.

Getting There

Oak Creek Canyon may be one of the easiest day trips you've ever taken. Simply head north of Uptown Sedona on State Route 89A; in minutes, you'll be wending your way through one of Arizona's most beautiful wooded canyons, with roadside views of red-rock formations and cool, running waters. Slide Rock State Park is less than 20 minutes from Sedona, and in another 30 minutes or so, you can reach the mountain town of Flagstaff, the unofficial capital of northern Arizona.

Jerome and the Verde Valley

When Spanish explorers first rode into this part of central Arizona in the 16th century, the verdant grass reached their horses' bellies and towering cottonwoods lined the banks of the river. The conquistadors named the area Verde Valley, a testament to its contrast with the Sonoran Desert lands they had just traveled.

The Sinagua people had known of this temperate oasis for hundreds of years, making their homes in pit houses, cliff dwellings, and hilltop pueblos until they moved on around A.D. 1400. By the late 19th century, Anglo settlers arrived and clashed with the Yavapai and Apache bands who roamed the land, prompting the army's intervention. In their zeal to appease the settlers, though, Fort Verde's civilian and military commanders changed the landscape forever. Local pioneers took full advantage of the Native Americans' relocation to reservations by moving more cattle onto the land to supply military encampments and mining towns. The booming mining industry further impacted the hills and valley, forcing many farmers to relocate in the early 1900s. Over time, the waist-high grasses that gave the Verde Valley its name disappeared, and topsoil washed away. Today low grasses, cacti, creosote, and mesquite bosques dominate the landscape.

And yet visitors will find rich reminders of the Verde Valley's dramatic history and natural diversity. Montezuma Castle and Tuzigoot national monuments preserve fascinating prehistoric Sinagua villages. Dead Horse Ranch State Park and the Verde River Greenway enclose a lush riparian reserve near Cottonwood. And for a taste of what life was really like in the Old West, explore the haunted mining town of Jerome or the frontier military installation at Fort Verde.

◖ JEROME

Jerome is a rough-and-tumble town with a colorful history and a penchant for surviving disaster. Once dubbed the "Wickedest Town in

SEDONA

© KATHLEEN BRYANT

The Verde Valley is home to vineyards, orchards, and markets.

SEDONA

the West," the hillside community has endured the ravages of fire, landslides, and an influenza epidemic—not to mention Prohibition and the boom-and-bust business of mining.

Despite its small, walkable size, Jerome packs a whole lot of history. The town was founded in 1876 after prospectors Angus McKinnon and M. A. Ruffner filed the first mining claims. In 1888, entrepreneur William Andrews Clark bought the United Verde Copper Company for $80,000. It became the richest individually owned mine in the world, and Clark made a fortune. Workers arrived in droves, and the city became a melting pot of cultures, with Irish, Greek, and Chinese immigrants showing up in search of jobs and opportunity. In 1912 James "Rawhide" Douglas purchased the UV extension, another bonanza mine that became known as the Little Daisy.

In its heyday, the city's population topped 15,000. Mine owners, engineers, and company

surgeons lived in elegant hillside homes. Saloons, opium dens, and brothels lined back alleys and mountainside gulches. Jerome flourished for decades, but after more than $1 billion had been unearthed from the mines, the bust came to town. The mines closed for good in 1953, and Jerome's population plummeted to about 50 (not counting ghosts). In the 1970s, settlers started to return, but this time they were hippies and artists who found the quaint atmosphere and cheap rent appealing.

Small shops, bars, and hotels still cling to the side of Cleopatra Hill, though today they mainly cater to tourists who are drawn to the town's artsy, quirky, colorful vibe. The past is always present in Jerome's winding streets and historic buildings, and some say literally so. The town is rumored to be haunted by an assortment of ghosts, including Jennie Banters, the former madam who was said to be the wealthiest woman in northern Arizona. Murdered by an opium-addicted boyfriend in 1905, Banters was regarded benevolently by Jeromites—at least in part because she was often the first to rebuild after the repeated fires that often consumed local businesses.

Plan to spend a couple of hours in Jerome, a National Historic Landmark. Explore the narrow streets and intriguing stairways that climb the town's steep slopes. Pop into its galleries and stores, pausing to read the plaques describing historic buildings and adjacent alleyways. It's entertaining to imagine what daily life here must have been like, and how it would have varied according to social standing and livelihood.

Sights
MINE MUSEUM
The local historical society operates the Mine Museum (200 Main St., 928/634-5477, www.jeromehistoricalsociety.com, 9 A.M.–5 P.M. daily, adults $2, children free) in a small storefront. Belying its size, the museum is

© KATHLEEN BRYANT

Take a side trip to Jerome for a day filled with art, history, and shopping.

jam-packed with information. Exhibitions trace the complex hierarchy of prostitutes, immigrants, and shopkeepers who made their home in Jerome, and the displays of rusty old tools quickly school onlookers in the rigors of life in the mines.

JEROME STATE HISTORIC PARK

For a look at how the other half lived, visit the Jerome State Historic Park (100 Douglas Road, 928/634-5381, http://azstateparks.com, 8:30 A.M.–5 P.M. daily, $5 adult, $2 ages 7–13), housed in the historic Douglas Mansion, a grand home of adobe bricks built in 1916 for the family who owned the Little Daisy Mine. Within the mansion's rooms are period furniture, mineral collections, a fascinating 3-D map of the mining tunnels beneath Jerome, and a small theater showing an entertaining film giving a great overview of Jerome's colorful past. Mining equipment is displayed outside,

where there are picnic tables with sweeping views of the Verde Valley and the red rocks beyond. To get to the mansion, look for the brown information sign on your right as you enter town on State Route 89A. You will fork right at Douglas Road just after crossing The Hogback, a narrow ridge with houses on both sides of the highway.

Entertainment and Events

When you're ready for a break, rub elbows with the locals at **The Spirit Room** (166 Main St., 928/634-8809, www.spiritroom. com, 11 A.M.–1 A.M. daily). Beers, bands, and bikes abound at this Jerome watering hole on the main floor of the restored 1898 Connor Hotel. To find it, just look for the line of Harleys parked outside or follow the sound of live music.

If you have a yen for something more refined, visit one of Jerome's three wine-tasting rooms, or time your visit for the **First Saturday Artwalk** (www.jeromeartwalk.com), when artists open their studios, galleries host receptions, and restaurants stay open late. A free shuttle runs 5–8 P.M. to help visitors navigate the hilly streets.

In May, Arizona's oldest **annual home tour** (www.jeromechamber.com) gives visitors an intriguing behind-the-scenes look at a select group of Jerome's historic gems, many of them private residences. And if you're visiting in late October, the community center known as **Spook Hall** (260 Hull Ave.) hosts the Verde Valley's biggest Halloween party, with live music and a costume contest. (Is it any surprise that a town haunted by ghosts lets it all hang out on Halloween?)

Shopping

Jerome's shops and galleries sell everything from kitschy souvenirs to fine art, and the buildings themselves have fascinating tales to tell. Jennie Banters's old brothel is now the home of **Nellie**

SEDONA

Sample a local wine in one of Jerome's tasting rooms.

Bly (136 Main St., 928/634-0255, http://nellyblyscopes.com, 10 A.M.–5:30 P.M. daily), a small store selling kaleidoscopes, jewelry, and arty gifts. The current incarnation of the **Liberty Theatre** (110 Jerome Ave., 928/649-9016, www.jeromelibertytheater.com), which opened in 1918 and hosted silent films and vaudeville acts, now sells souvenirs and movie memorabilia. A handful of delightfully girly stores sell lingerie, clothing, and jewelry: Ladies, if the menfolk and children get impatient while you browse, send them a mile down Perkinsville Road to the **Gold King Mine** (1000 Perkinsville Road, 928/634-0053, www.goldkingminehosttown.com, 10 A.M.–5 P.M. daily), home to a decades-old collection of mining equipment, vehicles, and other Americana, plus one very friendly burro.

Accommodations

A National Historic Landmark, the haunted **Jerome Grand Hotel** (200 Hill St., 928/634-8200, www.jeromegrandhotel.com, $120–205 d) sits high above town on Cleopatra Hill. The 12-room **Hotel Connor** (164 Main St., 928/634-5006, www.connorhotel.com, $90–165 d), built in 1898, offers respite from the high-spirited happenings in the Spirit Room saloon below.

The town is home to a handful of delightful B&Bs and guest apartments. A sophisticated throwback to Jerome's Victorian past, **The Miner's Cottage** (553 Main St., 928/254-1089, www.theminerscottage.com, $950 per week) has two master suites available for rental by the week. Shorter stays are possible on request. **The Surgeon's House** (100 Hill St., 928/639-1452, www.surgeonshouse.com, $145–195), built in 1916 for the UV mine's chief surgeon, is a gracious retreat with four guest suites and a lovely garden that has views all the way to Sedona's red rocks.

Food

The Asylum Restaurant and Lounge (200 Hill St., 928/639-3197, 11 A.M.–3:30 P.M. and 5–9 P.M. daily, $10–32) at the Jerome Grand Hotel features New American cuisine with a Southwestern twist. Meals are complemented by a terrific view of Verde Valley and an extensive wine list, which gets kudos from *Wine Spectator* magazine.

Mile High Grill & Spirits (309 Main St., 928/634-5094, www.milehighgrillandinn.com, lunch daily, breakfast Thurs.–Mon., dinner Fri.–Sat., $6–17) serves hearty breakfasts, followed by sandwiches, salads, wraps, and burgers for lunch. Weekend dinner entrées include updated classics like meatloaf, hanger steak, drunken shrimp, and salmon with chimichurri sauce.

◖**15.Quince** (363 Main St., 928/634-7087, 11 A.M.–8 P.M. Mon.–Thurs., 11 A.M.–9 P.M. Fri., 9 A.M.–9 P.M. Sat., 9 A.M.–8 P.M. Sun., $8–17) dishes up a lively atmosphere along with

New Mexican cuisine smothered in specialty salsas. Quince's owner/chef Vlad Costa has also reopened the beloved **Flat Iron Café** (416 Main St., 928/634-2733, www.flatironjerome.com, 8:30 A.M.–3 P.M. Wed.–Mon., $4–9), where you'll find breakfasts and lunches with a bit less spice than at Quince but every bit as delicious.

Named for the infamous madam Jennie Banters, **Belgian Jennie's Bordello Bistro & Pizzeria** (412 Main St., 928/639-3141, 11:30 A.M.–8 P.M. Thurs.–Mon.) fixes thin-crust pizzas and hearty pastas like fettuccine alfredo, lobster ravioli, and tortellini carbonara.

Getting There

From Sedona, take State Route 89A west to Cottonwood. You can turn left at the fourth stoplight to stay on State Route 89A (the "cut-off" to Jerome), or opt for a more leisurely drive by staying on Main Street and continuing through Old Town Cottonwood. This route passes Dead Horse Ranch State Park and Tuzigoot National Monument before traveling through the former mining company town of Clarkdale. It rejoins State Route 89A to wind up the side of Cleopatra Hill to Jerome.

COTTONWOOD

Backdropped by the Black Hills, Cottonwood was founded in 1879 along the tree-lined Verde River, becoming home to a half-dozen families who supplied Fort Verde and later the work-ers from Jerome's mines. By the 1920s, the flourishing commerce center was known as Arizona's "Biggest Little Town" because it had more businesses per capita than any other town in the state.

Now numbering 11,000 residents, Cottonwood still retains plenty of small-town charm, especially along Main Street in Old Town, the central historic district. The mean-dering path of the Verde, one of Arizona's last free-flowing rivers, is marked by a lush band of green, thanks to the towering cottonwood

© KATHLEEN BRYANT

Wine and dine along Main Street in Old Town Cottonwood.

SEDONA

trees that gave the town its name. And though the community has nurtured its connections to the past, modern Cottonwood also serves as a bedroom community for Sedona workers who can't afford to live in pricy Red Rock Country.

Dead Horse Ranch State Park

To catch a glimpse of what the Verde Valley looked like more than a century ago, head to Dead Horse Ranch State Park (675 Dead Horse Ranch Rd., 928/634-5283, http://azstateparks.com, 8 A.M.–5 P.M. daily, $7/vehicle), a nearly pristine stretch of Verde River that offers camping ($15–55), hiking, mountain biking, fishing, and equestrian areas. Officially classified as a cottonwood and willow riparian gallery forest—one of only 20 such ecosystems left in the world—the 423-acre park protects one of the last stretches of free-running river in the Sonoran Desert and more than 100 species of migrating birds, including the black hawks and golden eagles that come every year to feast on trout. Late in April, the park is home base for the region's premiere nature event, the **Verde Valley Birding and Nature Festival** (www.birdyverde.org), with workshops, exhibits, and field trips exploring the region's diverse habitats.

Look for the park's brown information sign along Main Street, after the road curves to the left (west) and approaches Old Town. Turn right (north) on 10th Street, continuing across the river and turning right on Dead Horse Ranch Road, which leads to the park entrance.

Old Town

Elvis walked here, and so can you. Strolling down Main Street in Old Town Cottonwood is a trip down memory lane, with brick storefronts and quaint signage offering a slice of Americana. Many buildings are undergoing restoration, and in recent years, boutiques and galleries have been joined by wine-tasting rooms and trendy cafés as Cottonwood rediscovers its agricultural roots. The four-block Old Town district (www.oldtown.org) is on the National Register of Historic Places, and the best way to see architectural details like hammered tin ceilings and river-rock masonry is to explore on foot. Three dozen buildings date to the 1920s and 1930s, some of them hiding underground rooms and tunnels used by Prohibition-era bootleggers. The proprietor of the **Cottonwood Hotel** (930 N. Main St., 928/634-9455, www.cottonwoodhotel.com) leads fascinating walking tours for $30–45. Or, for a self-guided nature walk, start at the **Old Jail** (1101 N. Main St.) and head down the mile-long Jail Trail to the Verde River Greenway. Check in at the **Pillsbury Wine Company** (1012 N. Main, 928/639-0646) for brochures and information about things to do in Old Town.

Entertainment and Events

Cottonwood boasts one of the finest concert venues in northern Arizona, the **Old Town Center for the Arts** (5th and Main St., 928/634-0940, www.oldtowncenter.org). Under the direction of musician and luthier William Eaton, OTCA has hosted musicians, comedy, and theater in its renovated historic building.

Housed in a former garage, **The Rendezvous in Old Town** (777 N. Main St., 928/634-3777, http://riotcottonwood.com, 2–9 P.M. Mon.–Thurs., 11 A.M.–midnight Fri.–Sat., 11 A.M.–9 P.M. Sun. $8–13) aka RIOT, keeps things hoppin' late with a small-but-creative fusion menu, two dozen beers on tap, a generous wine list, and nightly entertainment.

Blazin' M Ranch (1875 Mabery Ranch Rd., 928/634-0334, www.blazinm.com, 5–8:30 P.M. daily, closed Jan. and Aug., adults $35, children 3–12 $20) serves up "cowboy vittles, stories, tomfoolery." The dinner bell rings at 6:30, but arrive early to enjoy the full Wild West experience, including a shooting gallery, train ride, and petting zoo. Browse the old-fashioned shops—or dress up as rough-and-tumble cowboys and saloon madams for an "Olde Tyme" photo. Dinner includes barbecued meats, cowboy beans, chunky applesauce, and homemade biscuits. Afterward, the Blazin' M Cowboys carry on the Old West tradition of music and storytelling. Call for reservations.

In early May, the **Verde Valley Fair** (800 E. Cherry St., 928/634-3290, www.verdevalleyfair.com, $3–10) is a classic, with livestock exhibits, a carnival, and plenty of blue-ribbon quilts, jams, and pies. In November, a street fair with food and music, **Walkin' On Main** (928/639-3200), celebrates historic Main Street.

Following the annual **Christmas Parade** held on the first Saturday of December is the much-anticipated **Chocolate Walk** (4–8 P.M.). Participate by taking your chocolate collection bag from store to store, enjoying Christmas decorations and sampling sweet treats into the evening as you browse for holiday gifts. For more information about this and other events, contact the Chamber of Commerce (1010 S. Main St., 928/634-7593, www.cottonwoodchamberaz.org).

Shopping

The Verde Valley's largest commerce center, Cottonwood is home to the familiar big-box stores that don't fit into Jerome or Sedona, as well as many mom-and-pop service businesses. Antiques stores dot the main drag, with most galleries and boutiques centering in Old Town. Among them is **Art Institute Glitter** (712 N. Balboa St., 928/639-0805, www.artglitter.com, 9 A.M.–5 P.M. Mon.–Fri., 10 A.M.–3 P.M. Sat.), a must-stop for scrappers, crafters, and all who like shiny things. The store carries crafting supplies, but the mainstay is glitter, to the tune of 60,000 pounds a year. At **Bent River Books and Music** (1010 N. Main St., 928/634-8332, www.bentriverbm.com, winter

hours 10 A.M.–6 P.M. Mon. and Wed.–Sat., noon–5 P.M. Sun.), you can sip a cup of tea and browse new, used, and collectible books and ephemera for hours. The bookstore helps keep Old Town lively with author events and live acoustic music on weekends.

Pick up a bottle of local vino at any of the wine-tasting rooms on Main, and stop at **Orion Bread** (1028 N. Main St., 928/649-1557, www.orionbread.com, 8 A.M.–5 P.M. Mon.–Sat., 7 A.M.–4 P.M. Sun.) for a loaf of Rosemary Italian or Miner's Sourdough and some jumbo cookies. Add olive oil from **Verde Valley Olive Oil Traders** (1002 N. Main St., 928/634-9900, www.vvoliveoil.com, 10:30 A.M.–6 P.M. Mon.–Sat., 11 A.M.–6 P.M. Sun.) to create the perfect picnic.

Accommodations

You'll find a few chain motels in Cottonwood, which makes a convenient base if you're counting pennies or if rooms in Sedona or Jerome are booked. The **Pines Motel** (920 Camino Real, 928/634-9975, www.azpinesmotel.com, $50–90) has clean, bright rooms, and the mini-suites, equipped with full-size refrigerators, are great for larger groups or big families. Offering boutique accommodations in a restored 1925 grocery, **The Tavern Hotel** (904 N. Main, 928/639-1669, http://thetavernhotel.com, $150–170) is a stylish option with amenities that include breakfast vouchers for Old Town cafés.

Food

Willy's Burgers & Shakes (794 N. Main St., 928/634-6648, 11 A.M.–7 P.M. Mon.–Sat., 11 A.M.–3 P.M. Sun., $5–8) recreates the classic diner ambience of the 1950s, right down to the black-and-white checkered floor and swell jukebox. Look for the converted gas station's old pumps at out front, then refuel on classic burgers, gooey grilled cheese sandwiches, and malts or shakes.

Main Street's **Red Rooster** (901 N. Main St., 928/649-8100, http://oldtownredroostercafe.com, breakfast and lunch daily, $6–14) puts a gourmet touch on comfort food. The breakfast skillets (and coffee) are especially good; so are the homemade soups and quiche.

C Crema Café (917 N. Main St., 928/649-5785, www.cremacafe89a.com, breakfast and lunch daily, $5–10) has a simple menu with a Euro flair. Soups, salads, and sandwiches incorporate local organic ingredients, and the gelatos and sorbets are made from scratch.

Nic's Italian Steak & Crab House (925 N. Main St., 928/634-9626, www.nicsaz.com, diner nightly, $9–17) packs in locals with solid seafood dishes, top-notch steaks, and Italian classics like eggplant parmesan, lasagna, and chicken piccata.

Getting There

From Sedona, take State Route 89A west, which includes 6.5 miles known as the Dry Creek Scenic Road. As you descend toward the Verde Valley, the landscape changes from red-rock buttes and juniper woodland to high-desert chaparral and tawny grasslands. Scan the southern horizon for House Mountain, an extinct volcano with a house-shaped top, named by Cottonwood-area settlers in the 1870s. After you cross the Verde River and enter Cottonwood, the highway becomes Main Street.

TUZIGOOT NATIONAL MONUMENT

Between Old Town Cottonwood and Clarkdale, Tuzigoot National Monument (928/634-5564, www.nps.gov/tuzi, 8 A.M.–5 P.M. daily Sept.–May, 8 A.M.–6 P.M. daily June–Aug., $5 adults, children free) protects a 110-room hilltop pueblo that was once home to Sinagua villagers, who began its construction around A.D. 1100. The three-story pueblo formed an intricate complex of living,

Tuzigoot National Monument

© RANDY MIRAMONTEZ/123RF.COM

SEDONA

cooking, and storage spaces. Visitors can explore rooms up close, and the museum has the area's finest collection of prehistoric artifacts. The largest reconstructed room at the top of the complex has views of the Black Hills, Verde River, and Tavasci Marsh, a landscape that offered a large diversity of minerals, food, fuel, and other resources for the villagers, who traded with communities hundreds of miles away.

Getting There

From Sedona, take State Route 89A west to Cottonwood, where the highway becomes Main Street. Continue on Main Street through Old Town. Look for the turnoff to Tuzigoot Road on the right, marked by a brown information. Follow the road to the park entrance.

CLARKDALE

Below Jerome is the postcard-pretty town of Clarkdale (pop. 3,800), founded in 1912 and constructed almost entirely in one go as the company town for William Clark's UV mine smelter. Considered to be Arizona's first master-planned community, the town boasted cutting-edge technology for its time—telephone, telegraph, electricity, modern plumbing, and sewer. Amenities included a central park with a bandstand, and a handsome Spanish Colonial–style clubhouse with a library, bowling alley, and pool.

Today, the bandstand still hosts evening summertime concerts in the town square, surrounded by a collection of charming bungalows. The townsite is a National Historic District, encompassing 386 homes and businesses. The brick storefronts along Main Street look much the same as they did in 1928 when semiretired lawman Jim Roberts foiled a bank robbery amidst a flurry of bullets.

Find out more about the town's past at the **Clarkdale Historical Society and Museum** (900 1st N., 928/649-1198, http://

clarkdaleheritage.org, 10 A.M.–1 P.M. Wed.–Sun.), where you can pick up a map for a walking tour. The museum also has a gift shop with work by local artists.

Verde Canyon Railroad

Billed as Arizona's "longest-running nature show," the Verde Canyon Railroad (300 N. Broadway, 800/582-7245, http://verdecanyonrr.com, $55–80) leads into a steep-walled limestone canyon sheltering waterfowl and bald eagle nesting sites. Special events include the Grape Train Escape ($120), with first-class seats and wine-tasting on a twilight ride. Or you can rent the entire caboose ($600) for a group up of up to six. Packages with hotel accommodations are available.

Accommodations and Food

For a getaway that feels like home, settle into the **Blue Heron Guest House** (200 Main St., 982/634-3989, www.blueheronaz.com, $85–100), an early 20th-century workshop remodeled into a charming cottage/studio, equipped with a kitchenette. After a day of exploring, you can kick back on the shady front porch or warm up near the outdoor fireplace.

Presiding on Clarkdale's Main Street is **Su Casa** (1000 Main St., 928/634-2771, lunch and dinner daily, $8–16) a popular spot serving relatively tame Mexican fare.

Getting There

From Sedona, take State Route 89A west toward Cottonwood. Turn right (north) onto the Mingus Avenue extension, crossing the Verde River. At the next stoplight, turn right on Main Street, continuing through Old Town and passing Tuzigoot National Monument en route to Clarkdale. A left turn on Clarkdale's Main Street will take you through the town's historic center; staying to the right on Broadway leads to the Verde Canyon Railroad depot.

SEDONA

© KATHLEEN BRYANT

Visit the local wineries along Page Springs Road.

SEDONA

PAGE SPRINGS AND CORNVILLE

The creekside communities of Page Springs and Cornville are the heart of the Verde Valley's burgeoning agricultural revival. You can travel through both unincorporated areas (with a total population of about 4,500) on a pleasant loop drive from State Route 89A. Five miles of Page Springs Road have been designated by Yavapai County as a historic and scenic route. Cactus-covered hillsides sidle up to acres of lush vineyards as the route passes orchards, farms, wineries, and Cornville's **Windmill Park** (9950 E. Cornville Rd.), a pleasant eight-acre oasis along lower Oak Creek with picnic tables, horseshoes, and a working windmill. You won't see any cornfields in Cornville (the U.S. Postal Service misspelled the town's name, meant to acknowledge a pioneer family named Coan), but you will see creekside pastures.

Birders won't want to miss strolling around the 82-acre **Page Springs Fish Hatchery**

(1600 N. Page Springs Rd., 928/634-4805, 8 A.M.–4 P.M. daily, free), designated an Important Bird Area by the Audobon Society. The hatchery has a nature trail and an interpretive center. As well as trout, native fish species facing extinction in the Grand Canyon's Colorado River are nurtured here.

Accommodations

Lovely and peaceful **Lo Lo Mai Springs Resort** (11505 Lo Lo Mai Rd., 928/634-4700, www. lolomai.com) has shady RV spaces and tent sites (starting at $37) and camping cabins (kitchen needs are provided; towels and bedding are not, $75–140). Some of the cabins include bathrooms. The old-timey resort property along the creek has shower facilities, a seasonal pool and Jacuzzi, a playground, horseshoe pits, and a clubhouse. Though the resort operates on a membership basis, vacancies are often available for nonmembers. It's an ideal spot for a family reunion or large gathering.

Food

After a tasting flight or two at the vineyards along Page Springs Road, you may be ready for a meal nearby. The dining room at **Up the Creek** (1975 N. Page Springs Rd., 928/634-9954, 11 A.M.–9 P.M. Wed.–Sun., $8–30) juts over the lazy waters of lower Oak Creek for a treetop feel. Steaks and barbecue are the specialty, but vegetarians will appreciate the made-from-scratch tomato–sour cream–cornmeal pie.

The aptly named **Harry's Hideaway** (10990 E. Cornville Rd., 928/639-2222, http://harryshideaway.com, lunch and dinner Tues.–Sat., $8–18) may be a little hard to find—it's tucked into a small shopping center near Casey's Corner—but the owners will make you feel like family. The wine-friendly, wide-ranging menu runs the gamut from American comfort food to Mediterranean dishes.

Across the road from Cornville's post office, **Vince's Little Star** (9375 E. Cornville Rd., 928/634-4063, dinner Tues.–Sat., $8–15) is a classic small-town Italian joint, with red-checkered tablecloths, candles in chianti bottles, and Frank and Dean crooning on the stereo. Reservations are recommended.

Getting There

From Sedona, take State Route 89A west toward Cottonwood. Turn left (south) at Page Springs Road. After passing through Page Springs, the road intersects with the Cornville Road at Casey's Corner. Turn right and continue through the village of Cornville where the road loops back toward State Route 89A.

CAMP VERDE

At the end of the Civil War, farmers and ranchers began to settle around the confluence of the Verde River and West Clear Creek, aiming to supply food, cattle, hay, and other goods to the army at Fort Whipple and the growing mining community of Prescott. Historically, this prime location was used by seminomadic bands of Tonto Apaches and Yavapais for hunting game and gathering wild plants. Finding their traditional lands fenced and plowed, the Indians began raiding the settlers' crops and herds. In early 1865 the U.S. army established Camp Lincoln to deal with the escalating conflict, later moving the camp and renaming it Fort Verde.

Over the next decades, the fort and town became the center of Arizona's Indian Wars, associated with legendary scouts, chiefs, and commanders like General Crook. After the removal of many Yavapais and Apaches in 1875 and the surrender of Geronimo in 1886, the fort was abandoned. Concerned locals who recognized its historical importance joined together in the 1960s to rescue it from further disintegration. Camp Verde, the area's oldest settled community, takes an active role in preserving the past. The local historical society (435 S. Main, 928/567-9560) displays photographs, artifacts, and artwork in their small museum and maintains two historic buildings, the Clear Creek Church and the home of George Hance.

Today, more than 10,000 people live in the modern town of Camp Verde, and many families continue to farm and ranch along the river. February's Pecan and Wine Festival (www.pecanandwinefestival.com) spotlights two local crops, and July's CornFest (http://visit-campverde.com) celebrates a third. The main drag is lined with a few antiques shops and restaurants, and the town serves as the northern gateway to the Tonto National Forest, offering recreational activities from rafting the Verde River to exploring on horseback or by Jeep. The real highlight, however, is being able to step back into the past at this place where so many cultures intersected.

Fort Verde State Historic Park

See the real Old West at Fort Verde (125 E.

SEDONA

Hollamon, 928/567-3275, http://azstateparks. com, 9 A.M.–5 P.M. Thurs.–Mon., $5 adults, $2 ages 7–13), offering a glimpse of a frontier soldier's life during the Indian Wars of the late 1800s. Originally built in 1871, the fort housed as many as 300 soldiers who were stationed here to protect Anglo settlers from Apache and Yavapai raiders. What remains of the fort today is considered the best-preserved example of Indian War–era military architecture in the state.

Three historical houses still stand along the parade ground, decorated with 1880s-period furnishings. The Surgeon's Quarters was home to 27 army doctors over the years, and the downstairs office displays bonesaws and other medical equipment. The other two houses served as quarters for bachelor officers and the fort's commanding officer and his family. The former headquarters building now houses a museum with artifacts and photographs highlighting the soldiers, civilians, and Indian tribes who once lived in the region. Exhibits describe how Yavapai and Apache bands were pursued and incarcerated on a reservation in the Verde Valley, then force-marched to the San Carlos Apache reservation in 1875.

Several times a year, the fort hosts candelit tours, workshops, and other events. Mid-October brings Fort Verde Days, when reenactors representing Buffalo Soldiers (the army's African American cavalry regiments) ride into town.

Verde Valley Archaeology Center

Learn more about the prehistoric Sinagua Indians and the contemporary Yavapai and Apache tribes at the Verde Valley Archaeology Center (345 S. Main, 928/567-0066, www.verdevalleyarchaeology.org, 9:30 A.M.–4 P.M. Thurs.–Fri., 11 A.M.–4 P.M. Sat., noon–4 P.M. Sun., by donation). The volunteer-staffed museum displays artifacts from area sites, and it's a good idea to call first to verify hours. The center's research lab is used by a dedicated group of avocational archaeologists who educate locals and visitors about site preservation and assist professionals in stabilizing, monitoring, and investigating cultural sites from Camp Verde to Sedona. During March, the center hosts events for Arizona Archaeology Month, and in September, it holds a festival of American Indian arts.

Entertainment and Accommodations

Familiar motel and fast-food chains have staked out the freeway interchange at State Route 260. Travelers who want to add a cultural aspect to their visit can exit a couple miles north for **Cliff Castle Casino** (555 W. Middle Verde Rd., 928/567-7900, www.cliffcastle-casinohotel.com), conveniently situated near Montezuma Castle National Monument. The casino, owned by the Yavapai-Apache Nation, offers slots, poker, blackjack, and keno, as well as live entertainment at the outdoor **Stargazer Pavilion** and inside at its nightclub, **Dragonfly Lounge.** The casino has four restaurants (including the casual diner Johnny Rockets and the elegant Storyteller), a bowling alley, and a video arcade. Just downhill, you can find a clean, quiet room at **The Hotel at Cliff Castle** (928/567-6611 or 800/524-6343, $100–120 d).

Getting There

To get to Camp Verde from Sedona, drive south on State Route 179 through the Village of Oak Creek to I-17, where you'll merge right and head southwest. Take exit 287, and turn left onto State Route 260. Turn left to head toward downtown on the Finnie Flats Road, which becomes Main Street. You'll see signs directing you to the fort. If you are driving from Phoenix, drive I-17 north to exit 285, where you'll follow State Route 260 south (also known as the General Crook Trail) to Camp Verde's Main Street.

© KATHLEEN BRYANT

Montezuma Castle National Monument

❶ MONTEZUMA CASTLE NATIONAL MONUMENT

Walking up the shaded creekside path to view Montezuma Castle (I-17 exit 289, 928/567-3322, www.nps.gov/moca, 8 A.M.–5 P.M. daily, 8 A.M.–6 P.M. daily Jun.–Aug., $5 adults, children under 16 free), you can't help but imagine what it must have been like to live in the five-story pueblo, one of the best-preserved cliff dwellings in North America.

Built into a deep recess in the limestone cliff and sheltered from the elements, the 20-room pueblo and nearby Castle A, with 45–50 rooms, were occupied from about A.D. 1250 to the 1400s. Villagers cultivated fields along Beaver Creek and supplemented their diet by hunting and gathering native plants. The pueblos and their rooftop plazas—constructed of stone with wood timbers and mud mortar—were used for sleeping, preparing food, weaving, making pottery, and storing surplus food. The Sinagua participated in a vast trade network that reached as far south as present-day Mexico and as far west as the Pacific.

Explorers who discovered the site in the 1800s speculated (incorrectly) that the Aztecs and their legendary emperor Montezuma built the impressive structure. Museum exhibits inside the visitor center provide an overview of the site, the prehistoric Sinagua culture, and the contemporary Yavapai and Apache people who inhabit the Verde Valley today.

Montezuma Well

The Sinagua were experts at making the most of the Verde Valley's natural resources. Just 11 miles north of Montezuma Castle, you can witness their ingenuity at another of Arizona's natural wonders, Montezuma Well (I-17 exit 293, 928/567-4521, www.nps.gov/moca, 8 A.M.–5 P.M. daily, 8 A.M.–6 P.M. daily Jun.–Aug., $5 adults, children free). Small cliffside ruins and canals are clustered around the site, which provided a vital source of water to the

Sinagua farmers and also figures in Yavapai and Apache creation stories. You can imagine its importance in an area that averages 11 inches of rain annually. Underground springs still feed 1.5 million gallons of water every day into the well, which actually is a large sinkhole, 365 feet across and 55 feet deep. The constant supply of 74-degree water has created an ecosystem with several plants and animals not found anywhere else in the world. Unique species of crustaceans, water scorpions, and turtles thrive in the warm, carbon dioxide–rich water that is inhospitable to most fish and aquatic life. You can walk down to the ruins along the water's edge or to the well's tree-shaded outlet, where the temperature can be as much as 20 degrees cooler than in the surrounding grasslands. Nearby, a ramada protects the remains of a Hohokam-style pit house.

Getting There

From Sedona, head south on State Route 179 to I-17. Take exit 289, drive east through two roundabouts for less than a mile, and then turn left on Montezuma Castle Road. Plenty of signs will make navigating the narrow two-lane road quite easy. From Phoenix, follow I-17 north about an hour and turn right at exit 289, where signs will direct you through two traffic circles to the monument's entrance. To reach Montezuma Well, drive I-I7 to exit 293. Follow the signs through the towns of McGuireville and Rimrock to the park's entrance.

OUT OF AFRICA WILDLIFE PARK

Kids love animals, and they'll see plenty of them at Out of Africa Wildlife Park (3505 State Route 260, 928/567-2840, www.outo-fafricapark.com, 9:30 A.M.–5 P.M. daily, $36 adults, $20 ages 3–12), a 100-acre wildlife refuge with lions, tigers, giraffes, and other exotic beasts. Set aside a half-day for activities like the tiger splash or snake show and tours. Two of the tours use trams or safari vehicles, but you can walk to photo platforms and habitat areas at your own pace as well. There are a snack bar and gift shop on-site, and you'll often find discounted tickets online or at local hotels and businesses.

Getting There

From West Sedona, take State Route 89A to Cottonwood. Turn left on State Route 260 and travel 10 miles to Cherry Road. Turn right on Cherry, then right on Commonwealth Drive, which leads to the park entrance.

ARCOSANTI

Arcosanti (928/632-7135, www.arcosanti.org, 10 A.M.–4 P.M. daily) is a community designed and built by Italian architect Paolo Soleri as the embodiment of his principles of "arcology"— a mixture of architecture and ecology. Soleri's goal was to create a "lean alternative" to the wastefulness of modern cities by making them more compact and self-sustaining. His continuing real-world experiment began in 1970, more than two decades after he came to the Southwest to study with Frank Lloyd Wright at Taliesin West.

Perched on a high desert bluff, Arcosanti today is home to just a few hundred people at any one time. From a distance, it resembles an unlikely combination of Italian hill town and sci-fi movie set. But up close, the handcrafted details and perfectly human scale make this pioneering example of urban sustainability a delight to visit. Guided tours are $10, and special events include live music, art shows, and dinners under the arched concrete vaults, which are open to the desert skies.

Food

If your timing is right, you can join the community for a meal ($9) at the cafeteria, open daily at noon for lunch and reopening at 6 P.M. for dinner. Overnight stays ($40–100)

© KATHLEEN BRYANT

Sales of wind chimes and bells help fund Arcosanti's projects.

SEDONA

are available with prior arrangement. Special-interest tours and workshops can also be arranged, including weeklong learning programs.

Getting There

From Phoenix, drive north some 60 miles on I-17. Take exit 262 to State Route 69. Turn right on the Cordes Lakes Road. Signs for Arcosanti direct you north over 2.5 miles of unpaved roads to the site.

From Sedona, head south on State Route 179 to I-17. Drive the freeway 36 miles south, taking exit 262A to State Route 69. Turn left on the Cordes Lakes Road and follow the signs.

BACKGROUND

The Land

If the word "desert" conjures up images of sand dunes, camels, and parched, monochromatic landscapes, then get ready for a surprise. Phoenix and Scottsdale sit in the northeastern corner of the Sonoran Desert, the most ecologically diverse desert region on the planet. Stretching more than 100,000 square miles from central Arizona south into Mexico and west into California, the relatively lush Sonoran Desert is home to more than 1,000 native species of plants, 60 species of mammals, 350 kinds of birds, 20 amphibians, and 100 or so reptiles. It's the only place in the world where the iconic saguaro cactus—made famous in so many Western flicks—grows naturally.

GEOGRAPHY AND GEOLOGY

The Phoenix metro area is ringed with mountains, deep canyons, and broad, alluvial valleys watered by a few rivers and countless dry washes that can transform into raging torrents within minutes after a rain. This landscape is part of a vast basin-and-range region formed 15 million years ago when shifting tectonic plates beneath the Earth's crust in what is now the western United

States pulled it apart. It stretched as much as 50 percent, the land pushing up and pulling down to form a regular pattern of small but steep mountains and broad, flat valleys. A ring of such mountain ranges around metro Phoenix gives the area its nickname: the Valley of the Sun. The major ranges surrounding the Valley are the White Tank Mountains to the west, the Sierra Estrella to the southwest, South Mountain to the south, the Superstitions and Usery Mountains to the east, the McDowell Mountains to the northeast, and the Hieroglyphic Mountains to the northwest. Smaller ranges also ring the center of the city, including the Phoenix Mountains and the Papago Buttes. Most of the rock that forms these craggy peaks is volcanic, created by the inexorable seismic shifting.

To the north lies the high, flat Colorado Plateau, which covers the Four Corners area where northeastern Arizona, southeastern Utah, southwestern Colorado, and northwestern New Mexico meet. Sedona sits below the plateau's southwestern edge, which forms the Mogollon Rim, a long, snaking cliff that bisects the state from east to west. This dramatic drop-off separates the low desert surrounding Phoenix from the grasslands and ponderosa pine forests of the plateau. The area around Sedona is known as Red Rock Country, thanks to the red-tinged sandstone cliffs revealed by the uplifted plateau. The color comes from iron deposits that oxidize—rust—as the rock is weathered by air and water. In places, softer layers below are protected by a cap of harder rocks, allowing erosion to create buttes, spires, and other majestic formations. In fault-formed Oak Creek Canyon, higher cliffs are marked by basalt, lava from a volcanic eruption. An ancient river scoured lava deposits from the canyon, where springs now bubble up to form Oak Creek. The Verde Valley lies between Sedona and the Black Hills, which mark the edge of the basin-and-range province.

RIVERS AND LAKES

Phoenix owes its very existence to the Salt River (or Rio Salado as it is called in Spanish). The stream runs 200 miles from the White Mountains in eastern Arizona to join the Gila River about 15 miles west of downtown Phoenix, and farmers from ancient times to the present have come to the Valley of the Sun for its life-giving water. A series of dams has left the lower half of the riverbed mostly dry since the first, the Roosevelt Dam, was built in 1911, but the Salt's natural flow is more than 2,500 cubic feet per second, about three times the amount of water in the Rio Grande. Except for overflow released after storms, most of this water now goes into hundreds of miles of irrigation canals scattered around the region, and the dams themselves provide flood control and produce electricity. The one exception to this is the two-mile-long Tempe Town Lake, created in 1999 by building two inflatable dams in the bed of the Salt River and filling the area between them with a combination of upstream storm runoff and treated wastewater. Though no swimming is allowed, kayaking, rowing, sailing, and paddleboating are all popular pastimes, and the lake is regularly stocked with fish.

Central Arizona's other major river, the Gila, is even longer and more powerful than the Salt. It flows almost 650 miles from New Mexico's Black Range all the way to the Colorado River, which forms the border between Arizona and California. Dams and irrigation diversions reduce the river to a trickle in several areas, but in its natural state, the Gila carries more than 6,000 cubic feet of water per second and once was navigable from the Colorado nearly to the New Mexico border. For five years, from the end of the Mexican War to the Gadsden Purchase in 1853, the Gila River formed the border between the United States and Mexico. Today, significant portions of the river run through Native American communities.

Dams on the Salt and Gila Rivers have

An inflatable dam on the Salt River has created Tempe Town Lake.

created a number of reservoir lakes. An oft-repeated (but completely unverified) statistic is that Maricopa County has one of the highest per capita rates of boat ownership in the nation. Whether or not this is true, the somewhat incongruous sight of a large pickup truck towing a Jet Ski or fishing boat through the desert is surprisingly common, and it's possible to learn how to sail, kayak, and even scuba dive at Lake Pleasant and a few of the other large lakes in the area.

CLIMATE

Near-perfect weather is probably the Valley of the Sun's greatest claim to fame—well, at least for a good portion of the year. In February, blue, sunny skies and balmy temperatures in 70s and 80s delight residents and visitors alike. The good times last into April, as hiking trails, golf courses, and restaurant patios fill up with people hoping to spend every last second soaking in the spring nirvana. And because this is the desert, the arid climate's low humidity means nighttime temps fall 20 to 30 degrees, providing a cool counterpoint to the warm days.

The Sonoran Desert heats up quickly in May, and its reputation for sizzling summers isn't an exaggeration, with an average high in the 90s and lows in the 70s. Still, the low moisture means that it feels cooler than comparable days in New York, Miami, or Houston. By July, though, watch out. It's hot—as in a 115-degree kind of hot. Phoenix has the warmest climate of any major metropolitan area in the country, and its record high of 122 degrees on June 26, 1990, caused even the toughest of desert-tested Phoenicians to break out in one heck of a sweat. Most people cope by switching to an early morning or nocturnal schedule in the summer, when overnight lows drop into the 80s.

In late summer, monsoon storms roll into the city from the desert, bringing frequent breaks from the scorching heat and sunshine. These afternoon showers, caused by a seasonal change in weather patterns, can be sudden and torrential, stranding motorists and mountainside hikers. Dramatic bolts of lightning force golfers off the course and swimmers out of the pool.

Dry storms, called haboobs, send up towering clouds of dust that can smother the city at rush hour like something out of a big-budget sci-fi flick. Haboobs have occurred so frequently in recent summers that Valley of the Sun bartenders were asked to come up with a cocktail in

MONSOON MADNESS

© KATHLEEN BRYANT

The summer monsoons usher in fast-moving thunderstorms.

Triple-digit heat is to be expected during the summer months in Phoenix, but there's a weather phenomenon in the desert Southwest that makes the sweltering afternoons unpredictable. The Arizona monsoon season begins June 15 and ends September 30, bringing volatile afternoon storms that can range from blowing dust to torrential downpour. The term monsoon is taken from the Arabic word for season, *mausim,* referring to a seasonal shift in wind flow. In Arizona, typically westerly winds shift to a southerly flow, which pulls in moisture from the Gulf of California. Combine

that moisture with the intense afternoon heat, and you get thunderstorms.

In May, the average afternoon high temperature is about 93 degrees, with relative humidity averaging 15 percent or below. By July, the mercury will rise each afternoon to about 105 degrees, and relative humidity doubles to an average of about 30 percent. That makes it tougher for the human body to cool down during the sweltering heat. But heat is only one of the dangers of the monsoon.

About a third of Phoenix's yearly rainfall occurs in the summer, and sometimes it comes dangerously quickly. The sandy desert floor cannot absorb rainfall sometimes amounting to an inch or more in just a few hours. Flash floods become a problem as normally dry washes fill with water and careless drivers attempt to cross them. So-called "dry storms" are also dangerous, sparking lightning-caused fires and sending massive clouds of dust, called haboobs, across the desert. Their strong winds pick up the dry desert soil and sweep it into town, sometimes bringing traffic to a standstill as visibility hovers near zero. Thunderstorms often send hikers and golfers hurrying for cover, as lightning slashes across the desert horizon.

Monsoon thunderstorms are most likely during late afternoon but can erupt any time of the day. They are more common the farther south and east you go in Arizona. Although they can be very dangerous, they're essential to the desert ecosystem. Many desert creatures, including tarantulas, toads, and quail, have adapted their breeding cycles to benefit from the monsoon rain. And in May and June you will notice saguaro cacti blooming with beautiful white flowers, letting their fruit seeds ripen just in time to soak up the summer rains.

© KATHLEEN BRYANT

The Sonoran Desert is richly diverse due to twice-yearly rains.

their honor. (The winning haboob was mixed by Lon's at the Hermosa Inn.)

By October, a "second spring" emerges with lush, green plants and colorful wildflowers. Triple-digit temps become a memory, and fall temperatures drop back into the 80s, which means you'll be able to fit in plenty of outdoor time. In the high deserts of Sedona, which is typically 10 to 20 degrees cooler than Phoenix throughout the year, sycamores and maples along Oak Creek begin to turn, creating a golden yellow band with splashes of red leaves against evergreen forests.

Believe it or not, there is a winter in the Sonoran Desert. The 60-something highs and 40-something lows feel downright chilly to Phoenicians. Even so, Valley residents love nothing more than calling up snowed-in relatives in other parts of the country to gloat. Nighttime lows fall below freezing a few times a year, and a rare light snow does fall, more often in Sedona where the red rocks are dusted in white a few times each winter.

ENVIRONMENTAL ISSUES

In 2009 former mayor Phil Gordon announced an ambitious plan to make Phoenix "the greenest city in America." Though admirable, the initiative will have to solve at least two of the metro area's most daunting environmental problems—air pollution and suburban sprawl—if it's to be more than rhetoric. In winter, a brown cloud of dust, car exhaust, and other particulates often hangs over the city for days at a time, thanks to the surrounding mountains, which block the wind and trap warmer air near the ground. In summer, strong sunlight and extreme heat interact with chemicals in car exhaust to form ozone, a colorless pollutant that affects breathing and often leads to warnings from health officials for people with respiratory illnesses to stay inside. Poor air quality is a problem that defies easy solution in a metro area that sprawls over more than 1,000 square miles and forces residents to drive almost everywhere. And it's not the only problem resulting from the way Phoenix (one of the fastest-growing cities in the United States until the real estate bubble burst in 2008) was planned and built. During the long construction boom, new subdivisions, office parks, and shopping malls paved over the desert at the rate of more than an acre per hour, destroying wildlife habitat and native plants, not to mention impacting the views of pristine desert that draw so many people to Arizona in the first place.

Not surprisingly, one of the top concerns in the desert is water and where to get it. Metro Phoenix has fewer problems in this area than might be expected. Rivers and streams flowing out of the mountains to the north and east fill roughly half the metropolis's water needs, while a 350-mile canal from the Colorado River delivers the other half. Local officials say the billions of dollars spent on this water

Canals divert water from the Salt River and other sources in Phoenix.

infrastructure can supply more than the area currently needs, but a long drought could create serious problems. The complicated legal agreement that apportions water from the Colorado River to states along its banks is actually based on historically high levels of water, and with California at the front of the line, Arizona cities could get very thirsty if the mountain snows that feed all the rivers around the state get much lighter. Draining rivers so completely also creates a slew of environmental issues. Even under current conditions, very little of the water from the Salt and Gila Rivers makes it to the Colorado, and the mighty river itself now dries up miles before it reaches its mouth at the Sea of Cortez.

Another major problem comes from wildfires sparked by lightning, campers, vehicles, and other human-related activities. Huge blazes in recent years have charred hundreds of square miles at a time. Though none of the fires have reached inside the metro area,

the 2005 Cave Creek Complex destroyed 11 homes on the northeastern edge of the city, forcing evacuations before pushing north to the Tonto Forest and more remote communities. It burned nearly a quarter-million acres, the largest wildfire ever in the Sonoran Desert. (It also destroyed the state's largest saguaro cactus, a 46-footer estimated to be 200 years old.)

State and local officials have made efforts to address air quality and sprawl by changing the way people live and travel in the region. A light-rail line running through Phoenix, Tempe, and Mesa opened in 2008. It surpassed ridership expectations in its first six months, and has since eased congestion and attracted more businesses and residents in the neighborhoods it passes through. Abundant sunshine (286 days a year) makes the region a shoo-in for solar-power production, and many business leaders are hoping for clean solar-manufacturing plants too. Despite a state political climate that's often cool toward solar and other alternative energy initiatives, in 2011 more than 80 renewable energy projects were in the works for the Phoenix area.

Arizona Public Service partnered with the City of Phoenix to install a solar system on the roof of the Phoenix Convention Center that provides all the building's electricity. The recently approved Sonoran Solar Energy Project will trade 2,000 acres of desert southwest of Phoenix for 300 megawatts of solar power, enough to power 90,000 homes. In 2011, Riverpoint Solar Research Park launched an 18-acre test site near a stretch of I-10, marked by a 75-foot dish that takes in compressed solar-heated air. And it's not all sunshine: Two researchers at Arizona State University in Tempe have earned accolades for their work with algae as biofuel, and another venture will tap a closed landfill for biogas to power 2,000 homes. Projects like these will, it is hoped, attract high-paying engineering jobs to a metro area that's always been big in technology-related jobs, particularly computer-chip manufacturing. From the Hohokam's elaborate irrigation canals to the air-conditioning-inspired real estate boom of the 1950s and 1960s, metro Phoenix has been uniquely affected by new ideas and products—and there's no reason to think that the future won't repeat the cycle.

Flora and Fauna

FLORA
Cacti

They may seem prickly at first, but the Sonoran Desert's cacti are quite lovable once you get know them. Prime examples of form meeting function in Arizona's harsh environment, cacti have several resourceful means to mitigate the hot, arid climate. Their leaves have evolved into hard, slender spines, which provide shade and defend against animals foraging for food and water. Their trunks have become spongy repositories for water, and their green skins have taken on the duties of photosynthesis.

The saguaro (sah-WAH-roh) cactus is the undisputed king of the Sonoran Desert, an iconic figure that can be found only in this part of the world. The spiny giant can grow up to 60 feet tall and live to be more than 150 years old, with some of the oldest specimens surviving two centuries. Its clever root system tunnels only a few feet deep, but radiates out a distance equal to the saguaro's height, allowing the camel-like plant to capture the maximum amount of water possible after a rainstorm. These slow-growers can take up to 50 to 75 years to develop branches, or arms, with some sprouting as many as 25 and others never producing any. The saguaro is an important resource for the desert's ecosystem. In late spring, the cactus blooms with white flowers, taking advantage of nocturnal pollinators like moths and bats. They produce sweet, red fruits, which have been eaten by animals and indigenous people for thousands of years. The saguaro's thick trunk often provides a home for a burrowing Gila woodpecker—or the occasional desert owl that takes over an abandoned "apartment." Native people once used the plant's wooden ribs in the construction of their shelters, and desert animals still take up residence in their dry skeletons. (But for contemporary humans, damaging or even moving a saguaro cactus without a permit can result in hefty fines and even jail time.)

The desert's other barbed species include the paddle cactus, more commonly known as the prickly pear. It has flat, rounded pads (*nopales* in Spanish) that are edible once cooked, and a magenta-pink fruit (referred to as a pear, or *tuna*) that is used to make candy, jelly, and a

saguaros near Superstition Mountains

© ANTON FOLTIN/123RF.COM

prickly pear cactus

© KATHLEEN BRYANT

syrup that flavors iced tea, prickly-pear margaritas, and other concoctions. A traditional food in Hispanic and Indian cultures, the fruit is quite nutritious (if it's not made into candy, that is), and the pads' soluble fiber may prevent high cholesterol and diabetes.

The barrel cactus grows 1–3 feet wide and 2–4 feet high. The stout, barrel-shaped body is easy to recognize, though you won't want to get too close to its fishhook spines. The cactus is also known as the "compass barrel," as older plants frequently lean toward the southwest. Cholla cactus, another common inhabitant of the Sonoran Desert, comes in 20 varieties that bear descriptive names like pencil cholla, buckhorn cholla, chain-fruit cholla, teddy bear cholla, and jumping cholla, which doesn't so much jump as easily cling to anything that touches it.

Trees and Shrubs

First-time visitors to Arizona are often surprised by the numerous trees and shrubs that are native to the area. Arizona's official state tree, the green-barked paloverde, is a gorgeous example. Often found in floodplains and washes, it is drought-deciduous, shedding its tiny leaves during dry spells and leaving its green bark to take over photosynthesis. In the spring, the canopy blooms in an explosion of tiny yellow flowers. The hardy mesquite tree's desert adaptations include a deep taproot that can easily tunnel 25–50 feet underground. For generations, people have harvested the mesquite's seedpods for food and used the hard, dense wood in furniture. Like mesquites, acacia species have small compound leaves that slow evapotranspiration (water loss). In spring, several acacia species bear fragrant yellow flowers that look like small balls of fuzz. Farther north, in Sedona and Oak Creek Canyon, you'll see ponderosa pines, as well as white and Douglas firs, shrubby oaks, graceful sycamores, and distinctive species like the scaly alligator juniper.

© KATHLEEN BRYANT

The green-barked paloverde is Arizona's official state tree.

The creosote bush, a prevalent sight throughout the desert, has resinous leaves that exude a refreshing, herbal scent after much-appreciated rainstorms. In early spring, the silver-leafed brittlebush is topped with a crown of yellow flowers. The woody jojoba produces a seed that cosmetic companies covet for its natural oil. Not a cactus (though it bears plenty of spines), the ocotillo is easy to spot. Its long stems look like dried sticks until after a rain, when they are covered with small green leaves. In spring, clusters of red tubular flowers appear on the tips. The agave, a lily relative, is often used as a landscape plant. Its fleshy leaves radiate from a central core in a symmetrical pattern, ending in sharp points. The long-lived agave, also known as "century plant," flowers only once, its blooms atop a tall stalk that rises from the center of the plant. As dramatic as the heroine of a Western melodrama, the plant dies after it blooms.

Wildflowers

Nothing dispels the misperception of a lifeless, beige desert like wildflower season, when a torrent of psychedelic colors washes across the bajada and slopes. Thanks to *Arizona Highways* magazine, the Grand Canyon State is famous for its vibrant wildflowers, which typically appear after winter showers in late February or March and can last well into April or early May. Get your camera ready for the apricot-colored globe mallow, desert lavender, golden desert sunflower, violet purple mat, red-flowered chuparosa, orange-gold poppies, and lemon-yellow desert senna. It's not hard to find these seas of color, as any of the mountain preserves that surround the city will teem with polychromatic life, although the best spots are east of Phoenix in the Superstition Mountains at the far end of U.S. 60 or in North Scottsdale in the McDowell Mountains. You can also catch a secondary round of blooms in the fall when summer's hot weather gives way to spring-like temperatures.

FAUNA
Reptiles and Amphibians

The rattlesnake may be the Sonoran Desert's most famous resident, with some 20 species slithering around Arizona's rocky canyons and dusty desert floors, including the western diamondback, tiger, and sidewinder. They're best known for their ominous rattles, a series of hollow segments made of keratin—like fingernails—that rub against one another at the end of their tails. When threatened, rattlesnakes strike a defensive posture and shake their tails. Their potent venom has enzymes that destroy tissue and, in the case of the Mohave rattler, damage nerves. Rattlesnakes are pit vipers, named for heat-sensing pits—sensory organs near the eyes and nostrils that produce a "heat image" allowing the snakes to spot prey in the pitch black of a desert night. Other desert snakes include two nonvenomous constrictors, the king snake and the gopher snake, which prey on small creatures.

Lizards scurry around the desert as well, consuming insects, leaves, and springtime blossoms. Visitors are likely to see smaller lizards sunning themselves on mountainsides and rocks, or geckos searching for shade on patios. Larger varieties include the collared lizard and desert iguana, as well as chuckwallas, whiptails, and spiny lizards. North America's only venomous lizard, the Gila monster, also makes its home in Arizona. This large reptile, which can grow up to two feet long, spends most of its life underground. The black lizards are covered in spots or bands, in shades of pink, orange, or red. Desert tortoises (though threatened by off-road vehicles and bulldozers) also inhabit Arizona, as do a host of frogs and toads—like the noisy Couch's spadefoot, which crawls out

© KATHLEEN BRYANT

Lizards are the most frequently seen reptiles in the desert.

of the mud after monsoon showers to bellow loudly for a mate.

Mammals

Many warm-blooded mammals thrive in the desert, including mountain lions, bighorn sheep, and desert cottontail rabbits, a common sight in desert landscapes in and around the city. Bobcats look similar to domestic cats, though they're about two to three times larger, able to hunt down rabbits, squirrels, rodents, and even young mule deer and pronghorn. The howls and yips of coyotes are familiar nighttime sounds, pack members communicating with each other as they hunt. The coyote's tan and beige coat, along with keen hearing and sense of smell, help it search for prey. Collared peccaries, better known as javelinas, roam the desert in family groups, searching for cacti, grasses, and gardeners' prized flowers and vegetables.

© KATHLEEN BRYANT

The collared peccary, or javelina, is most active at dawn and dusk.

Bats, nature's only flying mammal, serve an important role in the desert's ecosystem. Migrating species, such as the lesser long-nosed bat from Mexico, travel to Arizona in the spring to pollinate plants and cacti, like the saguaro cactus. They also eat many of the small insects that could plague the desert without their hungry colonies. Several bat species live in rocky crevices—or underneath bridges—throughout the deserts of the Southwest.

Birds

Arizona is a bird-watcher's paradise, with more than 300 avian species soaring across the state's blue skies or nesting in its cliffs and cacti, including cardinals, finches, eagles, hawks, and sparrows. White-winged doves gorge themselves on saguaro fruits, and tiny hummingbirds sip from chuparosa or ocotillo blooms. A half-dozen owl species—such as burrowing owls and pygmy owls—hunt desert rodents. But if we've learned anything from cartoons, it's that where there are wily coyotes, there are speedy roadrunners. The long-legged cuckoos dash across the desert, chasing down lizards and insects. Their unique feet—with two toes facing forward and two facing backward—make X-shaped tracks that are easy to recognize.

Arizona's state bird, the brown-and-white cactus wren, is a frequent—and raucous—guest in backyard trees and on patios throughout the Valley of the Sun. Also fairly common in the urban landscape, Gila woodpeckers burrow into trees and cacti. Their black-and-white barred wings help distinguish them from other species, as does the small red "cap" on the top of the male's head. The ground-dwelling Gambel's quail, crowned by a curled "topknot," is often seen stopping traffic in the late spring with a line of small chicks following behind it.

Insects, Arachnids, and Centipedes

Once you get over the initial heebie-jeebies, you may be able to appreciate Arizona's insects. The easiest to love, of course, are the graceful butterflies that populate the desert in the spring or those that migrate from Mexico in late summer and early fall. The great purple hairstreak, orange sulphur, and scandalous painted lady are colorful specimens to keep an eye out for. It may be a bit harder, though, to channel the warm fuzzies for the giant desert centipede or the cactus longhorn beetle, which feasts on the cholla and prickly pear cacti.

A few spiders lurk in the desert, including the Arizona blond tarantula and the more common desert tarantula. Typically, they're hiding underground in their silk-lined holes, but like Scottsdale club-goers, they do come out in search of mates. The same is true of the unnerving scorpion, though fortunately, of the 30 species in Arizona, only the bark scorpion produces venom that can be lethal. Tracking down these stingers is a bit of a sport in Arizona, and hunters use an ultraviolet "black" light that causes scorpions to glow, or fluoresce.

History

ANCIENT CIVILIZATIONS

Despite its challenging terrain and climate, the Sonoran Desert has proven to be an irresistible temptation for waves of settlers. Generations of immigrants define much of Arizona's history, beginning with paleolithic hunters and followed by a succession of prehistoric and historic tribes, Spanish explorers, Catholic missionaries, 19th-century miners and ranchers, and modern-day pioneers, all searching for opportunity. The first to roam the area, at least 12,000 years ago, were small groups of Paleo-Indian hunters who followed big game around the region. Around 300 B.C. permanent civilizations began to form, thanks in large part to the development of agriculture, which requires a long-term, communal effort.

Two major groups emerged during this time, leaving a lasting legacy. The Hohokam culture laid the foundations for modern Phoenix. They migrated from Mesoamerica (present-day Mexico) just before the birth of Christ, bringing with them corn, beans, and other crops. Small groups settled along the banks of the Salt River and, over time, dug miles and miles of canals to create a dependable source of water for

their fields. Residents lived in pit houses, semi-subterranean structures that were built 1–2 feet below ground, covered by a dome of sticks and

© KATHLEEN BRYANT

The Sinaguan people drew pictographs in Coconino National Forest near Sedona.

brush, and then plastered with mud. As the population grew, a complex culture developed, with elaborate pottery, organized competitions on ball courts, and a sophisticated understanding of mathematics and astronomy, which allowed them to expanded their canals and track crop cycles.

To the north, the Sinagua people were developing their own civilization, expanding from northern Arizona into the Verde Valley and Sedona region. This complex society sustained itself by hunting, farming, and gathering indigenous plants. In red-rock country, Sinagua villagers began living in pit houses around A.D. 650, moving to cliffside dwellings in the mid-12th century, then later settling in large hilltop villages made of rock and mud. Their masonry dwellings are still standing in canyons and rocky outcroppings from Camp Verde to Flagstaff. The Sinagua culture, at the crossroads of several trade routes that stretched from California to the Four Corners region to villages in northern Mexico, thrived until 1350.

Around 1400, the Hohokam and Sinagua civilizations began to collapse. Anthropologists have posed several theories as to the cause, including drought, floods, disease, social change, or a combination of these factors. Some believe that the civilizations had grown too large, too complex, and too interdependent to sustain themselves. With as many as 50,000 people living in Phoenix alone, the desert's resources may have been stretched beyond their limits. By the end of the 1400s, Hohokam and Sinagua villagers had abandoned their pueblos and canals, with some establishing compact farming villages scattered across the region and others blending into smaller tribes. The modern Pima (Akimel O'odham) trace their roots to the Hohokam, as do the Papago (Tohono O'odham). The Hopi, Yavapai, and six other tribes count the Sinagua among their ancestors.

THE EUROPEANS ARRIVE

Spanish explorers swept through the Sonoran Desert in the 16th century, drawn by tales of the Seven Cities of Gold. In 1539, the viceroy of New Spain (now Mexico) organized a small expedition that included friar Marcos de Niza, who returned with stories confirming a golden city. A second expedition, headed by Francisco Vázquez de Coronado, was quickly dispatched, and the two-year odyssey stretched to the Grand Canyon and as far away as present-day Kansas. In the end, it revealed the legendary golden cities to be nothing more than myths—or perhaps the setting sun burnishing pueblo walls in a golden glow.

Coronado's failed expedition also fizzled most interest in Arizona for 150 years, with the exception of a few explorers and missionaries, the most famous being Father Eusebio Francisco Kino, an Italian Jesuit who in 1687 began his lifelong calling to spread Catholicism through the Sonoran Desert. He introduced 16 tribes to European plants, animals, and farming methods as he built a string of colonial missions, two of which became the first permanent European settlements in present-day southern Arizona. It was Padre Kino who mapped and named Phoenix's Salt River (Rio Salado), a moniker earned because of the salty taste of the water's high mineral content.

Mexico gained its independence from Spain in 1821, and a couple decades later, the Mexican-American War broke out. It ended in 1848, with Mexico ceding what is now the American Southwest, including most of Arizona, as a part of the Treaty of Guadalupe Hidalgo. The Mexican American population has shaped much of the state's art, culture, and cuisine.

THE TERRITORIAL BOOM

Prospectors, eager to strike it rich during the California Gold Rush that broke out in 1849, flooded across Arizona (then part of New

Mexico Territory). Gold discoveries in the 1850s and 1860s ignited boomtowns around Wickenburg and elsewhere, but calls to make Arizona a separate territory went unheeded as the country plunged into the Civil War. In 1862, residents of the southern half of New Mexico Territory formed the Confederate Arizona Territory, granting Confederate troops in Texas access to California. However, Union troops easily seized control of the desert renegades, prompting the establishment of Arizona Territory, with its current boundaries, the following year.

In 1867, former Confederate soldier Jack Swilling passed through the Salt River Valley and decided that it looked like a good place for farming. The broad, fertile landscape was filled with desert grasses and mesquite, willow, and cottonwood trees, all fed by a wide, winding river, prompting the onetime scout, gold miner, cattle rancher, and saloon owner to return home to Wickenburg, a mining town about 50 miles northwest of present-day Phoenix, to seek financial backing. He organized a company to dig irrigation canals and establish farms. It wasn't long before he and the dozens of settlers who followed discovered that digging up the Hohokam canal system was an easier way to bring water to their fields than starting from scratch. Swilling's friend, British-born Lord Darrell Duppa, suggested they name their new town Phoenix after the mythical bird that rises from its own ashes after being consumed by flame, a poetic tribute to the city's Hohokam roots.

Meanwhile, the Wild West was still alive and well in Arizona Territory. Fort Verde was built in 1871 to house as many 300 soldiers, stationed at the military outpost to protect Anglo settlers from Apache and Yavapai raiders, who were forced onto reservations. Just north, Jerome was founded in 1876 after prospectors filed the first mining claims. Workers arrived in droves, and soon saloons and brothels lined

the streets, transforming the mining camp into a lively boomtown. By comparison, Swilling's Phoenix seemed a "proper" Victorian town, so much so that Arizona's territorial capital was moved there from a Prescott log cabin in 1889. In just a decade, the young city's population grew to 5,554. During the 1800s, the old Black Canyon Trail linked Phoenix to Prescott, where wagon roads connected to Flagstaff from the west. Sedona remained relatively isolated until the 1930s, when the Oak Creek Canyon Highway (now State Route 89A) was completed.

STATEHOOD

By the early 20th century, Arizonans were clamoring for statehood. After rejecting a 1906 congressional decision that Arizona and New Mexico enter the Union as a single state, Arizonans took political matters into their own hands. In 1910, they elected 52 delegates (41 Democrats and 11 Republicans) to a state constitutional convention. Many of the representatives—who included Arizona's first governor, George W. P. Hunt, and Barry Goldwater's grandfather—had progressive, populist leanings. They drew up one of the nation's most liberal state constitutions, with provisions meant to give greater political voice to average Arizonans, including voter initiatives, referendums, and recalls. President William Howard Taft, who thought recalling judges would compromise judicial independence, threatened to veto Arizona's admission unless the provision was removed. It was, and Arizona was granted statehood. Voters, however, had the last laugh when they passed a constitutional amendment in the state's first general election in November 1912 that restored the controversial measure. It was Wild West democracy in action.

The Western landscape posed some of the new state's first problems. Snowmelt and rain regularly sent the Salt River over its banks. Luckily, President Theodore Roosevelt was ready to ride to the rescue with a bold plan and several million dollars. Roosevelt tasked the newly formed federal Bureau of Reclamation with building a hydroelectric dam on the Salt River in 1911 to control flooding and generate electricity. It was the first project the new agency tackled, and the Roosevelt Dam tamed the free-running river by diverting the whole flow from its banks into an expanded canal system, leading to one of the Phoenix area's first big boom periods. With an economy fueled by the "Five C's"—citrus, cotton, cattle, copper, and climate—Phoenix's population mushroomed to nearly 30,000 people by 1920, then added almost 20,000 more by 1930, matching the Hohokam's previous record of 50,000 inhabitants in just 50 years.

The state came of age during World War II. The Sonoran Desert's terrain was an ideal spot for training soldiers to fight in the deserts of North Africa, and thanks to the state's blue skies and open stretches of land, new airfields were constructed, 60 in all by the end of the war. Moreover, the large, land-locked state also provided space for 23 prisoner-of-war camps, which were scattered around Arizona, including one at Phoenix's Papago Park, the site of the largest mass escape of POWs in the United States during the war. When they weren't escaping, the German POWs helped with projects like canal maintenance and harvesting cotton crops. Also, due to the state's proximity to large Japanese American populations in California, several Japanese relocation and work camps were built, including one just south of Phoenix on the Pima–Maricopa Indian reservation.

During this time, one of the most important pieces of legislation in U.S. history was drafted by an Arizona senator, Ernest W. McFarland. The World War I veteran, having witnessed the poverty many soldiers were forced to endure after returning home, fought to pass a bill that granted tens of thousand of veterans financial

ARIZONA STATE FACTS

- **State Nickname:** The Grand Canyon State
- **Statehood:** February 14, 1912
- **Capital:** Phoenix
- **Area:** 113,998 square miles
- **State Flower:** Saguaro cactus flower
- **State Bird:** Cactus wren
- **State Tree:** Paloverde
- **State Fossil:** Petrified wood
- **State Gemstone:** Turquoise
- **State Amphibian:** Arizona tree frog
- **State Reptile:** Arizona ridge-nosed rattlesnake
- **State Neckwear:** Bola tie

© SCOTTSDALE CVB/ADAM RODRIGUEZ

The saguaro bloom is Arizona's state flower.

assistance for education and housing. As the primary sponsor of the GI Bill, McFarland was a major force behind its unanimous passage in the Senate and House, although it's unlikely he anticipated the sweeping effects it would have on the nation when President Franklin D. Roosevelt signed the bill into law in 1944. McFarland eventually served in the state's three highest offices: U.S. senator, governor, and chief justice of the Arizona Supreme Court.

THE NEW LAND RUSH

In its early days, the city's commercial and residential district was surrounded by thousands of square miles of farmland and undeveloped desert. Its churches, theaters, and department stores attracted distant farmers and ranchers who would "go into town" for supplies and entertainment, all of which lent itself to a lively downtown familiar to most American cities. The postwar building boom changed all of that. Soldiers captivated by Arizona's climate and landscape while stationed at one of the state's many military training facilities, returned to Phoenix with their Midwestern families and 1950s expectations of a three-bedroom home and a green lawn. The Valley of the Sun's burgeoning housing industry was happy to oblige, and developers conjured up cookie-cutter tract housing and large master-planned communities with amenities like parks and golf courses that appealed to young families as well as retirees.

As air-conditioning became widely available and technology-manufacturing companies moved to the city in search of cheap land, the population grew past 100,000 by 1950 and neared an almost-unimaginable 440,000 by 1960. Former agricultural land was quickly consumed by thousands of ranch houses, forcing new home buyers farther and farther out into the suburbs. All of this sprawl and, some would argue, poorly managed growth have created a few unexpected consequences. A brown smog cloud often chokes the Valley's famed blue skies in the winter, and the dry desert air that once attracted health-seekers suffering from asthma and tuberculosis is now burdened in the spring with pollen from non-indigenous plants brought in from other parts of the country. Formerly independent towns and suburbs now blend into one another, with regional malls and business districts that have sapped away much of downtown Phoenix's urban appeal.

Things are changing, though. Some 1.5 million people live in Phoenix, making it the country's sixth-largest city, and the U.S. Census Bureau estimates an additional 3 million residents in the surrounding communities. Many of these folks are driven by the same optimism and pioneering spirit that attracted the waves of settlers who preceded them, and these new Arizonans dream up solutions to 21st-century problems. Phoenix, Scottsdale, and Sedona are increasingly determined to grow responsibly, directing developers to be mindful of the desert landscape and considering green-minded enterprises like solar-powered energy. Downtown Phoenix is once again a center of activity, thanks to $3 billion worth of new projects, including condo and hotel towers, restaurants, stadiums, museums, and a 20-mile light-rail system that many hope will curb the city's love affair with the automobile. And it's anyone's guess what seemingly impossible feats the residents of this dynamic city will tackle next—a looming water crisis likely tops the list. Nevertheless, Arizona's landscape has sparked hope, art, and opportunity for generations. Now its citizens are working to ensure it inspires generations more.

Government and Economy

GOVERNMENT

In its relatively short history, Arizona has experienced no shortage of political milestones, defining moments, and shameful antics. For instance, more than 80 years before Bush vs. Gore, the state faced its own contentious court battle for chief executive. A gubernatorial fracas broke out in 1916 when Arizona's first governor, George W. P. Hunt, demanded a recount when his challenger, Thomas Campbell, was declared the winner by 30 votes. Hunt refused to vacate the governor's chair, and both men took the oath of office. The Arizona Supreme Court eventually settled the case, declaring Hunt the winner. However, both men would go on to serve multiple—and individual—terms as governor.

By the 1960s, Arizona's political titans were working hard to transform the Grand Canyon State into a national player. Morris "Mo" Udall took office in 1961 after winning the U.S. House seat vacated by his brother, Stewart, who had been appointed Secretary of the Interior by President John F. Kennedy. The Udall brothers, Representative John Rhodes, Senators Barry Goldwater and Carl T. Hayden, and Governor Paul Fannin formed a bipartisan group of political giants who reached across party lines and used their collective power to turn the state into a united political power.

Another Arizona highlight was precipitated by one of the state's political low points. When former car dealer Evan Mecham was removed from office in 1988, it extinguished the political firestorm that ignited almost as soon he was sworn in a year earlier. During his brief-but-infamous tenure, Mecham rescinded the Martin Luther King Jr. holiday, defended the

the Arizona State Capitol in Phoenix

use of the word "pickaninny," blamed working women for increasing divorce rates, and managed to insult minority groups from Asians to gays. But with Mecham's impeachment came one bright spot: Arizona swore in its first female governor—and the 10th in U.S. history—Rose Mofford. Strangely, it wasn't her first time in the chair. During the early days of Governor Bruce Babbitt's 1988 presidential bid, Mofford served as acting governor while he campaigned out of state.

Historically, women had a great deal of independence and opportunity in Arizona, thanks to the state's Wild West roots. They were granted the right to vote in the year of Arizona's statehood in 1912, eight years before the Nineteenth Amendment. In 1981, President Ronald Reagan made history—and fulfilled a campaign promise—when he appointed the first female Supreme Court justice, Arizonan Sandra Day O'Connor. Following her groundbreaking confirmation, O'Connor emerged as one of the most influential voices on the Court, serving as a swing vote in many of its most controversial and closely watched cases, from abortion to affirmative action. Nearly two decades later, in 1998, Arizona made national headlines again when voters elected the country's first all-female line of succession: governor, secretary of state, attorney general, treasurer, and superintendent of public instruction. The media dubbed the unprecedented lineup the "Fabulous Five," which included Attorney General Janet Napolitano, who would later serve as governor and U.S. Secretary of Homeland Security.

The release of the 2000 U.S. census heralded a demographic shift and strong new political voice in Arizona. Latinos accounted for 25 percent of Arizona's population that year, and that number has grown to nearly 30 percent. The controversial Arizona state senate bill, SB 1070, meant to address illegal immigration, served to ignite Latino activists and human-rights organizations in Arizona and across the United States. (Arizona voters recalled the state senator who introduced the bill in 2011, and parts of SB 1070 were overturned by the Supreme Court in 2012.) Latino voters will likely flex ever-more-considerable political influence in the coming decades, which is why they are being courted by both Republicans and Democrats. This swing group could prove to be a deciding voice as the once staunchly red, conservative Arizona turns purple.

ECONOMY

The "Five C's"—copper, cotton, cattle, citrus, and climate—fueled Arizona's early economy, signifying the state's early reliance on agriculture and mining as its main economic engine. The Valley of the Sun became an important farming center, thanks to the canals originally built by the Hohokam and resurrected by Jack Swilling—so much so that, at one time, the state was the country's largest producer of cotton. Even the small farming community of Gilbert—now a Phoenix suburb of 100,000 people—produced enough alfalfa in its fields during World War I to earn the title "Hay Capital of the World." Today, Arizona can still call itself the "Copper State," with its mammoth open-pit and underground mines producing about two-thirds of nation's total yield of the peachy-gold metal.

Thanks to nearly 300 days of sunshine a year, it's possible to grow oranges and grapefruit, but the endless sunny days also mean dining alfresco, lying by the pool, and playing golf year-round—in short, tourism, which accounts for $18.5 billion annually. The sun may even be the basis of a new sustainable solar economy as the country searches for energy independence—a particularly critical need for this region, which is dependent on air-conditioning during triple-digit summer temperatures. High-tech innovation in the desert isn't new, though. After World War II, early technology manufacturing companies set up shop in Phoenix, including Motorola, which opened a research and development laboratory in 1948. Other computer-chip manufacturers and engineering firms followed, and within the past decade, Arizona political and business leaders have enticed medical research and biotechnology firms, like T-Gen, to take the state's economy—and its health care—to new heights.

People and Culture

Phoenix is a city of immigrants, and that, perhaps more than any other factor, save the unrelenting sun, has shaped its character. Sydney has its convicts, and Boston its Puritans. Phoenix, though, was founded by a different breed: the pioneer. These trailblazing optimists left their homelands for the Wild West, an open frontier where opportunity and the promise of a better life outweighed the difficulties of a harsh terrain. And these expatriates continue to arrive, thousands every year, lured by warm winters or jobs in the high-tech or hospitality industries. Most are driven by a thirst for more and the adventurous spirit and independent attitude long associated with Arizona and the West.

So many people have pulled up stakes and moved to the Valley of the Sun that residents like to joke that a native Phoenician is hard to find. Some newbies are initially tempted by the warm climate, moving to Phoenix to attend school at Arizona State University or to spend their years on the golf course. Even visitors popping in to see their college kids or retired parents can be easily seduced to make a move, not

Folklórico dances and traditional foods are Cinco de Mayo highlights.

© KATHLEEN BRYANT

to mention the millions of tourists who travel to the state every year.

More than half of Arizona's 6.5 million residents live in the Greater Phoenix Metropolitan Area, and according to a Brookings Institution study, only about half are white, reflecting the city's changing demographics. Latinos make up most of the other half of the population. And though the city still attracts retirees, only 11 percent of the population is over age 65. Younger people are moving to Valley, and some 35 percent of adults are single, which may help explain Scottsdale's vibrant nightlife scene.

Several Native American communities govern tribal land around Phoenix and Sedona. These sovereign tribes act in many ways like independent nations, with the right to form their own governments, try legal cases within their borders, and levy taxes. Although these communities continue to honor their agricultural roots, many now own and operate successful casinos, which have expanded in recent years to include resorts, restaurants, golf courses, amusement parks, and museums. Among them, the Gila River Indian Community spans 584 square miles south of Phoenix, from the Sierra Estrella in the West Valley to the communities of Florence and Coolidge in the east. The 11,300 members are from the Pima (Akimel O'odham) and the Maricopa (Pee Posh) tribes. Its most famous son, Ira Hayes, was one of the five Marines depicted in the iconic 1945 photograph "Raising the Flag on Iwo Jima."

The Pima and the Maricopa also make their home on the Salt River Pima–Maricopa Indian Community just east of Scottsdale. More than 9,000 individuals are enrolled as tribal members, living on 52,000 acres surrounded by Scottsdale, Tempe, Mesa, and Fountain Hills. The adjacent Fort McDowell Yavapai Nation, with 950 members, is bordered by McDowell Mountain Park and the Tonto National Forest.

Just north, in the Verde Valley near Sedona, the Yavapai have also aligned with the Tonto Apache at the Yavapai-Apache Nation, where many of its 2,200 members live on four noncontiguous parcels of land.

RELIGION

Arizona has a rich religious tradition, beginning with the spiritual practices of the Native Americans who first worshipped in the region thousands of years ago. European missionaries introduced Catholicism to the Southwest in the 16th century, with Franciscan and Jesuit priests traveling throughout the Sonoran Desert to convert many of its indigenous people. Today, about 25 percent of Arizonans identify themselves as Catholic, according to the Pew Center, due in large part to the sizable Latino population. The Southwest's unique style of Catholicism incorporates indigenous customs, such as Día de los Muertos, or Day

© KATHLEEN BRYANT

The Old Adobe Mission was Scottsdale's first Catholic church.

of the Dead. Some Latino families celebrate the holiday October 31 through November 2 by visiting the graves of their ancestors or building small altars decorated with sugar skulls, artwork, flowers, and favorite foods. At Christmastime, luminarias, small votive candles in paper bags, are lit to celebrate the holiday season. Las posadas, commemorating Mary and Joseph's search for lodgings, precedes Christmas in many communities across the state, and nacimientos, elaborately detailed nativity scenes, are displayed in local homes.

More than a third of Arizona's population is Protestant. About 6 percent are Mormons, members of the Church of Jesus Christ of Latter-day Saints. Mormon pioneers settled the East Valley town of Mesa in 1878, and the Valley of the Sun has the nation's largest concentration of Mormons outside of Utah. Also, there are small Jewish, Muslim, Buddhist, Sikh, and Hindu populations throughout the state.

LANGUAGE

Language can be a hot topic in the Arizona desert, fueled largely by the controversial immigration debate that flares up on a regular basis in this border state. Nearly 75 percent of Arizonans speak only English at home, and the Modern Language Association estimates more than 20 percent speak Spanish. In addition to the occasional voter initiative to make English the state's official language, politicians have made efforts to revamp the public school system's English as a Second Language (ESL) program, which often faces opposition and produces mixed results. A recent Supreme Court case even debated if the state was spending enough to aid children who are learning to speak English, though it was kicked back down to a lower court. Travelers will hear Spanish spoken throughout the state, and in Phoenix, Spanish-language media are fairly commonplace. Native American languages may be heard on Indian lands, though almost all younger generations of Native Americans speak English.

THE ARTS

Arizona has been called a lot of things—the Wild West, retirement haven, desert oasis, sweltering inferno—but "cultural hotbed" is not one of them. Even among the air-conditioned locals who frequent malls and big-box stores chains, the state's rich artistic tradition seems hidden, if not forgotten. The truth is, Arizona's rich cultural tradition reaches back thousands of years, beginning with the state's original inhabitants, Native Americans. Some of the 20th century's greatest artists produced work here, from Ansel Adams and Max Ernst to Frank Lloyd Wright, having been inspired by the dramatic Sonoran Desert landscape.

Arts and Crafts

Arizona's arts and crafts trace their origins back to the earliest Native American residents, who graced everyday objects with symbols, patterns, and anthropomorphic images. Today, many artisans continue to create work that is firmly rooted in their tribal customs. Some may adhere to generations-old traditions, while others explore new techniques, materials, or contemporary imagery. Many have pushed the definitions of Native American art, ensuring that it continues to be dynamic, diverse, and relevant in a changing world.

Buyers shopping for authentic Native American arts and crafts should keep a few things in mind. First, when possible, buy directly from the artist. Throughout the year, events such as the Heard Museum's annual Indian Fair and Market showcase native artists. Ask artists or gallery representatives about the materials and how pieces were made, and be sure to get a certificate of authenticity. Quintessential arts and crafts include handwoven baskets, turquoise jewelry, pottery, Navajo rugs and sand paintings, and Hopi kachina carvings.

ARIZONA LUMINARIES

ARIZONANS WHO MADE (UNSUCCESSFUL) BIDS FOR PRESIDENT

- Barry Goldwater, Republican: 1964
- Morris "Mo" Udall, Democrat: 1976
- Bruce Babbitt, Democrat: 1988
- John McCain, Republican: 2000 and 2008

CABINET MEMBERS

- Morris "Mo" Udall, Democrat: Secretary of the Interior, Kennedy Administration
- Bruce Babbitt, Democrat: Secretary of the Interior, Clinton Administration
- Mary Peters, Republican: Secretary of Transportation, George W. Bush Administration
- Janet Napolitano, Democrat: Secretary of Homeland Security, Obama Administration

SUPREME COURT JUSTICES

- William Rehnquist
- Sandra Day O'Connor

CELEBRITIES

- Cartoonist Bil Keane
- Humorist Erma Bombeck
- Comedian David Spade
- Radio personality Paul Harvey
- Actress Emma Stone

MUSICIANS

- Alice Cooper
- Glen Campbell
- Waylon Jennings
- Linda Ronstadt
- Stevie Nicks

HISTORICAL FIGURES

- Apache chief Geronimo
- Labor leader César Chávez
- Environmentalist Edward Abbey
- Novelist Zane Grey
- Architect Frank Lloyd Wright
- Astronomer Percival Lowell

Architecture and Design

Arizona has suffered for years from a dearth of quality, geographically relevant architecture. Beginning with the Victorian buildings constructed in the original 1870s Phoenix townsite, architects tried to impose styles suited to the East or Midwest onto the Sonoran Desert. It took a Midwesterner, Frank Lloyd Wright, to break them of the habit—or at least introduce them to relevant ways of designing for the desert. Wright took his cues from the architecture of ancient Native Americans, building with materials from the desert and designing buildings around the sun's orientation.

But the Valley of the Sun grew rapidly, and developers responded to demand by building subdivisions of large, faceless houses. Sadly, many architectural icons were "remuddled" or torn down to be replaced by McMansions. Though Midcentury Modern is becoming more popular throughout the United States, local groups find it sometimes takes dedication and hard work to educate the public and promote preservation. As of late 2012, local historians and design aficionados were holding their breath as the home Frank Lloyd Wright designed for his son David in 1950 was slated to be demolished by a development company.

By the 1990s, a handful of architects—inspired by Wright and a group of Modernist designers like Al Beadle and Bennie Gonzales—pioneered a new style, Desert

Modernism, which respected Phoenix's harsh summer climate. These minimalist buildings blend indoor/outdoor spaces, use innovative materials, and embrace the desert's hallmark light and space. The best-known example, the Will Bruder–designed Burton Barr Central Library, features a rectangular, rusted-steel facade that resembles a red-hued mesa. In Sedona, Design Group's architects took their cues from the town's pioneer structures, incorporating low lines and red-rock masonry for projects, including the Sedona Public Library, that harmonize with, rather than detract from, the spectacular natural setting.

Interior designers have banished the howling coyotes, flute-playing Kokopellis, and pastel colors that had come to define "Southwestern design" in the 1980s. Instead, many of Valley's best designers are now employing a more subtle style that incorporates light as a central element. Large glass windows, natural stone and wood, and polished concrete floors that remain cool in the summer are turning posh restaurants and resorts into showplaces for chic desert style.

Literature

The myth of the West has proven to be a fertile source of literary inspiration. For generations, stories were often related orally, heightening their romance and intimacy. Native Americans passed their histories and folklore from one generation to the next, while cowboys shared stories over campfires or whiskies. Novelist Zane Grey may not have been the first to put these tales to paper, but he was certainly one of the most prolific, producing 60 books, from which 110 films were made. Many were set, and later filmed, at Arizona locations, including *Call of the Canyon* near Sedona. Grey's popular stories portrayed an idealized version of the Old West, with larger-than-life heroes and bigger landscapes.

These days, Arizona writers build on Grey's frontier legacy with equally adventurous stories. Local talent includes adventure writer Clive Cussler, historical novelist Diana Gabaldon, and Stephenie Meyer, author of the *Twilight* vampire series. And for stories with an intriguing Phoenix backdrop, look for mystery writer Jon Talton's series featuring David Mapstone, a historian turned police detective.

ESSENTIALS

Getting There and Around

BY AIR

Most visitors to the Valley of the Sun arriving by air land at **Phoenix Sky Harbor International Airport** (3400 E. Sky Harbor Blvd., 602/273-3300, www.phxskyharbor. com). It's one of the country's ten busiest airports in terms of traffic, with some 100,000 passengers arriving and departing every day. Tempe-based **US Airways** (800/428-4322, www.usairways.com) and **Southwest Airlines** (800/435-9792, www.southwest.com) account for more than half of Sky Harbor's traffic, though 15 other carriers provide service, including international airlines like **British Airways** (800/247-9297, www.britishairways. com), **Aeromexico** (800/237-6639, www.aero-mexico.com), and **Air Canada** (888/247-2262, www.aircanada.com). Free shuttles connect Terminals 2, 3, and 4, and visitors can also catch buses to the rental car center and the light-rail stop at 44th Street. Sky Harbor sits in the middle of the Valley, just three miles east of downtown Phoenix and 20 minutes from Old Town Scottsdale. Two entrances link the airport to the city: The west entrance connects to I-10 and 24th Street, and the east entrance

© KATHLEEN BRYANT

joins the Hohokam Expressway (State Route 143), 44th Street, and Loop 202.

Travelers arriving by private jet can use **Scottsdale Airport** (15000 N. Airport Dr., 480/312-2321, www.scottsdaleaz.gov/airport), a handy option. This North Scottsdale airpark, a frequent choice of celebrities, is one of the busiest single-runway airports in the country. **Phoenix-Mesa Gateway Airport** (6033 S. Sossaman Rd., 480/988-7600, www.phxmesagateway.org) in east Mesa serves as a small hub for regional carrier **Allegiant Air** (702/505-8888, www.allegiantair.com), with service to northern parts of the country; **Frontier Airlines** (800/432-1359, www.frontierairlines.com), with service to Denver; and **Spirit Airlines** (800/772-7117, www.spirit.com), with service to Chicago, Dallas, and Las Vegas. As the Valley continues to grow, the airport will likely relieve growing congestion at Sky Harbor.

BY CAR AND BUS

The car in some ways continues the grand tradition of exploring the West on horseback or by stagecoach, as it gives travelers the solitary experience of seeing the wide-open spaces that stretch between Arizona's towns and cities. That's the romantic take, at least. In truth, most visitors to Phoenix and Scottsdale will need a car. The Valley of the Sun is expansive, and unlike the densely populated centers of New York and San Francisco, there is too much space and too little public transportation to see it all in an efficient manner. Embrace the spirit of the Great American Road Trip, and be prepared to spend some time behind the wheel when plotting trips to the Apache Trail, Sedona, Jerome, Oak Creek Canyon, or Montezuma Castle.

Phoenix and Scottsdale were built with the car in mind. The streets follow an efficient and easy-to-navigate grid pattern, which is interconnected by a large web of highways. I-10 snakes from the southern part of the city, through downtown Phoenix, before heading to the West Valley. U.S. 60, also called the Superstition Freeway, provides an important artery to the East Valley, which is encircled by the Loop 202. Its counterpart, Loop 101, wends from Chandler to Tempe and Scottsdale, where it turns west and travels to the West Valley communities of Peoria and Sun City, before veering south through Glendale and connecting to I-10. Finally, State Route 51, known as the Piestewa Freeway, connects Central Phoenix to the northern part of the city and Loop 101.

This book covers only a small portion of the Grand Canyon State, and there is plenty to see within few hours' drive of Phoenix. Farther afield, I-10 connects Phoenix to Tucson in the south and Palm Springs and Los Angeles in the west. Scenic I-17 crosses Phoenix into the high deserts and grasslands of Camp Verde and Flagstaff, where you can catch other highways to the Grand Canyon and Las Vegas or to the other Four Corners states of New Mexico, Colorado, and Utah.

Arizona has a few quirky traffic laws to keep in mind. Many streets have a continuous turn lane in the center. Using it to make a left turn from the roadway seems obvious enough. But you can also legally use it to turn *into* a roadway from a side road or parking lot. If you do so, stop and wait in the continuous lane until a break in traffic allows you to enter the flow. (It is not, as some residents seem to think, an acceleration lane.) Some people refer to the two-way continuous turn lane as the "suicide lane," and yes, it is hazardous to have multiple uses for a single lane: Be courteous and cautious. At lighted intersections, it is legal (unless signage indicates) to turn right on a red light after stopping. In "enlightened" Scottsdale, lighted intersections have "lagging lefts"—the left turn arrow will turn green *after* the green light for through-traffic. On two-lane roads throughout the state, any vehicle (including bicycles) with five or more vehicles behind it must use the first safe pullout to allow the faster traffic to proceed.

If you'd prefer to leave the driving to someone else, **Greyhound** (2115 E. Buckeye Rd., 602/389-4200, www.greyhound.com) provides bus service to major cities throughout the state and Southwest, though you will not find terminals in Scottsdale or Sedona. To reach Red Rock Country without a car, you can catch a van service from Phoenix's Sky Harbor. **Sedona Phoenix Shuttle** (800/448-7988, www.sedona-phoenix-shuttle.com) offers a direct link to the Village of Oak Creek, West Sedona, Cottonwood, and Camp Verde.

Tips for Travelers

ECOTOURISM

It's only natural that tourists be mindful of the environment when visiting Arizona, as the state's main attraction is its rugged, yet surprisingly delicate, landscape. Increasingly, ecotourists—travelers who are drawn to a natural locale and try to minimize their environmental impact—are choosing to explore the Sonoran Desert. To capitalize on this movement and ensure that future generations are able to appreciate the desert, Arizona's tourism community has started to make green-minded changes to how they operate. For a list of green-certified hotels and businesses, contact the Arizona Lodging and Tourism Association (www.stayinaz.com). The Scottsdale Convention and Visitors Bureau has introduced its own online resource, **Scottsdale Green By Design** (www.scottsdalegreenbydesign.com), outlining environmentally conscious travel ideas and resources, including cultural attractions and outdoor activities. The site also provides a list of individual hotels, resorts, and restaurants that are incorporating sustainable tourism practices, from water conservation and recycling programs to organic menus and spa treatments. In Sedona, the **Institute of Ecotourism** (91 Portal Lane, 928/282-2720, www.ioet.org, 10 A.M.–6 P.M. Mon.–Fri.,) offers suggestions for travelers and hosts.

For travelers who like to leave things a little better than they found them, a volunteer vacation blends culture and landscape with service. The state's tourism board (www.arizonaguide.com) has ideas for volunteering trips to Phoenix, the Grand Canyon, and other locations.

FOREIGN TRAVELERS

International travelers should expect a warm welcome to Arizona, though you may encounter long lines and a little paperwork at immigration when entering the country. Citizens from most North American, European, and Latin American countries do not need a visa for stays up to 90 days. However, all international visitors, including Canadians, are required to show a valid passport. For more information about visas and requirements to enter the United States through the Visa Waiver Program, visit the U.S. State Department's website at www.travel.state.gov.

Travelers exchanging foreign currency can do so at small kiosks inside the airport or at most banks. ATMs (automated teller machines) offer the best exchange rates, charging a $2 fee for the convenience. Be sure to inquire at your home bank to see if they charge an exchange fee, which usually ranges 1–2 percent. You'll find ATMs at a host of locations, including banks, shopping centers, and gas stations. Also, almost all hotels, restaurants, and stores accept travelers checks from well-known institutions like American Express and Visa.

ETHICAL TRAVEL

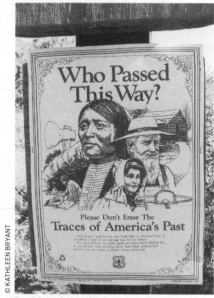

© KATHLEEN BRYANT

Prehistoric artifacts are an irreplaceable resource.

Travel is perhaps the most valuable means by which we learn about the world and our place within it. But as we explore desert trails, red-rock buttes, and ancient ruins, understanding the impact we make on the cultures and landscapes we encounter becomes increasingly important. Observe a responsible and sustainable approach to travel by following these guidelines:

- **Plan ahead and prepare:** Arriving with a sense of the social, political, and environmental issues at your destination makes your travels more meaningful. Educate yourself about the region's geography, customs, and cultures, and be respectful of local traditions.

- **Minimize your environmental impact:** Always follow designated trails. Don't bust "the crust"–delicate cryptobiotic soils that prevent erosion and support tiny organisms. Do not disturb animals, plants, or their natural habitats. Learn about local conservation programs and organizations working to preserve the environment.

- **Leave what you find:** Take only photographs. The impact of one person may seem minimal, but removing items from their native place can have unintended and unpleasant consequences, including fines or jail time (not to mention negative karma).

TRAVELERS WITH DISABILITIES

In the Valley of the Sun and Sedona, hotels, restaurants, attractions, and public transportation are easy to access thanks in large part to the Americans with Disabilities Act. However, the Sonoran Desert's rugged terrain can be difficult to navigate. That said, some state and city parks are building ADA-accessible trails, like the new **Gateway Access Area at the McDowell Sonoran Preserve** (480/998-7971, www.mcdowellsonoran.org) in Scottsdale. Up north, Sedona's Jeep tours offer an excellent opportunity to explore Red Rock Country's monolithic buttes up close. The off-the-highway trails can get quite bumpy, so those with disabilities may want to request a front seat, which offers a bit of neck and back support. Also, the National Park Service offers free admission to U.S. citizens with permanent disabilities via the lifetime **National Parks Access Pass** (www.nps.gov). The pass includes federal lands like Montezuma Castle and Coconino National Forest. They are available at any federal recreation site, and documentation is required. For more information, visit www.disabledtravelers.com, an Arizona-based website that offers advice, tips,

WHAT TO TAKE

A resort mentality and an independent Western attitude pervade much of Arizona, and overall, visitors will find Phoenix and Sedona to be pretty casual. Jeans are acceptable in most places, and in the summer shorts and sandals become de rigueur. That said, Scottsdale's nicer restaurants, bars, and clubs require that you "dress to impress," though that almost never means a suit or tie. If you plan to take advantage of Arizona's myriad outdoor activities, come prepared: hiking gear, swimsuits, and golf shoes and clubs.

The desert's arid climate can create a bit of confusion, as temperatures can swing as much as 20-30 degrees from an early-morning low to a late-afternoon high. Fall through early spring, be sure to bring along a sweater or jacket if you plan on staying out when the sun goes down. And it can be downright cold in the winter, with overnight temperatures sometimes falling below freezing.

The Sonoran Desert's powerful sun shouldn't be underestimated, particularly in the summer, when in late afternoons, the sun's rays are most intense and can cause fair skin to burn in less than 10 minutes. Wear a hat and be sure to cover up or wear a sunblock with a high SPF by the pool or on the golf course.

and recommendations for guided tours—and not just in Arizona.

TRAVELING WITH CHILDREN

With summer comes the all-important family vacation, and travelers with children shouldn't let the heat deter them from planning a trip to Arizona. In fact, most kids will revel in the season's prime attraction: the swimming pool. Families can easily spend days by the pool or at the Valley's water parks, which offer mammoth wave pools, multistoried slides, and lazy rivers for tubing. Also, most of the big resorts have built their own water parks, and the hotels offer adults a bit of respite thanks to well-organized kids' camps, which pack days full with morning hikes, arts and crafts, trips to the pool, and games in air-conditioned clubhouses. The whole family can enjoy one of the rafting trips on the Salt River northeast of Phoenix. These outdoor adventures are nothing more than a leisurely float, as the "rapids" never exceed a Class I (almost no white water). Kid-approved museums include the interactive Arizona Science Center and the Children's Museum of Phoenix.

In the cooler months, the state's parks and easy hiking trails can be fun to explore, especially on horseback. The Phoenix Zoo delights kids with 1,300 birds, slithering reptiles, and furry mammals, as well as a small petting area and the walk-through Monkey Village. For a taste of the Wild West, Rawhide Western Town delivers 1880s-themed family fun, with stunt shows, stagecoach rides, and old-fashioned chuck-wagon cookouts. A visit to Sedona may not wow the little ones, but older kids and teenagers will appreciate the bouncy Jeep tours and dozens of mountain-biking trails.

SENIOR TRAVELERS

Arizona's blissfully warm weather makes the state a popular destination for seniors, particularly active travelers who hit the tennis courts, swimming pools, and more than 200 golf courses. In the summer, many avoid the extreme heat at the half dozen casinos scattered around the Valley on Native American lands. Most Phoenix, Scottsdale, and Sedona attractions offer discounts for seniors, including the Desert Botanical Garden, which is an excellent way to survey the Sonoran Desert's diverse plant life without having to leave paved sidewalks. Also, travelers 62 and older can obtain the **National Parks Senior Pass,** a lifetime pass to all national parks. It can be purchased for $10 at any federal recreation site (www.nps.gov).

GAY AND LESBIAN TRAVELERS

Like most major metropolitan areas, the Valley has an active gay community that is centered around Central Phoenix, where travelers will find many of the city's gay-friendly restaurants and bars, including those on Central and 7th Avenues, between Indian School and Camelback Roads. The **Greater Phoenix Gay & Lesbian Chamber of Commerce** (602/266-5055, www.gpglcc.org) is a convenient resource for travelers, producing an online business directory that lists hotels and restaurants, as well as a thorough relocation guide for new residents. *Echo Magazine* (www.echomag.com) provides news and information on upcoming events.

Health and Safety

SUN AND HEAT

Phoenix is known as the Valley of the Sun for good reason. With around 300 days of sunshine a year, the fiery star can be hard to avoid—not that winter visitors trying to escape frozen climates will complain. Still, the Sonoran Desert's powerful sun shouldn't be underestimated, particularly in the summer, when in late afternoon the sun's UV rays are most intense, causing fair skin to burn in less than 10 minutes. Excessive exposure can cause real, and potentially fatal, health problems.

Shield yourself from the sun by covering up. Try to wear protective clothing, like long-sleeved shirts and pants. The sun easily damages sensitive skin on your face and neck, so be sure to bring a broad-rimmed hat and sunglasses when you are planning to spend extensive time outside, like on the golf course or while hiking. Poolside, long sleeves and pants may seem unreasonable, which makes a sunscreen with a high SPF a crucial ingredient. Be sure to slather on a thick coat 15 minutes before going out and reapply throughout the day. Also, seek shade when possible and get out of the sun occasionally. It's best to avoid the sun during the hottest part of the day, from 11 A.M. to 3 P.M., when the UV rays are at their peak.

Although everyone is at risk of getting a **sunburn,** no matter the skin tone, fair-skinned people and children are particularly susceptible. In fact, those with light skin, blue or green eyes, blond or red hair, freckles, or moles are at a greater risk of skin cancer. Should a burn occur, though, cool the skin by applying ice or taking a cold shower or bath. Apply an alcohol-free aloe vera gel and stay out of the sun.

The desert's hot, arid climate can take its toll on the body in other ways. You may not even feel particularly "sweaty" in Arizona, especially compared to more humid climates, but perspiration evaporates quickly in the dry air, depleting the body of moisture and leading to **dehydration.** Drink lots of water, about a gallon a day in the summer or when outside for long periods of time. Many Phoenicians carry a bottle of water with them and instinctively drink throughout the day. On the golf course, you'll see lots of drinking fountains and giant water coolers—take advantage of them. Again, try to limit exertion during the hottest parts of the day.

Should you find yourself dizzy, weak, or nauseated, it may be **heat exhaustion,** which is caused when the body is unable to replace fluids. Other symptoms include sweating profusely, paleness, muscle cramps, headaches, and fainting. Find a cool place immediately, sit down, and drink a beverage with electrolytes, like Gatorade. The next stage of heat-related illness is **heatstroke,** a potentially fatal form of hyperthermia. Heatstroke is marked by an elevated body temperature of 104 degrees and an inability to sweat or release heat. The skin may be red or hot to the touch. Other signs include increased heart rate, dizziness, fatigue, unconsciousness, or convulsions. Get immediate medical help, and try to cool the victim with water, ice, or cold compresses. Staying hydrated and avoiding the extreme heat will stave off these serious ailments.

FLOODS, LIGHTNING, AND DUST STORMS

The Sonoran Desert's weather, like its landscape, can be severe. Blue, sunny skies can quickly turn ominous when a storm rolls across the horizon, with sheets of rain and forked bolts of lightning that send motorists, golfers, and swimmers scurrying for cover. During monsoon season, a wall of dust may move in from the desert and sweep across the city with impressive speed and not a drop of rain despite a perceptible increase in moisture. These powerful storms, called haboobs, are impressive displays of the desert's strength. Should one of these climatic events occur, don't take any chances. Immediately get out of a swimming pool or any body of water if you see lightning or even hear thunder. You should also abandon any mountain biking or hiking expeditions (heights!) or rounds of golf (metal clubs!).

The monsoon's deluges can dump inches of rain on the dry desert floor, which is unable to absorb that much water quickly. As a result, dry washes become swiftly moving rivers, trapping cars that attempt to cross them. Freeways and underpasses may fill with water, stranding commuters. When pouring rain or dust storms limit visibility, pull over to the side of the road and wait for conditions to improve, as most storms sweep through quickly. Arizona's emergency information network (www.azein. gov) posts current conditions, road closures, and suggestions for safe travel.

REPTILES AND SCORPIONS

The Sonoran Desert's flora and fauna poke, scratch, and sometimes bite, but don't let the creepy-crawlies scare you away. If you stay on trails and use good judgment when hiking, a painful encounter with a snake or insect is unlikely. Don't put your hands or feet somewhere you can't see. Keep eyes—and ears—open for rattlesnakes; you are likely to hear them rattling before you spot them. Rattlesnakes usually don't defend themselves unless provoked, so give them a wide berth (five feet) and move on.

Scorpions tend to hide under rocks or in holes, and they typically sting people when they are inadvertently touched. Shake out your shoes before putting them on and pay attention to what you grab when exploring the desert. Gila monsters are also venomous, but bites from these slow-moving creatures are rare.

If you're stung or bitten by any poisonous desert dweller, don't panic. Remove constricting jewelry and limit movement of the affected area in order to minimize the flow of venom into the rest of the bloodstream. Seek medical attention immediately.

Information and Services

MAPS AND TOURIST INFORMATION

The **Arizona Office of Tourism** (866/275-5816, www.arizonaguide.com) will send helpful trip-planning information on request, and its comprehensive website, which includes videos and slide shows, is an excellent resource for tailoring a trip to your individual interests. The **Greater Phoenix Convention & Visitors Bureau** (602/254-6500, www.visitphoenix.com) offers loads of information about the Valley of the Sun to visitors and new residents. Its **Downtown Phoenix Visitor Information Center** (125 N. 2nd St. Ste. 120, 8 A.M.–5 P.M. Mon.–Fri.) is conveniently located across from the main entrance of the Hyatt Regency.

Arizona's top attraction is its diverse landscape, and there seems to be a stunning formation or unique geological feature off every highway exit. To chart out the state's national parks and monuments, visit the website for the **National Park Service** (www.nps.gov/state/az). The **Arizona State Parks** system (1300 W. Washington St., Phoenix, 602/542-4174, http://azstateparks.com, 8 A.M.–5 P.M. Mon.–Fri.) is among the best in the country. Learn more about the parks' diverse habitats and natural attractions by visiting the website or the office in downtown Phoenix.

AREA CODES AND TIME ZONES

The Grand Canyon State has five area codes, three of which are dedicated to the Phoenix metropolitan area: 602 for Phoenix proper, 623 for the West Valley, and 480 for the East Valley, including Scottsdale. Sedona and the rest of northern Arizona are assigned 928, while Tucson and southern Arizona use 520.

Independent-minded Arizona is never one to be told what to do by the rest of the country, and that sentiment extends to daylight saving time. The state lies within the mountain standard time (MST) zone, along with Utah, Colorado, New Mexico, Wyoming, Idaho, and Montana. But unlike the other mountain states, Arizona does not observe daylight saving time. Why? Well, in the hot desert, the last thing Arizonans need is more daylight. An "extra" hour of darkness at night means residents can take advantage of cooler temperatures earlier in the evening.

There is one exception to the exception: The Navajo reservation, which takes up a sizable portion of the northeastern part of Arizona, does observe daylight saving time, so that all of its land, which stretches into the neighboring Four Corners states, is on the same schedule.

LOCAL MEDIA

NEWSPAPERS
- *The Arizona Republic*
- *The East Valley Tribune*
- *Sedona Red Rock News*

NATIONAL PUBLIC RADIO
- KJZZ 91.5 FM
- KNAU 88.7 FM (in Sedona)

TELEVISION
- 3 KTVK (Independent)
- 5 KPHO (CBS)
- 8 KAET (PBS)
- 10 KSAZ (FOX)
- 12 KPNX (NBC)
- 15 KNXV (ABC)
- 45 KUTP (Independent)
- 61 KASW (CW)

RESOURCES

Glossary

Longtime residents often find it amusing to listen to the pronunciation struggles of DJs, news anchors, and reporters who are new to the Valley. From architectural styles to place-names to restaurant menus, local jargon is a mix of English, Spanish, and Indian words.

adobe (ah-DOH-bee): earthen building material, usually formed into bricks and dried in the sun

agua fresca (AH-wa FRES-cah): literally, "fresh water," referring to a beverage made with an infusion of mashed fruits or herbs and lightly sweetened

Anasazi (Ah-na-SAH-zee): a prehistoric farming culture in the Four Corners region; Ancestral Puebloan is preferred

ancho chile (AHN-cho CHILL-ee): a dried poblano chile that has turned a deep black-red color; its smoky-sweet flavor is found in many dishes

arroyo (ah-ROH-yo): a dry gully or small wash

asada (ah-SAH-dah): broiled over hot coals or roasted, such as carne asada

bajada (ba-HA-da): a sloping plain formed by the gravelly runoff that fans out from the base of a desert mountain range

burrito (buhr-REE-toh): a flour tortilla wrapped around any number of ingredients, from beans and cheese to meat, vegetables, and salsa; also called burro

camarón (cah-mah-ROHN): shrimp

carne (CAR-nay): meat, usually beef

cerveza (ser-VAY-sah): beer, the most popular Mexican brands in Arizona being Corona, Dos Equis, Modelo, Pacifico, and Tecate

ceviche (seh-VEE-chay): citrus-marinated seafood, raw or cooked, and tossed with spices and vegetables, like onions, chilies, and tomatoes

chile relleno (CHILL-ee ray-YAY-no): a mild green chile stuffed with cheese, lightly fried, and topped with a spicy red sauce

chimichanga (chih-mee-CHAHN-gah): a deep-fried burrito filled with meat and typically garnished with lettuce, salsa, sour cream, and guacamole

chipotle (chih-POHT-lay): a hot, smoke-dried jalapeño chile pepper

chorizo (CHOH-ree-zoh): a spicy pork (or sometimes beef) sausage, flavored with chilies and spices

churro (CHOOR-roh): a fried-dough pastry, coated with Mexican cinnamon and sugar

cilantro (SIH-lahn-troh): a fresh, slightly spicy herb used in salsas and as garnish

cotija (coh-TEE-ha): an aged, crumbly white Mexican cheese

elote (eh-LOH-tay): roasted corn on the cob, often topped with butter, *cotija* cheese, lime juice, and chile pepper

empanada (em-pah-NAH-da): a baked pastry filled with meat, cheese, or fruit

enchiladas (en-chih-LAH-das): corn or flour tortillas, dipped in red sauce and wrapped around shredded beef, chicken, or cheese; they are topped with more red sauce and cheese, and then baked

fajitas (fah-HEE-tas): grilled beef or chicken,

served on a sizzling platter with onions and green peppers; warm flour tortillas and fresh tomatoes and lettuce accompany the dish

flauta (FLOU-tah): a flour or corn tortilla stuffed with chicken or beef, then deep-fried

frijoles (free-HO-lays): beans, typically pinto or black; most dishes come with a side of frijoles, the most common being refried beans, which are fried, mashed, and "refried" with lard

Gila (HEE-lah): Probably a mix of Spanish and Yuman, Gila refers to a river that flows across Arizona, its valley or region, and the Indian reservation along part of the river.

guacamole (gwah-kah-MOH-lay): a dip or condiment made of mashed avocado, lime juice, and diced chilies, onions, tomatoes, and cilantro; served with tortilla chips

habanero (hah-bah-NEH-roh): Mexico's hottest pepper, used sparingly; adds a feisty kick to salsas and dishes

Hohokam (ho-HO-kum): Arizona's prehistoric desert culture, from the Pima (Akimel O'odham) *huhugam*, meaning "all used up"

horchata (or-CHAH-tah): a sweet, vanilla-and-cinnamon-flavored drink made with ground rice and water or milk

huevo (WAY-voh): egg

huevos rancheros (WAY-vose rahn-CHAIR-ohs): eggs, ranch-style–fried or scrambled eggs, topped with a red chile sauce or chunky salsa; served with tortillas and beans

huitlacoche (weet-lah-CO-chay): corn smut or corn truffle, a delicacy that is sometimes used as a taco stuffing

machaca (mah-CHA-ca): shredded beef

mariscos (mah-REE-skos): seafood, usually shellfish

masa (MAH-sah): a traditionally stone-ground corn dough, used in tamales

menudo (meh-NOO-doh): a spicy, chunky soup flavored with chiles, tripe, onion, and spices; routinely served with warm tortillas and fresh avocado and lime

mesa (MAY-sah): literally, "table," referring also to a flat-topped landform

mole (MOH-lay): a rich, dark sauce made with chilies, Mexican chocolate, nuts, fruit, spices, and vegetables

nopales (noh-PAHL-lays): prickly pear cactus pads that are stripped of their spines and then grilled or boiled; they're added to soups, served like fries, or stuffed into tacos

paleta (pah-LAY-tah): ice pops, a frozen treat often made with fruit

panela (pah-NAY-lah): cane sugar

panadería (pah-nah-day-REE-ah): a Mexican-style bakery

pico de gallo (PEE-coh dah GUY-yoh): a fresh chunky salsa, made from chopped tomato, onion, chiles, and cilantro

poblano (POH-blah-no): a dark-green, fresh chile pepper that is very mild

pollo (POY-yoh): chicken

posole (pah-SOHL-lay): a hearty, moderately spicy soup with pork or chicken, hominy, onions, and spices; a delicious red stew sometimes garnished with cabbage, radish, onion, avocado, and lime juice

pueblo (PWEB-loh): literally, "people," but also used to refer to a village

puerco (PWEAR-coh): pork

quesadilla (kay-sah-DEE-yah): a flour tortilla, stuffed with cheese, folded in half, pressed, and warmed; chicken or beef, onions, bell peppers, and chilies are sometimes added to the filling

queso (KAY-soh): cheese

saguaro (sah-WAH-ro): a columnar and often branched cactus growing up to 60 feet tall, endemic to the Sonoran Desert

salsa (SAHL-sah): literally, "sauce," though salsa usually describes the tomato-based condiment that includes chopped onions, chilies, and cilantro; many restaurants serve green tomatillo and mild red versions with tortilla chips

serrano chile (seh-RAH-no chill-ee): a small green chile from northern Mexico that can be quite hot; used in moderation in a host of dishes and salsas

slickrock: bare rock, usually sandstone

talus: loose rocks, usually sloping

tamale (TAH-mah-lay): masa dough, stuffed with meat or vegetables, wrapped in a corn-husk and steamed

taquería (tah-kay-REE-ah): a casual restaurant that specializes in Mexican "street food" like tacos and burritos

tomatillo (toh-mah-TEE-yo): a fruit similar in appearance to a small, green tomato; its bright, acidic flavor adds a pleasant punch to many dishes and salsas

torta (TORR-tah): a crusty Mexican sandwich, served hot or cold, and filled with any number of ingredients

tortilla (tor-TEE-yah): a thin, circular flatbread made of either corn or flour, and lightly cooked

tostada (tos-TAH-dah): a flat, fried corn tortilla topped with layer of beans, meat, lettuce, tomato, cheese, and salsa

Suggested Reading

HISTORY

Buscher, Linda, and Dick Buscher. *Historic Photos of Arizona.* Nashville: Turner Publishing Company, 2009. See how early pioneers, soldiers, and frontier families lived in the Wild West. The collection of 200 rare and historical images begins with Arizona's territorial days in 1850s and moves through statehood and the postwar population boom.

Dutton, Allen A. *Arizona: Then & Now.* Englewood, CO: Westcliffe Publishers, 2002. Get a sense of the Arizona's dramatic evolution from the 19th century to the 20th. Historical photographs, stories, and essays document the Grand Canyon State's cities and towns, mining industry, railroads, and ranching and farming traditions.

Johnson, James W. *Arizona Politicians: The Noble and the Notorious.* Tucson: University of Arizona Press, 2002. A former University of Arizona journalism professor sketches colorful portraits of the politicians who shaped the state and the country, including Barry Goldwater, Mo and Stewart Udall, Bruce Babbitt, John McCain, William Rehnquist, Sandra Day O'Connor, and disgraced former governors Evan Mecham and Fife Symington.

Lauer, Charles D. *Arrows, Bullets, and Saddle Sores: A Collection of True Tales of Arizona's Old West.* Phoenix: Golden West Publishers, 2005. The Wild West was built on a rich tradition of storytelling, from Native American myths to cowboy yarns. Hear about the events from the real West, including street-clearing gunfights, outlaw gangs, fatal poker games, stolen gold, and dirt-floored prisons.

Martin, Douglas D. *An Arizona Chronology: The Territorial Years, 1846–1912.* Tucson: University of Arizona Press, 1962. They didn't call it the Wild West for nothing. Learn how Arizona evolved from Mexican territory to America's 48th state.

Trimble, Marshall. *Roadside History of Arizona.* Missoula, MT: Mountain Press Publishing Company, 2004. Arizona's state historian takes a road-trip approach to exploring the Grand Canyon State's past. Because it's organized geographically and along highways, travelers can easily cruise to cultural sites, like old missions and Civil War battlefields.

NATIVE AMERICANS

Betancourt, Marian, Michael O'Dowd, and Jack Strong. *The New Native American Cuisine: Five-Star Recipes from the Chefs of Arizona's Kai restaurant.* Dallas: Three Forks Press, 2009. Only a handful of restaurants in the United States have earned AAA's Five Diamond rating and Mobil's Five Star designation, but it's little surprise given the innovative and elegant cuisine at Kai Restaurant at the Sheraton Wild Horse Pass Resort. Try out some of the Native American–inspired recipes at home, including those for cocktails, soups, salads, deserts, and entrées, like grilled elk chop with truffles and sweet corn panna cotta with venison carpaccio.

Circle of Light Navajo Education Project. *Our Fathers, Our Grandfathers, Our Heroes...The Navajo Code Talkers of World War II: A Photographic Exhibit.* Gallup, NM: Circle of Light Navajo Education Project, 2004. This rich collection of photographs chronicles the story of the Navajo Code Talkers, who transmitted U.S. Marine Corps messages in their native language during World War II. See the letters documenting the program's inception, newspaper clippings, a guide to the Navajo language, and historic photos of recruitment visits to the reservation and scenes from the Pacific Theater battlefields.

Hodge, Carle. *Ruins Along the River: Montezuma Castle, Tuzigoot, and Montezuma National Monuments.* Tucson: Western National Parks Association, 1986. Explore the rich history and heritage of the Sinagua people and learn how they were able to build a series of impressive monuments that still stand as a testament to their sophisticated civilization.

LITERATURE AND MEMOIRS

Bishop, James. *Epitaph for a Desert Anarchist: The Life and Legacy of Edward Abbey.* New York: Touchstone, 1995. Many books have been written by and about the desert's fiercest advocate, who is portrayed here, warts and all, through anecdotes and excerpts from his writings and personal papers. Bishop, a former journalist, interviews several of Abbey's acquaintances and draws on his own memories of a man who was as passionate about words and writing as he was about the landscape.

Guerrero, Pedro E. *Pedro E. Guerrero: A Photographer's Journey with Frank Lloyd Wright, Alexander Calder, and Louise Nevelson.* New York: Princeton Architectural Press, 2007. Guerrero, a Mexican American and Arizona native, documents the lives and work of some of the giants of the 20th-century art world. Here, 190 black-and-white photographs—some of them iconic images—tell the stories not only of these artists, but also of the mid-century Modernist movement that flourished during the photographer's heyday and Guerrero's incredible, seemingly impossible life.

O'Connor, Sandra Day, and H. Alan Day. *Lazy B: Growing up on a Cattle Ranch in the American Southwest.* New York: Random House, 2005. The former Supreme Court justice and her brother recount their lives growing up on an Arizona ranch near the New Mexican border, highlighting how their parents, fellow cowhands, and the environment taught them hard lessons and fundamental values. The warm, engaging memoir demonstrates how the Arizona landscape forged one of the country's greatest minds.

Summerhayes, Martha. *Vanished Arizona: Recollections of the Army Life of a New England Woman.* Lincoln, NE: Bison Books, 1979. An 1800s army officer's wife chronicles the hardships of traveling and living in the West. Her witty, wry, and perceptive account is a classic, combining travelogue with adventure and an insider's look at the everyday trials of frontier military life. Fort Verde, preserved today as a state park, was one of the places where she cast her lot with her soldier husband.

NATURE

Alcock, John. *When the Rains Come: A Naturalist's Year in the Sonoran Desert*. Tucson, AZ: University of Arizona Press, 2009. A naturalist and professor at ASU, Alcock shares his observations on the desert's interrelationships, from the tiniest insect to towering saguaros. Evocative and informative, as well as easy to read, Alcock's account of his hikes in the Usery Mountains east of Phoenix conveys the strange beauty and rich complexity of the Sonoran Desert landscape.

Chronic, Halka. *The Roadside Geology of Arizona*. Missoula, MT: Mountain Press Publishing Company, 1983. The road numbers may have changed, but the geology hasn't, and this book continues to be a favorite among those who like to learn about their natural surroundings. Chronic was a professional geologist with a gift for making science accessible for the layperson.

Maxa, Christine. *Arizona's Best Wildflower Hikes: The Desert*. Englewood, CO: Westcliffe Publishers, 2002. The noted travel writer and outdoor enthusiast shares her tips on where to find colorful wildflowers, from mountainside hideaways to the vast, open spaces carpeted with orange, yellow, pink, and violet blossoms.

Nabhan, Gary. *The Desert Smells Like Rain: A Naturalist in O'odham Country*. Tucson: University of Arizona Press, 2002. Ethnobotanist and educator Gary Nabhan has spearheaded movements focusing on sustainability, desert heritage foods, and local agriculture. He has written 24 books, and this is one of his classics, a lyrical account of the traditional lifeways of the Tohono O'odham Indians. One section describes the annual saguaro wine-drinking ceremony that brings rain.

Tessmer, Martin. *50 Hikes in Arizona*. Woodstock, VT: The Countryman Press, 2004. There's no shortage of great hikes in Arizona, and this illustrated guide highlights the state's diverse landscapes and best trails, including treks through the Grand Canyon and around the Valley of the Sun.

PHOENIX

Ellin, Nan. *Phoenix: 21st Century City*. London: Booth-Clibborn Editions, 2006. The richly photographed book chronicles Phoenix's evolution into a cosmopolitan metropolis, replete with cutting-edge architecture, a burgeoning fashion scene, modern design, and vibrant public art. Local writers, photographers, and designers create a rich tapestry that documents the city's cultural evolution.

Gober, Patricia. *Metropolitan Phoenix: Place Making and Community Building in the Desert*. Philadelphia: University of Pennsylvania Press, 2006. Phoenix, like its sister desert megalopolises in Las Vegas and Dubai, has transformed an arid landscape into a diverse, urban community. Learn how the Valley of the Sun and its citizens have tried to avoid becoming "another L.A." and what building a major metropolitan area in the desert means.

Scharbarch, Paul, and John H. Akers. *Phoenix: Then and Now*. San Diego, CA: Thunderbay Press, 2005. A fascinating before-and-after look at the Valley's growth, the richly illustrated book contrasts historical images against contemporary shots of Phoenix, Tempe, Mesa, and Glendale. The consistent theme: growth.

TRAVEL

Cheek, Lawrence W. *Arizona*. Oakland, CA: Compass American Guides, 1997. The dense guide takes a more literary approach to exploring Arizona, with a thoughtful collection of essays about the state's history and geographical regions, as well as its natural attractions, Native American culture, and art and architecture. The archival photos from Arizona's early territorial days are particularly fascinating.

Kutz, Jack. *Mysteries & Miracles of Arizona: Guide Book to the Genuinely Bizarre in the Grand Canyon State*. Corrales, NM: Rhombus Publishing Company, 1992. The Arizona desert hides a mystical side, or at least that's what generations of Native American shamans, fireside cowboys, and Sedona's New Agers say. Discover the curse of the Superstition Mountains east of Phoenix and the old ghost towns on the frontier.

Lindahl, Larry. *Secret Sedona: Sacred Moments in the Landscape*. Phoenix: Arizona

Highways, 2005. Sedona's red-hued landscape takes center stage in this lavishly illustrated book, with stunning photography and poetic descriptions that showcase the region's massive formations, ancient Native American history, and rich geology and wildlife.

Lowe, Sam. *Arizona Curiosities: Quirky Characters, Roadside Oddities, & Other Offbeat Stuff*. Guilford, CT: The Globe Pequot Press, 2003. Lowe, a former Arizona reporter, provides a humorous survey of the Grand Canyon State's kooky history, people, and roadside attractions. Most Arizonans don't know even half of the oddball stories about concrete religious shrines, alien abductions, and "wild" burros that roam the streets of one town.

Treat, Wesley. *Weird Arizona: Your Travel Guide to Arizona's Local Legends and Best Kept Secrets*. New York: Sterling, 2007. Uncover the Wild West's weird and wacky side, from outlaws and outhouses to rattlesnake-inspired bridges.

Internet Resources

TOURISM SITES

Arizona Office of Tourism
www.arizonaguide.com
Featuring video tours, itinerary options, travel deals, and a calendar of events, the AOT website is a valuable resource and great place to start planning your visit.

Arizona State Parks
www.azstateparks.com
This comprehensive guide to the state's 29 parks also describes volunteer programs, junior ranger activities, and upcoming events. Publications include maps, newsletters, and a Green Guide to Arizona.

Desert U.S.A.
www.desertusa.com
This excellent resource for the Sonoran Desert (and others) has news, travel tips, and natural history information, including a helpful spring wildflower update.

Greater Phoenix Convention & Visitors Bureau
www.visitphoenix.com
The Greater Phoenix CVB provides news and information on everything from golf to accommodations to assistance in relocating to Arizona. The site also hosts a blog called The

Hot Sheet, which is "written for Phoenix locals and visitors alike."

Red Rock Country
www.redrockcountry.org

If you're planning a hike or scenic drive in the Coconino National Forest surrounding Sedona, visit this site updated by the forest's Red Rock ranger district for trail descriptions and current conditions.

Scottsdale Convention and Visitors Bureau
www.scottsdalecvb.com

An outstanding resource for all things Scottsdale: attractions, shopping, resorts, and hotels, as well as tour packages and specials. Visitors can book their entire trip at this one-stop shop.

Sedona Chamber of Commerce
www.visitsedona.com

The definitive site for visiting Red Rock Country, it also provides information and assistance for planning your Sedona wedding. Something you'll be hard pressed to find elsewhere is its spiritual/personal enrichment webpage.

Sedona Verde Valley Travel Council
www.sedona-verdevalley.com

This visitor guide and information center includes Jerome and the Verde Valley communities around Sedona, suggesting arts and cultural activities, and providing news on events and festivals, hotels, dining, shopping, and tours.

Tonto National Forest
www.fs.usda.gov/tonto

This forest northeast of the Phoenix metro area encompasses Roosevelt and Apache Lakes and the Superstition Wilderness. Check for current conditions or to find a campground or hiking trail.

NEWS AND CULTURE

Arizona Highways
www.arizonahighways.com

Dazzling photography accompanies travel stories in this venerable monthly magazine. Feature articles are backed up by searchable lists of restaurants, lodgings, day trips, and hikes.

Arizona's Family
www.azfamily.com

Local television station 3TV's website features news, entertainment, and weather and traffic information, as well as stories on real estate, airport news, and flight maps. Slide shows and readers' photos make this hometown site a real Arizona "family" affair.

AZ Capitol Times
http://azcapitoltimes.com

Check here for the latest scoops from Arizona's political scene.

AZCentral
www.azcentral.com

The website for *The Arizona Republic* newspaper highlights local, state, national, and world news, along with the latest weather and sports. The food section includes restaurant reviews, and the "Things to Do" link serves as an essential resource for tourists.

KJZZ
www.kjzz.org

Phoenix's National Public Radio station offers this multimedia website, a great resource to learn more about the city's news, politics, people, and culture.

Index

List of Maps

www.moon.com

DESTINATIONS | ACTIVITIES | BLOGS | MAPS | BOOKS

MOON.COM is ready to help plan your next trip! Filled with fresh trip ideas and strategies, author interviews, informative travel blogs, a detailed map library, and descriptions of all the Moon guidebooks, Moon.com is all you need to get out and explore the world—or even places in your own backyard. While at Moon.com, sign up for our monthly e-newsletter for updates on new releases, travel tips, and expert advice from our on-the-go Moon authors. As always, when you travel with Moon, expect an experience that is uncommon and truly unique.

f 🐦 KEEP UP WITH MOON ON FACEBOOK AND TWITTER
JOIN THE MOON PHOTO GROUP ON FLICKR

MAP SYMBOLS

▭ Expressway	**C**	Highlight	✗	Airfield	⚓	Golf Course	
⋯ Primary Road	○	City/Town	✗	Airport	**P**	Parking Area	
⋯ Secondary Road	◉	State Capital	▲	Mountain	▲	Archaeological Site	
‑‑‑‑ Unpaved Road	⊛	National Capital	✛	Unique Natural Feature	⚑	Church	
‑ ‑ ‑ Trail	★	Point of Interest			⚑	Gas Station	
⋯ Ferry	●	Accommodation	⚐	Waterfall	⬭	Glacier	
‑▪‑ Railroad	▼	Restaurant/Bar	⬆	Park	▨	Mangrove	
▭ Pedestrian Walkway	▪	Other Location	**T**	Trailhead	▨	Reef	
▭ Stairs	Λ	Campground	⛷	Skiing Area	▨	Swamp	

CONVERSION TABLES

°C = (°F - 32) / 1.8
°F = (°C x 1.8) + 32
1 inch = 2.54 centimeters (cm)
1 foot = 0.304 meters (m)
1 yard = 0.914 meters
1 mile = 1.6093 kilometers (km)
1 km = 0.6214 miles
1 fathom = 1.8288 m
1 chain = 20.1168 m
1 furlong = 201.168 m
1 acre = 0.4047 hectares
1 sq km = 100 hectares
1 sq mile = 2.59 square km
1 ounce = 28.35 grams
1 pound = 0.4536 kilograms
1 short ton = 0.9078 metric ton
1 short ton = 2,000 pounds
1 long ton = 1,016 metric tons
1 long ton = 2,240 pounds
1 metric ton = 1,000 kilograms
1 quart = 0.94635 liters
1 US gallon = 3.7854 liters
1 Imperial gallon = 4.5459 liters
1 nautical mile = 1.852 km

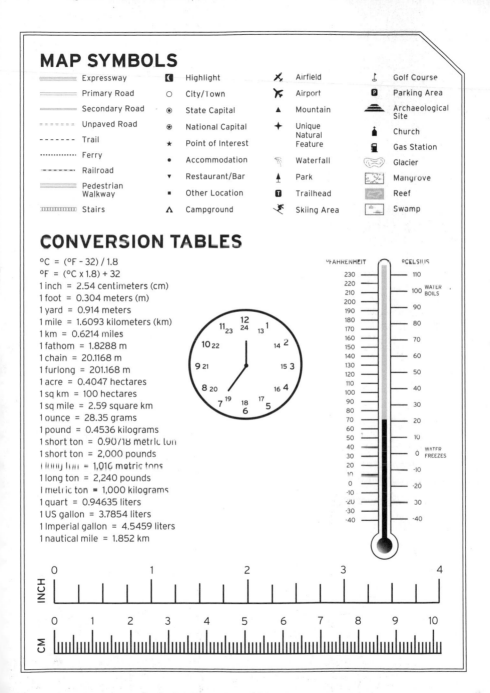

FAHRENHEIT / CELSIUS thermometer:
230 — 110
220
210 — 100 WATER BOILS
200 — 90
190
180 — 80
170
160 — 70
150
140 — 60
130
120 — 50
110
100 — 40
90 — 30
80
70 — 20
60
50 — 10
40
30 — 0 WATER FREEZES
20 — -10
10
0 — -20
-10
-20 — -30
-30 — -40
-40

MOON PHOENIX, SCOTTSDALE & SEDONA
Avalon Travel
a member of the Perseus Books Group
1700 Fourth Street
Berkeley, CA 94710, USA
www.moon.com

Editor: Erin Raber
Series Manager: Kathryn Ettinger
Copy Editor: Ashley Benning
Graphics Coordinator: Elizabeth Jang
Production Coordinator: Elizabeth Jang
Cover Designer: Elizabeth Jang
Map Editor: Albert Angulo
Cartographers: Kaitlin Jaffe, Heather Sparks,
   Andy Butkovic, Chris Henrick
Indexer: Greg Jewett

ISBN-13: 978-1-61238-347-7
ISSN: 2151-6138

Printing History
1st Edition – 2010
2nd Edition – May 2013
5 4 3 2 1

Text © 2013 by Kathleen Bryant.
Maps © 2013 by Avalon Travel.
All rights reserved.

Jeff Ficker wrote the first edition of *Moon Phoenix, Scottsdale & Sedona*.

Some photos and illustrations are used by permission and are the property of the original copyright owners.

Front cover photo: Cathedral Rock at sunrise © Tom Bol/Aurora Photos/Robert Harding

Title page photo: sunburst at Phoenix City Hall © Chris Curtis/123rf.com

Interior color photos: p. 4 red rocks of Sedona © Chris Curtis/123rf.com; p. 5 (top) saguaros in the Sonoran Desert © Anton Foltin/123rf.com, (right) agave bloom © Kathleen Bryant; p. 6 (inset) cactus at the Desert Botanical Garden © Kathleen Bryant, (bottom) Phoenix skyline at night © Greater Phoenix CVB; p. 7 (top left) sign at Usery Pass © Anton Foltin/123rf.com, (top right) prickly pear with bee © Kathleen Bryant, (bottom left) the distinctive architecture of Cosanti © Kathleen Bryant, (bottom right) desert boulders and cholla cactus © Kathleen Bryant, pp. 8-9 all © Kathleen Bryant; p. 10 (left) Kathleen Bryant, (right) © Adam Rodriguez/Scottsdale Convention and Visitors Bureau (SCVB); p. 11 © Kathleen Bryant; p. 12 © Greater Phoenix CVB; pp. 13-15 © Kathleen Bryant; p. 16 © Scott Prokop/123rf.com; p. 17 © Kathleen Bryant; p. 18 (top) © Greater Phoenix CVB; (bottom) © William Perry/123rf.com; p. 19 © Kathleen Bryant; p. 20 © Adam Rodriguez/Desert Botanical Garden; p. 21 © Natalia Bratslavsky/123rf.com; p. 22 (top) © Richard Mayer, (bottom) © Kathleen Bryant; pp. 23-24 © Kathleen Bryant

Printed in Canada by Friesens

CENTRAL ARKANSAS LIBRARY SYSTEM
ADOLPHINE FLETCHER TERRY BRANCH
LITTLE ROCK, ARKANSAS

KEEPING CURRENT

If you have a favorite gem you'd like to see included in the next edition, or see anything that needs updating, clarification, or correction, please drop us a line. Send your comments via email to feedback@moon.com, or use the address above.